MODEL CHECKING QUANTUM SYSTEMS

Model checking is one of the most successful verification techniques and has been widely adopted in traditional computing and communication hardware and software industries.

This book provides the first systematic introduction to model-checking techniques applicable to quantum systems, with broad potential applications in the emerging industry of quantum computing and quantum communication as well as quantum physics.

Suitable for use as a course textbook and for self-study, graduate and senior undergraduate students will appreciate the step-by-step explanations and the exercises included. Researchers and engineers in the related fields can further develop these techniques in their own work, with the final chapter outlining potential future applications.

MINGSHENG YING is Distinguished Professor in the Centre for Quantum Software and Information, University of Technology Sydney; Deputy Director for Research of the Institute of Software, Chinese Academy of Sciences; and Cheung Kong Chair Professor in the Department of Computer Science and Technology, Tsinghua University. His research interests are quantum computing, programming theory and logics in artificial intelligence. He is the author of the books *Foundations of Quantum Programming* (2016) and *Topology in Process Calculus: Approximate Correctness and Infinite Evolution of Concurrent Programs* (2001). Currently, he serves as (Co-)Editor-in-Chief of *ACM Transactions on Quantum Computing*.

YUAN FENG is Professor in the Centre for Quantum Software and Information, University of Technology Sydney. His research interests include formal verification of quantum systems, the theory of quantum programming, quantum information and computation and probabilistic systems. He has published more than 70 research papers in international leading journals and mainstream conferences. He was awarded an ARC (Australian Research Council) Future Fellowship in 2010.

MODEL CHECKING QUANTUM SYSTEMS

Principles and Algorithms

MINGSHENG YING

University of Technology Sydney

YUAN FENG

University of Technology Sydney

CAMBRIDGE
UNIVERSITY PRESS

CAMBRIDGE
UNIVERSITY PRESS

University Printing House, Cambridge CB2 8BS, United Kingdom

One Liberty Plaza, 20th Floor, New York, NY 10006, USA

477 Williamstown Road, Port Melbourne, VIC 3207, Australia

314–321, 3rd Floor, Plot 3, Splendor Forum, Jasola District Centre, New Delhi – 110025, India

79 Anson Road, #06–04/06, Singapore 079906

Cambridge University Press is part of the University of Cambridge.

It furthers the University's mission by disseminating knowledge in the pursuit of education, learning, and research at the highest international levels of excellence.

www.cambridge.org
Information on this title: www.cambridge.org/9781108484305
DOI: 10.1017/9781108613323

First published 2021

Printed in the United Kingdom by TJ Books Limited, Padstow Cornwall

A catalogue record for this publication is available from the British Library.

Library of Congress Cataloging-in-Publication Data
Names: Ying, Mingsheng, author. | Feng, Yuan, 1977– author.
Title: Model checking quantum systems : principles and algorithms / Mingsheng Ying, University of Technology, Sydney, Yuan Feng, University of Technology, Sydney.
Description: Cambridge, UK ; New York, NY : Cambridge University Press, 2020. | Includes bibliographical references and index.
Identifiers: LCCN 2020041998 (print) | LCCN 2020041999 (ebook) | ISBN 9781108484305 (hardback) | ISBN 9781108613323 (epub)
Subjects: LCSH: Quantum computing. | Computer systems–Verification.
Classification: LCC QA76.889 .Y564 2020 (print) | LCC QA76.889 (ebook) | DDC 006.3/843–dc23
LC record available at https://lccn.loc.gov/2020041998
LC ebook record available at https://lccn.loc.gov/2020041999

ISBN 978-1-108-48430-5 Hardback

Contents

Preface

Model checking is an algorithmic technique for verification of dynamic properties of (mainly) finite state systems. After the development of more than 35 years, it has become a prominent verification technique for both hardware and software systems and has found numerous successful applications in the information and communications technology industries. The special attractiveness of model checking is due mainly to the following two features:

- It is completely automatic.
- It provides counterexamples whenever the properties are not satisfied and thus is very useful in debugging.

Since various stochastic phenomena occur in computing and communication systems, model checking has been systematically extended for verifying probabilistic systems, such as Markov chains and Markov decision processes.

With the emergence of quantum computing and quantum communication and, in particular, their rapid progress in the past few years, one may naturally expect to further extend the model-checking technique for verification of quantum systems. Indeed, research on model checking quantum systems has already been conducted for more than 10 years, starting from directly applying probabilistic model checking to quantum systems, in particular, quantum communication protocols. In dealing with more and more general quantum systems, it has been gradually realised that model checking quantum systems requires certain principles fundamentally different from those for classical systems (including probabilistic systems). Some basic principles for model checking quantum systems have been developed in recent research, but they are scattered in various conference and journal papers.

This book attempts to provide a systematic exposition of the principles for model checking quantum systems and the algorithms based on them, which have been proposed up to the writing of this book. Some potential applications and topics for future research are briefly discussed at the end of the book. We hope that the book can serve as an introduction to this new area for researchers and provide a basis for further development of the area.

The book is also intended to serve as a textbook for graduate students. It is therefore organised with a careful pedagogical consideration. Since the students in quantum computing and information may come from either a computer science or physics background, two preliminary chapters are given at the beginning of the book: the first briefly introduces model checking for those from physics, and the second briefly introduces quantum theory for those from computer science. After that, model-checking technique for quantum systems is presented step by step, from simpler models and checked properties to more sophisticated ones.

Acknowledgements

The materials of this book mainly come from a series of articles by the authors and their collaborators. The authors would like to thank Drs Nengkun Yu, Yangjia Li, Shenggang Ying and Ji Guan for pleasant and fruitful collaborations. Without their contributions, this book would not have been possible.

The work presented in this book has been partially supported by the National Key R&D Program of China (Grant No. 2018YFA0306701), the Australian Research Council (Grant Nos. DP160101652 and DP180100691), the National Natural Science Foundation of China (Grant No. 61832015) and the Key Research Program of Frontier Sciences, Chinese Academy of Sciences. All of them are gratefully acknowledged.

1

Introduction

1.1 Second Quantum Revolution Requires New Verification Techniques

We are currently in the midst of a second quantum revolution: *transition from quantum theory to quantum engineering* [41]. The aim of quantum theory is to find fundamental rules that govern the physical systems already existing in the nature. Instead, quantum engineering intends to design and implement new systems (machines, devices, etc.) that did not exist before to accomplish some desirable tasks, based on quantum theory. Active areas of quantum engineering include quantum computing, quantum cryptography, quantum communication, quantum sensing, quantum simulation, quantum metrology and quantum imaging.

Experiences in today's engineering indicate that it is not guaranteed that a human designer completely understands the behaviours of the systems she or he designed, and a bug in her or his design may cause some serious problems and even disasters. So, correctness, safety and reliability of complex engineering systems have attracted wide attention and have been systematically studied in various engineering fields. In particular, in the past four decades, computer scientists have developed various verification techniques for correctness of both hardware and software as well as security of communication protocols.

As is well known, human intuition is much better adapted to the classical world than to the quantum world. This implies that human engineers will commit many more faults in designing and implementing complex quantum systems such as quantum computer hardware and software and quantum communication protocols. Thus, correctness, safety and reliability problems will be even more critical in quantum engineering than in today's engineering. However, because of the essential differences between the classical and quantum worlds, verification techniques developed for classical engineering systems cannot be directly used to quantum systems. Novel verification techniques will be indispensable for the coming era of quantum engineering and quantum technology [32].

1

1.2 Model-Checking Techniques for Classical Systems

Model checking is an effective automated technique that checks whether a desired property is satisfied by a system, for example, a computing or communication system. The properties that are checked are usually specified in a logic, in particular, temporal logic; typical properties are deadlock freedom, invariants, safety and request–response properties. The systems under checking are mathematically modelled as, for example (finite-state) automata, transition systems, Markov chains and Markov decision processes [7, 35].

Model checking has become one of the dominant techniques for verification of computer (hardware and software) systems 30 years after its inception. Many industrial-strength systems have been verified by employing model-checking techniques. Recently, it has also successfully been used in systems biology; see [68] for example.

With quantum engineering and quantum technology emerging, a question then naturally arises: *Is it possible to use model-checking techniques to verify correctness and safety of quantum engineering systems* and if so, how?

1.3 Difficulty in Model Checking Quantum Systems

Unfortunately, it seems that the current model-checking techniques cannot be directly applied to quantum systems because of some essential differences between the classical world and the quantum world. To develop model-checking techniques for quantum systems, the following three problems must be systematically addressed:

- *System modelling and property specification*: The classical system modelling method cannot be used to describe the behaviours of quantum systems, and the classical specification language is not suited to formalise the properties of quantum systems to be checked. So, we need to carefully and clearly define a conceptual framework in which we can properly reason about quantum systems, including *formal models of quantum systems* and *formal description of temporal properties of quantum systems*.
- *Quantum measurements*: Model checking is usually applied to check long-term behaviours of the systems. But to check whether a quantum system satisfies a certain property at a time point, one has to perform a quantum measurement on the system, which can change the state of the system. This makes studies of the long-term behaviours of quantum systems much harder than those of classical systems [22, 23, 60].
- *Algorithms*: The state spaces of the classical systems that model-checking algorithms can be applied to are usually finite or countably infinite. However, the

state spaces of quantum systems are inherently continuous even when they are finite dimensional. To develop algorithms for model checking quantum systems, we have to exploit some deep mathematical properties of the systems so that it suffices to examine only a finite number of (or at most countably infinitely many) representative elements, for example, those in an orthonormal basis, of their state spaces. Also, a linear algebraic structure always resides in the state space of a quantum system. So, an algorithm checking a quantum system should be carefully developed so that the linear algebraic structure is nicely preserved and fully exploited.

1.4 Current Research on Model Checking of Quantum Systems

Despite the difficulties discussed in the previous section, quite a few model-checking techniques for quantum systems have been developed in the past 10 years. The earliest work mainly targeted checking quantum communication protocols:

- Taking the probabilism arising from quantum measurements into account, [54] used the probabilistic model-checker PRISM [75] to verify the correctness of quantum protocols, including superdense coding, quantum teleportation and quantum error correction.
- A branching-time temporal extension (called quantum computation tree logic or QCTL for short) of exogenous quantum propositional logic [88] was introduced and then the model-checking problem for this logic was studied in [8, 9], with verification of the correctness of quantum key distribution BB84 [15] as an application.
- A linear temporal extension QLTL of exogenous quantum propositional logic [88] was then defined and the corresponding model-checking problem was investigated in [87].
- Model-checking techniques were developed in [38, 39] for quantum communication protocols modelled in process algebra CQP (Communicating Quantum Processes) [56]. The checked properties are specified by the quantum computation tree logic QCTL defined in [8].
- A model checker for quantum communication protocols was also developed in [55, 57, 96], where the checked properties are specified by QCTL [8] too, but only the protocols that can be modelled as quantum circuits expressible in the stabiliser formalism [59] were considered. In [5, 6], this technique was extended beyond stabiliser states and used to check equivalence of quantum protocols.

A research line pursued by the authors and their collaborators is to develop model-checking techniques that can be used not only for quantum communication protocols but also for quantum computing hardware and software and other quantum engineering systems:

- In retrospect, our research on model checking quantum systems stemmed from termination analysis of quantum programs. The termination problem of quantum loop programs with unitary transformation as loop bodies (in a finite-dimensional state Hilbert space) was first examined in [118]. The semantics of this class of quantum programs can be modelled by *quantum automata*. The main results of [118] were generalised in [123] to quantum loops with general quantum operations (or super-operators) as loop bodies by introducing *quantum Markov chains* as their semantic models. These researches naturally motivated us to the studies of model checking quantum systems, because termination can be seen as a kind of reachability, which is central to model-checking algorithms.

- The model-checking problem for *quantum automata* was first considered in [119], where closed subspaces of the state Hilbert space are used as the atomic propositions about the behaviour of the system, following the basic idea of Birkhoff-von Neumann quantum logic, and the checked linear-time properties are defined as infinite sequences of sets of atomic propositions. Furthermore, decidability or undecidability of several reachability problems (eventually reachable, globally reachable, ultimately forever reachable and infinitely often reachable) for quantum automata were proved in [82].

- The reachability problem of *quantum Markov chains* was first investigated in [123], where an algorithm for computing the reachable space of a quantum Markov chain was presented and applied to termination analysis of concurrent quantum programs. A more systematic study in this direction was carried out in [120] by developing a new graph theory in Hilbert spaces; in particular, an algorithm for computing several kinds of reachability probabilities of quantum Markov chains was found based on the BSCC (bottom strongly connected components) decomposition of their state Hilbert spaces, and undecidability of some other reachability problems were proved. The same problems for *quantum Markov decision processes* were studied in [121].

- The notion of a *super-operator-valued Markov chain* was introduced in [51] as a higher-level model of quantum programs and quantum cryptographic protocols, where the (classical) control flow of a quantum program is depicted as a (classical) directed graph, but each edge is associated with a super-operator that describes one step of quantum computation. A corresponding computation tree logic (CTL) was also defined, and algorithms for checking CTL properties of super-operator-valued Markov chains are developed. Furthermore, the reachability of the recursive extension of super-operator-valued Markov chains was studied in [52].

1.5 Structure of the Book

This book is a systematic exposition of the currently existing principles and algo-rithms for model checking quantum systems. The remainder of this book is divided into the following chapters:

- **Chapters 2 and 3** are the preliminary part of this book. For convenience of the reader, we briefly review model checking in Chapter 2, from mathematical *models of systems* to *temporal logics* for specifying properties of systems and basic *model-checking algorithms*. In Chapter 3, we review the basics of quantum theory needed in the subsequent chapters, including *static* and *dynamic* descriptions of a quantum system and quantum *measurements*.
- **Chapter 4:** From this chapter on, we develop the techniques for model checking quantum systems step by step, from a simple model of quantum systems to more and more complicated ones.

  This chapter starts from defining *linear time properties* of quantum systems and then focuses on the study of a special linear time property, namely *reach-ability* of *quantum automata*, in which the system's transition is modelled as a unitary transformation that is a discrete-time description of the dynamics of a closed quantum system.
- **Chapter 5:** In this chapter, we consider reachability problems of *quantum Markov chains* and *quantum Markov decision processes*, which, as suggested by their names, are the quantum counterparts of Markov chains and Markov decision processes. Their dynamics is described as a super-operator rather than a unitary transformation. We first introduce some necessary mathematical tools, in particular graph theory in Hilbert spaces, and then present several algorithms solving these reachability problems.
- **Chapter 6:** In this chapter, we first define the notion of a super-operator-valued Markov chain (SVMC) and both a computation tree logic (CTL) and a linear temporal logic (LTL) for specifying properties of SVMCs. The majority of this chapter is devoted to introducing a series of algorithms for checking CTL or LTL properties of SVMCs.
- **Chapter 7:** This is the concluding chapter, where we discuss some possible improvements and potential applications of the model-checking techniques for quantum systems introduced in this book and point out several directions for the further developments of this area.
- **Appendices:** For readability, the proofs of some technical lemmas are omitted in Chapters 4–6. But we provide these proofs in the appendices for the readers who are interested in them.

2

Basics of Model Checking

Model checking is an algorithmic technique for verifying certain properties of (mainly) finite state systems. The systems are usually modelled as a transition system (or a finite state automaton, a labelled graph). The properties are specified in a temporal logic. The checking algorithm is based mainly on systematic inspection of all reachable states of the model. Because of its complete automation and ability of finding counterexamples, model checking has been successfully and widely adopted in the information and communications technology industries. On the other hand, it has a major drawback, namely the *state space explosion* problem – the number of states can grow exponentially in the number of variables. Several techniques have been introduced to mitigate this drawback, including symbolic model checking, bounded model checking, abstraction and partial order reduction. In real-world applications, model checking is facing the *validation* problem that all branches of science have: are the model and the properties being checked a proper and adequate description of the system's behaviour?

Model checking was first proposed for verification of classical non-probabilistic systems and then extended for probabilistic systems. In this book, we will further extend the technique of model checking for quantum systems. As preliminaries, this chapter introduces basics of model checking for both classical non-probabilistic and probabilistic systems.

The ideas and techniques introduced in this chapter cannot be directly applied to quantum systems, but they provide us with a guideline to develop an appropriate framework and to ask the right questions in the later chapters.

2.1 Modelling Systems

First of all, we need a formal model describing the possible behaviour of the system under consideration. One of the most commonly used models is a transition system.

Definition 2.1 A transition system is a 6-tuple

$$\mathcal{M} = (S, Act, \rightarrow, I, AP, L),$$

where

   (i) S is a (finite) set of states;
   (ii) $I \subseteq S$ is a set of initial states;
  (iii) Act is a set of (the names of) actions;
  (iv) $\rightarrow \subseteq S \times Act \times S$ is a transition relation;
   (v) AP is a set of atomic propositions;
  (vi) $L : S \rightarrow 2^{AP}$ is a labelling function, where 2^{AP} stands for the power set of AP, that is, the set of all subsets of AP.

Several ingredients in the foregoing definition deserve careful explanation:

- $(s, \alpha, s') \in \rightarrow$, usually written as $s \xrightarrow{\alpha} s'$, means that the action α causes the system's state to change from s to s'.
- The transition relation $\rightarrow$ can be equivalently represented by a family of transition relations indexed by action names:

$$\rightarrow = \left\{ \xrightarrow{\alpha} : \alpha \in Act \right\},$$

where for each $\alpha \in Act$,

$$\xrightarrow{\alpha} = \left\{ (s, s') : s \xrightarrow{\alpha} s' \right\} \subseteq S \times S$$

is the set of transitions enabled by action α.
- Elements of AP are atomic propositions chosen to describe the basic properties of the system's states.
- For each $s \in S$, $L(s)$ denotes the set of those atomic propositions that hold in state s.

For each $s \in S$ and $\alpha \in Act$, let

$$post(s, \alpha) = \{s' \in S : s \xrightarrow{\alpha} s'\}$$

be the set of α-successors of s. We write $|X|$ for the number of elements in X.

Definition 2.2 A transition system $\mathcal{M}$ is called deterministic if

  (i) there is at most one initial state; that is, $|I| \leq 1$;
  (ii) for each action α, each state s has at most one α-successor; that is, it holds that $|post(s, \alpha)| \leq 1$ for every $s \in S$ and $\alpha \in Act$.

Otherwise, it is non-deterministic.

Definition 2.3 A state $s \in S$ is called a terminal state of the transition system $\mathcal{M}$ if it has no outgoing transition; that is, $post(s, \alpha) = \emptyset$ for every $\alpha \in Act$.

A transition system $\mathcal{M}$ runs in the following way: it starts from some initial state $s_0 \in I$ and then evolves according to the transition relation $\rightarrow$. Formally, we have:

Definition 2.4 A path in the transition system $\mathcal{M}$ is a (finite or infinite) sequence $\pi = s_0 s_1 \ldots s_{i-1} s_i \ldots$ of states such that

$$s_0 \xrightarrow{\alpha_1} s_1 \xrightarrow{\alpha_2} \cdots s_{i-1} \xrightarrow{\alpha_i} s_i \xrightarrow{\alpha_{i+1}} \cdots ,$$

where $s_{i-1} \xrightarrow{\alpha_i} s_i$ is a transition in $\mathcal{M}$ for each $i \geq 1$.

Note that for a non-deterministic transition system, the initial state s_0 and the next state s_i at the ith step in Definition 2.4 may be chosen non-deterministically. For a path $\pi = s_0 s_1 \ldots$ and $i \geq 0$, we write

$$\pi[i] = s_i, \qquad\qquad \pi[i) = s_i s_{i+1} \ldots$$

for the $(i+1)$th state s_i and the suffix of π starting in state s_i, respectively.

Definition 2.5 A state $s \in S$ is called reachable in $\mathcal{M}$ if there is a path $\pi = s_0 s_1 \ldots s_{n-1} s_n$ in $\mathcal{M}$ starting at an initial state $s_0 \in I$ and ending at $s_n = s$.

As stated at the beginning of this chapter, model checking is done by inspecting all reachable states of the system. This central notion of reachable state will therefore be generalised into various quantum systems, and computing (the space of) reachable states of a quantum system will be one of the central issues discussed in this book.

2.2 Temporal Logics

We also need a formal language to specify the required properties of the system. Since we are interested in its dynamic properties, a temporal logic(al language) is often adopted, which is an extension of propositional logic with some operators that can describe the behaviour over time. Mainly, two types of temporal logics are used in model checking. They are chosen according to two different views on the notion of (discrete) time.

2.2.1 Linear Temporal Logic

Linear temporal logic (LTL) is employed to describe linear-time properties. The linearity means:

• *Each time point has a unique possible future.*

We assume that the reader is familiar with propositional logic. The LTL language is an expansion of propositional logical language. Its alphabet consists of

- A set AP of atomic propositions, ranged over by meta-variables $a, a_1, a_2, \ldots$
- Propositional connectives: $\neg$ (not), $\wedge$ (and)
- Temporal operators: O (next), U (until)

It is worth noting that a set AP of atomic propositions is also assumed in a transition system (see Definition 2.1). Indeed, AP is the point where a temporal logical formula is connected to a transition system. More precisely, the labelling function $L : S \to 2^{AP}$ in the transition system gives an interpretation of atomic propositions:

$$\text{Atomic proposition } a \in AP \text{ is true in state } s \Leftrightarrow a \in L(s). \tag{2.1}$$

The LTL formulas are generated from atomic propositions by a finite number of applications of connectives $\neg, \wedge$ and temporal operators O, U.

Definition 2.6 (Syntax) The LTL formulas over AP are defined by the grammar

$$\varphi ::= a \mid \neg\varphi \mid \varphi_1 \wedge \varphi_2 \mid O\varphi \mid \varphi_1 U \varphi_2.$$

The meanings of $\neg\varphi$ and $\varphi_1 \wedge \varphi_2$ are the same as in propositional logic. Intuitively, $O\varphi$ is true at the current point of time if φ is true at the next, $\varphi_1 U \varphi_2$ holds at the current time point if there is a future point of time at which φ_2 is true and φ_1 holds at all moments from the current to that future point.

The following abbreviations are often used to simplify the presentation of LT formulas:

$$\mathbf{true} : = a \vee \neg a;$$
$$\varphi_1 \vee \varphi_2 : = \neg(\neg\varphi_1 \wedge \neg\varphi_2);$$
$$\Diamond\varphi : = \mathbf{true}\ U\varphi;$$
$$\Box\varphi : = \neg\Diamond\neg\varphi.$$

Again, the meanings of **true** and $\varphi_1 \vee \varphi_2$ are the same as in propositional logic. Moreover, we can see that $\Diamond\varphi$ means that φ will be true eventually (sometime in the future), and $\Box\varphi$ means that φ will be true always (from now on forever). It is worth noting that the derived formulas introduced earlier do not increase the expressive power of LTL, but LTL formulas can often be shortened using these abbreviations.

Example 2.7

(i) $\Box\Diamond\varphi$: for every time point i, there exists some $j \geq i$ such that φ is true at time point j; that is, φ holds infinitely often.

(ii) $\Diamond\Box\varphi$: there is a time point i such that φ is true at all time points $j \geq i$; that is, φ holds eventually forever.

(iii) $\Box(\text{request} \to \Diamond\text{response})$: every request will eventually have a response.

The semantics of the logic is obtained by extending interpretation (2.1) of atomic propositions to all LTL formulas.

Definition 2.8 (Semantics) Let $\mathcal{M} = (S, Act, \rightarrow, I, AP, L)$ be a transition system, π a path in $\mathcal{M}$, $s \in S$ and φ an LTL formula over AP. Then

(i) The satisfaction $\pi \models \varphi$ is defined by induction on the structure of φ:

(a) $\varphi = a$: $\pi \models \varphi$ iff $a \in L(\pi[0])$;
(b) $\varphi = \neg\varphi'$: $\pi \models \varphi$ iff $\pi \not\models \varphi'$;
(c) $\varphi = \varphi_1 \wedge \varphi_2$: $\pi \models \varphi$ iff $\pi \models \varphi_1$ and $\pi \models \varphi_2$;
(d) $\varphi = O\varphi'$: $\pi \models \varphi$ iff $\pi[1] \models \varphi'$;
(e) $\varphi = \varphi_1 U \varphi_2$: $\pi \models \varphi$ iff there exists $i \geq 0$ such that $\pi[i] \models \varphi_2$ and $\pi[j] \models \varphi_1$ for all $0 \leq j < i$.

(ii) $s \models \varphi$ iff $\pi \models \varphi$ for all paths π starting in s.
(iii) $\mathcal{M} \models \varphi$ iff $s_0 \models \varphi$ for all initial states $s_0 \in I$.

Essentially, Definition 2.8 is a formal description of the intuitive explanations of LTL formulas given after Definition 2.6.

Note that in (2.1), we directly considered whether a state s satisfies an atomic proposition a. In Definition 2.8, however, the satisfaction of a general LTL formula by a state needs to be formulated in two steps. In clause (i), we first consider whether an LTL formula φ is satisfied by a path which represents the notion of linear time, since φ may contain some temporal operators. Then in clause (ii), the satisfaction of an LTL formula by a state can be defined in terms of satisfaction by all paths starting from the state.

Let us further carefully explain the sub-clauses of clause (i) as follows:

- Sub-clause (a) is indeed a restatement of (2.1), with s being the initial state $\pi[0]$ of path π.
- The interpretations of connectives $\neg, \wedge$ in sub-clauses (b) and (c) are the same as in the standard propositional logic.
- Sub-clause (d) means that $O\varphi'$ is satisfied by path π iff φ' is satisfied by the tail $\pi[1]$ of π starting at the next point of time.
- Sub-clause (e) states that $\varphi_1 U \varphi_2$ is satisfied by π iff φ_2 is satisfied at some point i of time in path π, and before that point, φ_1 is satisfied.

Example 2.9 Consider transition system $\mathcal{M} = (S, Act, \rightarrow, I, AP, L)$ depicted in Figure 2.1, where

- $S = \{s_1, s_2, s_3\}$;
- $Act = \{F, B, C\}$;
- $s_1 \xrightarrow{F} s_2 \xrightarrow{F} s_3$, $s_2 \xrightarrow{B} s_1$ and $s_3 \xrightarrow{C} s_3$;

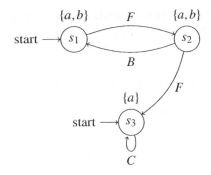

Figure 2.1 An example transition system.

- $I = \{s_1, s_3\}$;
- $L(s_1) = L(s_2) = \{a, b\}$ and $L(s_3) = \{a\}$.

Then

$$\mathcal{M} \models \Box(\neg b \rightarrow \Box(a \wedge \neg b)),$$
$$\mathcal{M} \not\models bU(a \wedge \neg b).$$

Two different LTL formulas may have the same semantics; that is, they are satisfied by the same transition systems.

Definition 2.10 (Equivalence) Let φ and ψ be two LTL formulas over AP. Then φ and ψ are equivalent, written $\varphi \equiv \psi$, if

$$\mathcal{M} \models \varphi \text{ iff } \mathcal{M} \models \psi$$

for any transition system $\mathcal{M} = (S, Act, \rightarrow, I, AP, L)$.

Exercise 2.1 Prove the expansion law:

$$\varphi U \psi \equiv \psi \vee (\varphi \wedge O(\varphi U \psi)). \tag{2.2}$$

2.2.2 Computation Tree Logic

Computation tree logic (CTL) is a branching temporal logic – a temporal logic based on a notion of branching time:

- A tree of states rather than a sequence of states, in which each point of time may split into more than one future.

To specify branching time, the syntax of CTL is a little bit more complicated than that of LTL – CTL formulas are classified into two categories: state formulas and path formulas.

Definition 2.11 (Syntax) Given a set AP of atomic propositions, the CTL formulas are defined by the following grammar:

- State formulas:

$$\Phi ::= a \mid \exists\varphi \mid \forall\varphi \mid \neg\Phi \mid \Phi_1 \wedge \Phi_2,$$

where $a \in AP$ and φ is a path formula.
- Path formulas:

$$\varphi ::= O\Phi \mid \Phi_1 U \Phi_2,$$

where Φ, Φ_1, Φ_2 are state formulas.

Path quantifiers $\exists, \forall$ are used to describe the branching structure of a computation tree. As in first-order logic, quantifier $\exists$ and $\forall$ means 'for at least one' and 'for all', respectively. But they are applied over individuals (e.g. states) in first-order logic, and in contrast they are applied over paths here; that is, $\exists\varphi$ is true in a state if φ is true for some path starting from the state, and $\forall\varphi$ is true in a state if φ is true for all paths starting from the state. The temporal operators O, U are used to describe properties of a single path in the tree. Their interpretation here in CTL is similar to those in LTL.

We sometimes use the following abbreviations:

$$\text{eventually}: \exists\Diamond\Phi := \exists(\textbf{true } U\,\Phi);$$
$$\forall\Diamond\Phi := \forall(\textbf{true } U\,\Phi);$$
$$\text{always}: \exists\Box\Phi := \neg\forall\Diamond\neg\Phi;$$
$$\forall\Box\Phi := \neg\exists\Diamond\neg\Phi.$$

Example 2.12

(i) Safety of a traffic light – each red light must be preceded by a yellow light:

$$\forall\Box(yellow \vee \forall O\neg red).$$

(ii) Every request will eventually receive a response:

$$\forall\Box(request \rightarrow \forall\Diamond response).$$

The intuitive explanations of CTL formulas given after Definition 2.11 can be more precisely formulated as their formal semantics. Accordingly, the semantics of CTL is defined for state formulas and path formulas separately.

Definition 2.13 (Semantics) Let $\mathcal{M} = (S, Act, \rightarrow, I, AP, L)$ be a transition system, $s \in S$, π a path in $\mathcal{M}$, Φ a state formula and φ a path formula over AP. Then:

(i) The satisfaction relation $s \models \Phi$ for state formulas is defined by induction on the structure of Φ:

(a) $s \models a$ iff $a \in L(s)$;
(b) $s \models \exists \varphi$ iff $\pi \models \varphi$ for some path π starting in state s;
(c) $s \models \forall \varphi$ iff $\pi \models \varphi$ for all paths π starting in state s;
(d) $s \models \neg \Phi$ iff $s \not\models \Phi$;
(e) $s \models \Phi_1 \wedge \Phi_2$ iff $s \models \Phi_1$ and $s \models \Phi_2$.

(ii) The satisfaction relation $\pi \models \varphi$ for path formulas is defined as follows:

(a) $\pi \models O\Phi$ iff $\pi[1] \models \Phi$;
(b) $\pi \models \Phi_1 U \Phi_2$ iff for some $i \geq 0$, $\pi[i] \models \Phi_2$ and $\pi[j] \models \Phi_1$ for all $0 \leq j < i$.

(iii) $\mathcal{M} \models \Phi$ iff $s_0 \models \Phi$ for all initial states $s_0 \in I$.

The reader should already have noticed that the definitions of semantics of state formulas and path formulas are indeed intertwined. Quantifiers $\exists, \forall$ and propositional connectives $\neg, \wedge$ are interpreted in the standard way, but once again, it is worth noting that here the quantifiers $\exists, \forall$ are taken over paths rather than over states as in first-order logic. Satisfaction of CTL path formulas is then defined in a way similar to that of LTL formulas.

The notion of equivalence can be introduced for CTL state formulas.

Definition 2.14 (Equivalence) Let Φ and Ψ be two state formulas over AP. Then Φ and Ψ are equivalent, written $\Phi \equiv \Psi$, if

$$\mathcal{M} \models \Phi \text{ iff } \mathcal{M} \models \Psi$$

for any transition system $\mathcal{M} = (S, Act, \rightarrow, I, AP, L)$.

Exercise 2.2

(i) Prove the expansion laws:

$$\exists(\Phi U \Psi) \equiv \Psi \vee (\Phi \wedge \exists O \exists (\Phi U \Psi)); \tag{2.3}$$

$$\exists \Box \Phi \equiv \Phi \wedge \exists O \exists \Box \Phi. \tag{2.4}$$

(ii) Find expansion laws for $\forall(\Phi U \Psi)$, $\forall \Diamond \Phi$, $\forall \Box \Phi$ and $\exists \Diamond \Phi$.

It should be noted that the left-hand side of an expansion law occurs as a subformula in the right-hand side. Thus, an expansion law can be understood as an equation of which the left-hand side is a solution (fixed point). The foregoing expansion laws will be used as a key step in model checking the properties expressed as CTL formulas.

A crucial idea for model checking CTL properties is to transform every CTL formula into a formula in a special form so that it is convenient to compute the states that satisfy the formula and are reachable in the transition system. One of such special forms is given in the following:

Definition 2.15 (Existential Normal Form) The state formulas in existential normal form (ENF) are defined by the following grammar:

$$\Phi ::= a \mid \neg\Phi \mid \Phi_1 \wedge \Phi_2 \mid \exists O\Phi \mid \exists\Box\Phi \mid \exists(\Phi_1 U \Phi_2).$$

The following theorem guarantees that the transformation of a CTL state formula into ENF is always possible.

Theorem 2.16 *Each state formula is equivalent to a state formula in ENF.*

Proof Let Φ be an arbitrary state formula. We proceed by induction on the structure of Φ.

(i) $\Phi = a \mid \neg\Psi \mid \Phi_1 \wedge \Phi_2 \mid \exists\varphi$: Obvious.
(ii) $\Phi = \forall\varphi$, where $\varphi = O\Psi \mid \Phi_1 U \Phi_2$. Then the following duality laws enable us to transform Φ into an ENF:

$$\forall O\Psi \equiv \neg\exists O\neg\Psi; \tag{2.5}$$

$$\forall(\Phi_1 U \Phi_2) \equiv \neg\exists(\neg\Phi_2 U(\neg\Phi_1 \wedge \neg\Phi_2)). \tag{2.6}$$

$\Box$

Exercise 2.3 Prove duality laws (2.5) and (2.6).

2.3 Model-Checking Algorithms

After introducing transition systems as the system's model and LTL and CTL formulas for specifying the system's properties in the previous sections, we are now ready to define our central problem:

- **Model-Checking Problem**: Given a (finite) transition system M and an LTL φ (resp. a CTL state formula Φ) over the same atomic propositions AP. The problem is to check whether $M \models \varphi$ (resp. Φ).

An algorithm solving the model-checking problem is required to return the answer:

- *'yes'* if $M \models \varphi$ (resp. Φ);
- *'no'* plus a counterexample: a finite path (resp. state) in M that violates φ (resp. Φ), if $M \not\models \varphi$ (resp. Φ)

As mentioned before, essentially, a model-checking algorithm exhaustively inspects all reachable states (of the model) of the system being checked in a systematic, but usually brute-force way.

The remainder of this section is divided into two subsections devoted to present two standard model-checking algorithms for LTL and CTL formulas, respectively. As we will see, both LTL and CTL model checking heavily depend on graph-theoretic algorithms, in particular, the algorithm for computing strongly connected components (SCCs) of graphs.

2.3.1 LTL Model Checking

In this subsection, we introduce the automata-based method for checking LTL formulas. For a simple presentation (but without any loss of generality), we consider only transition systems without terminal states.

The basic idea of this method is to transform the model-checking problem:

$$\mathcal{M} \models \varphi?$$

to a problem about the (infinite) words accepted by a certain automaton which is well studied in automata theory. The alphabet of these words is $\Sigma = 2^{AP}$. Thus, an infinite word over Σ is an infinite sequence of sets of atomic propositions:

$$\sigma = A_0 A_1 A_2 \ldots \in \left(2^{AP}\right)^{\omega},$$

where $A_0, A_1, A_2, \ldots \subseteq AP$. The solution to the LTL model-checking problem consists of the following three steps:

Step I. Constructing Büchi Automata from LTL Formulas Let us first see how an LTL formula can describe a linear-time property represented by (an ω-language of) infinite words.

> **Definition 2.17** Let φ be an LTL formula over atomic propositions AP. Then the ω-language defined by φ is
>
> $$Words(\varphi) = \left\{\sigma \in \left(2^{AP}\right)^{\omega} : \sigma \models \varphi\right\},$$
>
> where satisfaction $\sigma \models \varphi$ for infinite word $\sigma = A_0 A_1 A_2 \ldots$ is defined inductively as follows:
>
> (i) $\sigma \models a$ iff $a \in A_0$;
> (ii) $\sigma \models \neg\varphi'$ iff $\sigma \not\models \varphi'$;
> (iii) $\sigma \models \varphi_1 \wedge \varphi_2$ iff $\sigma \models \varphi_1$ and $\sigma \models \varphi_2$;
> (iv) $\sigma \models O\varphi'$ iff $\sigma[1] \models \varphi'$;
> (v) $\sigma \models \varphi_1 U \varphi_2$ iff there exists $i \geq 0$ such that $\sigma[i] \models \varphi_2$ and $\sigma[j] \models \varphi_1$ for all $0 \leq j < i$.
>
> Here, for any $i \geq 0$, $\sigma[i] = A_i A_{i+1} \ldots$ is the tail of σ starting from the $(i+1)$th element.

It is suggested that the reader compare this definition with Definition 2.8 and to observe the connection between them.

Next, we introduce the notion of generalised Büchi automaton accepting an ω-language.

Definition 2.18 A (non-deterministic) generalised Büchi automaton is a 5-tuple:

$$\mathcal{A} = (Q, \Sigma, \rightarrow, Q_0, \mathcal{F})$$

where

- Q is a finite set of states.
- Σ is a finite set of symbols, called the alphabet.
- $\rightarrow \subseteq Q \times \Sigma \times Q$ is the transition relation.
- $Q_0 \subseteq Q$ is the set of initial states.
- $\mathcal{F} \subseteq 2^Q$ is a collection of accepting sets.

In particular, if $\mathcal{F}$ consists of a single accepting set, then $\mathcal{A}$ is called a Büchi automaton.

Readers might already notice the similarity between Büchi automaton $\mathcal{A}$ and transition system $\mathcal{M}$, but they should not be confused: the latter is used to model the system, but the former will be used to represent (i.e. enumerate) the system's properties.

We write Σ^ω for the set of infinite sequences of elements in Σ. Each element σ of Σ^ω is called a (an infinite) word over Σ. An infinite sequence $\pi = q_0 q_1 q_2 \ldots$ of states in Q is called a path in $\mathcal{A}$ accepting $\sigma = \sigma_1 \sigma_2 \ldots$ if $q_i \overset{\sigma_{i+1}}{\rightarrow} q_{i+1}$; that is, $(q_i, \sigma_{i+1}, q_{i+1}) \in \rightarrow$ is a transition in $\mathcal{A}$, for every $i \geq 0$. Then the ω-language accepted by the generalised Büchi automaton $\mathcal{A}$ is defined as

$$\mathcal{L}_\omega(\mathcal{A}) = \left\{ \sigma \in \Sigma^\omega : \exists \text{ path } \pi = q_0 q_1 q_2 \ldots \text{ accepting } \sigma \text{ s.t. } (\forall F \in \mathcal{F})(\overset{\infty}{\exists} i) q_i \in F \right\},$$

where $\overset{\infty}{\exists} i$ stands for 'for infinitely many index i'.

Essentially, the basic idea of constructing a generalised Büchi automaton representing an LTL formula comes from a commonly used technique in model theory – a branch of mathematical logic:

- *constructing a model (semantics) from maximally consistent set of formulas (syntax).*

For each LTL formula φ, its closure is defined as

$$closure(\varphi) = \{\psi, \neg\psi : \psi \text{ is a subformula of } \varphi\}$$

where for every formula ψ, $\neg\neg\psi$ is identified with ψ.

Definition 2.19 Let $B \subseteq closure(\varphi)$. Then B is called maximally consistent if

(i) B is consistent with propositional connectives and temporal operators: for any $\varphi', \varphi_1, \varphi_2 \in closure(\varphi)$,

    (a) $\varphi' \in B \Rightarrow \neg\varphi' \notin B$;
    (b) $\varphi_1 \wedge \varphi_2 \in B \Leftrightarrow \varphi_1 \in B$ and $\varphi_2 \in B$;
    (c) $\varphi_2 \in B \Rightarrow \varphi_1 U \varphi_2 \in B$;
    (d) $\varphi_1 U \varphi_2 \in B$ and $\varphi_2 \notin B \Rightarrow \varphi_1 \in B$.

(ii) B is maximal: for any $\varphi' \in closure(\varphi)$,

    • $\varphi' \notin B \Rightarrow \neg\varphi' \in B$.

Subclauses (i) (a), (b) and clause (ii) in Definition 2.19 are the same as in the definition of maximally consistent sets of propositional logical formulas. It is obvious that subclauses (i) (c), (d) reflect the semantics of until operator U. The reader may notice that the semantics of next step operator O is not embodied in the above definition. But it will be embodied in the transition relation of the automaton constructed next.

Now an LTL formula φ over atomic propositions AP is given. We are ready to present the algorithm that constructs a generalised Büchi automaton:

$$\mathcal{A}_\varphi = \left(Q, 2^{AP}, \rightarrow, Q_0, \mathcal{F} \right),$$

with alphabet $\Sigma = 2^{AP}$ from φ. The ingredients of $\mathcal{A}_\varphi$ are computed as follows:

- $Q = \{$maximally consistent $B \subseteq closure(\varphi)\}$;
- $Q_0 = \{B \in Q : \varphi \in B\}$;
- The accepting sets $\mathcal{F} = \left\{ F_{\varphi_1 U \varphi_2} : \varphi_1 U \varphi_2 \in closure(\varphi) \right\}$, where

$$F_{\varphi_1 U \varphi_2} = \{B \in Q : \varphi_1 U \varphi_2 \notin B \text{ or } \varphi_2 \in B\}. \tag{2.7}$$

- The transition relation $\rightarrow \subseteq Q \times 2^{AP} \times Q$ is defined as follows:

    – If $A \neq B \cap AP$, then $B \overset{A}{\nrightarrow}$.
    – If $A = B \cap AP$, then $B \overset{A}{\rightarrow} B'$ for every $B' \in Q$ satisfying the following two conditions:

    (i) For each $O\varphi' \in closure(\varphi)$:

$$O\varphi' \in B \Leftrightarrow \varphi' \in B'. \tag{2.8}$$

    (ii) For each $\varphi_1 U \varphi_2 \in closure(\varphi)$:

$$\varphi_1 U \varphi_2 \in B \Leftrightarrow \varphi_2 \in B \vee \left(\varphi_1 \in B \wedge \varphi_1 U \varphi_2 \in B' \right). \tag{2.9}$$

Obviously, Eqs. (2.7), (2.8) and (2.9) reflect the semantics of next step and until operators O and U. In particular, (2.9) is an incarnation of the expansion law (2.2). The design idea of automaton $\mathcal{A}_\varphi$ can be further understood through the proof of Lemma 2.20.

The complexity of the algorithm for constructing $\mathcal{A}_\varphi$ is given in the following:

Exercise 2.4 Show that in the automaton $\mathcal{A}_\varphi$:

(i) The number $|Q|$ of states is $O(2^{|\varphi|})$.
(ii) The number $|\mathcal{F}|$ of accepting sets is $O(|\varphi|)$.

The following lemma shows that as intended, generalised Büchi automaton $\mathcal{A}_\varphi$ constructed earlier accepts exactly the ω-language defined by LTL formula φ.

Lemma 2.20 $\mathcal{L}_\omega(\mathcal{A}_\varphi) = Words(\varphi)$.

Proof (1) We first prove $Words(\varphi) \subseteq \mathcal{L}_\omega(\mathcal{A}_\varphi)$: Let $\sigma = A_1 A_2 \ldots \in Words(\varphi)$. Then we set:

$$B_i = \{\psi \in closure(\varphi) : A_{i+1} A_{i+2} \ldots \models \psi\}$$

for $i = 0, 1, 2, \ldots$.

Claim 1: Each $B_i \in Q$; that is, B_i is maximally consistent.

Claim 2: $B_0 \xrightarrow{A_1} B_1 \xrightarrow{A_2} B_2 \ldots$ is a path in $\mathcal{A}_\varphi$:

- $B_0 \in Q_0$; that is, $\varphi \in B_0$;
- $A_{i+1} = B_i \cap AP$ for $i = 0, 1, 2, \ldots$;
- for every $O\varphi' \in closure(\varphi)$ and $i \geq 0$: $O\varphi' \in B_i \Leftrightarrow \varphi' \in B_{i+1}$;
- for every $\varphi_1 U \varphi_2 \in closure(\varphi)$ and $i \geq 0$: $\varphi_1 U \varphi_2 \in B_i \Leftrightarrow \varphi_2 \in B_i \vee ((\varphi_1 \in B_i \wedge \varphi_1 U \varphi_2 \in B_{i+1})$.

Claim 3: For any $\varphi_1 U \varphi_2 \in closure(\varphi)$, it holds that $B_i \in F_{\varphi_1 U \varphi_2}$ for infinitely many i.

If not, then we set $i_0 = \max\{i : B_i \in F_{\varphi_1 U \varphi_2}\}$, and for each $i > i_0$:

$$A_{i+1} A_{i+2} \ldots \models \varphi_1 U \varphi_2 \text{ and } A_{i+1} A_{i+2} \ldots \not\models \varphi_2,$$

a contradiction.

(2) Now we prove $\mathcal{L}_\omega(\mathcal{A}_\varphi) \subseteq Words(\varphi)$: Let $\sigma = A_1 A_2 \ldots \in \mathcal{L}_\omega(\mathcal{A}_\varphi)$. Then there exists a path $B_0 \xrightarrow{A_1} B_1 \xrightarrow{A_2} B_2 \ldots$ in $\mathcal{A}_\varphi$ such that $B_0 \in Q_0$; that is $\varphi \in B_0$, and for each $F \in \mathcal{F}$, $B_i \in F$ for infinitely many i. Indeed, by induction on the length of ψ we can prove:

Claim 4: If $B_0, B_1, B_2, \ldots$ in Q satisfy

- $B_0 \overset{A_1}{\to} B_1 \overset{A_2}{\to} B_2 \ldots$ in $\mathcal{A}_\varphi$;
- for all $F \in \mathcal{F}$: $B_i \in F$ for infinitely many i,

then for all $\psi \in closure(\varphi)$:

$$\psi \in B_0 \Leftrightarrow A_1 A_2 \ldots \models \psi.$$

Then it follows immediately that $\sigma = A_1 A_2 \ldots \models \varphi$ and $\sigma \in Words(\varphi)$. □

Exercise 2.5 Complete the proof by verifying Claims 1, 2 and 4.

Step II. Transforming LTL Model Checking to Intersection Emptiness Problem The infinite words over 2^{AP} described by an LTL formula φ were defined in Definition 2.17. Now we define the infinite words over 2^{AP} that characterise the linear-time properties of a transition system $\mathcal{M}$. Then one can anticipate that an LTL formula φ and a transition system $\mathcal{M}$ can be linked to each other through these words.

Definition 2.21 Let $\mathcal{M} = (S, Act, \to, I, AP, L)$ be a transition system.

(i) The trace of a path $\pi = s_0 s_1 s_2 \ldots$ in $\mathcal{M}$ is the sequence

$$trace(\pi) = L(s_0) L(s_1) L(s_2) \ldots \in \left(2^{AP} \right)^\omega$$

of subsets of atomic propositions AP.

(ii) The set of traces of $\mathcal{M}$ is

$$Traces(\mathcal{M}) = \{trace(\pi) : \pi \text{ is a path starting in an initial state } s_0 \in I\}.$$

The following lemma establishes a connection between the LTL model-checking problem and the intersection emptiness problem in automata theory:

Lemma 2.22 *For any transition system $\mathcal{M}$ and LTL formula φ over the same atomic propositions; we have*

$$\mathcal{M} \models \varphi \Leftrightarrow Traces(\mathcal{M}) \cap Words(\neg\varphi) = \emptyset. \tag{2.10}$$

Proof First, we observe from Definitions 2.8 and 2.17 that for any path π in $\mathcal{M}$:

$$\pi \models \varphi \Leftrightarrow trace(\pi) \models \varphi. \tag{2.11}$$

Then it follows that

$$\mathcal{M} \models \varphi \Leftrightarrow \pi \models \varphi \text{ for all paths } \pi \text{ starting in some initial state in } I$$
$$\Leftrightarrow trace(\pi) \models \varphi \text{ for all paths } \pi \text{ starting in some initial state in } I$$
$$\Leftrightarrow Traces(\mathcal{M}) \subseteq Words(\varphi)$$
$$\Leftrightarrow Traces(\mathcal{M}) \cap Words(\neg\varphi) = \emptyset. \qquad \square$$

Exercise 2.6 Prove (2.11) by induction on the length of π.

Step III. Solving the Intersection Emptiness Problem   Now we can assemble
the techniques developed earlier to solve the LTL model-checking problem. We
are given a transition system $\mathcal{M}$ and an LTL formula φ over the same atomic
propositions AP. Using the technique developed in Step I, we can construct a
generalised Büchi automaton $\mathcal{A}_{\neg\varphi}$ such that $\mathcal{L}_\omega\left(\mathcal{A}_{\neg\varphi}\right) = Words(\neg\varphi)$. Combining
it with Eq. (2.10) in Step II, we obtain

$$\mathcal{M} \models \varphi \Leftrightarrow Traces(\mathcal{M}) \cap \mathcal{L}_\omega\left(\mathcal{A}_{\neg\varphi}\right) - \emptyset.$$

Therefore, checking whether $\mathcal{M} \models \varphi$ can be reduced to the following:

Intersection Emptiness Problem: Given a transition system $\mathcal{M} = (S, Act, \rightarrow,$
$I, AP, L)$ and a generalised Büchi automaton $\mathcal{A} = (Q, \Sigma, \rightarrow, Q_0, \mathcal{F})$ with $\Sigma =$
2^{AP}, determine whether $Traces(\mathcal{M}) \cap \mathcal{L}_\omega(\mathcal{A}) = \emptyset$.

There is a standard solution to the intersection emptiness problem for finite
state automata. It is based on the fact that the language accepted by the product
of two finite state automata is the intersection of the languages accepted by the two
automata. With the hope that this result is also true for Büchi automata, we first
construct a generalised Büchi automaton from transition system $\mathcal{M}$ and generalised
Büchi automaton $\mathcal{A}$ – the product of $\mathcal{M}$ and $\mathcal{A}$:

$$\mathcal{M} \times \mathcal{A} = (S \times Q, \Sigma, \rightarrow, I \times Q_0, \mathcal{G}),$$

where

- $(s, q) \xrightarrow{A} (s', q')$ if

    (i) $s \xrightarrow{\alpha} s'$ in $\mathcal{M}$ for some $\alpha \in Act$,
    (ii) $L(s) = A$, and
    (iii) $q \xrightarrow{A} q'$;

- $\mathcal{G} = \{S \times F : F \in \mathcal{F}\}$.

The following lemma shows that the language accepted by the product of $\mathcal{M}$ and
$\mathcal{A}$ is really the intersection of the languages accepted by $\mathcal{M}$ and $\mathcal{A}$.

Lemma 2.23 $\mathcal{L}_\omega(\mathcal{M} \times \mathcal{A}) = Traces(\mathcal{M}) \cap \mathcal{L}_\omega(\mathcal{A})$.

Exercise 2.7 Prove Lemma 2.23.

Next we show that each generalised Büchi automaton can be simulated by an
ordinary Büchi automaton.

Lemma 2.24 *For any generalised Büchi automaton $\mathcal{A}$, there exists a Büchi automaton $\mathcal{A}'$ such that $\mathcal{L}_\omega(\mathcal{A}') = \mathcal{L}_\omega(\mathcal{A})$.*

Proof Assume that generalised Büchi automaton $\mathcal{A} = (Q, \Sigma, \rightarrow, Q_0, \mathcal{F})$ with $\mathcal{F} = \{F_0, \dots, F_{k-1}\}$. Then we define Büchi automaton $\mathcal{A}' = (Q', \Sigma, \rightarrow, Q'_0, F')$, where

- $Q' = Q \times \{0, \dots, k-1\}$; $Q'_0 = Q_0 \times \{0\}$; $F' = F_1 \times \{0\}$;
- transitions:

$$(q, i) \xrightarrow{\sigma} (q', i) \text{ if } q \xrightarrow{\sigma} q' \text{ and } q \notin F_i,$$

$$(q, i) \xrightarrow{\sigma} (q', i \oplus 1) \text{ if } q \xrightarrow{\sigma} q' \text{ and } q \in F_i,$$

where $\oplus$ stands for addition modulo k. Then it is easy to verify that $\mathcal{L}_\omega(\mathcal{A}') = \mathcal{L}_\omega(\mathcal{A})$. $\square$

By combining Lemmas 2.23 and 2.24, the intersection emptiness problem is reduced to the following:

Emptiness Problem: Given a Büchi automaton $\mathcal{A} = (Q, \Sigma, \rightarrow, Q_0, F)$, determine whether $\mathcal{L}_\omega(\mathcal{A}) = \emptyset$.

A crucial observation for solving the emptiness problem is given as the following:

Lemma 2.25 *For any Büchi automaton $\mathcal{A}$, the following two statements are equivalent:*

(i) $\mathcal{L}_\omega(\mathcal{A}) \neq \emptyset$.
(ii) *There exists a state $q \in Q$ satisfying the following:*

   (a) *q is reachable; that is, $q_0 \xrightarrow{\sigma_1} q_1 \dots \xrightarrow{\sigma_{n-1}} q_{n-1} \xrightarrow{\sigma_n} q$ for some $q_0 \in Q_0$, $n \geq 0$, $q_1, \dots, q_{n-1} \in Q$ and $\sigma_1, \dots, \sigma_n \in \Sigma$;*
   (b) *q is accepted; that is, $q \in F$; and*
   (c) *q belongs to a cycle in $\mathcal{A}$; that is, $q \xrightarrow{\sigma_1} q_1 \dots \xrightarrow{\sigma_{n-1}} q_{n-1} \xrightarrow{\sigma_n} q$ for some $n \geq 1$, $q_1, \dots, q_{n-1} \in Q$ and $\sigma_1, \dots, \sigma_n \in \Sigma$.*

Exercise 2.8 Prove Lemma 2.25.

The above lemma enables us to solve the emptiness problem by a standard graph-theoretic algorithms – computing the strongly connected components (SCCs) of a graph.

Definition 2.26 Let G be a (directed) graph. Then

(i) A subgraph H of G is called strongly connected if any two nodes in H are connected by a path within H; in particular, if H has only one node, then this node must have a self-loop.
(ii) Every maximal strongly connected subgraph of G is called a strongly connected component (SCC).

Finally, the emptiness problem for a Büchi automaton $\mathcal{A} = (Q, \Sigma, \rightarrow, Q_0, F)$ can be solved in time $O(|Q| + |\rightarrow|)$ as follows:

- Compute the SCCs of the underlying graph of $\mathcal{A}$, that is the graph with elements of Q as vertices and elements of $\rightarrow$ as edges. The reader can find an algorithm for this from any textbook on algorithms, for example, [2].
- Check whether there is a nontrivial SCC that is reachable and contains an accepting state.

2.3.2 CTL Model Checking

In this section, we present an algorithm solving the CTL model-checking problem:

$$\mathcal{M} \models \Phi?$$

where $\mathcal{M}$ is a transition system and Φ a CTL state formula. This algorithm is based on the notion of satisfaction set defined in the following:

Definition 2.27 Let $\mathcal{M} = (S, Act, \rightarrow, I, AP, L)$ be a transition system and Φ a CTL state formula over AP. Then the satisfaction set of Φ in $\mathcal{M}$ is

$$Sat(\Phi) := \{s \in S : s \models \Phi\}.$$

Obviously, $\mathcal{M} \models \Phi$ if and only if $I \subseteq Sat(\Phi)$. Therefore, the essential part of checking $\mathcal{M} \models \Phi$ is the computation of satisfaction set $Sat(\Phi)$, which can be done by induction on the structure of Φ:

$$
\begin{cases}
Sat(a) & = \{s : a \in L(s)\} \text{ for every } a \in AP; \\
Sat(\neg\Phi) & = S \setminus Sat(\Phi); \\
Sat(\Phi_1 \wedge \Phi_2) & = Sat(\Phi_1) \cap Sat(\Phi_2); \\
Sat(\exists O \Phi) & = Pre(Sat(\Phi)); \\
Sat(\exists \Box \Phi) & = \nu T.[T = Sat(\Phi) \cap Pre(T)] \\
& \qquad \text{(greatest fixed point)} \\
& = \bigcup\{T \subseteq Sat(\Phi) : T \subseteq Pre(T)\}; \\
Sat(\exists(\Phi_1 U \Phi_2)) & = \mu T.[T = Sat(\Phi_2) \cup (Sat(\Phi_1) \cap Pre(T))] \\
& \qquad \text{(least fixed point)} \\
& = \bigcap\{T \supseteq Sat(\Phi_2) : Sat(\Phi_1) \cap Pre(T) \subseteq T\},
\end{cases}
\tag{2.12}
$$

where $Pre(T)$ is the set of predecessors of $T \subseteq S$:

$$Pre(T) = \{s' \in S : s' \xrightarrow{\alpha} s \text{ for some } s \in T \text{ and } \alpha \in Act\}.$$

Exercise 2.9 Prove the formulas in Eq. (2.12) for computing $Sat(\cdot)$ [Hint: use expansion laws (2.3) and (2.4) for the cases of $\exists\Box\Phi$ and $\exists(\Phi_1 U \Phi_2)$].

It is easy to see from Eq. (2.12) that the hard part in the computation of satisfaction sets is computing $Sat(\exists\Box\Phi)$ and $Sat(\exists(\Phi_1 U \Phi_2))$, which requires computing the greatest and least fixed points.

Case I. Algorithm for Computing $Sat(\exists(\Phi_1 U \Phi_2))$: The basic idea of this algorithm is as follows:

(i) We find all states that satisfy Φ_2.
(ii) We work backwards step by step using the converse of transition relation $\rightarrow$ to find all states reachable by a path where each state satisfies Φ_1.

It is easy to see that the time complexity of this algorithm is $O(|S| + | \rightarrow |)$.

Case II. Algorithm for Computing $Sat(\exists\Box\Phi)$: This algorithm can be conveniently described in terms of SCCs. First, the following lemma establishes a connection between satisfaction of formula $\exists\Box\Phi$ and SCCs.

Lemma 2.28 *We set $S' = Sat(\Phi)$, and let transition relation $\rightarrow'$ be the restriction of $\rightarrow$ on S'. Then $\mathcal{M},s \models \exists\Box\Phi$ if and only if*

(i) *$s \in S'$; and*
(ii) *$(S', \rightarrow')$ has an SCC reachable from s through a path within S'.*

Proof ($\Leftarrow$) Easy by definition.
($\Rightarrow$) If $\mathcal{M},s \models \exists\Box\Phi$, then there exists a path π starting at s such that Φ is satisfied at each state in π. Since S is a finite set, and π an infinite sequence, we can write $\pi = \pi_0\pi_1$ where π_0 is a (finite) prefix, and π_1 an infinite suffix of π such that each state in π_1 occurs infinitely often. Let C be the set of states in π_1. Then C must be strongly connected and thus contained in an SCC. $\qquad\Box$

The algorithm computing $Sat(\exists\Box\Phi)$ then works as follows:

(i) All SCCs of graph $(S', \rightarrow')$ are computed using a standard graph-theoretic algorithm.
(ii) We work backward using the converse of $\rightarrow'$ to find all states that can reach some state in an SCC.

It is easy to see that the time complexity of this algorithm is $O(|S| + | \rightarrow |)$.

2.4 Model Checking Probabilistic Systems

The model-checking techniques introduced in the previous sections have been systematically generalised to probabilistic systems with applications in, for example, analysis and verification of randomised algorithms and unreliable communication systems and performance evaluation of computer systems.

As is well known, the behaviour of quantum systems (observed by measurements) is essentially statistical. So, some ideas in model checking probabilistic systems can serve as a stepping stone in developing model-checking techniques for quantum systems. In this section, we briefly review the basics of probabilistic model checking.

2.4.1 Markov Chains and Markov Decision Processes

Two of the most popular models used in model checking probabilistic systems are (discrete-time) Markov chains and Markov decision processes. Essentially, they are probabilistic extensions of transition systems and (non-deterministic) finite state automata.

Definition 2.29 A (discrete-time) Markov chain is a 5-tuple:

$$\mathcal{M} = (S, P, I, AP, L),$$

where

- S, AP and L are the same as in Definition 2.1.
- $P : S \times S \rightarrow [0,1]$ is the transition probability function such that for every $s \in S$:

$$\sum_{s' \in S} P(s, s') = 1.$$

- $I : S \rightarrow [0, 1]$ is the initial distribution such that $\sum_{s \in S} I(s) = 1$.

Intuitively, for each $s \in S$, $I(s)$ is the probability that the system starts in state s, and for any $s, s' \in S$, $P(s, s')$ is the probability that the system moves from state s to s' in one step.

Comparing Definition 2.29 with Definitions 2.1 and 2.2 should be helpful for the reader. In a deterministic transition system (Definition 2.2), an action changes it from a state to at most one next state. An action allows a (non-deterministic) transition system (Definition 2.1) to move from one state to more than one next states, which are chosen non-deterministically. In contrast, a Markov chain moves from a state s to the next states according to a probability distribution $P(s, \cdot)$ (note that actions are not specified explicitly).

Markov chains can be generalised to Markov decision processes in order to model concurrent probabilistic systems, where interleaving behaviours may occur.

Definition 2.30 A (discrete-time) Markov decision process is a 6-tuple:

$$\mathcal{M} = (S, Act, P, I, AP, L),$$

where

- S, Act, AP, L are the same as in Definition 2.1, and I is as in Definition 2.29.
- $P : S \times Act \times S \to [0,1]$ is the transition probability function such that for every $s \in S$ and every $\alpha \in Act$:

$$\sum_{s' \in S} P(s, \alpha, s') = 1 \text{ or } 0.$$

An action α is enabled in a state s if $\sum_{s' \in S} P(s, \alpha, s') = 1$. We write $Act(s)$ for the set of enabled actions in s. Intuitively, if $Act(s) = \emptyset$, then no action can be performed in state s. Otherwise, on entering state s, an enabled action $\alpha \in Act(s)$ is chosen non-deterministically. After performing action α, the system moves from s to the next state according to the probability distribution $P(s, \alpha, \cdot)$. Here, non-deterministic and probabilistic choices are combined together. Obviously, Markov chains can be seen as a special class of Markov decision processes.

2.4.2 Probabilistic Temporal Logics

The properties of probabilistic systems verified by model-checking techniques mainly include

- *Qualitative properties* — a certain event will happen almost surely (with probability 1) or never (with probability 0)
- *Quantitative properties* — constraints on the probability or expectation of certain events

The temporal logics defined in the previous sections can be expanded to specify these properties.

Probability Measure over Infinite Paths A key step in defining probabilistic temporal logics is to properly define a probability measure over (infinite) paths in a Markov chain or decision process. Here, we assume the reader is familiar with the basic measure theory. We only give an outline of the procedure for defining a probability space $(Paths(\mathcal{M}), \mathcal{B}_\mathcal{M}, Pr_\mathcal{M})$ in a Markov chain $\mathcal{M} = (S, P, I, AP, L)$:

- The sample space is $Paths(\mathcal{M})$ — the set of all infinite paths $s_0 s_1 s_2 \ldots$ such that $P(s_i, s_{i+1}) > 0$ for all $i \geq 0$.
- For each finite path $\hat{\pi} = s_0 s_1 \ldots s_n$, the cylinder set spanned by it is defined as:

$$C(\hat{\pi}) = \{ \pi \in Paths(\mathcal{M}) : \hat{\pi} \text{ is a prefix of } \pi \}.$$

Then all cylinder sets generate a σ-algebra $\mathcal{B}_\mathcal{M}$ such that $(Paths(\mathcal{M}), \mathcal{B}_\mathcal{M})$ is a measurable space.

- The probability of the cylinder set spanned by $\hat{\pi} = s_0 s_1 \ldots s_n$ is naturally defined as

$$Pr_{\mathcal{M}}(C(\hat{\pi})) = I(s_0) \cdot \prod_{i=0}^{n-1} P(s_i, s_{i+1}).$$

Furthermore, by the Carathéodory–Hahn theorem, the probabilities of cylinder sets can be uniquely extended to a probability measure $Pr_{\mathcal{M}}$ over $\mathcal{B}_{\mathcal{M}}$ because $\mathcal{B}_{\mathcal{M}}$ is generated from cylinder sets.

The above procedure can be further generalised to define a probability measure over infinite paths in a Markov decision process.

Probabilistic Extension of Temporal Logics: Probabilities can be introduced into temporal logics at either the semantic or syntactic level:

- For an LTL formula φ and a state $s \in S$, one can show that

$$[\![\varphi]\!]_s = \{\pi \in Paths(\mathcal{M}) \text{ starting in } s : \pi \models \varphi\}$$

is measurable; that is, $[\![\varphi]\!]_s \in \mathcal{B}_{\mathcal{M}}$. Therefore, the probability that φ is satisfied by state s in $\mathcal{M}$ is well defined:

$$Pr_{\mathcal{M}}(s \models \varphi) = Pr_{\mathcal{M}_s}([\![\varphi]\!]_s),$$

where $\mathcal{M}_s$ is the Markov chain obtained from $\mathcal{M}$ by replacing the initial distribution with the point distribution δ_s:

$$\delta_s(s') = \begin{cases} 1 & \text{if } s' = s, \\ 0 & \text{otherwise.} \end{cases}$$

- Probabilistic computation tree logic (PCTL) is defined through replacing the universal and existential quantification $\forall \varphi$ and $\exists \varphi$ in the syntax of CTL by a *probabilistic quantifier* $\mathbb{P}_J(\varphi)$, where J is a subinterval of $[0, 1]$ (with rational ends). Its satisfaction is defined as follows: for a state $s \in S$,

  - $s \models \mathbb{P}_J(\varphi)$ iff $Pr_{\mathcal{M}}(s \models \varphi) \in J$.

  For example, qualitative properties of a probabilistic system can be specified as $\mathbb{P}_J(\varphi)$ with $J = \{1\}$ or $\{0\}$.

2.4.3 *Probabilistic Model-Checking Algorithms*

The models and logical languages introduced in the preceding two subsections enable us to formulate model-checking problems for probabilistic systems. Here, we focus on Markov chains, but the ideas presented in the text that follows can be generalised to Markov decision processes.

Two typical probabilistic model-checking problems are as follows. Given a Markov chain $\mathcal{M}$,

- **Quantitative Problem:** Compute the probability $Pr_{\mathcal{M}}(s \models \varphi)$, where φ is an LTL formula, and s a state of $\mathcal{M}$.
- **Qualitative Problem:** Check whether $\mathcal{M} \models \Phi$ or not, where Φ is a PCTL state formula.

Various algorithms for checking probabilistic systems against quantitative and qualitative temporal properties have been developed. We saw in the preceding section that computing reachable states is a crucial step in both non-probabilistic LTL and CTL model checking, which can be in turn solved by graph-theoretic algorithms, in particular BSCC decomposition. Reachability analysis plays a similar role in model checking probabilistic systems. Now the question is turned to compute the probability of reaching a certain set B of states in a Markov chain.

I. Algorithm for Quantitative Problems   LTL model-checking algorithms for Markov chains are usually automata based, just as the one presented in the last section for (non-probabilistic) transition systems. The core idea of automata-based model checking is to connect the system under checking and its property to be checked by taking a product of the system's model and the Büchi automaton representing the property. However, this idea cannot be directly applied to Markov chains, because a Büchi automaton can be non-deterministic, but non-determinism (rather than probabilism) is not involved in a Markov chain, and thus the product of a Markov chain and a Büchi automaton may not be a Markov chain. One way to overcome this difficulty is to introduce a deterministic variant of Büchi automaton, say, a deterministic Rabin automaton.

Definition 2.31 A deterministic Rabin automaton is a 5-tuple:

$$\mathcal{A} = (Q, \Sigma, \delta, q_0, Acc),$$

where

- Q is a finite set of states;
- Σ is the alphabet;
- $\delta : Q \times \Sigma \to Q$ is the transition function;
- $q_0 \in Q$ is the initial state; and
- $Acc \subseteq 2^Q \times 2^Q$ is a collection of accepting pairs from 2^Q.

A path of $\mathcal{A}$ for an infinite word $\sigma = \sigma_1 \sigma_2 \ldots \in \Sigma^{\omega}$ is an infinite sequence $\pi = q_0 q_1 q_2 \ldots$ of states in Q such that $\delta(q_i, \sigma_{i+1}) = q_{i+1}$ for every $i \geq 0$. The path π is accepting if there exists a pair $(L, K) \in Acc$ such that

$$\left[(\exists i)(\forall j \geq i)\, q_j \notin L \right] \wedge \left[(\overset{\infty}{\exists} i)\, q_i \in K \right].$$

The ω-language accepted by $\mathcal{A}$ is defined as

$$\mathcal{L}_{\omega}(\mathcal{A}) = \{\sigma \in \Sigma^{\omega} : \text{the path of } \mathcal{A} \text{ for } \sigma \text{ is accepting}\}.$$

Product of Rabin Automata and Markov Chains   Now we are given a Markov chain $\mathcal{M} = (S, P, I, AP, L)$ and a deterministic Rabin automaton $\mathcal{A} = (Q, 2^{AP}, \delta, q_0, Acc)$ with $Acc = \{(L_i, K_i) : 1 \leq i \leq n\}$; we can then construct the product of $\mathcal{M}$ and $\mathcal{A}$, which is again a Markov chain, as follows:

$$\mathcal{M} \times \mathcal{A} = (S \times Q, P', I', AP', L'),$$

where

- $P'((s, q), (s', q')) = \begin{cases} P(s, s') & \text{if } q' = \delta(q, L(s')), \\ 0 & \text{otherwise}; \end{cases}$

- $I'((s, q)) = \begin{cases} I(s) & \text{if } q = \delta(q_0, L(s)), \\ 0 & \text{otherwise}; \end{cases}$

- $AP' = \{L_i, K_i : 1 \leq i \leq n\};$
- $L'((s, q)) = \{R \in AP' : q \in R\}.$

Checking Algorithm   As a generalisation of Definition 2.26, a notion of BSCC (bottom strongly connected component) can be defined for Markov chains. Furthermore, a BSCC B of $\mathcal{M} \times \mathcal{A}$ is called accepting if there exists i such that

$$B \cap (S \times L_i) = \emptyset \qquad \text{and} \qquad B \cap (S \times K_i) \neq \emptyset.$$

Then the following results can be shown from which an algorithm for LTL model checking follows naturally:

(i) For any LTL formula φ over atomic propositions AP, there is a deterministic Rabin automaton $\mathcal{A}_{\varphi}$ with alphabet 2^{AP}, which can be constructed in time $O(2^{2^{|\varphi|}})$, such that $\mathcal{L}_{\omega}(\mathcal{A}_{\varphi}) = Words(\varphi)$.

(ii) For any Markov chain $\mathcal{M}$ and a deterministic Rabin automaton $\mathcal{A}$, let U be the union of all accepting BSCCs of $\mathcal{M} \times \mathcal{A}$. Then

$$Pr_{\mathcal{M}}(s \models \varphi) = Pr_{\mathcal{M} \times \mathcal{A}}((s, q_s) \models \Diamond U),$$

where $q_s = \delta(q_0, L(s))$. Furthermore, the reachability probability on the right can be computed with time complexity $poly(|\mathcal{M}| \cdot |\mathcal{A}|)$ (see II. Algorithm for Qualitative Problems for PCTL model checking).

In summary, the time complexity of the preceding algorithm to compute the probability $Pr_{\mathcal{M}}(s \models \varphi)$ is $O(poly(2^{2^{|\varphi|}} \cdot |\mathcal{M}|))$. Note that more efficient (single exponential in $|\varphi|$) but more conceptually involved algorithms exist for probabilistic LTL model checking. A detailed discussion of these algorithms is beyond the scope of this book.

II. Algorithm for Qualitative Problems: Similar to non-probabilistic CTL model checking presented in the preceding section, PCTL model checking for Markov chains also boils down to the computation of satisfaction sets. The only difference is that here we are required to compute

$$Sat(\mathbb{P}_J(\varphi)) := \{s \in S : Pr_{\mathcal{M}}(s \models \varphi) \in J\},$$

for probabilistic quantification over a path formula φ. There are two cases to consider:

(i) $\varphi \equiv O\Phi$. This case is easy, since

$$Pr_{\mathcal{M}}(s \models O\Phi) = \sum_{s' \in Sat(\Phi)} P(s, s').$$

(ii) $\varphi = \Phi_1 U \Phi_2$. This case requires to solve a certain linear equation system. To be specific, let

$$S_0 = \{s \in S : Pr_{\mathcal{M}}(s \models \varphi) = 0\}$$
$$S_1 = \{s \in S : Pr_{\mathcal{M}}(s \models \varphi) = 1\},$$

which are computable efficiently (with linear time complexity in the size of $\mathcal{M}$) by simple graph algorithms. Let $S_? = S \backslash S_0 \backslash S_1$. We construct a linear equation system:

$$(\mathbf{I} - \mathbf{A})\mathbf{x} = \mathbf{b},$$

where

$$\mathbf{A} = \left[P(s, s') \right]_{s, s' \in S_?}, \qquad \mathbf{b} = \left[\sum_{s' \in S_1} P(s, s') \right]_{s \in S_?}.$$

Then it can be shown that the equation system has a unique solution $\mathbf{x}^* = \left[x_s^* \right]_{s \in S_?}$ with

$$x_s^* = Pr_{\mathcal{M}}(s \models \varphi)$$

for all $s \in S_?$.

The time complexity of the preceding algorithm to check whether $\mathcal{M} \models \Phi$ is $O(|\Phi| \cdot poly(|\mathcal{M}|))$.

2.5 Bibliographic Remarks

Model checking was invented by Clarke and Emerson [33] and Queille and Sifakis [101] in the early 1980s. Now it has been developed into a large area with a huge number of papers presented in conferences or published in journals. Fortunately, there are two standard textbooks [7, 35] for it. A major later development is bounded model checking, which is not included in [7, 35], but is nicely surveyed in [19].

The automata-based LTL model-checking algorithm presented in Subsection 2.3.1 was proposed by Vardi and Wolper [110], and the CTL model-checking algorithm presented in Subsection 2.3.2 was given in the original paper [33], but our exposition of them largely follows [7, 35]. The comparison of the expressive powers of LTL and CTL as well as the complexity of LTL- and CTL-model checking are not considered in this chapter, model checking probabilistic systems is only very briefly discussed, and timed systems are untouched. The interested reader can find a careful discussion of them in [7].

3

Basics of Quantum Theory

This chapter is intended to introduce some basic notions of quantum theory needed in the subsequent chapters for the reader who is not familiar with them.

Quantum mechanics is a fundamental physics subject that studies phenomena at the atomic and subatomic scales. It has been built based on several basic postulates. We introduce the required mathematical tools and then present these postulates mainly through their mathematical formalisms. Their interpretation in terms of physics is only very briefly discussed; for more details, we recommend the reader consult chapter 2 of the excellent textbook [93].

3.1 State Spaces of Quantum Systems

Let us start from a static description of a quantum system, that is, how its states can be modelled mathematically.

3.1.1 Hilbert Spaces

A quantum system is associated with a Hilbert space, which is called the state space of the system. The main aim of this book is to present algorithms for checking quantum systems, so we only deal with finite-dimensional Hilbert spaces, which are essentially complex vector spaces equipped with an inner product.

Let $\mathbb{C}$ stand for the set of complex numbers. For a complex number $\lambda = a + bi \in \mathbb{C}$, we write λ^* for its conjugate; that is, $\lambda^* = a - bi$. The standard Dirac notation in quantum mechanics is adopted in this book; we use $|\varphi\rangle, |\psi\rangle, \ldots$ to denote vectors in Hilbert spaces.

Definition 3.1 A (complex) vector space is a non-empty set $\mathcal{H}$ with two operations:

- Vector addition $(+) : \mathcal{H} \times \mathcal{H} \to \mathcal{H}, (|\varphi\rangle, |\psi\rangle) \mapsto |\varphi\rangle + |\psi\rangle$
- Scalar multiplication $(\cdot) : \mathbb{C} \times \mathcal{H} \to \mathcal{H}, (\lambda, |\psi\rangle) \mapsto \lambda \cdot |\psi\rangle \equiv \lambda|\psi\rangle$

satisfying the following conditions: for any $|\varphi\rangle, |\psi\rangle, |\chi\rangle \in \mathcal{H}$, and $\lambda, \mu \in \mathbb{C}$,

(i) (+ is commutative) $|\varphi\rangle + |\psi\rangle = |\psi\rangle + |\varphi\rangle$;

(ii) (+ is associative) $|\varphi\rangle + (|\psi\rangle + |\chi\rangle) = (|\varphi\rangle + |\psi\rangle) + |\chi\rangle$;

(iii) + has a zero element 0, called the zero vector, such that $0 + |\varphi\rangle = |\varphi\rangle$;

(iv) there exists a vector $-|\varphi\rangle$ such that $|\varphi\rangle + (-|\varphi\rangle) = 0$;

(v) $1|\varphi\rangle = |\varphi\rangle$;

(vi) $\lambda(\mu|\varphi\rangle) = \lambda\mu|\varphi\rangle$;

(vii) $(\lambda + \mu)|\varphi\rangle = \lambda|\varphi\rangle + \mu|\varphi\rangle$;

(viii) $\lambda(|\varphi\rangle + |\psi\rangle) = \lambda|\varphi\rangle + \lambda|\psi\rangle$.

Example 3.2 For any integer $n \geq 1$, the n-dimensional vector space $\mathcal{H}_n = \mathbb{C}^n$ consists of all n-dimensional column vectors:

$$\begin{pmatrix} \alpha_1 \\ \cdots \\ \alpha_n \end{pmatrix},$$

with $\alpha_1, \ldots, \alpha_n \in \mathbb{C}$. The vector addition and scalar multiplication are defined as follows:

$$\begin{pmatrix} \alpha_1 \\ \cdots \\ \alpha_n \end{pmatrix} + \begin{pmatrix} \beta_1 \\ \cdots \\ \beta_n \end{pmatrix} = \begin{pmatrix} \alpha_1 + \beta_1 \\ \cdots \\ \alpha_n + \beta_n \end{pmatrix},$$

$$\lambda \cdot \begin{pmatrix} \alpha_1 \\ \cdots \\ \alpha_n \end{pmatrix} = \begin{pmatrix} \lambda\alpha_1 \\ \cdots \\ \lambda\alpha_n \end{pmatrix}.$$

Definition 3.3 An inner product space is a vector space $\mathcal{H}$ equipped with an inner product

$$\langle \cdot | \cdot \rangle : \mathcal{H} \times \mathcal{H} \to \mathbb{C}$$

such that for any $|\varphi\rangle, |\psi\rangle, |\psi_1\rangle, |\psi_2\rangle \in \mathcal{H}$ and $\lambda_1, \lambda_2 \in \mathbb{C}$,

(i) $\langle \varphi | \varphi \rangle \geq 0$ with equality holds if and only if $|\varphi\rangle = 0$;

(ii) $\langle \varphi | \psi \rangle = \langle \psi | \varphi \rangle^*$;

(iii) $\langle \varphi | \lambda_1 \psi_1 + \lambda_2 \psi_2 \rangle = \lambda_1 \langle \varphi | \psi_1 \rangle + \lambda_2 \langle \varphi | \psi_2 \rangle$.

Sometimes, we write $(|\varphi\rangle, |\psi\rangle)$ for $\langle \varphi | \psi \rangle$. Two vectors $|\varphi\rangle$ and $|\psi\rangle$ are said to be orthogonal, denoted $|\varphi\rangle \perp |\psi\rangle$, if $\langle \varphi | \psi \rangle = 0$. The length of a vector $|\psi\rangle \in \mathcal{H}$ is defined to be

$$\||\psi\| = \sqrt{\langle \psi | \psi \rangle}.$$

It is called a unit vector if its length equals 1.

Example 3.4 The inner product in $\mathbb{C}^n$ is defined as follows:

$$\langle \varphi | \psi \rangle = \sum_{i=1}^{n} \alpha_i^* \beta_i$$

for any

$$|\varphi\rangle = \begin{pmatrix} \alpha_1 \\ \ldots \\ \alpha_n \end{pmatrix}, \quad |\psi\rangle = \begin{pmatrix} \alpha_1 \\ \ldots \\ \alpha_n \end{pmatrix}$$

in $\mathbb{C}^n$. It is easy to see that the length of $|\varphi\rangle$ is

$$\|\varphi\| = \sqrt{\sum_{i=1}^{n} |\alpha_i|^2}.$$

Definition 3.5 A family $\{|\psi_i\rangle\}$ of unit vectors is called an orthonormal basis of $\mathcal{H}$ if

(i) $\{|\psi_i\rangle\}$ are pairwise orthogonal: $|\psi_i\rangle \perp |\psi_j\rangle$ for all $i \neq j$;
(ii) $\{|\psi_i\rangle\}$ span the whole space $\mathcal{H}$; that is, each $|\psi\rangle \in \mathcal{H}$ can be written as a linear combination of $\{|\psi_i\rangle\}$: $|\psi\rangle = \sum_i \lambda_i |\psi_i\rangle$ for some $\lambda_i \in \mathbb{C}$.

Example 3.6 For $1 \le i \le n$, let

$$|i - 1\rangle = \begin{pmatrix} 0 \\ \ldots \\ 0 \\ 1 \\ 0 \\ \ldots \\ 0 \end{pmatrix} \quad (1 \text{ appears only at row } i).$$

Then $\{|i - 1\rangle\}_{i=1}^{n}$ is an orthonormal basis of $\mathbb{C}^n$.

For a given Hilbert space $\mathcal{H}$, the numbers of vectors in any two orthonormal bases are the same. It is called the dimension of $\mathcal{H}$ and denoted $\dim \mathcal{H}$. If $\dim \mathcal{H} = n$, and we consider a *fixed* orthonormal basis $\{|\psi_1\rangle, |\psi_2\rangle, \ldots, |\psi_n\rangle\}$, then each vector $|\psi\rangle = \sum_{i=1}^{n} \lambda_i |\psi_i\rangle \in \mathcal{H}$ can be represented by the vector in $\mathbb{C}^n$:

$$\begin{pmatrix} \lambda_1 \\ \vdots \\ \lambda_n \end{pmatrix}.$$

In this way, every n-dimensional vector space is isomorphic to $\mathbb{C}^n$.

3.1.2 Subspaces

Definition 3.7 Let $\mathcal{H}$ be a vector space and $X \subseteq \mathcal{H}$. If for any $|\varphi\rangle, |\psi\rangle \in X$ and $\lambda \in \mathbb{C}$,

(i) $|\varphi\rangle + |\psi\rangle \in X$; and
(ii) $\lambda|\varphi\rangle \in X$,

then X is called a subspace of $\mathcal{H}$.

For any subset $X \subseteq \mathcal{H}$,

$$spanX = \left\{ \sum_{i=1}^{n} \lambda_i |\psi_i\rangle : n \geq 1, \text{and } \forall i.(\lambda_i \in \mathbb{C} \wedge |\psi_i\rangle \in X) \right\} \qquad (3.1)$$

is the smallest subspace of $\mathcal{H}$ containing X, called the space spanned by X. In other words, $spanX$ is the subspace of $\mathcal{H}$ generated by X.

The orthogonality between two states can be naturally generalised to orthogonality between two sets of states.

Definition 3.8 Let $\mathcal{H}$ be a vector space and $X, Y \subseteq \mathcal{H}$. Then we say that X and Y are orthogonal, written $X \perp Y$, if $|\varphi\rangle \perp |\psi\rangle$ for all $|\varphi\rangle \in X$ and $|\psi\rangle \in Y$. In particular, we simply write $|\varphi\rangle \perp Y$ if X is the one-dimensional space spanned by $\{|\varphi\rangle\}$.

Definition 3.9 Let $\mathcal{H}$ be a vector space. Then the orthocomplement of a subspace X of $\mathcal{H}$ is

$$X^{\perp} = \{|\varphi\rangle \in \mathcal{H} : |\varphi\rangle \perp X\}.$$

The orthocomplement $X^{\perp}$ is also a subspace of $\mathcal{H}$, and we have $(X^{\perp})^{\perp} = X$ for every subspace X of $\mathcal{H}$.

Definition 3.10 Let $\mathcal{H}$ be a vector space, and X, Y two subspaces of $\mathcal{H}$. Then

$$X \oplus Y = \{|\varphi\rangle + |\psi\rangle : |\varphi\rangle \in X \text{ and } |\psi\rangle \in Y\}$$

is called the sum of X and Y.

Similarly, we can define $\bigoplus_{i=1}^{n} X_i$ of subspaces X_i for any $n \geq 2$. If X_i $(1 \leq i \leq n)$ are orthogonal to each other, then $\bigoplus_{i=1}^{n} X_i$ is called an orthogonal sum.

Exercise 3.1 Prove or disprove the following statements:

(i) $spanX \oplus spanY = span(X \cup Y)$ for any $X, Y \subseteq \mathcal{H}$.
(ii) $(X \oplus Y)^{\perp} = X^{\perp} \cap Y^{\perp}$ for any subspaces X, Y of $\mathcal{H}$.

3.1.3 Postulate of Quantum Mechanics I

Now we are ready to introduce the postulate about the states of a quantum system:

- **Postulate I:** The state space of an isolated quantum system (i.e. a system without interactions with its environment) is represented by a Hilbert space, and a pure state of the system is described by a unit vector in its state space.

A linear combination

$$|\psi\rangle = \sum_{i=1}^{n} \lambda_i |\psi_i\rangle$$

of states $|\psi_1\rangle, \ldots, |\psi_n\rangle$ is often called their *superposition*, and the complex coefficients λ_i are called probability amplitudes.

Example 3.11 A qubit – quantum bit – is the quantum counterpart of a bit. Its state space is the 2-dimensional vector space

$$\mathcal{H}_2 = \mathbb{C}^2 = \{\alpha|0\rangle + \beta|1\rangle : \alpha, \beta \in \mathbb{C}\}.$$

The inner product in $\mathcal{H}_2$ is defined by

$$(\alpha|0\rangle + \beta|1\rangle, \alpha'|0\rangle + \beta'|1\rangle) = \alpha^*\alpha' + \beta^*\beta'$$

for all $\alpha, \alpha', \beta, \beta' \in \mathbb{C}$. Then $\{|0\rangle, |1\rangle\}$ is an orthonormal basis of $\mathcal{H}_2$, called the computational basis. The vectors $|0\rangle, |1\rangle$ themselves are represented as

$$|0\rangle = \begin{pmatrix} 1 \\ 0 \end{pmatrix}, \quad |1\rangle = \begin{pmatrix} 0 \\ 1 \end{pmatrix}$$

in this basis.

A state of a qubit is described by a unit vector $|\psi\rangle = \alpha|0\rangle + \beta|1\rangle$ with $|\alpha|^2 + |\beta|^2 = 1$. The two vectors

$$|+\rangle = \frac{|0\rangle + |1\rangle}{\sqrt{2}} = \frac{1}{\sqrt{2}} \begin{pmatrix} 1 \\ 1 \end{pmatrix}, \quad |-\rangle = \frac{|0\rangle - |1\rangle}{\sqrt{2}} = \frac{1}{\sqrt{2}} \begin{pmatrix} 1 \\ -1 \end{pmatrix}$$

form another orthonormal basis. Both of these vectors are superpositions of $|0\rangle$ and $|1\rangle$.

3.2 Dynamics of Quantum Systems

Now we turn to consider how can we describe the dynamics of a quantum system. The evolution of an isolated quantum system is mathematically modelled by a unitary transformation, which is a special linear operator on its state vector space.

3.2.1 Linear Operators

Definition 3.12 Let $\mathcal{H}$ be a Hilbert space. A mapping

$$A : \mathcal{H} \rightarrow \mathcal{H}$$

is called an (a linear) operator on $\mathcal{H}$ if it satisfies the following conditions:

(i) $A(|\varphi\rangle + |\psi\rangle) = A|\varphi\rangle + A|\psi\rangle$; and
(ii) $A(\lambda|\psi\rangle) = \lambda A|\psi\rangle$

for all $|\varphi\rangle, |\psi\rangle \in \mathcal{H}$ and $\lambda \in \mathbb{C}$.

We write $\mathcal{L}(\mathcal{H})$ for the set of operators in a Hilbert space $\mathcal{H}$.

Example 3.13

(i) The identity operator in $\mathcal{H}$ maps each vector in $\mathcal{H}$ to itself and is denoted $I_{\mathcal{H}}$.

(ii) The zero operator in $\mathcal{H}$ maps every vector in $\mathcal{H}$ to the zero vector and is denoted $0_{\mathcal{H}}$.

(iii) For any vectors $|\varphi\rangle, |\psi\rangle \in \mathcal{H}$, their outer product is the operator $|\varphi\rangle\langle\psi|$ on $\mathcal{H}$ defined by

$$(|\varphi\rangle\langle\psi|)|\chi\rangle = \langle\psi|\chi\rangle|\varphi\rangle$$

for every $|\chi\rangle \in \mathcal{H}$.

A class of very useful operators are projectors (or projection operators). Let X be a subspace of $\mathcal{H}$ and $|\psi\rangle \in \mathcal{H}$. Then there exist uniquely $|\psi_0\rangle \in X$ and $|\psi_1\rangle \in X^{\perp}$ such that

$$|\psi\rangle = |\psi_0\rangle + |\psi_1\rangle.$$

The vector $|\psi_0\rangle$ is called the projection of $|\psi\rangle$ onto X and written $|\psi_0\rangle = P_X|\psi\rangle$.

Definition 3.14 For each subspace X of $\mathcal{H}$, the operator

$$P_X : \mathcal{H} \to X, \quad |\psi\rangle \mapsto P_X|\psi\rangle$$

is called the projector onto X.

Exercise 3.2 Show that $P_X = \sum_i |\psi_i\rangle\langle\psi_i|$ whenever $\{|\psi_i\rangle\}$ is an orthonormal basis of X.

Another class of useful operators are positive operators defined in the following:

Definition 3.15 An operator $A \in \mathcal{L}(\mathcal{H})$ is positive if for all states $|\psi\rangle \in \mathcal{H}$, $\langle\psi|A|\psi\rangle \geq 0$.

Various operations of operators can be defined in order to combine several operators to produce a new one.

Definition 3.16 For any operators $A, B \in \mathcal{L}(\mathcal{H})$ and $\lambda \in \mathbb{C}$, the addition, scalar multiplication and composition are defined as follows: for every $|\psi\rangle \in \mathcal{H}$,

$$(A + B)|\psi\rangle = A|\psi\rangle + B|\psi\rangle,$$
$$(\lambda A)|\psi\rangle = \lambda(A|\psi\rangle),$$
$$(BA)|\psi\rangle = B(A|\psi\rangle).$$

Exercise 3.3 Show that $\mathcal{L}(\mathcal{H})$ equipped with addition and scalar multiplication forms a vector space.

Based on the notion of positivity, we can define an order between operators.

Definition 3.17 The Löwner order $\sqsubseteq$ is defined as follows: for any $A, B \in \mathcal{L}(\mathcal{H})$, $A \sqsubseteq B$ if and only if $B - A = B + (-1)A$ is positive.

Matrix Representation of Operators. The preceding discussions about operators are given in an abstract manner. Indeed, in a finite-dimensional space, operators can be described in a concrete way that the reader is more familiar with. Let $\dim \mathcal{H} = n$. For a given orthonormal basis $\{|\psi_1\rangle, \ldots, |\psi_n\rangle\}$, each linear operator A on $\mathcal{H}$ can be represented by an $n \times n$ complex matrix:

$$A = (a_{ij})_{n \times n} = \begin{pmatrix} a_{11} & \cdots & a_{1n} \\ \vdots & \ddots & \vdots \\ a_{n1} & \cdots & a_{nn} \end{pmatrix},$$

where

$$a_{ij} = \langle \psi_i | A | \psi_j \rangle = (|\psi_i\rangle, A|\psi_j\rangle)$$

for every $i, j = 1, \ldots, n$. Moreover, the image of a vector $|\psi\rangle = \sum_{i=1}^{n} \alpha_i |\psi_i\rangle \in \mathcal{H}$ under operator A is represented by the product of matrix $A = (a_{ij})_{n \times n}$ and vector $(\alpha_i)_{n \times 1}$:

$$A|\psi\rangle = A \begin{pmatrix} \alpha_1 \\ \vdots \\ \alpha_n \end{pmatrix} = \begin{pmatrix} \beta_1 \\ \vdots \\ \beta_n \end{pmatrix},$$

where $\beta_i = \sum_{j=1}^{n} a_{ij}\alpha_j$ for every $i = 1, \ldots, n$.

Example 3.18

(i) The identity operator $I_\mathcal{H}$ is represented by the unit matrix.
(ii) The zero operator $0_\mathcal{H}$ is represented by the zero matrix.
(iii) If

$$|\varphi\rangle = \begin{pmatrix} \alpha_1 \\ \vdots \\ \alpha_n \end{pmatrix}, \quad |\psi\rangle = \begin{pmatrix} \beta_1 \\ \vdots \\ \beta_n \end{pmatrix},$$

then their outer product is the matrix $|\varphi\rangle\langle\psi| = (a_{ij})_{n \times n}$ with $a_{ij} = \alpha_i \beta_j^*$ for every $i, j = 1, \ldots, n$.

3.2.2 Unitary Operators

Definition 3.19 For any operator A on a Hilbert space $\mathcal{H}$, there exists a unique operator $A^\dagger$ on $\mathcal{H}$ such that

$$(A|\varphi\rangle, |\psi\rangle) = \left(|\varphi\rangle, A^\dagger|\psi\rangle \right)$$

for all $|\varphi\rangle, |\psi\rangle \in \mathcal{H}$. The operator $A^\dagger$ is called the adjoint of A.

Let $\dim \mathcal{H} = n$. If A is represented by the matrix $A = (a_{ij})_{n \times n}$ in a given orthonormal basis, then its adjoint is represented by the transpose conjugate of A:

$$A^\dagger = (b_{ij})_{n \times n},$$

with $b_{ij} = a_{ji}^*$ for every $i, j = 1, \ldots, n$.

Definition 3.20 An operator $U \in \mathcal{L}(\mathcal{H})$ is called a unitary transformation if the adjoint of U is its inverse:

$$U^\dagger U = U U^\dagger = I_\mathcal{H}.$$

Exercise 3.4 Let $\mathcal{H}$ be a finite-dimensional Hilbert space. Prove that $U^\dagger U = I_\mathcal{H}$ if and only if $U U^\dagger = I_\mathcal{H}$.

Every unitary transformation U preserves the inner product: for any $|\varphi\rangle, |\psi\rangle \in \mathcal{H}$,

$$(U|\varphi\rangle, U|\psi\rangle) = (|\varphi\rangle, |\psi\rangle).$$

In particular, it preserves the length of vectors: for any $|\psi\rangle \in \mathcal{H}$,

$$\|U|\psi\rangle\| = \|\psi\|.$$

If $\dim \mathcal{H} = n$, then a unitary operator in $\mathcal{H}$ is represented by an $n \times n$ unitary matrix U; that is, a matrix U with $U^\dagger U = I_n$, where I_n is the n-dimensional unit matrix.

A useful procedure for defining a unitary operator is as follows: we first define it partially in a subspace of its domain and then extend it to the entire domain. The following lemma warrants the reasonableness of this procedure.

Lemma 3.21 *Suppose that $\mathcal{K}$ is a subspace of Hilbert space $\mathcal{H}$. If linear operator $U : \mathcal{K} \to \mathcal{H}$ preserves the inner product of vectors in its domain:*

$$(U|\varphi\rangle, U|\psi\rangle) = (|\varphi\rangle, |\psi\rangle)$$

for any $|\varphi\rangle, |\psi\rangle \in \mathcal{K}$, then there exists a unitary operator V on $\mathcal{H}$ which extends U; that is, $V|\psi\rangle = U|\psi\rangle$ for all $|\psi\rangle \in \mathcal{K}$.

Exercise 3.5 Prove Lemma 3.21.

3.2.3 Postulate of Quantum Mechanics II

We now can present the postulate about the evolution of a (closed) quantum system.

- **Postulate II:** Suppose that the states of an isolated quantum system at times t_0 and t are $|\psi_0\rangle$ and $|\psi\rangle$, respectively. Then they are related to each other by a unitary operator U which depends only on the times t_0 and t:

$$|\psi\rangle = U|\psi_0\rangle.$$

Example 3.22 We consider several frequently used unitary transformation on a qubit, that is, unitary operators in the 2-dimensional Hilbert space $\mathcal{H}_2$ or 2×2 unitary matrices:

(i) Hadamard transformation:

$$H = \frac{1}{\sqrt{2}} \begin{pmatrix} 1 & 1 \\ 1 & -1 \end{pmatrix}.$$

It transforms a qubit in the computational basis states $|0\rangle$ and $|1\rangle$ into their superpositions:

$$H|0\rangle = H \begin{pmatrix} 1 \\ 0 \end{pmatrix} = \frac{1}{\sqrt{2}} \begin{pmatrix} 1 \\ 1 \end{pmatrix} = |+\rangle,$$

$$H|1\rangle = H \begin{pmatrix} 0 \\ 1 \end{pmatrix} = \frac{1}{\sqrt{2}} \begin{pmatrix} 1 \\ -1 \end{pmatrix} = |-\rangle.$$

(ii) Pauli matrices:

$$X = \sigma_x = \begin{pmatrix} 0 & 1 \\ 1 & 0 \end{pmatrix}, \quad Y = \sigma_y = \begin{pmatrix} 0 & -i \\ i & 0 \end{pmatrix}, \quad Z = \sigma_z = \begin{pmatrix} 1 & 0 \\ 0 & -1 \end{pmatrix}.$$

(iii) Rotation operators:

$$R_x(\theta) = \cos\frac{\theta}{2} \cdot I - i \sin\frac{\theta}{2} \cdot X = \begin{pmatrix} \cos\frac{\theta}{2} & -i\sin\frac{\theta}{2} \\ -i\sin\frac{\theta}{2} & \cos\frac{\theta}{2} \end{pmatrix},$$

$$R_y(\theta) = \cos\frac{\theta}{2} \cdot I - i \sin\frac{\theta}{2} \cdot Y = \begin{pmatrix} \cos\frac{\theta}{2} & -\sin\frac{\theta}{2} \\ \sin\frac{\theta}{2} & \cos\frac{\theta}{2} \end{pmatrix},$$

$$R_z(\theta) = \cos\frac{\theta}{2} \cdot I - i \sin\frac{\theta}{2} \cdot Z = \begin{pmatrix} e^{-i\frac{\theta}{2}} & 0 \\ 0 & e^{i\frac{\theta}{2}} \end{pmatrix}.$$

3.3 Quantum Measurements

The information about a quantum system is acquired through measurements. There is a fundamental difference between a quantum measurement and a classical measurement: performing a measurement on the same quantum system can produce different outcomes with certain probabilities, and the measurement may change the state of the measured system.

3.3.1 Postulate of Quantum Mechanics III

The aforementioned idea can be more precisely formulated as the following:

- **Postulate III:** A quantum measurement on a system with state Hilbert space $\mathcal{H}$ is described by a collection $\{M_m\}$ of operators in $\mathcal{L}(\mathcal{H})$ satisfying the normalisation condition:

$$\sum_m M_m^\dagger M_m = I_{\mathcal{H}}, \tag{3.2}$$

where M_m are called measurement operators, and the index m stands for the measurement outcomes that may occur in the experiment. If the system's state is $|\psi\rangle$ immediately before the measurement, then for each m, the probability that result m occurs in the measurement is

$$p(m) = \|M_m|\psi\rangle\|^2 = \langle\psi|M_m^\dagger M_m|\psi\rangle \quad \text{(Born rule)}$$

and the post-measurement state of the system when outcome m is observed is

$$|\psi_m\rangle = \frac{M_m|\psi\rangle}{\sqrt{p(m)}}.$$

Exercise 3.6 Show that the normalisation condition (3.2) implies that the probabilities for all outcomes sum up to 1; that is, $\sum_m p(m) = 1$.

Example 3.23 The measurement of a qubit in the computational basis has outcomes 0 and 1 defined respectively by the measurement operators:

$$M_0 = |0\rangle\langle0|, \quad M_1 = |1\rangle\langle1|.$$

If the qubit was in state $|\psi\rangle = \alpha|0\rangle + \beta|1\rangle$ before the measurement, then the probability of obtaining outcome 0 is

$$p(0) = \langle\psi|M_0^\dagger M_0|\psi\rangle = \langle\psi|M_0|\psi\rangle = |\alpha|^2,$$

and in this case the post-measurement state is

$$\frac{M_0|\psi\rangle}{\sqrt{p(0)}} = |0\rangle.$$

Similarly, the probability of observing outcome 1 is $p(1) = |\beta|^2$ and in this case the post-measurement state is $|1\rangle$.

Exercise 3.7 The measurement in basis $\{|+\rangle, |-\rangle\}$ is defined as $M = \{M_+, M_-\}$, where $M_+ = |+\rangle\langle+|$ and $M_- = |-\rangle\langle-|$. Compute the probability of outcome $+$ when M is performed on a qubit in state $|\psi\rangle = \alpha|0\rangle + \beta|1\rangle$.

3.3.2 Projective Measurements

A particularly important class of quantum measurements are projective measurements. A projective measurement can be defined by a physical observable, and vice versa.

Definition 3.24 An operator M is called Hermitian if it is self-adjoint:

$$M^\dagger = M.$$

In physics, a Hermitian operator is also called an observable.

Exercise 3.8 Prove that an operator P is a projector; that is, $P = P_X$ for some subspace X of $\mathcal{H}$, if and only if P is Hermitian and $P^2 = P$.

A quantum measurement can be constructed from an observable based on the spectral decomposition of a Hermitian operator.

Definition 3.25

(i) An eigenvector of an operator $A \in \mathcal{L}(\mathcal{H})$ is a non-zero vector $|\psi\rangle \in \mathcal{H}$ such that $A|\psi\rangle = \lambda|\psi\rangle$ for some $\lambda \in \mathbb{C}$, where λ is called the eigenvalue of A corresponding to $|\psi\rangle$.
(ii) The set of eigenvalues of A is called the (point) spectrum of A and denoted $spec(A)$.
(iii) For each eigenvalue $\lambda \in spec(A)$, the set

$$\{|\psi\rangle \in \mathcal{H} : A|\psi\rangle = \lambda|\psi\rangle\}$$

is a subspace of $\mathcal{H}$, called the eigenspace of A corresponding to λ.

Exercise 3.9 Let M be an observable (i.e. a Hermitian operator). Prove:

(i) The eigenspaces corresponding to different eigenvalues of M are orthogonal.
(ii) All eigenvalues of M are real numbers.

It is well known that every observable has the spectral decomposition:

$$M = \sum_{\lambda \in spec(M)} \lambda P_\lambda,$$

where P_λ is the projector onto the eigenspace corresponding to λ. Then it defines a measurement $\{P_\lambda : \lambda \in spec(M)\}$, called a projective measurement, because all measurement operators P_λ are projectors.

Postulate of quantum mechanics III implies that upon measuring a system in state $|\psi\rangle$, the probability of getting result λ is

$$p(\lambda) = \langle\psi|P_\lambda^\dagger P_\lambda|\psi\rangle = \langle\psi|P_\lambda^2|\psi\rangle = \langle\psi|P_\lambda|\psi\rangle, \quad (3.3)$$

and in this case the state of the system after the measurement is

$$\frac{P_\lambda|\psi\rangle}{\sqrt{p(\lambda)}}. \quad (3.4)$$

The expectation – average value – of M in state $|\psi\rangle$ is calculated as

$$\langle M\rangle_\psi = \sum_{\lambda \in spec(M)} p(\lambda) \cdot \lambda$$

$$= \sum_{\lambda \in spec(M)} \lambda\langle\psi|P_\lambda|\psi\rangle$$

$$= \langle \psi | \sum_{\lambda \in spec(M)} \lambda P_\lambda | \psi \rangle$$

$$= \langle \psi | M | \psi \rangle.$$

3.4 Composition of Quantum Systems

The aforementioned three postulates of quantum mechanics deal with a single quantum system. Now we move on to consider how several subsystems can be combined to form a composite system.

3.4.1 Tensor Products

The main mathematical tool for describing composite quantum systems is the tensor product of Hilbert spaces.

Definition 3.26 For each $i = 1, \ldots, n$, let $\mathcal{H}_i$ be a Hilbert space, with $\{|\psi_{ij_i}\rangle\}$ being an orthonormal basis. We write $\mathcal{B}$ for the set of elements:

$$|\psi_{1j_1}, \ldots, \psi_{nj_n}\rangle = |\psi_{1j_1} \otimes \ldots \otimes \psi_{nj_n}\rangle = |\psi_{1j_1}\rangle \otimes \ldots \otimes |\psi_{nj_n}\rangle.$$

Then the tensor product of $\mathcal{H}_i$ $(i = 1, \ldots, n)$ is the Hilbert space with $\mathcal{B}$ as an orthonormal basis:

$$\bigotimes_i \mathcal{H}_i = span\mathcal{B}.$$

It follows from Eq. (3.1) that each element in $\bigotimes_i \mathcal{H}_i$ can be written in the form of linear combination (i.e. superposition):

$$\sum_{j_1, \ldots, j_n} \alpha_{j_1, \ldots, j_n} |\varphi_{1j_1}, \ldots, \varphi_{nj_n}\rangle,$$

where $|\varphi_{1j_1}\rangle \in \mathcal{H}_1, \ldots, |\varphi_{nj_n}\rangle \in \mathcal{H}_n$ and $\alpha_{j_1, \ldots, j_n} \in \mathbb{C}$ for all $j_1, \ldots, j_n$.

It can be shown by linearity that the choice of basis $\{|\psi_{ij_i}\rangle\}$ of each factor space $\mathcal{H}_i$ is not essential in Definition 3.26. Furthermore, the vector addition, scalar multiplication and inner product in $\bigotimes_i \mathcal{H}_i$ can be naturally defined.

To depict dynamics of and measurements on composite quantum systems, we need linear operators on the tensor products of Hilbert spaces. A simple class of such operators is introduced in the following:

Definition 3.27 Let $A_i \in \mathcal{L}(\mathcal{H}_i)$ for $i = 1, \ldots, n$. Then their tensor product is the operator $\bigotimes_{i=1}^n A_i = A_1 \otimes \ldots \otimes A_n \in \mathcal{L}\left(\bigotimes_{i=1}^n \mathcal{H}_i\right)$ defined by

$$(A_1 \otimes \ldots \otimes A_n)|\varphi_1, \ldots, \varphi_n\rangle = A_1|\varphi_1\rangle \otimes \ldots \otimes A_n|\varphi_n\rangle$$

for all $|\varphi_i\rangle \in \mathcal{H}_i$ $(i = 1, \ldots, n)$ together with linearity.

However, we will see in the text that follows that some interesting unitary transformations of a composite system are not the tensor products of operators on its subsystems. The reader can also construct measurements on a composite system that cannot be defined as tensor products.

3.4.2 Postulate of Quantum Mechanics IV

The preceding mathematical preparation enables us to present the following:

- **Postulate IV:** The state space of a composite quantum system is the tensor product of the state spaces of its components.

Suppose that S is a quantum system composed by subsystems $S_1, \ldots, S_n$ with state Hilbert spaces $\mathcal{H}_1, \ldots, \mathcal{H}_n$. If for each $1 \leq i \leq n$, S_i is in state $|\psi_i\rangle \in \mathcal{H}_i$, then S is in the product state $|\psi_1, \ldots, \psi_n\rangle$. Furthermore, S can be in a superposition (i.e. linear combination) of several product states.

A state of the composite system is called *entangled* if it is not a product of states of its component systems. The existence of entanglement is one of the major differences between the classical world and the quantum world.

Example 3.28 The state space of the system of n qubits is

$$\mathcal{H}_2^{\otimes n} = \mathbb{C}^{2^n} = \left\{ \sum_{x \in \{0,1\}^n} \alpha_x |x\rangle : \alpha_x \in \mathbb{C} \text{ for all } x \in \{0,1\}^n \right\}.$$

In particular, a two-qubit system can be in a product state such as $|00\rangle, |1\rangle|+\rangle$; but it can also be in an entangled state such as the Bell states or the EPR (Einstein–Podolsky–Rosen) pairs:

$$|\beta_{00}\rangle = \frac{1}{\sqrt{2}}(|00\rangle + |11\rangle), \quad |\beta_{01}\rangle = \frac{1}{\sqrt{2}}(|01\rangle + |10\rangle),$$

$$|\beta_{10}\rangle = \frac{1}{\sqrt{2}}(|00\rangle - |11\rangle), \quad |\beta_{11}\rangle = \frac{1}{\sqrt{2}}(|01\rangle - |10\rangle).$$

Operators rather than tensor products introduced in Definition 3.27 are indispensable in quantum computation to create entanglement.

Example 3.29 The controlled-NOT or CNOT operator C in the state Hilbert space $\mathcal{H}_2^{\otimes 2} = \mathbb{C}^4$ of a two-qubit system is defined by

$$C|00\rangle = |00\rangle, \quad C|01\rangle = |01\rangle, \quad C|10\rangle = |11\rangle, \quad C|11\rangle = |10\rangle$$

or equivalently as the 4×4 matrix

$$C = \begin{pmatrix} 1 & 0 & 0 & 0 \\ 0 & 1 & 0 & 0 \\ 0 & 0 & 0 & 1 \\ 0 & 0 & 1 & 0 \end{pmatrix}.$$

It can transform product states into entangled states:

$$C|+\rangle|0\rangle = \beta_{00}, \quad C|+\rangle|1\rangle = \beta_{01}, \quad C|-\rangle|0\rangle = \beta_{10}, \quad C|-\rangle|1\rangle = \beta_{11}.$$

3.5 Mixed States

The situation we considered in the previous sections is that a quantum system is exactly in a (pure) state represented by a vector $|\psi\rangle$. Sometimes, however, the state of a quantum system is not completely known. Instead, what we only know is that it is in one of a number of pure states $|\psi_i\rangle$, with respective probabilities p_i. In this section, we introduce the mathematical tools for dealing with this new situation.

3.5.1 Density Operators

Let us first precisely define the notion of mixed state.

Definition 3.30 Let $|\psi_i\rangle \in \mathcal{H}$, $p_i \geq 0$ for each i, and $\sum_i p_i = 1$. Then

$$\{(|\psi_i\rangle, p_i)\}$$

is called an ensemble of pure states or a mixed state.

Then we can present an elegant characterisation of mixed states in terms of operators.

Definition 3.31 The trace $\text{tr}(A)$ of operator $A \in \mathcal{L}(\mathcal{H})$ is defined to be

$$\text{tr}(A) = \sum_i \langle \psi_i | A | \psi_i \rangle,$$

where $\{|\psi_i\rangle\}$ is an orthonormal basis of $\mathcal{H}$.

It can be shown that $\text{tr}(A)$ is independent of the choice of basis $\{|\psi_i\rangle\}$.

Definition 3.32 A density operator ρ in a Hilbert space $\mathcal{H}$ is a positive operator (see Definition 3.15) with $\text{tr}(\rho) = 1$.

Every mixed state $\{(|\psi_i\rangle, p_i)\}$ defines a density operator:

$$\rho = \sum_i p_i |\psi_i\rangle\langle\psi_i|. \tag{3.5}$$

In particular, a pure state $|\psi\rangle$ may be seen as a special mixed state $\{(|\psi\rangle, 1)\}$ and its density operator is $\rho = |\psi\rangle\langle\psi|$. Conversely, for any density operator ρ, there exists a (but not necessarily unique) mixed state $\{(|\psi_i\rangle, p_i)\}$ such that Eq. (3.5) holds.

3.5.2 Evolution of and Measurement on Mixed States

The postulates about evolution of and measurement on a quantum system can be straightforwardly generalised into the case of mixed states and elegantly formulated in the language of density operators:

- Suppose that the evolution of an isolated quantum system from time t_0 to t is described by unitary operator U (see Postulate of Quantum Mechanics II). If the system is in mixed states ρ_0, ρ at times t_0 and t, respectively, then

$$\rho = U\rho_0 U^\dagger. \tag{3.6}$$

- If the state of a quantum system was ρ immediately before measurement $\{M_m\}$ is performed on it, then the probability that result m occurs is

$$p(m) = \mathrm{tr}\left(M_m^\dagger M_m \rho\right), \tag{3.7}$$

and in this case the post-measurement state of the system is

$$\rho_m = \frac{M_m \rho M_m^\dagger}{p(m)}. \tag{3.8}$$

This should be compared with Postulate of Quantum Mechanics III in Subsection 3.3.

Exercise 3.10 Derive Eqs. (3.6), (3.7) and (3.8) from Eq. (3.5) and Postulates of Quantum Mechanics I and II.

Exercise 3.11 Let M be an observable (a Hermitian operator) and $\{P_\lambda : \lambda \in spec(M)\}$ the projective measurement defined by M. Show that the expectation of M in a mixed state ρ is

$$\langle M \rangle_\rho = \sum_{\lambda \in spec(M)} p(\lambda) \cdot \lambda = \mathrm{tr}(M\rho).$$

3.5.3 Reduced Density Operators

We often need to describe a subsystem of a quantum system. It is possible that a composite system is in a pure state, but some of its subsystems must be seen as in a mixed state. This phenomenon is another major difference between the classical world and the quantum world. Consequently, a proper description of a subsystem of a composite quantum system can be achieved only after introducing the notion of density operator. The mathematical tool for this purpose is defined in the following:

> **Definition 3.33** Let $\mathcal{H}_1$ and $\mathcal{H}_2$ be two Hilbert spaces. The partial trace tr_2 over system $\mathcal{H}_2$ is a mapping from operators in $\mathcal{H}_1 \otimes \mathcal{H}_2$ to operators in $\mathcal{H}_1$ defined by
>
> $$tr_2(|\varphi_1\rangle\langle\psi_1| \otimes |\varphi_2\rangle\langle\psi_2|) = \langle\psi_2|\varphi_2\rangle \cdot |\varphi_1\rangle\langle\psi_1|$$
>
> for all $|\varphi_1\rangle, |\psi_1\rangle \in \mathcal{H}_1$ and $|\varphi_2\rangle, |\psi_2\rangle \in \mathcal{H}_2$ together with linearity.

The partial trace tr_1 over $\mathcal{H}_1$ can be defined in a symmetric way.

> **Exercise 3.12** Let ρ be a density operator in $\mathcal{H}_1 \otimes \mathcal{H}_2 \otimes \mathcal{H}_3$. Show that $tr_3(tr_2(\rho)) = tr_{23}(\rho)$, where tr_{23} stands for the partial trace over $\mathcal{H}_2 \otimes \mathcal{H}_3$.

Now let A and B be two quantum systems with respective state Hilbert spaces $\mathcal{H}_A$ and $\mathcal{H}_B$, and let the composite system AB be in a mixed state represented by density operator ρ on $\mathcal{H}_A \otimes \mathcal{H}_B$. Then the states of subsystems A and B are described by the reduced density operators:

$$\rho_A = tr_B(\rho), \qquad \rho_B = tr_A(\rho),$$

respectively.

3.6 Quantum Operations

As said before, unitary transformations are suited only to describe the dynamics of closed (isolated) quantum systems. For open quantum systems, a more general notion of quantum operation is required to describe their state transformations.

3.6.1 A Generalisation of Postulate of Quantum Mechanics II

A linear operator on the space $\mathcal{L}(\mathcal{H})$ of operators on a Hilbert space $\mathcal{H}$ is called a *super-operator* on $\mathcal{H}$. Then the postulate for the evolution of closed quantum systems can be generalised to open systems as follows:

Generalised Postulate II: If the states of a system at times t_0 and t are ρ_0 and ρ, respectively, then they must be related by a super-operator $\mathcal{E}$ which depends only on the times t_0 and t,

$$\rho = \mathcal{E}(\rho_0).$$

The dynamics between times t_0 and t can be seen as a physical process: ρ_0 is the initial state before the process, and $\rho = \mathcal{E}(\rho_0)$ is the final state after the process happens. It is not the case that all super-operators are suited to model such a process. To identify those eligible super-operators, let us first introduce the following:

Definition 3.34 Let $\mathcal{H}$ and $\mathcal{K}$ be Hilbert spaces. For any super-operator $\mathcal{E}$ on $\mathcal{H}$ and super-operator $\mathcal{F}$ on $\mathcal{K}$, their tensor product $\mathcal{E} \otimes \mathcal{F}$ is a super-operator on $\mathcal{H} \otimes \mathcal{K}$ defined by

$$(\mathcal{E} \otimes \mathcal{F})(A \otimes B) = \mathcal{E}(A) \otimes \mathcal{F}(B) \tag{3.9}$$

for all $A \in \mathcal{L}(\mathcal{H})$ and $B \in \mathcal{L}(\mathcal{K})$ together with linearity; that is,

$$(\mathcal{E} \otimes \mathcal{F})(C) = \sum_k \alpha_k (\mathcal{E}(A_k) \otimes \mathcal{F}(B_k)) \tag{3.10}$$

for each operator

$$C = \sum_k \alpha_k (A_k \otimes B_k) \tag{3.11}$$

on $\mathcal{H} \otimes \mathcal{K}$, where $A_k \in \mathcal{L}(\mathcal{H})$ and $B_k \in \mathcal{L}(\mathcal{K})$ for all k.

It should be noted that the linearity of $\mathcal{E}$ and $\mathcal{F}$ guarantees that $\mathcal{E} \otimes \mathcal{F}$ is well defined; that is, $(\mathcal{E} \otimes \mathcal{F})(C)$ is independent of the choice of A_k and B_k in Eq. (3.10).

Now we can define the super-operators that can be used to describe the dynamics of open quantum systems.

Definition 3.35 A quantum operation in a Hilbert space $\mathcal{H}$ is a super-operator on $\mathcal{H}$ satisfying the following conditions:

(i) $\mathrm{tr}[\mathcal{E}(\rho)] \leq \mathrm{tr}(\rho) = 1$ for each density operator ρ in $\mathcal{H}$; and
(ii) (Complete positivity) For any extra Hilbert space $\mathcal{H}_R$, $(\mathcal{I}_R \otimes \mathcal{E})(A)$ is positive provided A is a positive operator on $\mathcal{H}_R \otimes \mathcal{H}$, where $\mathcal{I}_R$ is the identity super-operator on $\mathcal{H}_R$ (i.e. the identity operator on $\mathcal{L}(\mathcal{H}_R)$); that is, $\mathcal{I}_R(A) = A$ for each operator $A \in \mathcal{L}(\mathcal{H}_R)$.

The following two examples show that both unitary transformations and quantum measurements can be seen as special quantum operations.

Example 3.36 Let U be a unitary transformation in a Hilbert space $\mathcal{H}$. We define

$$\mathcal{E}(\rho) = U\rho U^\dagger$$

for every density operator ρ. Then $\mathcal{E}$ is a quantum operation in $\mathcal{H}$.

Example 3.37 Let $M = \{M_m\}$ be a quantum measurement in $\mathcal{H}$.

(i) For each m, if for any system state ρ before measurement, we define

$$\mathcal{E}_m(\rho) = p_m \rho_m = M_m \rho M_m^\dagger,$$

where p_m is the probability of outcome m and ρ_m is the post-measurement state corresponding to m, then $\mathcal{E}_m$ is a quantum operation.

(ii) For any system state ρ before measurement, the post-measurement state is

$$\mathcal{E}(\rho) = \sum_m \mathcal{E}_m(\rho) = \sum_m M_m \rho M_m^\dagger$$

whenever the measurement outcomes are ignored. Then $\mathcal{E}$ is also a quantum operation.

The next example shows that quantum noises can be modelled as quantum operations.

Example 3.38 Let X, Y, Z be the Pauli matrices (see Example 3.22).

(i) The bit flip noise flips the state of a qubit from $|0\rangle$ to $|1\rangle$ and vice versa with probability $1 - p$. It is modelled by a quantum operation:

$$\mathcal{E}_{BF}(\rho) = E_0 \rho E_0 + E_1 \rho E_1 \tag{3.12}$$

for all ρ, where

$$E_0 = \sqrt{p}I = \sqrt{p}\begin{pmatrix} 1 & 0 \\ 0 & 1 \end{pmatrix} \quad E_1 = \sqrt{1-p}X = \sqrt{1-p}\begin{pmatrix} 0 & 1 \\ 1 & 0 \end{pmatrix}.$$

(ii) The phase flip noise is modelled by a quantum operation $\mathcal{E}_{PF}$ defined by Eq. (3.12) with

$$E_0 = \sqrt{p}I = \sqrt{p}\begin{pmatrix} 1 & 0 \\ 0 & 1 \end{pmatrix} \quad E_1 = \sqrt{1-p}Z = \sqrt{1-p}\begin{pmatrix} 1 & 0 \\ 0 & -1 \end{pmatrix}.$$

(iii) The bit-phase flip noise is modelled by a quantum operation $\mathcal{E}_{BPF}$ defined by Eq. (3.12) with

$$E_0 = \sqrt{p}I = \sqrt{p}\begin{pmatrix} 1 & 0 \\ 0 & 1 \end{pmatrix} \quad E_1 = \sqrt{1-p}Y = \sqrt{1-p}\begin{pmatrix} 0 & -i \\ i & 0 \end{pmatrix}.$$

Remark 3.39 *In the remaining part of this book, all super-operators are assumed to be quantum operations, and we will use the terms quantum operation and super-operator interchangeably.*

3.6.2 Representations of Quantum Operations

The abstract definition of quantum operations (Definition 3.35) is not easy to use in applications. But Example 3.38 hints that there are perhaps some concrete representations of quantum operations that are convenient to manipulate in calculations. This observation is confirmed by the following:

Theorem 3.40 *The following statements are equivalent:*

(i) *$\mathcal{E}$ is a quantum operation in a Hilbert space $\mathcal{H}$.*

(ii) *(System-environment model) There are an environment system E with state Hilbert space $\mathcal{H}_E$, a unitary transformation U in $\mathcal{H}_E \otimes \mathcal{H}$ and a projector P onto some closed subspace of $\mathcal{H}_E \otimes \mathcal{H}$ such that*

$$\mathcal{E}(\rho) = \text{tr}_E\left[PU(|e_0\rangle\langle e_0| \otimes \rho)U^\dagger P\right]$$

for all density operator ρ in $\mathcal{H}$, where $|e_0\rangle$ is a fixed state in $\mathcal{H}_E$;

(iii) *(Kraus operator-sum representation) There exists a finite set of operators $\{E_i : i \in I\}$ in $\mathcal{H}$ such that $\sum_{i \in I} E_i^\dagger E_i \sqsubseteq I_\mathcal{H}$ and*

$$\mathcal{E}(\rho) = \sum_{i \in I} E_i \rho E_i^\dagger$$

for all density operators ρ in $\mathcal{H}$. In this case, we often write $\mathcal{E} = \{E_i : i \in I\}$ directly.

Here, we are not going to present the lengthy proof of Theorem 3.40, but the reader can find it in chapter 8 of [93].

Matrix Representation for Quantum Operations (Super-Operators). The Kraus operator-sum representation in Theorem 3.40 employs a family of matrices on $\mathcal{H}$ to represent a quantum operation on the same space $\mathcal{H}$. We can further combine this family of matrices into a single matrix but on $\mathcal{H} \otimes \mathcal{H}$. More precisely, let $\mathcal{E} = \{E_i : i \in I\}$ be a quantum operation on $\mathcal{H}$. The matrix representation of $\mathcal{E}$ is defined as

$$M_\mathcal{E} = \sum_{i \in I} E_i \otimes E_i^*. \tag{3.13}$$

Here the complex conjugate is taken according to a given orthonormal basis $\{|k\rangle : k \in K\}$ of $\mathcal{H}$. It is easy to check that $M_\mathcal{E}$ is independent of the choice of orthonormal basis and the Kraus operators E_i of $\mathcal{E}$.

This matrix representation will be widely used in the algorithms for model checking quantum systems presented in later chapters.

3.7 Bibliographic Remarks

The materials in this chapter are standard and can be found in almost all (advanced) textbooks of quantum mechanics. The presentation of these materials here largely follows either the standard quantum computation and information textbook [93] or chapter 2 of a recent quantum programming book [117] by one of the authors. This chapter only provides a brief introduction to the mathematical formalism of quantum mechanics. The reader is encouraged to read chapters 1, 2 and 8 of [93] for a better understanding of the physical interpretations of the notions introduced in this chapter.

4

Model Checking Quantum Automata

From this chapter on, we study model-checking techniques for quantum systems. We strongly suggest the reader keep thinking about the following two problems throughout reading the book:

- Why does this or that model-checking technique for classical systems fail to apply to quantum systems?
- How can we remould it in order to deal with quantum systems?

Quantum systems are modelled as different mathematical structures, depending on their nature and complexity. In this chapter, we consider one of the simplest (discrete-time) models of quantum systems, namely quantum automata. The actions of a quantum automaton are defined by a family of unitary transformations. Remember from Section 3.2 that unitary operators are the mathematical formalism of dynamics of closed quantum systems, which have no interactions with or disturbance from the environment.

We shall introduce a way of describing linear-time (dynamic) properties of quantum systems. It can be seen as a dynamic (temporal logical) extension of Birkhoff–von Neumann quantum logic, where atomic propositions for describing (static) properties of a quantum system are interpreted as (closed) subspaces of the system's state Hilbert space.

We shall present several algorithms for checking certain linear-time properties of quantum automata, for example, invariants. As we saw in Section 2.3, the core of various model-checking algorithms for classical systems is reachability analysis. A large part of this chapter is indeed devoted to reachability analysis of quantum automata.

4.1 Quantum Automata

Let us start from a formal definition of quantum automata, which will serve as the model of quantum systems considered in this chapter. It is a straightforward quantum generalisation of the notion of classical transition system (or finite-state automaton) introduced in Definition 2.1 and its probabilistic extensions – Markov chain (see Definition 2.29) and Markov decision process (see Definition 2.30).

Definition 4.1 A quantum automaton is a 4-tuple

$$\mathcal{A} = (\mathcal{H}, Act, \{U_\alpha : \alpha \in Act\}, \mathcal{H}_0),$$

where

(i) $\mathcal{H}$ is a finite-dimensional state Hilbert space;
(ii) Act is a finite set of action names;
(iii) for each $\alpha \in Act$, U_α is a unitary operator in $\mathcal{H}$; and
(vi) $\mathcal{H}_0$ is a subspace of $\mathcal{H}$, called the space of initial states.

A comparison between Definition 4.1 and Definitions 2.1, 2.29 and 2.30 should be helpful for a better understanding:

- The set S of states in a transition system (Definition 2.1) and a Markov chain or decision process (Definitions 2.29 and 2.30) is replaced in Definition 4.1 by a Hilbert space $\mathcal{H}$ of quantum states. It is worth noting that S is a finite set, but $\mathcal{H}$ is a continuum and thus uncountably infinite, although it is finite dimensional. Roughly speaking, the correspondence between S and $\mathcal{H}$ is as follows: S can be seen as an orthonormal basis of $\mathcal{H}$, and $\mathcal{H}$ is thus the Hilbert space spanned by S. Therefore, a generic element in $\mathcal{H}$ can be understood as a superposition of elements in S.
- In a transition system, the transition relation $\rightarrow$ is modelled by a family of binary relations $\xrightarrow{\alpha}$ ($\alpha \in Act$) between states, indexed by the names α of actions; in both a Markov chain and a Markov decision process, such a binary relation $\xrightarrow{\alpha}$ is generalised to a probabilistic relation, or equivalently, a mapping that sends a state to a probability distribution of states. In a quantum automaton, each action α is then described by a unitary transformation, which sends a basis state to a superposition of basis states, a quantum counterpart of probability distribution. We remember from Section 3.2 that unitary operators are used to model the dynamics of *closed* quantum systems. So, a quantum automaton is treated at this stage as a *closed* quantum system.

Now we consider the dynamic behaviour of a quantum automaton, that is, how it runs. A path of $\mathcal{A}$ is a finite or infinite sequence $|\psi_0\rangle|\psi_1\rangle|\psi_2\rangle \ldots$ of (pure) states in $\mathcal{H}$ such that $|\psi_0\rangle \in \mathcal{H}_0$, and

$$|\psi_{n+1}\rangle = U_{\alpha_n}|\psi_n\rangle$$

for some $\alpha_n \in Act$, for all $n \geq 0$. This means that a path starts in an initial state $|\psi_0\rangle$, and for each $n \geq 0$, at the beginning of the nth step the machine is in state

$|\psi_n\rangle$. Then it performs an action described by unitary operator U_{α_n} and evolves into state $|\psi_{n+1}\rangle$.

Example 4.2 Let us consider a qubit system with the following possible actions: Hadamard operator H and Pauli operators X, Y, Z. The system starts from the basis state $|0\rangle$. Then it can be modelled as a quantum automaton $\mathcal{A} = (\mathcal{H}, Act, \{U_\alpha : \alpha \in Act\}, \mathcal{H}_0)$, where:

(i) $\mathcal{H} = \mathcal{H}_2$ is the 2-dimensional Hilbert space;
(ii) $Act = \{h, x, y, z\}$;
(iii) $U_h = H, U_x = X, U_y = Y, U_z = Z$; and
(iv) $\mathcal{H}_0 = \text{span}\{|0\rangle\}$.

A path of $\mathcal{A}$ is

$$|0\rangle \xrightarrow{x} |1\rangle \xrightarrow{h} |-\rangle \xrightarrow{y} i|+\rangle \xrightarrow{z} i|-\rangle,$$

and an infinite path of $\mathcal{A}$ is

$$|0\rangle \xrightarrow{x} |1\rangle \xrightarrow{h} |-\rangle \xrightarrow{z} |+\rangle \xrightarrow{h} |0\rangle \xrightarrow{x} |1\rangle \xrightarrow{h} |-\rangle \xrightarrow{z} |+\rangle \xrightarrow{h} |0\rangle \ldots.$$

The simple reachability in transition systems introduced in Definition 2.5 can be easily generalised into quantum automata. Let $\mathcal{A} = (\mathcal{H}, Act, \{U_\alpha : \alpha \in Act\}, \mathcal{H}_0)$ be a quantum automaton. We use Act^ω to denote the set of infinite sequences of actions. A schedule of $\mathcal{A}$ is defined as an element $w = \alpha_0\alpha_1\alpha_2\ldots$ of Act^ω. For a given initial state $|\psi_0\rangle$ and a schedule $w \in Act^\omega$, we write $\pi = \pi(|\psi_0\rangle, w)$ for the path generated by w from $|\psi_0\rangle$. We further write $\sigma(\pi) = |\psi_0\rangle|\psi_1\rangle|\psi_2\rangle\ldots$ for the sequence of states in π. Sometimes, we simply call $\sigma(\pi)$ a path of $\mathcal{A}$.

Definition 4.3 Let $|\psi\rangle \in \mathcal{H}_0$ and let $|\varphi\rangle$ be a state in $\mathcal{H}$.

(i) $|\varphi\rangle$ is reachable from $|\psi\rangle$ in quantum automaton $\mathcal{A}$ if $\mathcal{A}$ has a path $|\psi_0\rangle|\psi_1\rangle\ldots|\psi_n\rangle$ such that $|\psi_0\rangle = |\psi\rangle$ and $|\psi_n\rangle = |\varphi\rangle$.
(ii) The reachable space of quantum automaton $\mathcal{A}$ is

$$R(\mathcal{A}) = \text{span}\{|\varphi\rangle \in \mathcal{H} : |\psi\rangle \text{ is reachable from some initial state } |\psi\rangle \in \mathcal{H}_0\}.$$

Note that the states reachable from some initial state in $\mathcal{H}_0$ may not form a subspace of $\mathcal{H}$. So, $R(\mathcal{A})$ is defined as the subspace spanned by them. The following lemma gives a simple characterisation of the reachable space.

Lemma 4.4 *$R(\mathcal{A})$ is the intersection of all subspaces $\mathcal{X}$ of $\mathcal{H}$ satisfying the following conditions:*

(i) *$\mathcal{H}_0 \subseteq \mathcal{X}$; and*
(ii) *$U_\alpha(\mathcal{X}) \subseteq \mathcal{X}$ for all $\alpha \in Act$.*

That is, $R(\mathcal{A})$ is the smallest of such $\mathcal{X}$.

Exercise 4.1 Prove Lemma 4.4.

4.2 Birkhoff-von Neumann Quantum Logic

In the following sections, we are going to define a language for specifying properties of quantum systems that we are interested in. Before dealing with dynamic properties, we need to first choose a way for describing the static properties of a quantum system; that is, its properties at a fixed time point. We decide to use Birkhoff–von Neumann quantum logic for this purpose.

Propositions in Quantum Logic. Let $\mathcal{H}$ be the state Hilbert space of a quantum system. A (closed) subspace of $\mathcal{H}$ is viewed in the quantum logic as an atomic proposition about this system; more precisely, we mainly consider the basic properties of the system of the form

$$|\psi\rangle \in \mathcal{X},$$

where $\mathcal{X}$ is a subspace of $\mathcal{H}$, and $|\psi\rangle$ is a state of the system. So, for a subspace $\mathcal{X}$ of $\mathcal{H}$, the atomic proposition represented by $\mathcal{X}$ specifies a constraint on the behaviour of the system that its state is within the given region $\mathcal{X}$. We write $S(\mathcal{H})$ for the set of (closed) subspaces of $\mathcal{H}$.

> **Example 4.5** An atomic proposition about a quantum system is a physical description of the system at a single instant. Consider
>
> (i) $\mathcal{X} = $ 'at time t, the quantum particle has its x position coordinate in the interval $[a,b]$';
> (ii) $\mathcal{Y} = $ 'at time t, the quantum particle has its y momentum coordinate in the interval $[a,b]$'.
>
> These statements $\mathcal{X}, \mathcal{Y}$ can be represented by certain subspaces of the state Hilbert space of the particle.

The aforementioned idea of using subspaces as atomic propositions can also be interpreted in terms of quantum measurements. Assume that a basic property of the system is described by a (closed) subspace $\mathcal{X}$ of $\mathcal{H}$. In quantum mechanics, to check whether or not this property is satisfied, a binary (yes–no) measurement $\{P_{\mathcal{X}}, P_{\mathcal{X}^\perp}\}$ should be performed on the system's current state $|\psi\rangle$, where $P_{\mathcal{X}}$ and $P_{\mathcal{X}^\perp}$ are the projections onto $\mathcal{X}$ and its orthocomplement $\mathcal{X}^\perp$, respectively. The measurement outcome is generally non-deterministic: $\mathcal{X}$ is considered as being satisfied in $|\psi\rangle$ with probability $\langle\psi|P_{\mathcal{X}}|\psi\rangle$, and it is not satisfied with probability $\langle\psi|P_{\mathcal{X}^\perp}|\psi\rangle = 1 - \langle\psi|P_{\mathcal{X}}|\psi\rangle$. A quantitative satisfaction relation can be defined by setting a threshold $\lambda \in [0,1]$ to the probability of satisfaction:

$$\mathcal{X} \text{ is } (\lambda, \rhd)\text{-satisfied in } |\psi\rangle \text{ if } \langle\psi|P_{\mathcal{X}}|\psi\rangle \rhd \lambda, \tag{4.1}$$

where $\rhd \in \{<, \leq, >, \geq\}$. Here, we only consider the *qualitative* satisfaction, namely, the $(\lambda, \rhd)$-satisfaction with the threshold λ being 0 or 1. Obviously, we have for any pure state $|\psi\rangle$ and subspace $\mathcal{X}$,

- $\mathcal{X}$ is $(1, \geq)$-satisfied in $|\psi\rangle$ if and only if $|\psi\rangle \in \mathcal{X}$;
- $\mathcal{X}$ is $(0, \leq)$-satisfied in $|\psi\rangle$ if and only if $|\psi\rangle \in \mathcal{X}^{\perp}$.

Connectives in Quantum Logic.   After identifying atomic propositions, we need to introduce several connectives that can be used to construct composite propositions from atomic ones in order to specify more sophisticated properties of quantum systems. Semantically, they can be seen as algebraic operations in $\mathcal{S}(\mathcal{H})$. First of all, the inclusion $\subseteq$ between subspaces is a partial order in $\mathcal{S}(\mathcal{H})$. It can be understood as implication in the (meta-logic of) quantum logic. Second, the orthocomplement $\mathcal{X}^{\perp}$ of a subspace $\mathcal{X}$ serves as the interpretation of negation in the quantum logic. Third, it is easy to see that $\mathcal{S}(\mathcal{H})$ is closed under intersection; that is, for any family $\{\mathcal{X}_i\}$ of elements in $\mathcal{S}(\mathcal{H})$, it holds that

$$\bigcap_i \mathcal{X}_i \in \mathcal{S}(\mathcal{H}).$$

The conjunction in the quantum logic is interpreted as intersection. Furthermore, we have:

Definition 4.6 For a (finite or an infinite) family $\{\mathcal{X}_i\}$ of subspaces of $\mathcal{H}$, their join is defined by

$$\bigvee_i \mathcal{X}_i = \mathrm{span}\left(\bigcup_i \mathcal{X}_i\right).$$

In particular, we write $\mathcal{X} \vee \mathcal{Y}$ for the join of two subspaces $\mathcal{X}$ and $\mathcal{Y}$ of $\mathcal{H}$.

The disjunction in the quantum logic is interpreted as join. It is well known that $(\mathcal{S}(\mathcal{H}), \cap, \vee, \perp)$ is an orthomodular lattice with $\subseteq$ as its ordering, which is an algebraic model of Birkhoff–von Neumann quantum logic. Here, we are not going to discuss more details of quantum logic; the reader can consult [20, 71] if interested.

In practical applications, we usually only choose a subset AP of $\mathcal{S}(\mathcal{H})$ as the set of atomic propositions. The elements of AP can be thought of as those propositions that really concern us, and others may be irrelevant. For algorithmic purpose, we often assume AP to be a countable or even finite subset of $\mathcal{S}(\mathcal{H})$ rather than $\mathcal{S}(\mathcal{H})$ itself as the set of atomic propositions because $\mathcal{S}(\mathcal{H})$ is uncountably infinite.

Satisfaction in Quantum Logic. Now we further define when a (quantum logical) proposition is satisfied by a quantum state. For any atomic proposition $X \in AP$ and state $|\psi\rangle \in \mathcal{H}$, if $|\psi\rangle \in X$, then we say that state $|\psi\rangle$ satisfies X. We write $L(|\psi\rangle)$ for the set of atomic propositions satisfied in state $|\psi\rangle$:

$$L(|\psi\rangle) = \{X \in AP : |\psi\rangle \in X\}.$$

Sometimes, we need a more general satisfaction relation between a state $|\psi\rangle$ and a proposition X that is not in AP; for example, in some application we may be interested in whether a proposition X is satisfied in a state $|\psi\rangle$ or not, but for consideration of memory a quantum model checker chooses only a very limited number of atomic propositions that do not include X.

Definition 4.7 Given a set AP of atomic propositions. Let $X \in \mathcal{S}(\mathcal{H})$. Then we say that state $|\psi\rangle$ satisfies X, written $|\psi\rangle \models_{AP} X$ or simply $|\psi\rangle \models X$, if

$$\bigcap_{\mathcal{Y} \in L(|\psi\rangle)} \mathcal{Y} \subseteq X. \tag{4.2}$$

Intuitively, $\bigcap_{\mathcal{Y} \in L(|\psi\rangle)} \mathcal{Y}$ is the weakest statement characterising the state $|\psi\rangle$ definable in terms of atomic propositions. Thus, the inclusion (4.2) means that the atomic propositions that hold in state $|\psi\rangle$ collectively imply proposition X. In particular, if $X \in AP$, then $|\psi\rangle \models X$ if and only if $|\psi\rangle \in X$.

Example 4.8 Let $\mathcal{H}$ be an n-dimensional Hilbert space with orthonormal basis $\{|0\rangle, |1\rangle, \ldots, |n-1\rangle\}$ $(n \geq 2)$, and let $|\psi\rangle = \frac{1}{\sqrt{2}}(|0\rangle + |1\rangle)$.

(i) If we take AP to be the subspaces orthogonal to the basis state $|0\rangle$:

$$AP = \{\mathcal{Y} \in \mathcal{S}(\mathcal{H}) : |0\rangle \perp \mathcal{Y}\},$$

then $L(|\psi\rangle) = \emptyset$ and

$$\bigcap_{\mathcal{Y} \in L(|\psi\rangle)} \mathcal{Y} = \mathcal{H}.$$

Thus, for any $X \in \mathcal{S}(\mathcal{H})$, $|\psi\rangle \models X$ if and only if $X = \mathcal{H}$.

(ii) Let AP be the 2-dimensional subspaces of $\mathcal{H}$. For the case of $n = 2$,

$$\bigcap_{\mathcal{Y} \in L(|\psi\rangle)} \mathcal{Y} = \mathcal{H},$$

and $|\psi\rangle \models X$ if and only if $X = \mathcal{H}$. For the case of $n > 2$,

$$\bigcap_{\mathcal{Y} \in L(|\psi\rangle)} \mathcal{Y} = \text{span } \{|\psi\rangle\},$$

and $|\psi\rangle \models X$ if and only if $|\psi\rangle \in X$.

(iii) If AP is the subspaces containing the basis state $|2\rangle$, i.e. $AP = \{\mathcal{X} \in S(\mathcal{H}) : |2\rangle \in \mathcal{X}\}$, then

$$\bigcap_{\mathcal{Y} \in L(|\psi\rangle)} \mathcal{Y} = \text{span } \{|\psi\rangle, |2\rangle\},$$

and $|\psi\rangle \models \mathcal{X}$ if and only if $|\psi\rangle, |2\rangle \in \mathcal{X}$.

Some Special Sets of Propositions. In general, a set of propositions in quantum logic cannot be treated in the same way as in the case of classical propositional logic. One of the main reasons is the non-commutativity between propositions about quantum systems. To conclude this subsection, we identify a very special class of sets of atomic quantum propositions that are relatively easy to deal with.

Definition 4.9 A set $AP \subseteq S(\mathcal{H})$ of atomic propositions is called *proper* if it satisfies the following two conditions.

(i) Any two elements $\mathcal{X}_1, \mathcal{X}_2$ of AP commute:

$$P_{\mathcal{X}_1} P_{\mathcal{X}_2} = P_{\mathcal{X}_2} P_{\mathcal{X}_1},$$

where $P_{\mathcal{X}_1}, P_{\mathcal{X}_2}$ are the projections onto $\mathcal{X}_1$ and $\mathcal{X}_2$, respectively; and
(ii) AP is closed under join: if $\mathcal{X}_1, \mathcal{X}_2 \in AP$, then $\mathcal{X}_1 \vee \mathcal{X}_2 \in AP$.

The following lemma shows that for a proper set AP of atomic propositions, we only need to check its basis states in order to verify that a property (definable in terms of AP) is satisfied by all states in a subspace.

Lemma 4.10 *Given a proper set AP of atomic propositions in $\mathcal{H}$. Let $\mathcal{Y}$ be a (closed) subspace of $\mathcal{H}$ with $\{|\psi_i\rangle\}$ as its basis. Then the following two statements are equivalent:*

(i) *$|\xi\rangle \models \mathcal{X}$ for all $|\xi\rangle \in \mathcal{Y}$.*
(ii) *$|\psi_i\rangle \models \mathcal{X}$ for all i.*

Proof Obviously, (i) implies (ii). Now we show that (ii) implies (i). For any $|\xi\rangle \in \mathcal{Y}$, we can write:

$$|\xi\rangle = \sum_{i \in J} a_i |\psi_i\rangle$$

for a finite index set J and for some complex numbers a_i $(i \in J)$ because $\{|\psi_i\rangle\}$ is a basis of $\mathcal{Y}$. By the assumption that $|\psi_i\rangle \models \mathcal{X}$, we have

$$\bigcap_{\mathcal{Z} \in L(|\psi_i\rangle)} \mathcal{Z} \subseteq \mathcal{X}$$

for all $i \in J$. Therefore,

$$\bigvee_{i \in J} \bigcap_{\mathcal{Z} \in L(|\psi_i\rangle)} \mathcal{Z} \subseteq \mathcal{X}.$$

Since any two elements of AP commute, distributivity is valid among AP (see Proposition 2.5 in [24]) and we have

$$\bigvee_{i \in J} \bigcap_{\mathcal{Z} \in L(|\psi_i\rangle)} \mathcal{Z} = \bigcap_{\mathcal{Z} \in \prod_{i \in J} L(|\psi_i\rangle)} \bigvee_{i \in J} \mathcal{Z}(i).$$

Thus, we only need to show that

$$\bigcap_{\mathcal{Z} \in L(|\xi\rangle)} \mathcal{Z} \subseteq \bigcap_{\mathcal{Z} \in \prod_{i \in J} L(|\psi_i\rangle)} \bigvee_{i \in J} \mathcal{Z}(i). \tag{4.3}$$

In fact, for any

$$\mathcal{Z} \in \prod_{i \in J} L(|\psi_i\rangle),$$

by definition it holds that $|\psi_i\rangle \in \mathcal{Z}(i)$ for all $i \in J$. Then

$$|\xi\rangle = \sum_{i \in J} a_i |\psi_i\rangle \in \bigvee_{i \in J} \mathcal{Z}(i).$$

In addition, it is assumed that AP is closed under join. This implies

$$\bigvee_{i \in J} \mathcal{Z}(i) \in L(|\xi\rangle)$$

and

$$\bigcap_{\mathcal{Z} \in L(|\xi\rangle)} \mathcal{Z} \subseteq \bigvee_{i \in J} \mathcal{Z}(i).$$

So, we complete the proof. $\qquad\qquad\qquad\qquad\qquad\qquad\qquad\square$

4.3 Linear-Time Properties of Quantum Systems

Section 4.2 has provided us with a way for describing the static properties of a quantum system. In this section, we further consider how to describe the dynamic properties of quantum systems. We shall introduce the notion of a linear-time property of quantum systems and define its satisfaction by a quantum automaton; that is, when does a quantum automaton satisfy a given linear-time property?

4.3.1 Basic Definitions

Let us start from defining the notion of a general linear property, and more specific ones will be discussed in the subsequent subsections.

Traces of Quantum Automata.   Let $\mathcal{H}$ be the state Hilbert space of a quantum system, and let a set AP of atomic propositions in $\mathcal{H}$ be fixed. We write

$$\left(2^{AP}\right)^* = \bigcup_{n=0}^{\infty} \left(2^{AP}\right)^n$$

for the set of finite sequences of subsets of AP and $\left(2^{AP}\right)^{\omega}$ for the set of infinite sequences of subsets of AP, where $\omega = \{0, 1, 2, \ldots\}$ is the set of natural numbers. Then we can use elements of $\left(2^{AP}\right)^{\omega}$ (or $\left(2^{AP}\right)^*$) to represent the dynamic behaviour of quantum systems.

Now we consider a quantum automaton $\mathcal{A}$ with state Hilbert space $\mathcal{H}$. For a path $\pi = |\psi_0\rangle|\psi_1\rangle|\psi_2\rangle \ldots$ in $\mathcal{A}$, we denote

$$L(\pi) = L(|\psi_0\rangle)L(|\psi_1\rangle)L(|\psi_2\rangle)\ldots \in \left(2^{AP}\right)^* \cup \left(2^{AP}\right)^{\omega}. \tag{4.4}$$

Thus, path π is described by a sequence of sets of atomic propositions, where $L(|\psi_i\rangle)$ is the set of atomic propositions that are satisfied in the ith state of the path. Furthermore, we collect all such sequences as a specification of the dynamic behaviour of the quantum automaton.

> **Definition 4.11** The set of traces and the set of finite traces of a quantum automaton $\mathcal{A}$ are defined respectively by
>
> $$Traces(\mathcal{A}) = \{L(\pi)|\pi \text{ is a path in } \mathcal{A}\},$$
> $$Traces_{fin}(\mathcal{A}) = \{L(\pi)|\pi \text{ is a finite path in } \mathcal{A}\}.$$

> **Exercise 4.2** Consider the quantum automaton $\mathcal{A}$ in Example 4.2 and let atomic propositions $AP = \{\mathcal{H}_0, \mathcal{H}_1, \mathcal{H}_+, \mathcal{H}_-\}$, where $\mathcal{H}_x = \text{span}\{|x\rangle\}$ for $x \in \{0, 1, +, -\}$. Compute $Traces(\mathcal{A})$ and $Traces_{fin}(\mathcal{A})$.

Linear Properties.   The foregoing discussion motivates us to introduce a general notion of linear-time properties.

> **Definition 4.12** A linear-time property in Hilbert space $\mathcal{H}$ is a subset P of
>
> $$\left(2^{AP}\right)^* \cup \left(2^{AP}\right)^{\omega};$$
>
> that is, an element of P is a finite or infinite sequence $A_0 A_1 A_2 \ldots$ such that A_n is a subset of AP for all $n \geq 0$.

Here, it is worth comparing linear-time properties of classical and quantum systems. At the top, both of them are defined as a set of finite or infinite sequences of sets of atomic propositions. But at the bottom, they are quite different: atomic propositions about a quantum system are chosen in the view of Birkhoff–von Neumann quantum logic; that is, they are certain (closed) subspaces of the state Hilbert space of the quantum system under consideration.

Satisfaction. The satisfaction relation between a quantum state and an atomic proposition introduced in Definition 4.7 can be naturally lifted to a satisfaction relation between a quantum automaton and a linear-time property through Eq. (4.4). Obviously, the aforementioned definition of linear-time property is independent of any quantum automaton. But for a given quantum automaton $\mathcal{A}$, we can consider when a linear-time property is satisfied by it. More precisely, a property P specifies the admissible behaviours of automaton $\mathcal{A}$:

- A path $\pi = |\psi_0\rangle|\psi_1\rangle|\psi_2\rangle\ldots$ of $\mathcal{A}$ is admissible whenever there exists $A_0 A_1 A_2 \ldots \in P$ such that $L(|\psi_n\rangle) = A_n$ for all $n \geq 0$; otherwise the path π is prohibited by P.

This observation leads to the following:

> **Definition 4.13** A quantum automaton $\mathcal{A}$ satisfies a linear-time property P, written $\mathcal{A} \models P$, if *Traces*$(\mathcal{A}) \subseteq P$.

4.3.2 Safety Properties

In the remaining subsections, we examine several special classes of linear-time properties of quantum systems. Safety is one of the most important kinds of linear-time properties studied in the literature of model checking classical systems. Intuitively, a safety property specifies that 'something bad never happens'. The notion of safety property can be straightforwardly generalised into the quantum setting. Let

$$\widehat{\sigma} \in \left(2^{AP}\right)^* \text{ and } \sigma \in \left(2^{AP}\right)^* \cup \left(2^{AP}\right)^\omega.$$

If $\sigma = \widehat{\sigma}\sigma'$ for some $\sigma' \in \left(2^{AP}\right)^* \cup \left(2^{AP}\right)^\omega$, then $\widehat{\sigma}$ is called a prefix of σ, and we write $\widehat{\sigma} \sqsubseteq \sigma$.

> **Definition 4.14** A finite sequence $\widehat{\sigma} \in \left(2^{AP}\right)^*$ is a bad prefix of a property P if $\widehat{\sigma}\sigma \notin P$ for all $\sigma \in \left(2^{AP}\right)^\omega$.

Intuitively, a bad prefix $\widehat{\sigma}$ is used to indicate a time point where the 'bad thing' happens. The condition that $\widehat{\sigma}\sigma \notin P$ for all $\sigma \in \left(2^{AP}\right)^\omega$ in Definition 4.14 means that the 'bad thing' is irremediable.

We write $BPref(P)$ for the set of bad prefixes of P.

Definition 4.15 A property P is a safety property if any $\sigma \notin P$ has a prefix $\widehat{\sigma} \in BPref(P)$.

This abstract definition of safety is not easy to understand and deserves a careful explanation. Intuitively, the condition that $\sigma \notin P$ has a prefix $\widehat{\sigma} \in BPref(P)$ says a 'bad event' for a safety property occurs in a finite amount of time, if it occurs at all. In other words, either the 'bad thing' is unconditionally prohibited, or if it happens during a run of the system, there must be an identifiable point at which it happens.

The following lemma gives a simple characterisation of satisfaction of safety properties.

Lemma 4.16 *For any quantum automaton A and any safety property P,*

$$A \models P \text{ if and only if } Traces_{fin}(A) \cap BPref(P) = \emptyset.$$

Exercise 4.3 Prove Lemma 4.16.

We write $MBPref(P)$ for the set of minimal bad prefixes of P; that is, minimal elements of $BPref(P)$ according to the order $\sqsubseteq$. It is easy to see that $BPref(P)$ in Definition 4.15 and Lemma 4.16 can be replaced by $MBPref(P)$.

A reader who is familiar with the formalism of safety properties of classical systems (from, e.g. [7]) should have noted that the preceding discussion about safety properties of quantum systems is exactly the same as that of classical systems. The reason is that it does not touch the bottom level of atomic propositions.

4.3.3 Invariants

We now further consider a special class of safety properties, namely, invariants. The problem of model checking a large class of safety properties of classical systems can be reduced to the problem of checking their invariants. The notion of invariant can also be easily generalised from the classical setting to the quantum setting.

Definition 4.17 A property P is called an invariant if there exists a subspace X of $\mathcal{H}$ such that

$$P = \left\{ A_0 A_1 A_2 \ldots \in \left(2^{AP}\right)^{\omega} : \bigcap_{y \in A_n} y \subseteq X \text{ for all } n \geq 0 \right\}. \tag{4.5}$$

Intuitively, the condition

$$\bigcap_{y \in A_n} y \subseteq X \tag{4.6}$$

means that all of the atomic propositions in A_n together imply the proposition X. The invariance of X is defined by requiring that (4.6) holds for all n. In other words, X is a property that is true in all steps n.

We call P in Definition 4.17 the invariant defined by X and write

$$P = inv\ X,$$

and X is often called the invariant condition of $inv\ X$. Given a subspace X of $\mathcal{H}$, the invariant $P = inv\ X$ defined by X contains all of the sequences $A_0 A_1 A_2 \ldots$ satisfying condition (4.6). So, $P = inv\ X$ is uniquely determined by X.

Example 4.18 We write $\mathcal{H}_2$ for the 2-dimensional Hilbert space, that is, the state space of a single qubit. Let $\mathcal{H} = \mathcal{H}_2^{\otimes n}$ be the state space of n qubits. We write I_2 for the identity operator in $\mathcal{H}_2$. The set

$$G_1 = \{\pm I_2, \pm i I_2, \pm X, \pm i X, \pm Y, \pm i Y, \pm Z, \pm i Z\}$$

forms a group with the composition of operators as its group operation, called the Pauli group on a single qubit. More generally, the Pauli group on n qubits is

$$G_n = \{A_1 \otimes \ldots \otimes A_n : A_1, \ldots, A_n \in G_1\}.$$

Let S be a subgroup of G_n generated by $g_1, \ldots, g_l$. A state $|\psi\rangle \in \mathcal{H}_2^{\otimes n}$ is stabilised by S, or S is a stabiliser of $|\psi\rangle$, if

$$g|\psi\rangle = |\psi\rangle$$

for all $g \in S$. Let $Act = \{\alpha_k : k = 1, \ldots, l\}$, $U_{\alpha_k} = g_k$ for $1 \leq k \leq l$, and $\mathcal{H}_0 = \text{span}\ \{|\psi\rangle\}$. Then

$$\mathcal{A} = (\mathcal{H}, Act, \{U_\alpha : \alpha \in Act\}, \mathcal{H}_0)$$

is a quantum automaton. We choose AP to contain all 1-dimensional subspaces of $\mathcal{H}$. If S is a stabiliser of $|\psi\rangle$, then span $\{|\psi\rangle\}$ is an invariant of $\mathcal{A}$, that is,

$$\mathcal{A} \models inv\ \text{span}\ \{|\psi\rangle\}. \tag{4.7}$$

Conversely, if (4.7) holds, then S is a stabiliser of $|\psi\rangle$ modulo a phase shift; that is, for every $g \in S$, we have

$$g|\psi\rangle = e^{i\alpha}|\psi\rangle$$

for some real number α.

Satisfaction of Invariants. Now we are going to give some conditions under which an invariant holds in a quantum automaton

$$\mathcal{A} = (\mathcal{H}, Act, \{U_\alpha : \alpha \in Act\}, \mathcal{H}_0).$$

First, we observe that to check whether $A \models inv\ \mathcal{X}$, one needs to consider all infinite paths starting from $\mathcal{H}_0$. But the space $\mathcal{H}_0$ of initial states is uncountably infinite in general. This makes checking an invariant in a quantum system much harder than that in a classical system. The following lemma shows that we only need to consider the states reachable from a basis of $\mathcal{H}_0$, which is a finite set, under the assumption of proper set of atomic propositions.

Lemma 4.19 *Suppose the initial states $\mathcal{H}_0$ of a quantum automaton A are spanned by $\{|\psi_i\rangle\}_i$ and AP is proper. Then the following two statements are equivalent:*

(i) $A \models inv\ \mathcal{X}$.
(ii) $|\psi\rangle \models \mathcal{X}$ *for any state $|\psi\rangle$ reachable in A from some $|\psi_i\rangle$.*

Proof   The '(i) $\Rightarrow$ (ii)' part is obvious. To prove the '(ii) $\Rightarrow$ (i)' part, it suffices to prove the following:

• Claim: If $|\xi\rangle \models \mathcal{X}$ for all state $|\xi\rangle$ reachable from some $|\psi_i\rangle$, then $|\psi\rangle \models \mathcal{X}$ for any state $|\psi\rangle$ reachable from some state $|\varphi\rangle \in \mathcal{H}_0$.

In fact, for any $|\varphi\rangle \in \mathcal{H}_0$, we can write

$$|\varphi\rangle = \sum_i a_i |\psi_i\rangle$$

for some complex numbers a_i because $\mathcal{H}_0 = \text{span}\ \{|\psi_i\rangle\}$. If $|\psi\rangle$ is reachable from $|\varphi\rangle$, then there are $\alpha_1, \ldots, \alpha_n \in Act, n \geq 0$ such that

$$|\psi\rangle = U_{\alpha_n} \ldots U_{\alpha_1} |\varphi\rangle.$$

We write

$$|\xi_i\rangle = U_{\alpha_n} \ldots U_{\alpha_1} |\psi_i\rangle$$

for each i. Then

$$|\psi\rangle = \sum_i a_i |\xi_i\rangle,$$

and $|\xi_i\rangle$ is reachable from $|\psi_i\rangle$. It immediately follows from Lemma 4.10 that $|\psi\rangle \models \mathcal{X}$ provided that $|\xi_i\rangle \models \mathcal{X}$ for all i. This completes the proof.   □

The following simple corollary gives a sufficient condition for invariant, which meets our intuition of invariant of a system very well.

Corollary 4.20 *Suppose AP is proper and $\mathcal{H}_0 = \text{span}\{|\psi_i\rangle\}_i$. If*

(i) $|\psi_i\rangle \models \mathcal{X}$ *for all i; and*
(ii) $U_\alpha \mathcal{Y} \subseteq \mathcal{Y}$ *for all $\mathcal{Y} \in AP$ and for all $\alpha \in Act$,*

then $A \models inv\ \mathcal{X}$.

Proof We first have the following:

• Claim: $|\psi\rangle \models \mathcal{X}$ implies $U_\alpha|\psi\rangle \models \mathcal{X}$ for all $\alpha \in Act$.

In fact, it follows from condition (ii) that

$$L(|\psi\rangle) = \{\mathcal{Y} \in AP : |\psi\rangle \in \mathcal{Y}\} \subseteq \{\mathcal{Y} \in AP : U_\alpha|\psi\rangle \in \mathcal{Y}\} = L(U_\alpha|\psi\rangle).$$

Thus, if $|\psi\rangle \models \mathcal{X}$, then

$$\bigcap_{\mathcal{Y} \in L(U_\alpha|\psi\rangle)} \mathcal{Y} \subseteq \bigcap_{\mathcal{Y} \in L(|\psi\rangle)} \mathcal{Y} \subseteq \mathcal{X}$$

and $U_\alpha|\psi\rangle \models \mathcal{X}$. Now the proof is completed by simply combining the preceding claim, condition (i) and Lemma 4.19. □

4.3.4 Liveness Properties

Liveness properties are another important kind of linear-time properties that are in a sense dual to safety properties. A liveness property specifies that 'something good will happen eventually'. The notion of liveness property can also be easily generalised into the quantum case.

Definition 4.21 A linear-time property $P \subseteq (2^{AP})^\omega$ is called a liveness property if for any $\widehat{\sigma} \in (2^{AP})^*$, there exists $\sigma \in (2^{AP})^\omega$ such that $\widehat{\sigma}\sigma \in P$.

This abstract definition of liveness also needs a careful explanation. A finite sequence $\widehat{\sigma} \in (2^{AP})^*$ represents a partial run of the system. We say that $\widehat{\sigma}$ is live for a property P if it can be extended to a full run that satisfies P; that is, $\widehat{\sigma}\sigma \in P$ for some $\sigma \in (2^{AP})^\omega$, which means that some 'good thing' eventually happens. Then a liveness property P requires that every partial run of the system must be live for it.

Example 4.22 Let $\mathcal{H}$ be a Hilbert space and $\mathcal{U}$ be a set of unitary operators in $\mathcal{H}$. It is unnecessary that $\mathcal{U}$ contains all unitary operators in $\mathcal{H}$. The elements of $\mathcal{U}$ can be understood as the operations allowed in the scenario under consideration. For any $U \in \mathcal{U}$ and $1 \leq i \leq n$,

$$U_i = U \otimes \bigotimes_{j \neq i} I_\mathcal{H}$$

performs U on the ith copy of $\mathcal{H}$ and does nothing on the other copies, where $I_\mathcal{H}$ is the identity operator in $\mathcal{H}$. So, U_i can be seen as a local operation in $\mathcal{H}^{\otimes n}$. For any two n-partite states $|\varphi\rangle, |\psi\rangle \in \mathcal{H}^{\otimes n}$, if there exists a sequence $U_{i_1}^{(1)}, \ldots, U_{i_m}^{(m)}$ of local operations such that

$$|\psi\rangle = U_{i_1}^{(1)} \ldots U_{i_m}^{(m)}|\varphi\rangle,$$

then we say that $|\varphi\rangle$ and $|\psi\rangle$ are locally $\mathcal{U}$-equivalent.

We construct a quantum automaton in $\mathcal{H}^{\otimes n}$ that starts in state $|\varphi\rangle$ and performs local $\mathcal{U}$-operations:

$$\mathcal{A} = (\mathcal{H}^{\otimes n}, Act = \{U_i | U \in \mathcal{U} \text{ and } 1 \leq i \leq n\}, \mathcal{H}_0 = \text{span } \{|\varphi\rangle\})$$

and set

$$P = \left\{ A_0 A_1 A_2 \ldots \in (2^{AP})^\omega : (\exists n \geq 0) \ A_n = \{\text{span}\{|\psi\rangle\}\} \right\}.$$

Obviously, P is a liveness property. It is easy to see that if $\mathcal{A} \models P$, then $|\varphi\rangle$ and $|\psi\rangle$ are locally $\mathcal{U}$-equivalent modulo a phase shift, that is,

$$|\psi\rangle = e^{i\alpha} U_{i_1}^{(1)} \ldots U_{i_m}^{(m)} |\varphi\rangle$$

for some real number α and local operations $U_{i_1}^{(1)}, \ldots, U_{i_m}^{(m)}$.

4.3.5 Persistence Properties

Persistence properties are a useful class of liveness properties. A persistence property asserts that a certain condition always holds from some moment on. Again, the notion of persistence property can be straightforwardly generalised to quantum systems.

Definition 4.23 A property P is called a persistence property if there exists $\mathcal{X} \in S(\mathcal{H})$ such that

$$P = \left\{ A_0 A_1 A_2 \ldots \in \left(2^{AP}\right)^\omega : (\exists m)(\forall n \geq m) \bigcap_{\mathcal{Y} \in A_n} \mathcal{Y} \subseteq \mathcal{X} \right\}. \tag{4.8}$$

We call P in Eq. (4.8) the persistence property defined by $\mathcal{X}$ and write $P = pers \ \mathcal{X}$.

Exercise 4.4 Prove that $P = pers \ \mathcal{X}$ is a liveness property provided that $P \neq \emptyset$.

Satisfaction of Persistence Properties. Although the definitions of the persistence property for classical and quantum systems are the same, checking it in the quantum case needs some new ideas. As in the case of invariants, to check whether a persistence property is satisfied by a quantum automaton, we have to examine the behaviour of the automaton starting in all initial states, which form a continuum. But the next lemma shows that for a proper set of atomic propositions, it suffices to consider the behaviour of the automaton starting in some basis states of the space of initial states.

Lemma 4.24 *Let AP be proper and* $\mathcal{H}_0 = \text{span } \{|\psi_1\rangle, \ldots, |\psi_k\rangle\}$. *Then* $\mathcal{A} \models \text{pers } \mathcal{X}$ *if and only if for each* $1 \leq i \leq k$, *and for each path*

$$|\psi_i\rangle = |\zeta_0\rangle \xrightarrow{U_{\alpha_0}} |\zeta_1\rangle \xrightarrow{U_{\alpha_1}} |\zeta_2\rangle \xrightarrow{U_{\alpha_2}} \ldots$$

starting in a basis state $|\psi_i\rangle$, *there exists* $m \geq 0$ *such that* $|\zeta_n\rangle \models \mathcal{X}$ *for all* $n \geq m$.

Proof We only need to prove the "if" part. By Definition 4.23 it suffices to show that for any path

$$|\eta_0\rangle \xrightarrow{U_{\alpha_0}} |\eta_1\rangle \xrightarrow{U_{\alpha_1}} |\eta_2\rangle \xrightarrow{U_{\alpha_2}} \ldots,$$

where $|\eta_0\rangle \in \mathcal{H}_0$, we can find $m \geq 0$ such that $|\eta_n\rangle \models \mathcal{X}$ for all $n \geq m$. Since $|\eta_0\rangle \in \mathcal{H}_0 = \text{span } \{|\psi_1\rangle, \ldots, |\psi_k\rangle\}$, we have

$$|\eta_0\rangle = \sum_{i=1}^{k} a_i |\psi_i\rangle$$

for some complex numbers a_i $(1 \leq i \leq k)$. Put

$$|\zeta_{ij}\rangle = U_{\alpha_{j-1}} \ldots U_{\alpha_1} U_{\alpha_0} |\psi_i\rangle$$

for all $1 \leq i \leq k$ and $j \geq 0$. A simple calculation shows that

$$|\eta_j\rangle = \sum_{i=1}^{k} a_i |\zeta_{ij}\rangle$$

for all $j \geq 0$. On the other hand, for each $1 \leq i \leq k$, we have the following transitions:

$$|\psi_i\rangle = |\zeta_{i0}\rangle \xrightarrow{U_{\alpha_0}} |\zeta_{i1}\rangle \xrightarrow{U_{\alpha_1}} |\zeta_{i2}\rangle \xrightarrow{U_{\alpha_2}} \ldots.$$

By the assumption, there is $m_i \geq 0$ such that $|\zeta_{in}\rangle \models \mathcal{X}$ for all $n \geq m_i$. Let $m = \max_{i=1}^{k} m_i$. Then for all $n \geq m$, we have $|\zeta_{in}\rangle \models \mathcal{X}$ for all $1 \leq i \leq k$ and

$$|\eta_n\rangle = \sum_{i=1}^{k} a_i |\zeta_{in}\rangle.$$

By Lemma 4.10 we obtain $|\eta_n\rangle \models \mathcal{X}$ and thus complete the proof. □

Furthermore, the following lemma shows that persistence properties and invariants coincide whenever the state Hilbert space is finite dimensional and the set AP of atomic proposition is proper.

Lemma 4.25 *If the state Hilbert space* $\mathcal{H}$ *is finite dimensional and AP is proper, then* $\mathcal{A} \models \text{pers } \mathcal{X}$ *if and only if* $\mathcal{A} \models \text{inv } \mathcal{X}$.

Proof The 'if' part is obvious. We now prove the 'only if' part. Assume that $\mathcal{A} \models pers\ \mathcal{X}$ and we want to show that $\mathcal{A} \models inv\ \mathcal{X}$. It suffices to demonstrate that $|\psi\rangle \models \mathcal{X}$ for all $|\psi\rangle \in R(\mathcal{A})$. We complete the proof by proving the following two claims:

- Claim 1: There exist $m \geq 0$ and unitary operator U such that $|\psi\rangle \models \mathcal{X}$ for all $|\psi\rangle \in U^m R(\mathcal{A})$.

Since $R(\mathcal{A})$ is finite dimensional and is spanned by the reachable states of $\mathcal{A}$, we can find a basis $\{|\psi_1\rangle, \ldots, |\psi_l\rangle\}$ of $R(\mathcal{A})$ such that for each i, there exists a path $|\varphi_0\rangle|\varphi_1\rangle \ldots |\varphi_n\rangle$ in $\mathcal{A}$ with $|\varphi_0\rangle \in \mathcal{H}_0$ and $|\varphi_n\rangle = |\psi_i\rangle$. We arbitrarily choose a unitary operator $U \in \{U_\alpha : \alpha \in Act\}$, and put

$$|\varphi_{n+k}\rangle = U^k |\varphi_n\rangle$$

for all $k \geq 1$. Then the path $|\varphi_0\rangle|\varphi_1\rangle \ldots |\varphi_n\rangle$ is extended to a path:

$$|\varphi_0\rangle|\varphi_1\rangle \ldots |\varphi_n\rangle|\varphi_{n+1}\rangle \ldots.$$

It follows from the assumption of $\mathcal{A} \models pers\ \mathcal{X}$ that there exists $m_i \geq 0$ with

$$U^k |\psi_i\rangle = |\varphi_{n+k}\rangle \models \mathcal{X}$$

for all $k \geq m_i$. Put $m = \max_{i=1}^l m_i$. Then $U^m |\psi_i\rangle \models \mathcal{X}$ for all $1 \leq i \leq l$. By Lemma 4.10 we obtain that $|\psi\rangle \models \mathcal{X}$ for all

$$|\psi\rangle \in span\ \{U^m |\psi_i\rangle | 1 \leq i \leq l\} = U^m R(\mathcal{A}).$$

- Claim 2: $U^m R(\mathcal{A}) = R(\mathcal{A})$.

By definition we have $U R(\mathcal{A}) \subseteq R(\mathcal{A})$. On the other hand, $\dim(U R(\mathcal{A})) = \dim(R(\mathcal{A}))$ because U is a unitary operator. Then it follows that $U R(\mathcal{A}) = R(\mathcal{A})$. Consequently, it holds that $U^m R(\mathcal{A}) = R(\mathcal{A})$.   □

It should be noted that the equivalence of persistence properties and invariants holds only in finite-dimensional Hilbert spaces. The following counterexample explicitly shows that it is not true in an infinite-dimensional Hilbert space.

Example 4.26 Consider the space $\mathcal{L}_2$ of square summable sequences:

$$\mathcal{L}_2 = \left\{ \sum_{n=-\infty}^{\infty} \alpha_n |n\rangle : \alpha_n \in \mathbb{C} \text{ for all } n, \text{ and } \sum_{n=-\infty}^{\infty} |\alpha_n|^2 < \infty \right\}.$$

The inner product in $\mathcal{L}_2$ is defined by

$$\left(\sum_{n=-\infty}^{\infty} \alpha_n |n\rangle, \sum_{n=-\infty}^{\infty} \alpha'_n |n\rangle \right) = \sum_{n=-\infty}^{\infty} \alpha_n^* \alpha'_n$$

for all $\alpha_n, \alpha'_n \in \mathbb{C}$, $-\infty < n < \infty$. The translation operator T_+ in $\mathcal{L}_2$ is defined by

$$T_+|n\rangle = |n+1\rangle$$

for all n. It is easy to verify that T_+ is a unitary operator. Let $Act = \{+\}$ consist of a single action and $\mathcal{H}_0 = \text{span}\{|0\rangle\}$. Then $\mathcal{A} = (\mathcal{L}_2, Act, \{U_\alpha : \alpha \in Act\}, \mathcal{H}_0)$ is a quantum automaton.

Let k be a fixed integer, and let

$$[k) = \text{span}\{|n\rangle : n \geq k\}, \quad (k-1] = \text{span}\{|n\rangle : n \leq k-1\}.$$

Put $AP = \{[k), (k-1], \mathcal{L}_2\}$. Then AP is proper. It is easy to see that $\mathcal{A} \models pers\ [k)$, but $\mathcal{A} \models inv\ [k)$ does not hold provided $k > 0$.

4.4 Reachability of Quantum Automata

In the previous section, we defined the general notion of linear properties of quantum systems and saw several interesting examples of it. In this section, we continue to consider a large class of linear properties. As we saw in Chapter 2, most of the model-checking problems for classical systems can be reduced to certain reachability problems. Reachability will play a similar role in the studies of model-checking techniques for quantum systems. A simple version of reachability in quantum automata was already introduced at the end of Section 4.1. This section aims to define and carefully examine several more sophisticated notions of reachability for quantum automata.

4.4.1 A (Meta-)Propositional Logic for Quantum Systems

Reachability is a kind of dynamic property of a system, but it is defined based on a certain static property, that is, the property satisfied by the states reached in the systems. In this subsection, we prepare a logical language for specifying the static properties that can be used to define our notions of reachbility.

Given a Hilbert space $\mathcal{H}$, for specifying static properties of quantum systems, we defined in Section 4.2 the quantum logic $(\mathcal{S}(\mathcal{H}), \perp, \cap, \vee)$, where elements of $\mathcal{S}(\mathcal{H})$, that is, (closed) subspaces of $\mathcal{H}$, are considered as propositions about a quantum system with $\mathcal{H}$ as its state space, and $\perp, \cap, \vee$ are the interpretations of logical connectives 'not', 'and', 'or', respectively. But sometimes when we say that 'the current state of the quantum system is in subspace $\mathcal{X}$ or in subspace $\mathcal{Y}$', we do not mean that the state is in the join $\mathcal{X} \vee \mathcal{Y}$, or equivalently, the state is a linear combination of a state in $\mathcal{X}$ and a state in $\mathcal{Y}$; instead we simply mean that the state is in $\mathcal{X} \cup \mathcal{Y}$. However, $\mathcal{X} \cup \mathcal{Y}$ is not in general in $\mathcal{S}(\mathcal{H})$. Therefore, we need to extend this quantum logic in order to specify such a property.

We choose to treat $(\mathcal{S}(\mathcal{H}), \bot, \cap, \vee)$ as our object logic and beyond it we define a meta-propositional logic. We assume a set $AP \subseteq \mathcal{S}(\mathcal{H})$ of atomic propositions. The meta-logical formulas are generated from AP by using traditional Boolean connectives $\neg$, $\wedge$ and $\vee$. Their semantics are inductively defined as follows: for any state $|\psi\rangle \in \mathcal{H}$,

- If $f \in AP$, then $|\psi\rangle \models f$ if $|\psi\rangle \in f$;
- $|\psi\rangle \models \neg f$ if $|\psi\rangle \models f$ does not hold;
- $|\psi\rangle \models f_1 \wedge f_2$ if $|\psi\rangle \models f_1$ and $|\psi\rangle \models f_2$; and
- $|\psi\rangle \models f_1 \vee f_2$ if $|\psi\rangle \models f_1$ or $|\psi\rangle \models f_2$.

> **Remark 4.27** *It is worth noting that here we abuse a little bit of notation: $\vee$ is used to denote both the disjunction in the object logic and that in the meta-logic with different semantics. But its correct semantics can be easily recognised from the context. Also, the negation $\neg$ in the meta-logic and the negation $\bot$ in the object logic have different semantics. However, the interpretation of conjunction $\wedge$ in the meta-logic coincides with the conjunction $\cap$ in the object logic.*

For a meta-logical formula f, we write $[\![f]\!]$ for the set of states that satisfy f:

$$[\![f]\!] = \{|\psi\rangle \in \mathcal{H} : |\psi\rangle \models f\}.$$

For example, for a subspace V of $\mathcal{H}$, we have:

- $[\![\neg V]\!] = \{|\psi\rangle \in \mathcal{H} : V \text{ is } (1, \, <) - \text{satisfied in } |\psi\rangle)\}$;
- $[\![\neg(V^{\bot})]\!] = \{|\psi\rangle \in \mathcal{H} : V \text{ is } (0, \, >) - \text{satisfied in } |\psi\rangle)\}$,

where $(\lambda, \triangleright)$-satisfaction is defined according to Eq. (4.1). In general, $[\![f]\!]$ is a Boolean combination of subspaces of $\mathcal{H}$, but it might not be a subspace of $\mathcal{H}$ because $\vee$ and $\neg$ may appear in f.

4.4.2 Satisfaction of Reachability by Quantum Automata

In Subsection 4.4.1, we introduced meta-logical formulas to specify more complicated static properties of quantum systems. In this subsection, we use them to define several interesting notions of reachability in quantum automata.

Let us start by recalling the simple notion of reachability introduced in Section 4.1. Assume that $\mathcal{A} = (\mathcal{H}, Act, \{U_\alpha : \alpha \in Act\}, \mathcal{H}_0)$ is a quantum automaton. A path of $\mathcal{A}$ is generated by a sequence $\alpha_0\alpha_1\alpha_2 \ldots \in Act^\omega$ of actions, starting from an initial state:

$$\pi = |\psi_0\rangle \overset{U_{\alpha_0}}{\to} |\psi_1\rangle \overset{U_{\alpha_1}}{\to} |\psi_2\rangle \overset{U_{\alpha_2}}{\to} \cdots,$$

where $|\psi_0\rangle \in \mathcal{H}_0$, and $\alpha_n \in Act$, $|\psi_{n+1}\rangle = U_{\alpha_n}|\psi_n\rangle$ for all $n \geq 0$. Then a state $|\varphi\rangle \in \mathcal{H}$ is reachable from $|\psi\rangle \in \mathcal{H}_0$ if $\mathcal{A}$ has a path $|\psi_0\rangle|\psi_1\rangle \ldots |\psi_n\rangle$ such that

$|\psi_0\rangle = |\psi\rangle$ and $|\psi_n\rangle = |\varphi\rangle$. Furthermore, the reachable space of quantum automaton $\mathcal{A}$ is the subspace of $\mathcal{H}$:

$$R(\mathcal{A}) = \text{span } \{|\varphi\rangle \in \mathcal{H} : |\psi\rangle \text{ is reachable from some initial state } |\psi\rangle \in \mathcal{H}_0\}.$$

More sophisticated reachability can be defined by lifting the meta-logical formulas introduced in Subsection 4.4.1. Let f be a meta-logical formula representing a Boolean combination of some subspaces of the state Hilbert space $\mathcal{H}$, and let $\sigma = |\psi_0\rangle|\psi_1\rangle|\psi_2\rangle \dots$ be an infinite sequence of states in $\mathcal{H}$. We define:

- (Eventually reachable):

$$\sigma \models \mathbf{F}f \text{ if } \exists i \geq 0. |\psi_i\rangle \models f. \tag{4.9}$$

- (Globally reachable):

$$\sigma \models \mathbf{G}f \text{ if } \forall i \geq 0. |\psi_i\rangle \models f. \tag{4.10}$$

- (Ultimately forever reachable):

$$\sigma \models \mathbf{U}f \text{ if } \overset{\infty}{\forall} i \geq 0. |\psi_i\rangle \models f. \tag{4.11}$$

- (Infinitely often reachable):

$$\sigma \models \mathbf{I}f \text{ if } \overset{\infty}{\exists} i \geq 0. |\psi_i\rangle \models f. \tag{4.12}$$

Here, $\overset{\infty}{\forall} i \geq 0$ means '$\exists j \geq 0, \forall i \geq j$', and $\overset{\infty}{\exists} i \geq 0$ means '$\forall j \geq 0, \exists i \geq j$'.

Moreover, satisfaction of these reachability properties by quantum automata can be defined straightforwardly:

Definition 4.28 Let $\mathcal{A}$ be a quantum automaton. Then for reachability property $\Delta \in \{\mathbf{F}, \mathbf{G}, \mathbf{U}, \mathbf{I}\}$, satisfaction of Δ by $\mathcal{A}$ is defined as follows:

$$\mathcal{A} \models \Delta f \text{ if } \sigma(\pi) \models \Delta f \text{ for all paths } \pi \text{ in } \mathcal{A}.$$

To illustrate that the reachability properties defined earlier can actually be used to specify some interesting properties of quantum physical systems, let us consider the following example.

Example 4.29 Let $\mathcal{A}$ be a quantum walk on a quadrilateral with the state Hilbert space $\mathcal{H}_4 = \text{span}\{|0\rangle, |1\rangle, |2\rangle, |3\rangle\}$. Its behaviour is described as follows.

(i) Initialise the system in state $|0\rangle$.
(ii) Non-deterministically apply one of the two unitary operators

$$W_\pm = \frac{1}{\sqrt{3}} \begin{pmatrix} 1 & 1 & 0 & \mp 1 \\ \pm 1 & \mp 1 & \pm 1 & 0 \\ 0 & 1 & 1 & \pm 1 \\ 1 & 0 & -1 & \pm 1 \end{pmatrix}.$$

(iii) Perform a measurement $\{P_{yes}, P_{no}\}$, where

$$P_{yes} = |2\rangle\langle 2|, \qquad P_{no} = I_4 - |2\rangle\langle 2|,$$

and I_4 is the 4×4 unit matrix. If the outcome is 'yes', then the walk terminates; otherwise go back to step (ii).

It was proved in [83] that this walk terminates with a probability less than 1 if and only if a diverging state (i.e. a state with terminating probability 0) can be reached, and the set of diverging states is $PD_1 \cup PD_2$, where

$$PD_1 = \mathrm{span}\{|0\rangle, (|1\rangle - |3\rangle)/\sqrt{2}\},$$
$$PD_2 = \mathrm{span}\{|0\rangle, (|1\rangle + |3\rangle)/\sqrt{2}\}.$$

So, termination of the walk can be expressed as a reachability property:

$$\mathcal{A} \models \mathbf{G}\neg(PD_1 \vee PD_2). \tag{4.13}$$

Remark 4.30 *Example 4.29 shows that the Boolean disjunction in our meta-logic is really needed in some applications. Obviously, '$\vee$' in (4.13) should be understood as the Boolean disjunction rather than the disjunction in Birkhoff–von Neumann quantum logic.*

Remark 4.31 *The quantum walk in Example 4.29 is actually not a quantum automaton in the strict sense according to Definition 4.1. But it can be seen as a system consisting of a quantum automaton with two unitary actions $W_{\pm}$ and a measurement performed at the end of each step.*

A Characterisation of Reachability Properties. The reachability properties discussed earlier can be viewed in a different way, which should be helpful for the reader to understand these properties better. For any finite sequence $s = \alpha_0\alpha_1 \ldots \alpha_n \in Act^*$ of actions, we write the corresponding unitary operator

$$U_s = U_{\alpha_n} \ldots U_{\alpha_1} U_{\alpha_0}.$$

If $U_s|\psi_0\rangle \models f$ for some initial state $|\psi_0\rangle \in \mathcal{H}_0$, we say that s is accepted by $\mathcal{A}$ with f. The set of all such accepted action sequences is called the language accepted by $\mathcal{A}$ with condition f, and denoted by $\mathcal{L}(\mathcal{A}, f)$. For any $S \subseteq Act^*$, we write $\omega(S)$ for the set of infinite action sequences such that infinitely many of their initial segments lie in S; that is,

$$\omega(S) = \{w = \alpha_0\alpha_1\alpha_2 \ldots \in Act^{\omega} : \overset{\infty}{\exists} n \geq 0, \alpha_0\alpha_1 \ldots \alpha_n \in S\}.$$

We say that $S \subseteq Act^*$ satisfies the *liveness* (respectively, *deadness*) property, if $\omega(S) = Act^{\omega}$ (respectively, $\omega(S) = \emptyset$).

The following lemma gives a characterisation of reachability of quantum automata in terms of accepted languages.

Lemma 4.32 *Let $\mathcal{A}$ be a quantum automaton with* $\dim \mathcal{H}_0 = 1$. *Then*

(i) $\mathcal{A} \models \mathbf{F}f$ *iff* $Act^{\omega} = \mathcal{L}(\mathcal{A}, f) \cdot Act^{\omega}$. *Here, $X \cdot Y$ stands for the set the concatenations of elements of X and Y;*

(ii) $\mathcal{A} \models \mathbf{I}f$ *iff* $\mathcal{L}(\mathcal{A}, f)$ *satisfies the liveness;*

(iii) $\mathcal{A} \models \mathbf{G}f$ *iff* $\mathcal{L}(\mathcal{A}, f) = Act^*$ (*i.e.* $\mathcal{L}(\mathcal{A}, \neg f) = \emptyset$); *and*

(iv) $\mathcal{A} \models \mathbf{U}f$ *iff* $Act^* - \mathcal{L}(\mathcal{A}, f)$ (*i.e.* $\mathcal{L}(\mathcal{A}, \neg f)$) *satisfies the deadness.*

Exercise 4.5 Prove Lemma 4.32.

4.5 Algorithm for Checking Invariants of Quantum Automata

We have already defined various linear-time properties in the previous sections. In this and the next sections, we develop algorithms for checking whether they are satisfied by a given quantum automaton. Let us start from a class of simple linear-time properties, namely invariants. The model-checking problem here can be formulated as follows:

- **Problem of Checking Invariants:** Given a (finite-dimensional) quantum automaton $\mathcal{A} = (\mathcal{H}, Act, \{U_\alpha : \alpha \in Act\}, \mathcal{H}_0)$ and a subspace X of its state Hilbert space $\mathcal{H}$, check whether $\mathcal{A} \models inv\ X$.

Under the assumption that the set AP of atomic propositions is proper (see Definition 4.9 and Lemma 4.19), an algorithm solving the foregoing problem is presented as Algorithm 1. The design idea of this algorithm is based on Lemmas 4.4 and 4.19 as well as the following observation:

- If $\{|\psi_1\rangle, \dots |\psi_l\rangle\}$ is a basis of the reachable space $R(\mathcal{A})$, then $\mathcal{A} \models inv\ X$ if and only if $|\psi_i\rangle \models X$ for all $1 \leq i \leq l$.

Moreover, the condition that $|\psi_i\rangle \models X$ for all $1 \leq i \leq l$ can be checked by a forward depth-first search.

For a better understanding of this algorithm, let us carefully analyse it from several different angles:

Termination of the Algorithm. First, we show that Algorithm 1 actually terminates for a finite-dimensional Hilbert space $\mathcal{H}$. It can be observed that in the algorithm, for a candidate state $|\xi\rangle$, if it is in span B, then it would not be added into B. So, the elements in B are always linear independent, and there are at most $d = \dim \mathcal{H}$ elements in B. Furthermore, note that a state would be pushed into S if and only if it has been added into B. Then S would become empty after popping at most d states. This implies that the algorithm terminates after at most d iterations of the **while** loop.

Correctness of the Algorithm. Second, we show that Algorithm 1 is correct. It is easy to check that all elements in B are reachable. In fact, the initial states $|\psi_i\rangle$ are reachable, and if some $|\psi\rangle \in B$ is reachable, then all candidate states $|\xi\rangle = U_\alpha|\psi\rangle$ are reachable. So, if an execution of the algorithm returns '*false*', then there must be a reachable state $|\psi_i\rangle$ or some candidate state $|\xi\rangle$ that does not satisfy $\mathcal{X}$. If the output is '*true*', then according to Lemma 4.10, all states in B, further in span B, satisfy $\mathcal{X}$. Therefore, correctness of the algorithm comes immediately from the following:

Algorithm 1: Invariant checking

---

input:

    (i) The set $\{U_\alpha : \alpha \in Act\}$ of the unitary operators in $\mathcal{A}$;

    (ii) A basis $\{|\psi_1\rangle, |\psi_2\rangle, \ldots, |\psi_k\rangle\}$ of the space $\mathcal{H}_0$ of initial states;

    (iii) A subspace $\mathcal{X}$ of $\mathcal{H}$ (invariant condition).

output: true if $\mathcal{A} \models inv\ \mathcal{X}$, and false otherwise.

begin

    set of states $B \leftarrow \emptyset$;   (*a basis of $R(\mathcal{A})$*)

    stack of states $S \leftarrow \varepsilon$;   (*the empty stack*)

    bool $b \leftarrow$ true;   (*all states in B satisfy $\mathcal{X}$*)

    for $i = 1, 2, \ldots, k$ **do**

        $B \leftarrow B \cup \{|\psi_i\rangle\}$;   (*initial states are reachable*)

        $push(|\psi_i\rangle, S)$;   (*start a depth-first search with initial states*)

        $b \leftarrow b \wedge (|\psi_i\rangle \models \mathcal{X})$;   (*check if all initial states satisfy $\mathcal{X}$*)

    end

    while $(b \wedge S \neq \varepsilon)$ **do**

        $|\psi\rangle \leftarrow top(S)$;   (*consider a reachable state*)

        $pop(S)$;

        for *all* $\alpha \in Act$ **do**

            $|\xi\rangle \leftarrow U_\alpha|\psi\rangle$;   (*get a candidate state*)

            $b \leftarrow b \wedge (|\xi\rangle \models \mathcal{X})$;   (*check if X is satisfied*)

            if $b \wedge |\xi\rangle \notin$ span B **then**

                (*check if it has not been considered*)

                $B \leftarrow B \cup \{|\xi\rangle\}$; (*extend B by adding new reachable states*)

                $push(|\xi\rangle, S)$

        end

        end

    end

    return b

end

Lemma 4.33 *Reachable space* $R(\mathcal{A}) \subseteq \text{span } B$.

Proof We only need to check that span B satisfies conditions (i) and (ii) in Lemma 4.4. Condition (i) is satisfied as $|\psi_i\rangle \in B$ for all $1 \leq i \leq k$. Note that for any $|\psi\rangle \in B$ and any $\alpha \in Act$, $U_\alpha|\psi\rangle$ was a candidate state at some time, and then either $U_\alpha|\psi\rangle \in \text{span } B$ or it would be added into B. So, we always have $U_\alpha|\psi\rangle \in \text{span } B$. Consequently,

$$U_\alpha(\text{span } B) = \text{span } (U_\alpha B) \subseteq \text{span } (\text{span } B) = \text{span } B$$

and condition (ii) is satisfied.   □

Implementation of the Algorithm. To ensure that Algorithm 1 can be actually executed, the quantum states, unitary operations U_α, subspace $\mathcal{X}$ and subspaces in AP should be given in some effective forms. We fix an orthonormal basis of the state space $\mathcal{H}$ as the computational basis. Then all of the system's states can be represented by column vectors with complex numbers in this basis. We identify a subspace of $\mathcal{H}$ with the projection operator onto it, and assume that all the projection operators and unitary operators are represented by complex matrices in the computational basis. To record them with a finite storage space, it is reasonable to assume that the real and imaginary parts of the complex numbers involved are rational.

The aforementioned idea (or a similar idea) works in the implementation of other algorithms presented in this book.

> **Remark 4.34** *An improvement of Algorithm 1 was given in [119] for the case where all unitary operators U_α have no degenerate eigenvectors by reducing invariant checking of quantum automata to a problem of classical invariant checking.*

The algorithms for checking liveness and persistence can be developed using some ideas similar to that for invariants presented earlier. We leave them as

> **Exercise 4.6** Find algorithms for checking liveness and persistence properties (see Definitions 4.21 and 4.23) of quantum automata.

4.6 Algorithms for Checking Reachability of Quantum Automata

Now we move on to develop algorithms for checking a larger class of linear-time properties, namely reachability properties, of quantum automata. This problem can be formally formulated as follows:

- **Problem of Checking Reachability:** Given a (finite-dimensional) quantum automaton $\mathcal{A} = (\mathcal{H}, Act, \{U_\alpha : \alpha \in Act\}, \mathcal{H}_0)$ and a meta-logic formula f, that is, a Boolean combination of atomic propositions in AP (using $\neg$, $\wedge$, $\vee$). Check whether $\mathcal{A} \models \Delta f$, where reachability property $\Delta \in \{\mathbf{F}, \mathbf{G}, \mathbf{U}, \mathbf{I}\}$ (eventually, globally, ultimately forever, infinitely often reachable; see their defining equations (4.9), (4.10), (4.11) and (4.12)).

As we will see in the next section, this problem is in general undecidable. But for $\Delta \neq \mathbf{F}$ and with the restriction that f is a positive logical formula; that is, $\neg$ is not present in f, this problem becomes decidable. More precisely, we have

Theorem 4.35 *(Decidability) For reachability property $\Delta \in \{\mathbf{G}, \mathbf{U}, \mathbf{I}\}$, if f contains no negation $\neg$, then the problem whether or not $\mathcal{A} \models \Delta f$ is decidable.*

This section is devoted to gradually developing algorithms solving the reachability checking problem in the case considered in Theorem 4.35. Before doing it, let us present several technical preparations.

- As discussed at the end of Section 4.5, for the algorithmic purpose, it is reasonable to make the following assumption: we identify a subspace of $\mathcal{H}$ with the projection operator onto it, and assume that all the projection operators and unitary operators in automaton $\mathcal{A}$ and formula f are represented by complex matrices in a fixed orthonormal basis. Furthermore, we assume that all involved complex numbers have rational real and imaginary parts.
- The (meta-)logical formula f can be written in the disjunctive normal form:

$$f = \bigvee_{i=1}^{m} f_i,$$

where each f_i is a conjunctive clause. As it contains no negation and the intersection of a family of subspaces is a subspace, for each i, $[\![f_i]\!]$ is a subspace, say V_i, of the state Hilbert space $\mathcal{H}$ of quantum automaton $\mathcal{A}$. Then

$$[\![f]\!] = \bigcup_{i=1}^{m} V_i$$

is a union of finitely many subspaces of $\mathcal{H}$.
- We are going to decide whether or not $\mathcal{A} \models \Delta f$ for a quantum automaton

$$\mathcal{A} = (\mathcal{H}, Act, \{U_\alpha : \alpha \in Act\}, \mathcal{H}_0).$$

We show that this can be done by computing certain predecessor states in $\mathcal{A}$. To this end, for each $|\psi\rangle \in \mathcal{H}$, we introduce automaton

$$\mathcal{A}(\psi) = (\mathcal{H}, Act, \{U_\alpha : \alpha \in Act\}, \text{span}\{|\psi\rangle\}),$$

which can be thought of as a restriction of $\mathcal{A}$ on the paths starting from $|\psi\rangle$. Moreover for any $\wedge \in \{\mathbf{G}, \mathbf{U}, \mathbf{I}\}$, we write the set of all states satisfying $\wedge f$ as

$$Sat(\wedge f) = \{|\psi\rangle \in \mathcal{H} : \mathcal{A}(\psi) \models \wedge f\}.$$

Then it is easy to see that $\mathcal{A} \models \wedge f$ can be decided by checking whether or not $\mathcal{H}_0 \subseteq Sat(\wedge f)$.

4.6.1 Checking $\mathcal{A} \models \mathbf{I} f$ for the Simplest Case

Now we are ready to develop our algorithms for checking various reachability properties. We first present an algorithm for checking whether $\mathcal{A} \models \mathbf{I} f$ (infinitely often reachability). The preceding analysis shows that we only need to construct the satisfaction set $Sat(\mathbf{I} f)$. For a better understanding, we will do this in two steps. In this subsection, we consider the simplest case where $|Act| = 1$ and $m = 1$; that is, $\mathcal{A}$ has a single unitary operator and $f = V$ is a subspace. The general case will be discussed in the next subsection.

Lemma 4.36 *For any unitary operator U on $\mathcal{H}$, there exists an integer $p \geq 1$ such that for any subspace K of $\mathcal{H}$, one of the following two cases holds:*

(i) *$U^p K = K$; or*
(ii) *$U^n K \neq K$ for any $n \geq 1$.*

Furthermore, the smallest such integer, called the period of U and denoted p_U, can be computed in $O(d^3)$ where $d = \dim \mathcal{H}$.

Proof See Appendix 1, Section A1.1. ☐

The next theorem shows that if the quantum automaton $\mathcal{A}$ has a single action and the logic formula f corresponds to a subspace, then the satisfaction set $Sat(\mathbf{I} f)$ is simply the union of a cycle of subspaces.

Theorem 4.37 *Let $\mathcal{A} = (\mathcal{H}, Act, \{U_\alpha : \alpha \in Act\}, \mathcal{H}_0)$ be a quantum automaton where $Act = \{\alpha\}$ is a singleton and $p = p_{U_\alpha}$, and f a meta-logic formula f with $[\![f]\!] = V$ for some subspace V.*

(i) *Let $K_0 = V$, and for any $n \geq 0$,*

$$K_{n+1} = K_n \cap U_\alpha^p K_n.$$

Then $K_{m+1} = K_m$ for some $m \leq \dim V$. Denote K_m by K, or $K(U_\alpha, V)$ to show the dependence of K on U_α and V. Then

$$K = \bigcup \{X \text{ a subspace of } V : U_\alpha^p X = X\};$$

that is, K is the largest subspace of V satisfying $U_\alpha^p K = K$.

(ii)

$$Sat(\mathbf{I}f) = \bigcup_{r=0}^{p-1} U_\alpha^r K.$$

Proof We leave the proof of (i) as an exercise. Now we prove (ii). For each positive integer q, denote by K_q the largest subspace of V such that $U_\alpha^q K_q = K_q$. Then $K_p = K$. On the other hand, we can show that

$$K_q = \{|\psi\rangle \in V : \forall n \in \mathbb{N}, \, U_\alpha^{qn}|\psi\rangle \in V\}. \tag{4.14}$$

In fact, it is easy to verify that any state in K_q is also in the right-hand side of Eq. (4.14). Conversely, for any state $|\psi\rangle$ in the right-hand side of (4.14), $\text{span}\{U_\alpha^{qn}|\psi\rangle : n = 0, 1, \ldots\}$ is an invariant subspace of U_α^q included in V. Then it must be a subspace of K_q according to the definition of K_q, and so $|\psi\rangle \in K_q$. Therefore, (4.14) is proved.

Now for each $|\psi\rangle \in \mathcal{H}$, it follows from Lemma 4.32 (ii) that $\mathcal{A}(\psi) \models \mathbf{I}f$ if and only if

$$\mathcal{L}(\mathcal{A}(\psi), V) = \{n \geq 0 : U_\alpha^n|\psi\rangle \in V\}$$

satisfies liveness condition; that is, it is infinite in this special case. Note that

$$U_\alpha^n|\psi\rangle \in V \text{ iff } \text{tr}(P_{V^\perp}\mathcal{U}^n(\psi)) = 0,$$

where $\psi = |\psi\rangle\langle\psi|$ is the density operator corresponding to pure state $|\psi\rangle$, $P_{V^\perp}$ is the projection operator onto $V^\perp$ and $\mathcal{U}$ is the super-operator defined by unitary operator U_α, that is, $\mathcal{U}(\rho) = U_\alpha\rho U_\alpha^\dagger$ for every density operator ρ. Since

$$\{\text{tr}(P_{V^\perp}\mathcal{U}^n(\psi))\}_{n=0}^{\infty} \tag{4.15}$$

is a linear recurrence sequence, it follows from Theorem A1.1 that $\mathcal{L}(\mathcal{A}(\psi), V)$ is semi-linear. Thus it is infinite if and only if it contains an arithmetic progression $\{qn + r\}_{n=0}^{\infty}$ for some integers $q > 0$ and $r \geq 0$. Therefore,

$$\begin{aligned}
Sat(\mathbf{I}f) &= \{|\psi\rangle : \mathcal{L}(\mathcal{A}(\psi), V) \text{ is infinite}\} \\
&= \{|\psi\rangle : \exists q > 0, r \geq 0, \forall n \geq 0. \, U_\alpha^{qn+r}|\psi\rangle \in V\} \\
&= \{|\psi\rangle : \exists q > 0, r \geq 0. \, U_\alpha^r|\psi\rangle \in K_q\} \\
&= \{|\psi\rangle : \exists q > 0, r \geq 0. \, |\psi\rangle \in U_\alpha^{q-r}K_q\} \\
&= \bigcup_{q>0, r\geq 0} U_\alpha^r K_q = \bigcup_{r=0}^{\infty} U_\alpha^r K_p = \bigcup_{r=0}^{p-1} U_\alpha^r K.
\end{aligned} \tag{4.16}$$

Algorithm 2: Checking $\mathcal{A} \models \mathbf{I}f$ for the simplest case

---

input:

    (i) A quantum automaton $\mathcal{A} = (\mathcal{H}, Act, \{U_\alpha : \alpha \in Act\}, \mathcal{H}_0)$ where $Act = \{\alpha\}$ is a singleton;

    (ii) A meta-logic formula f with $[\![f]\!] = V$ for some subspace V of $\mathcal{H}$.

output: true if $\mathcal{A} \models \mathbf{I}f$, and false otherwise.

begin

    $p \leftarrow p_U$, the period of U;   (*Use Lemma 4.36*)

    $K_0 \leftarrow V$;

    $K \leftarrow \mathcal{H}$;

    while $K \neq K_0$ **do**

        $K_0 \leftarrow K$;

        $K \leftarrow K \cap U_\alpha^p K$;

    end

    return $\bigvee_{r=0}^{p-1} (\mathcal{H}_0 \subseteq U_\alpha^r K)$

end

The last two equalities in Eq. (4.16) come from the following observation: for each integer q, since $U_\alpha^q K_q = K_q$, it follows that $U_\alpha^p K_q = K_q$ by Lemma 4.36. Thus, by the definition of K we obtain $K_q \subseteq K_p = K$. $\square$

Exercise 4.7 Prove Theorem 4.37 (i).

Exercise 4.8 Prove that the sequence in Eq. (4.15) is a linear recurrence sequence.

Employing Lemma 4.36 and Theorem 4.37, we design Algorithm 2 to check whether $\mathcal{A} \models \mathbf{I}f$ for the simplest case. It is easy to see that the algorithm runs in time $O(d^3)$ where $d = \dim \mathcal{H}$.

4.6.2 Checking $\mathcal{A} \models \mathbf{I}f$ for the General Case

In Subsection 4.6.1, we only presented an algorithm for checking $\mathcal{A} \models \mathbf{I}f$ in the simplest case where automaton $\mathcal{A}$ only has a single action, and reachability condition f simply corresponds to a subspace V. Now we further consider the general case of arbitrary quantum automaton $\mathcal{A}$ and $[\![f]\!] = \bigvee_{i=1}^{m} V_i$. Fortunately, the idea used in Subsection 4.6.1 can be generalised to the general case. Recall that to check whether $\mathcal{A} \models \mathbf{I}f$, we only need to construct the set $Sat(\mathbf{I}f)$.

The next theorem, which is a generalisation of Theorem 4.37, shows that $Sat(\mathbf{I}f)$ can be written as a union of finitely many subspaces.

Theorem 4.38 *Let A be a quantum automaton, and f a mega-logic formula with $[\![f]\!] = \bigvee_{i=1}^{m} V_i$. There exists a family $\mathbb{X} = \{Y_1, Y_2, \ldots, Y_q\}$ of subspaces of $\mathcal{H}$ satisfying the following conditions:*

(i) *For any i and $\alpha \in Act$, there exists j such that $U_\alpha Y_i = Y_j$. In other words, under the unitary transformations, these subspaces form a more general directed graph than a simple cycle graph in the case of a single unitary operator.*

(ii) *For any simple loop (namely, $Y_{r_i} \neq Y_{r_j}$ for different i and j in the loop)*

$$Y_{r_0} \overset{U_{\alpha_0}}{\to} Y_{r_1} \overset{U_{\alpha_1}}{\to} \cdots \overset{U_{\alpha_{k-2}}}{\to} Y_{r_{k-1}} \overset{U_{\alpha_{k-1}}}{\to} Y_{r_0},$$

there exists some $i \in \{0, 1, \ldots, k-1\}$ and $j \in \{1, 2, \ldots, m\}$ such that $Y_{r_i} \subseteq V_j$.

(iii)

$$Sat(\mathbf{I}f) = \bigcup \mathbb{X} = Y_1 \cup Y_2 \cup \ldots \cup Y_q.$$

To prove this theorem, we need two technical lemmas.

Lemma 4.39 *Given a family $\mathbb{X} = \{Y_1, Y_2, \ldots, Y_q\}$ of subspaces of $\mathcal{H}$ with $Y_i \not\subseteq Y_j$ for all $i \neq j$, and $Sat(\mathbf{I}f) \subseteq \bigcup \mathbb{X}$. If $\mathbb{X}$ does not satisfy condition (i) or condition (ii) of Theorem 4.38, then we can algorithmically find some $Y_i \in X$ and its proper subspaces $W_1, W_2, \ldots, W_l$ such that*

$$Sat(\mathbf{I}f) \cap Y_i \subseteq W_1 \cup W_2 \cup \ldots \cup W_l. \tag{4.17}$$

Proof See Appendix 1, Section A1.2.   □

Lemma 4.40 *Suppose that for each k, X_k is the union of a finite number of subspaces of a finite-dimensional Hilbert space $\mathcal{H}$, and*

$$X_0 \supseteq X_1 \supseteq \cdots \supseteq X_k \supseteq \cdots.$$

Then there exists $n \geq 0$ such that $X_k = X_n$ for all $k \geq n$.

Exercise 4.9 Prove Lemma 4.40. (A proof of this lemma can be found in [83].)

With the help of Lemmas 4.39 and 4.40, we can prove Theorem 4.38 as follows.

Proof of Theorem 4.38: We initially put $\mathbb{X} \leftarrow \{\mathcal{H}\}$, and apply the procedure shown in the proof of Lemma 4.39 to obtain some $Y_i \in \mathbb{X}$ and its subspaces $W_1, W_2, \ldots, W_l$ satisfying Eq. (4.17). Let

$$\mathbb{X}' = \mathbb{X} \cup \{W_k : 1 \leq k \leq l\} \backslash \{Y_i\}$$

and eliminate all subspaces from $\mathbb{X}'$ which are included in some other subspaces in $\mathbb{X}'$. Then $\bigcup \mathbb{X}' \subseteq \bigcup \mathbb{X}$. Furthermore, from $Sat(\mathbf{I}f) \subseteq \bigcup \mathbb{X}$, we have $Sat(\mathbf{I}f) \subseteq \bigcup \mathbb{X}'$ as well from Eq. (4.17).

Repeating the foregoing procedure, we can finally get a family $\mathbb{X} = \{Y_1, Y_2, \ldots, Y_q\}$ of subspaces of $\mathcal{H}$ satisfying conditions (i) and (ii), with the termination guaranteed by Lemma 4.40. We now prove that such $\mathbb{X}$ also satisfies condition (iii).

Note that $Sat(\mathbf{I}f) \subseteq \bigcup \mathbb{X}$. It suffices to prove that for any $|\psi_0\rangle \in \bigcup \mathbb{X}$, we have $|\psi_0\rangle \in Sat(\mathbf{I}f)$, namely, $\mathcal{A}(\psi_0) \models \mathbf{I}f$.

Choose $Y_{r_0} \in \mathbb{X}$ such that $|\psi_0\rangle \in Y_{r_0}$. For any $\alpha_0\alpha_1 \ldots \in Act^\omega$, let $|\psi_{n+1}\rangle = U_{\alpha_n}|\psi_n\rangle$ for $n = 0, 1, \ldots$. According to condition (i), we can assume $|\psi_n\rangle \in Y_{r_n}$ where all $Y_{r_n} \in \mathbb{X}$. Note that $q < \infty$. We immediately know from condition (ii) that the set $\{n \geq 0 : |\psi_n\rangle \in [\![f]\!]\}$ is infinite. $\qquad\qquad\square$

Employing Theorem 4.38, we design Algorithm 3 to check whether $\mathcal{A} \models \mathbf{I}f$ for the general case.

Algorithm 3: Checking $\mathcal{A} \models \mathbf{I}f$

---

input:
  (i) A quantum automaton $\mathcal{A} = (\mathcal{H}, Act, \{U_\alpha : \alpha \in Act\}, \mathcal{H}_0)$;
  (ii) A meta-logic formula f with $[\![f]\!] = \bigvee_{i=1}^m V_i$ for some subspaces V_i of $\mathcal{H}$.

output: true if $\mathcal{A} \models \mathbf{I}f$, and false otherwise.
begin
    $\mathbb{X} \leftarrow \{\mathcal{H}\}$;
    while *Conditions (i) and (ii) of Theorem 4.38 is not satisfied by* $\mathbb{X}$ **do**
        if *Conditions (i) not satisfied* **then**
            $Y \leftarrow$ a subspace in $\mathbb{Y}$ with the maximal dimension; (*$\mathbb{Y}$ defined in
            Eq (A1.1)*)
            $\alpha \leftarrow$ an action with $U_\alpha Y \notin \mathbb{X}$;
            $\mathbb{X} \leftarrow \mathbb{X} \cup \{U_\alpha^{-1}X \cap Y : X \in \mathbb{X}\}$;
        else
            Take a simple loop as in Eq. (A1.2);
            for $0 \leq i < k$ **do**
                $T_i \leftarrow U_{\alpha_i} \ldots U_{\alpha_1} U_{\alpha_k} \ldots U_{\alpha_{i+1}}$;
                $p_i \leftarrow p_{T_i}$, the period of T_i;   (*Use Lemma 4.36*)
                for $0 \leq n < p_i, 1 \leq t \leq m$ **do**
                    $\mathbb{X} \leftarrow \mathbb{X} \cup \{Y_{r_0} \cap U_{\alpha_1}^{-1} U_{\alpha_2}^{-1} \ldots U_{\alpha_i}^{-1} T_i^n K(T_i, V_t)\}$;
                    (*$K(T_i, V_t)$ computed in Algorithm 2*)
                end
            end
        end
        Simplify $\mathbb{X}$ by deleting all subspaces which are included in some
            others;
    end
    return $(\mathcal{H}_0 \subseteq \bigcup \mathbb{X})$
end

4.6.3 Checking $\mathcal{A} \models \mathbf{G}f$ and $\mathcal{A} \models \mathbf{U}f$

In this subsection, we turn to develop algorithms for checking whether $\mathcal{A} \models \mathbf{G}f$ (global reachability) and $\mathcal{A} \models \mathbf{U}f$ (ultimately forever reachability).

Checking $\mathcal{A} \models \mathbf{G}f$. We first consider global reachability $\mathcal{A} \models \mathbf{G}f$. As discussed at the beginning of this section, checking $\mathcal{A} \models \mathbf{G}f$ can be done by computing $Sat(\mathbf{G}f)$. Furthermore, with Lemma 4.32 (iii), we have

$$Sat(\mathbf{G}f) = \{|\psi\rangle \in \mathcal{H} : \forall s \in Act^*, U_s|\psi\rangle \in [\![f]\!]\}. \tag{4.18}$$

Thus, for every $\alpha \in Act$, we have

$$U_\alpha \cdot Sat(\mathbf{G}f) \subseteq Sat(\mathbf{G}f) \subseteq [\![f]\!] = V_1 \cup V_2 \cup \ldots \cup V_m.$$

An algorithm to check if $\mathcal{A} \models \mathbf{G}f$ is presented as Algorithm 4, whose correctness is shown as follows. We write $Y_0, Y_1, \ldots$ for the instances of Y during the execution of the algorithm. Then $Y_0 = V_1 \cup V_2 \cup \ldots \cup V_m$ and

$$Y_{n+1} = U_\alpha^{-1} Y_n \cap Y_n$$

for some $\alpha \in Act$. It can be proved by induction on n that each Y_n is a union of finitely many subspaces of $\mathcal{H}$. Note that $Y_0 \supseteq Y_1 \supseteq Y_2 \supseteq \ldots$ is a descending

---

Algorithm 4: Checking $\mathcal{A} \models \mathbf{G}f$

---

input:

    (i) A quantum automaton $\mathcal{A} = (\mathcal{H}, Act, \{U_\alpha : \alpha \in Act\}, \mathcal{H}_0)$;

    (ii) A meta-logic formula f with $[\![f]\!] = \bigvee_{i=1}^{m} V_i$ for some subspaces V_i of $\mathcal{H}$.

output: true if $\mathcal{A} \models \mathbf{G}f$, and false otherwise.

begin

    $Y \leftarrow V_1 \cup V_2 \cup \ldots \cup V_m$;

    $Y' \leftarrow \{0\}$;

    while $Y \neq Y'$ **do**

        $Y' \leftarrow Y$;

        for $\alpha \in Act$ **do**

            if $U_\alpha Y \neq Y$ **then**

                $Y \leftarrow U_\alpha^{-1} Y \cap Y$;

            end

        end

    end

    return $(\mathcal{H}_0 \subseteq Y)$

end

---

chain. According to Lemma 4.40, this chain would terminate at some Y_n. Then we have $U_\alpha Y_n = Y_n$ for all $\alpha \in Act$. Now we prove $Y_n = Sat(\mathbf{G}f)$. First, since $Sat(\mathbf{G}f) \subseteq [\![f]\!] = Y_0$ and

$$Sat(\mathbf{G}f) \subseteq U_\alpha^{-1} Sat(\mathbf{G}f)$$

for all $\alpha \in Act$, it can be proved by induction on k that $Sat(\mathbf{G}f) \subseteq Y_k$ for all k, and particularly, $Sat(\mathbf{G}f) \subseteq Y_n$. On the other hand, as

$$U_s Y_n = Y_n \subseteq [\![f]\!]$$

for all $s \in Act^*$, we have $Y_n \subseteq Sat(\mathbf{G}f)$. So $Y_n = Sat(\mathbf{G}f)$.

Checking $\mathcal{A} \models \mathbf{U}f$. To conclude this section, let us consider how to check ultimately forever reachability $\mathcal{A} \models \mathbf{U}f$. As the following lemma shows, for a positive (meta-)logical formula f, ultimately forever reachability $\mathbf{U}f$ and global reachability $\mathbf{G}f$ are equivalent to each other, and thus the algorithm for checking $\mathcal{A} \models \mathbf{G}f$ presented earlier can also be used to check $\mathcal{A} \models \mathbf{U}f$.

Lemma 4.41 *If f is positive, then for any quantum automaton $\mathcal{A}$, we have:*

$$\mathcal{A} \models \mathbf{U}f \text{ iff } \mathcal{A} \models \mathbf{G}f.$$

Proof The 'if' part is obvious. So, we only need to prove the 'only if' part. Assume that $\mathcal{A} \models \mathbf{U}f$. Then for any $|\psi_0\rangle \in \mathcal{H}_0$, we have $\mathcal{A}(\psi_0) \models \mathbf{U}f$. We claim that there exists some $s \in Act^*$ such that $U_s|\psi_0\rangle \models \mathbf{G}f$. In fact, if it is not the case, then for all $s \in Act^*$, there exists some $s' \in Act^*$ such that $U_{ss'}|\psi_0\rangle \not\models f$. Then we can find a sequence of strings $s_0, s_1, s_2, \dots$ in Act^* such for any $k \geq 0$,

$$U_{s_0 s_1 \dots s_k}|\psi_0\rangle \not\models f,$$

contradicting the assumption that $\mathcal{A} \models \mathbf{U}f$.

Now suppose $U_s|\psi_0\rangle \in Sat(\mathbf{G}f)$ for some $s \in Act^*$. Note that

$$U_\alpha Sat(\mathbf{G}f) = Sat(\mathbf{G}f)$$

for all $\alpha \in Act$. So we have

$$|\psi_0\rangle \in U_s^{-1} Sat(\mathbf{G}f) = Sat(\mathbf{G}f),$$

which completes the proof. $\qquad\square$

4.7 Undecidability of Checking Reachability of Quantum Automata

In Section 4.6, we presented algorithms checking $\mathcal{A} \models \Delta f$ for reachability $\Delta \in \{\mathbf{G}, \mathbf{U}, \mathbf{I}\}$ and positive (meta-)logical formula f. In general, however, we have

Theorem 4.42 *(Undecidability) For reachability* $\Delta \in \{F, G, U, I\}$ *and a general (meta-)logical formula* f, *the problem whether or not* $\mathcal{A} \models \Delta f$ *is undecidable.*

This section is devoted to proving Theorem 4.42. If the reader is only interested in algorithms for checking reachability of quantum systems, she or he can skip this section and jump to the next chapter.

4.7.1 Undecidability of $\mathcal{A} \models Gf$, $\mathcal{A} \models Uf$ and $\mathcal{A} \models If$

We first prove undecidability of reachability $\mathcal{A} \models \Delta f$ for $\Delta \in \{G, U, I\}$. Essentially, it is a corollary of the Blondel–Jeandel–Koiran–Portier theorem on undecidability of the language emptiness problem for quantum automata, which was proved based on undecidability of Skolem's problem for linear recurrence sequences. For convenience of the reader, a brief exposition of Skolem's problem and the Blondel–Jeandel–Koiran–Portier theorem is given in Appendix 1, Sections A1.3 and A1.4.

Undecidability of $\mathcal{A} \models Gf$. Let quantum automaton $\mathcal{A}$ be the same as in the Blondel–Jeandel–Koiran–Portier theorem (see Theorem A1.3 in Appendix 1, Section A1.4) and put $f = \neg V$. Then by Lemma 4.32, we see that $\mathcal{A} \models Gf$ is equivalent to the emptiness of language $\mathcal{L}(\mathcal{A}, \neg(\neg V)) = \mathcal{L}(\mathcal{A}, V)$. The undecidability of $\mathcal{A} \models Gf$ then follows immediately from the Blondel–Jeandel–Koiran–Portier theorem.

It is worth noting that $\mathcal{A} \models Gf$ is undecidable even for a simple (meta-)logical formula $f = \neg V$, with V being an atomic proposition.

Undecidability of $\mathcal{A} \models Uf$ and $\mathcal{A} \models If$. To prove this result, we need to slightly modify the quantum automaton $\mathcal{A} = (\mathcal{H}, Act, \{U_\alpha : \alpha \in Act\}, \mathcal{H}_0)$ by adding a silent action τ. Assume that $\tau \notin Act$ is a new action name. We put $U_\tau = I$ (the identity operator on $\mathcal{H}$) and

$$\mathcal{A}' = (\mathcal{H}, Act \cup \{\tau\}, \{U_\alpha : \alpha \in Act \cup \{\tau\}\}, \mathcal{H}_0).$$

We claim that

$$\mathcal{A} \models Gf \text{ iff } \mathcal{A}' \models Uf \text{ iff } \mathcal{A}' \models If. \tag{4.19}$$

Then undecidability of $\mathcal{A} \models Uf$ and $\mathcal{A} \models If$ follows immediately from Eq. (4.19) and undecidability of $\mathcal{A} \models Gf$. Now what we need to do is to prove Eq. (4.19). In fact, it is obvious that

$$\mathcal{A} \models Gf \text{ implies } \mathcal{A}' \models Uf \text{ implies } \mathcal{A}' \models If$$

because U_τ does not change any quantum state. Conversely, if $\mathcal{A} \not\models \mathbf{G}f$, then there exists $s = \alpha_0\alpha_1 \ldots \alpha_n \in \Lambda ct^*$ such that $U_s|\psi_0\rangle \not\models f$. Obviously, the infinite sequence of actions $w = s\tau^\omega \in (\Lambda ct \cup \{\tau\})^\omega$ serves as a witness for both $\mathcal{A}' \not\models \mathbf{U}f$ and $\mathcal{A}' \not\models \mathbf{I}f$.

4.7.2 Undecidability of $A \models Ff$

The proof of undecidability of $A \models \mathbf{F}f$ is relatively more difficult. Our strategy is a reduction from the halting problem for 2-counter Minsky machines [89] to reachability of quantum automata.

2-Counter Minsky Machines. For convenience of the reader, we first briefly review the notion of 2-counter Minsky machine and its halting problem. A 2-counter Minsky machine is a program $\mathcal{M}$ consisting of two variables (counters) a and b of natural numbers and a finite set of instructions, labeled by $l_0, l_1, \ldots, l_m$. This program starts at l_0 and halts at l_m. Each of instructions $l_0, l_1, \ldots, l_{m-1}$ is one of the following two types:

$$\begin{array}{lll} \textbf{increment} & l_i : & c \leftarrow c + 1; \text{ goto } l_j; \text{ or} \\ \textbf{test-and-decrement} & l_i : & \text{if } c = 0 \text{ then goto } l_{j_1}; \\ & & \text{else } c \leftarrow c - 1; \text{ goto } l_{j_2}, \end{array}$$

where $c \in \{a, b\}$ is one of the counters.

The halting problem for 2-counter Minsky machines is as follows:

- Given a 2-counter Minsky machine $\mathcal{M}$ together with the initial values of a and b, decide whether the computation of $\mathcal{M}$ will terminate or not.

This problem is well known to be undecidable.

Modified Minsky Machines. A 2-counter Minsky machine $\mathcal{M}$ defined earlier cannot directly used for our purpose. But we can slightly modify the definition of $\mathcal{M}$ as follows without changing its termination:

 (i) Without loss of generality, we assume the initial values of a and b to be both 0. This can be done because any value can be achieved from zero by adding some instructions of increment at the beginning.
 (ii) For each instruction l_i of test-and-decrement of c, we rewrite it as

$$\begin{array}{ll} l_i : & \text{if } c = 0 \text{ then goto } l_i'; \text{ else goto } l_i''; \\ l_i' : & \text{goto } l_{j_1}; \\ l_i'' : & c \leftarrow c - 1; \text{ goto } l_{j_2}, \end{array} \qquad (4.20)$$

where l_i' and l_i'' are new instructions. For $c \in \{a, b\}$, we write L_{1c} for the set of all instructions of increment of c; and we write L_{2c}, L_{2c}' and L_{2c}'' for the set of instructions l_i, the set of instructions l_i' and the set of instructions l_i'' given in Eq. (4.20), respectively. Now the set of all instructions of $\mathcal{M}$ becomes

$$L = L_{1a} \cup L_{1b} \cup L_{2a} \cup L_{2b} \cup L_{2a}' \cup L_{2b}' \cup L_{2a}'' \cup L_{2b}'' \cup \{l_m\}.$$

(iii) We further rewrite the last instruction l_m as

$$l_m : \quad \text{goto } l_m;$$

and we say $\mathcal{M}$ terminates if l_m is reachable during the computation.

Obviously, the halting problem is also undecidable for such modified 2-counter Minsky machines.

Encoding 2-Counter Minsky Machines into Quantum Automata. Now we are ready to encode 2-counter Minsky machines into quantum automata so that undecidability of $\mathcal{A} \models \mathbf{F}f$ is derived from the undecidability of halting problem. More precisely, for any given 2-counter Minsky machine $\mathcal{M}$, we will construct a quantum automaton $\mathcal{A}$ and find two subspaces V and W of $\mathcal{H}$ such that

$$\mathcal{M} \text{ terminates} \Leftrightarrow \mathcal{A} \models \mathbf{F}(V \wedge \neg W). \tag{4.21}$$

For readability, here, we only outline the basic ideas of this construction. The detailed construction of quantum automaton $\mathcal{A}$ is postponed to Appendix 1, Section A1.5.

(i) A state of $\mathcal{M}$ is of the form (a, b, x), where $a, b \in \mathbb{N}$ are the values of the two counters, and $x \in L$ is the instruction to be executed immediately. We will use quantum states $|\phi_n\rangle$ and $|l\rangle$ to encode nature numbers n and instructions l, respectively. Then the corresponding quantum state in $\mathcal{A}$ is chosen as the product state $|\psi\rangle = |\phi_a\rangle|\phi_b\rangle|l\rangle$.

(ii) The computation of $\mathcal{M}$ is represented by the sequence of its states:

$$\sigma_{\mathcal{M}} = (a_0, b_0, x_0)(a_1, b_1, x_1)(a_2, b_2, x_2)\ldots, \tag{4.22}$$

where $(a_0, b_0, x_0) = (0, 0, l_0)$ is the initial state and $(a_{i+1}, b_{i+1}, x_{i+1})$ is the successor of (a_i, b_i, x_i) for all $i \geq 0$. We will construct unitary operators of $\mathcal{A}$ to encode the transitions from a state to its successor. Then by successively taking the corresponding unitary operators, the quantum computation

$$\sigma_0 = |\psi_0\rangle|\psi_1\rangle\ldots, \ \forall i \geq 0 \ |\psi_i\rangle = |\phi_{a_i}\rangle|\phi_{b_i}\rangle|x_i\rangle \tag{4.23}$$

is achieved in $\mathcal{A}$ to encode $\sigma_{\mathcal{M}}$.

(iii) From the correspondence between $\sigma_{\mathcal{M}}$ and σ_0, termination of $\mathcal{M}$ will be encoded as certain reachability property of σ_0 (see Lemma A1.4 in Appendix 1, Section A1.5).

(iv) Besides σ_0, infinitely many computation paths are achievable in $\mathcal{A}$. So there is still a gap between reachability of σ_0 and that of $\mathcal{A}$. Our solution is to construct two subspaces V and W such that $\sigma \models \mathbf{F}(V \wedge \neg W)$ for all paths σ of $\mathcal{A}$ except σ_0 (see Lemma A1.5 in Appendix 1, Section A1.5). Then

$$\mathcal{A} \models \mathbf{F}(V \wedge \neg W) \Leftrightarrow \sigma_0 \models \mathbf{F}(V \wedge \neg W),$$

and Eq. (4.21) will be proved from this equivalence.

4.8 Final Remark

To conclude this chapter, we would like to point out that the study of model checking quantum automata is still at a very early stage. Comparing this chapter with Chapter 2, we should find that quantum counterparts of several crucial parts of classical model checking are still missing. In particular:

- We do not have a full-fledged temporal logical language like LTL (linear temporal logic) and CTL (computation tree logic) for specifying complicated dynamic properties of quantum automata. For example, eventual reachability $\mathbf{F}f$, global reachability $\mathbf{G}f$, ultimately forever reachability $\mathbf{U}f$ and infinitely often reachability $\mathbf{I}f$ were defined in a natural language together with mathematical notations rather than in a formal logical language.
- A more fundamental question is whether a linear-time logic is enough for specifying dynamic properties of quantum automata, given that all actions of them are unitary transformations and thus reversible. Obviously, if quantum measurements can be performed in the middle of an execution path of a quantum automaton, then a branching-time logic will be needed for describing its behaviours.

Several quantum temporal logics have been defined in both the physics literature [70] and computer science literature [87, 112]. But we need to understand how they can be properly used to specify interesting properties of quantum automata. More recently, a new quantum temporal logic (QTL) was defined by Yu [122]; in particular, he proved decidability of basic QTL formulas for a system model which is much more general than the quantum automata considered in this chapter, and essentially equivalent to quantum Markov decision processes to be discussed in the next chapter.

4.9 Bibliographic Remarks

The system model employed in this chapter is quantum automata. Two early references for quantum automata are [72, 92]. A large number of results on quantum automata have been published since then. For a good survey about quantum automata, see [4].

The properties of quantum systems considered in this chapter are linear-time properties defined based on Birkhoff–von Neumann quantum logic [20], which has a history of more than 80 years. A thorough exposition of quantum logic can be found in the handbook [44].

The lifting from Birkhoff–von Neumann quantum logic to temporal properties of quantum systems in Section 4.3 is adapted from [119]. The notions of invariants, liveness and persistence for quantum automata introduced in Section 4.3 and the algorithm for checking invariants of quantum automata given in Section 4.5 also come from [119].

The definitions of quantum reachability properties in Section 4.4, the algorithms for checking quantum reachability in Section 4.6 and the undecidability results in Section 4.7 are exposed entirely based on Li et al. [82]. But the decidability of $A \models \mathbf{I}f$ for the special case of $|Act| = 1$ and $m = 1$ (see Subsection 4.6.1) was first proved in [18] in a different way as the decidability of finiteness of Skolem's problem in the single matrix form.

A related topic that is not discussed in this chapter is equivalence checking of quantum automata, which has been extensively studied in the literature; see, for example, [79, 80, 100, 113].

5
Model Checking Quantum Markov Chains

In Chapter 4, we studied model-checking techniques for quantum automata. The actions of a quantum automaton are described by unitary transformations, and thus the automaton is seen as a closed quantum system. In this chapter, we will develop model-checking techniques for a much larger class of quantum systems modelled as quantum Markov chains or more generally, quantum Markov decision processes. The structures of a quantum automaton and a quantum Markov chain or decision process are very similar. Their differences come from the actions allowed to be performed by them: the actions of the latter are described as quantum operations or super-operators, and thus the latter should be treated as open quantum systems that can interact with their environments.

As we saw in Example 3.36, unitary operators can be seen as a special class of super-operators. So, quantum automata can be thought of as a special kind of quantum Markov decision processes. However, the mathematical properties of unitary operators and super-operators are quite different; in particular, the former are reversible, but the latter are not. These differences require us to develop new model-checking techniques for quantum Markov systems that are fundamentally different from those exposed in the last chapter.

As we have seen before, reachability analysis is always central to model-checking techniques, either for classical systems or for quantum automata. The emphasis of this chapter will also be algorithms for analysing various reachability of quantum Markov chains and decision processes. It is well known that reachability analysis techniques for classical Markov chains and decision processes heavily rely on algorithms for graph-reachability problems. Likewise, a kind of graph structures can be defined from quantum Markov chains and decision processes in their state Hilbert spaces, and they will play a crucial role in these systems' reachability analysis.

5.1 Quantum Markov Chains

Let us start from formally defining the notion of quantum Markov chain. To motivate the definition of quantum Markov chain, we briefly recall again that a classical
Markov chain is a pair $\langle S, P \rangle$, where S is a finite set of states, and P is a matrix of
transition probabilities, that is, a mapping $P : S \times S \to [0, 1]$ such that

$$\sum_{t \in S} P(s, t) = 1$$

for every $s \in S$, where $P(s, t)$ is the probability of the system going from s to t.

A quantum Markov chain is a straightforward quantum generalisation of a
Markov chain, where the state space of a Markov chain is replaced by a Hilbert
space and its transition matrix is replaced by a quantum operation which, as we
saw in Subsection 3.6, is a mathematical formalism of the discrete-time evolution
of (open) quantum systems.

> **Definition 5.1** A quantum Markov chain is a pair $\mathcal{C} = \langle \mathcal{H}, \mathcal{E} \rangle$, where
>
>   (i) $\mathcal{H}$ is a finite-dimensional Hilbert space;
> (ii) $\mathcal{E}$ is a quantum operation (or super-operator) in $\mathcal{H}$.

Note that a quantum automaton considered in Chapter 4 can have more than
one action. However, a quantum Markov chain has a single action described as a
super-operator $\mathcal{E}$. A quantum system with more than one action modelled by super-
operators will be introduced in Section 5.5 as a quantum Markov decision process,
and it can be seen as a generalisation of quantum automata.

The behaviour of a quantum Markov chain can be roughly described as follows:
if currently the process is in a mixed state ρ, then it will be in state $\mathcal{E}(\rho)$ in the next
step. Moreover, the system can repeat this procedure many times:

$$\rho \to \mathcal{E}(\rho) \to \cdots \to \mathcal{E}^n(\rho) \to \mathcal{E}^{n+1}(\rho) \to \cdots$$

So, a quantum Markov chain $\langle \mathcal{H}, \mathcal{E} \rangle$ is a discrete-time quantum system of which the
state space is $\mathcal{H}$ and the dynamics is described by quantum operation $\mathcal{E}$.

> **Example 5.2** Recall from Example 3.38 that three typical models of noise on qubits
> are described as the following quantum operations:
>
>   (i) The bit flip noise flips the state of a qubit from $|0\rangle$ to $|1\rangle$ and vice versa with
>   probability $1 - p$, and can be modelled by the super-operator
>
> $$\mathcal{E}_{BF}(\rho) = E_0 \rho E_0^{\dagger} + E_1 \rho E_1^{\dagger} \qquad (5.1)$$
>
> for all ρ, where
>
> $$E_0 = \sqrt{p}I = \sqrt{p} \begin{pmatrix} 1 & 0 \\ 0 & 1 \end{pmatrix} \qquad E_1 = \sqrt{1-p}\,\sigma_x = \sqrt{1-p} \begin{pmatrix} 0 & 1 \\ 1 & 0 \end{pmatrix}.$$

(ii) The phase flip noise can be modelled by the super-operator $\mathcal{E}_{PF}$ with

$$E_0 = \sqrt{p}I = \sqrt{p}\begin{pmatrix} 1 & 0 \\ 0 & 1 \end{pmatrix} \quad E_1 = \sqrt{1-p}\,\sigma_z = \sqrt{1-p}\begin{pmatrix} 1 & 0 \\ 0 & -1 \end{pmatrix}.$$

(iii) The bit-phase flip noise is modelled by the super-operator $\mathcal{E}_{BPF}$ with

$$E_0 = \sqrt{p}I = \sqrt{p}\begin{pmatrix} 1 & 0 \\ 0 & 1 \end{pmatrix} \quad E_1 = \sqrt{1-p}\,\sigma_y = \sqrt{1-p}\begin{pmatrix} 0 & -i \\ i & 0 \end{pmatrix},$$

where $\sigma_x, \sigma_y, \sigma_z$ are Pauli matrices.

Let $\mathcal{H}$ be the 2-dimensional Hilbert space, that is, the state space of a qubit. Then $\langle\mathcal{H}, \mathcal{E}_{BF}\rangle, \langle\mathcal{H}, \mathcal{E}_{PF}\rangle$ and $\langle\mathcal{H}, \mathcal{E}_{BPF}\rangle$ are all quantum Markov chains.

Exercise 5.1 Consider quantum Markov chain $\langle\mathcal{H}, \mathcal{E}_{BPF}\rangle$ in Example 5.2. Assume its initial state is $|+\rangle = \frac{1}{\sqrt{2}}(|0\rangle + |1\rangle)$. Compute its state after three steps; that is, $\mathcal{E}_{BPF}^3(\rho)$, where $\rho = |+\rangle\langle+|$.

Notations. Before we move on to study reachability of quantum Markov chains, we need to introduce several mathematical notations. Let $\mathcal{H}$ be a Hilbert space. We write $\mathcal{D}(\mathcal{H})$ for the set of all partial density operators on $\mathcal{H}$. First, we see that each density operator ρ in a Hilbert space $\mathcal{H}$ determines a subspace of $\mathcal{H}$, namely its support $\text{supp}(\rho)$, that can be seen as a qualitative representation of ρ. Conversely, ρ can be regarded as a quantitative refinement of $\text{supp}(\rho)$.

Definition 5.3 The support $\text{supp}(\rho)$ of a partial density operator $\rho \in \mathcal{D}(\mathcal{H})$ is the subspace of $\mathcal{H}$ spanned by the eigenvectors of ρ associated with non-zero eigenvalues.

Exercise 5.2 Compute the support of $\mathcal{E}_{BPF}^3(\rho)$ in Example 5.2.

We present several simple properties of the supports of density operators in the following.

Proposition 5.4

(i) *If a density operator ρ is defined by a family of pure states*

$$\rho = \sum_k \lambda_k |\psi_k\rangle\langle\psi_k|,$$

where all $\lambda_k > 0$ (but $|\psi_k\rangle$'s are not required to be pairwise orthogonal), then $\text{supp}(\rho) = \text{span}\{|\psi_k\rangle\}_k$;

(ii) $\text{supp}(\rho + \sigma) = \text{supp}(\rho) \vee \text{supp}(\sigma)$.

Exercise 5.3 Prove Proposition 5.4.

A super-operator is a mapping $\mathcal{E}$ from mixed states (density operators) to mixed states in a Hilbert space $\mathcal{H}$. Recall that for each ordinary mapping $f : X \to X$, we can define the image and pre-image of a subset $Y \subseteq X$ under f:

$$f(Y) = \{f(x) : x \in Y\}, \qquad f^{-1}(Y) = \{x \in X : f(x) \in Y\}.$$

The notions of image and pre-image of a subspace of $\mathcal{H}$ under a super-operator $\mathcal{E}$ can be similarly defined.

Definition 5.5 The image of a subspace X of Hilbert space $\mathcal{H}$ under a quantum operation $\mathcal{E}$ is defined as

$$\mathcal{E}(X) = \bigvee_{|\psi\rangle \in X} \text{supp}(\mathcal{E}(|\psi\rangle\langle\psi|)),$$

where $\bigvee$ stands for the join of a family of subspaces; see Definition 4.6.

Intuitively, $\mathcal{E}(X)$ is the subspace of $\mathcal{H}$ spanned by the images under $\mathcal{E}$ of all states in X. Note that in the defining equation of $\mathcal{E}(X)$, $|\psi\rangle\langle\psi|$ is the density operator corresponding to pure state $|\psi\rangle$. We said in Definition 5.3 that support $\text{supp}(\rho)$ can be seen as a qualitative representation of density operator ρ. In a similar sense, $\mathcal{E}$ as a mapping from subspaces to subspaces defined earlier can be thought of as a qualitative approximation of $\mathcal{E}$ itself (as a mapping from density operators to density operators).

Definition 5.6 The pre-image of a subspace X of $\mathcal{H}$ under a super-operator $\mathcal{E}$ is defined as

$$\mathcal{E}^{-1}(X) = \{|\psi\rangle \in \mathcal{H} : \text{supp}(\mathcal{E}(|\psi\rangle\langle\psi|)) \subseteq X\}. \tag{5.2}$$

It is easy to see that $\mathcal{E}^{-1}(X)$ is well defined as a subspace of $\mathcal{H}$; that is, the right-hand side of (5.2) is indeed a subspace. Actually, it is the maximal subspace Y satisfying that $\mathcal{E}(Y) \subseteq X$.

Some properties of images and pre-images of quantum operations are given in the following propositions. They will be very useful in proving various properties of quantum Markov chains.

Proposition 5.7

(i) $\mathcal{E}(\text{supp}(\rho)) = \text{supp}(\mathcal{E}(\rho))$.
(ii) $\mathcal{E}(X_1 \vee X_2) = \mathcal{E}(X_1) \vee \mathcal{E}(X_2)$. Thus, $X \subseteq Y$ implies $\mathcal{E}(X) \subseteq \mathcal{E}(Y)$;
(iii) *Let super-operator $\mathcal{E}$ have the Kraus operator-sum representation $\mathcal{E} = \{E_i : i \in I\}$. We write $\mathcal{E}^*$ for its (Schrödinger–Heisenberg) dual; that is, $\mathcal{E}^* = \{E_i^\dagger : i \in I\}$. Then*

$$\mathcal{E}(X) = \text{span}\{E_i|\psi\rangle : i \in I \text{ and } |\psi\rangle \in X\}$$

and

$$\mathcal{E}^{-1}(X) = (\mathcal{E}^*(X^\perp))^\perp,$$

where $X^\perp$ stands for the ortho-complement of X.

Exercise 5.4 Prove Proposition 5.7.

5.2 Quantum Graph Theory

In this section, we define a graph structure from a quantum Markov chain. It provides us with a geometric picture, which is often very helpful for understanding the correspondence between reachability properties of a classical Markov chain and a quantum Markov chain.

We first observe that there is a directed graph underlying a Markov chain $\langle S, P \rangle$. The elements of S are vertices of the graph. The adjacency relation of the graph is defined as follows:

- For any $s, t \in S$, if $P(s, t) > 0$, then the graph has an edge from s to t.

Such a graph structure is often very useful for qualitative analysis of Markov chain $\langle S, P \rangle$ itself.

5.2.1 Adjacency and Reachability

Adjacency Relation. Now we assume that $\mathcal{C} = \langle \mathcal{H}, \mathcal{E} \rangle$ is a quantum Markov chain. An idea similar to that briefly described earlier for deriving a graph structure from a classical Markov chain can be used to naturally define a graph structure in $\mathcal{C}$. Based on Definitions 5.3 and 5.5, we can define the adjacency relation between (pure and mixed) states in $\mathcal{H}$.

> **Definition 5.8** Given a quantum Markov chain $\mathcal{C} = \langle \mathcal{H}, \mathcal{E} \rangle$. Let $|\varphi\rangle, |\psi\rangle \in \mathcal{H}$ be pure states and $\rho, \sigma \in \mathcal{D}(\mathcal{H})$ be density operators (i.e. mixed states) in $\mathcal{H}$. Then
>
> (i) $|\varphi\rangle$ is adjacent to $|\psi\rangle$ in $\mathcal{C}$, written $|\psi\rangle \to |\varphi\rangle$, if $|\varphi\rangle \in \mathrm{supp}(\mathcal{E}(|\psi\rangle\langle\psi|))$.
> (ii) $|\varphi\rangle$ is adjacent to ρ, written $\rho \to |\varphi\rangle$, if $|\varphi\rangle \in \mathcal{E}(\mathrm{supp}(\rho))$.
> (iii) σ is adjacent to ρ, written $\rho \to \sigma$, if $\mathrm{supp}(\sigma) \subseteq \mathcal{E}(\mathrm{supp}(\rho))$.

Intuitively, $\langle \mathcal{H}, \to \rangle$ can be thought of as a 'directed graph'. However, there are two major differences between this graph and a classical graph:

- The set of vertices of a classical graph is usually finite, whereas the state Hilbert space $\mathcal{H}$ is a continuum.
- A classical graph has no other mathematical structure rather than the adjacency relation, but the space $\mathcal{H}$ possesses a linear algebraic structure that must be preserved by an algorithm searching through the graph $\langle \mathcal{H}, \to \rangle$.

As we will see in the text that follows, these differences between a quantum graph and a classical graph make analysis of the former much harder than that of the latter.

Graph Reachability.   With the adjacency relation defined earlier, we can introduce the notion of reachability in a quantum graph in the same way as in the classical graph theory.

> **Definition 5.9** Let C be a quantum Markov chain. Then
>
> (i) A path from density operator ρ to density operator σ in C is a sequence
>
> $$\rho_0 \to \rho_1 \to \cdots \to \rho_n \ (n \geq 0)$$
>
> of adjacent density operators in C such that $\rho_0 = \rho$ and $\rho_n = \sigma$.
> (ii) For any density operators ρ and σ, if there is a path from ρ to σ then we say that σ is reachable from ρ in C.

The notion of reachable space of a quantum automaton introduced in Definition 4.3(ii) can be generalised to the case of quantum Markov chain.

> **Definition 5.10** Let $C = \langle \mathcal{H}, \mathcal{E} \rangle$ be a quantum Markov chain. For any $\rho \in \mathcal{D}(\mathcal{H})$, its reachable space in C is the subspace of $\mathcal{H}$ spanned by the states reachable from ρ:
>
> $$\mathcal{R}_C(\rho) = \text{span}\{|\psi\rangle \in \mathcal{H} : |\psi\rangle \text{ is reachable from } \rho \text{ in } C\}. \tag{5.3}$$

It should be noted that in Eq. (5.3), $|\psi\rangle$ is identified with its density operator $|\psi\rangle\langle\psi|$.

> **Exercise 5.5** Consider a quantum Markov chain $(\mathcal{H}, \mathcal{E}_{BPF})$ modelling the bit-phase flip in Example 5.2 and Exercise 5.1. Compute the reachable space $\mathcal{R}_C(\rho)$ for $\rho = |+\rangle\langle+|$.

Reachability in classical graph theory is transitive; that is, if a vertex v is reachable from u, and w is reachable from v, then w is also reachable from u. As one can expect, the following lemma shows that reachability in a quantum Markov chain is transitive too.

> **Lemma 5.11** *(Transitivity of Reachability) For any $\rho, \sigma \in \mathcal{D}(\mathcal{H})$, if* $\text{supp}(\rho) \subseteq \mathcal{R}_C(\sigma)$, *then* $\mathcal{R}_C(\rho) \subseteq \mathcal{R}_C(\sigma)$.

> **Exercise 5.6** Prove Lemma 5.11.

Transitive Closure and Reachable Space.   A reader who did Exercise 5.5 should have noticed that computing the reachable space $\mathcal{R}_C(\rho)$ of a state in a quantum Markov chain can be very involved. We now develop a general method for this purpose. To motivate our method, let us consider a classical directed graph $\langle V, E \rangle$, where V is the set of vertices and $E \subseteq V \times V$ is the adjacency relation. The (reflective and) transitive closure of E is defined as the set of pairs of vertices in which the second vertex can be reached from the first one through 0 or a finite number of edges in E:

$$t(E) = \bigcup_{n=0}^{\infty} E^n = \{\langle v, v' \rangle : v' \text{ is reachable from } v \text{ in } \langle V, E \rangle\}.$$

It is well-known that the transitive closure can be computed as

$$t(E) = \bigcup_{n=0}^{|V|-1} E^n, \tag{5.4}$$

where $|V|$ is the number of vertices; that is, all elements of $t(E)$ can be obtained from E within at most $|V|$ steps.

The above fact has an elegant quantum generalisation:

Theorem 5.12 *Let $C = \langle \mathcal{H}, \mathcal{E} \rangle$ be a quantum Markov chain. If $d = \dim \mathcal{H}$, then for any $\rho \in D(\mathcal{H})$, we have*

$$\mathcal{R}_C(\rho) = \bigvee_{i=0}^{d-1} \mathrm{supp} \left(\mathcal{E}^i(\rho) \right), \tag{5.5}$$

where $\mathcal{E}^i$ is the ith power of $\mathcal{E}$; that is, $\mathcal{E}^0 = \mathcal{I}$ (the identity operation in $\mathcal{H}$) and

$$\mathcal{E}^{i+1} = \mathcal{E} \circ \mathcal{E}^i$$

for $i \geq 0$.

It is worth noting the correspondence between the number $|V|$ of vertices in Eq. (5.4) and the dimension d of Hilbert space $\mathcal{H}$ in Eq. (5.5). Although $\mathcal{H}$ is always an uncountably infinite set, its dimension d is assumed here to be finite.

Proof We first show that $|\psi\rangle$ is reachable from ρ if and only if $|\psi\rangle \in \mathrm{supp}\left(\mathcal{E}^i(\rho) \right)$ for some $i \geq 0$. In fact, if $|\psi\rangle$ is reachable from ρ, then there exist $\rho_1, \ldots, \rho_{i-1}$ such that

$$\rho \rightarrow \rho_1 \rightarrow \cdots \rightarrow \rho_{i-1} \rightarrow |\psi\rangle.$$

Using Propositions 5.4 and 5.7, we obtain

$$\begin{aligned}
|\psi\rangle \in \mathrm{supp}(\mathcal{E}(\rho_{i-1})) &= \mathcal{E}(\mathrm{supp}(\rho_{i-1})) \\
&\subseteq \mathcal{E}(\mathrm{supp}(\mathcal{E}(\rho_{i-2})) \\
&= \mathrm{supp}\left(\mathcal{E}^2(\rho_{i-2}) \right) \subseteq \ldots \subseteq \mathrm{supp}\left(\mathcal{E}^i(\rho) \right).
\end{aligned}$$

Conversely, if $|\psi\rangle \in \mathrm{supp}(\mathcal{E}^i(\rho))$, then

$$\rho \to \mathcal{E}(\rho) \to \cdots \to \mathcal{E}^{i-1}(\rho) \to |\psi\rangle$$

and $|\psi\rangle$ is reachable from ρ. Therefore, it holds that

$$\mathcal{R}_C(\rho) = \mathrm{span}\{|\psi\rangle : |\psi\rangle \text{ is reachable from } \rho\}$$

$$= \mathrm{span}\left[\bigcup_{i=0}^{\infty} \mathrm{supp}\left(\mathcal{E}^i(\rho)\right)\right]$$

$$= \bigvee_{i=0}^{\infty} \mathrm{supp}\left(\mathcal{E}^i(\rho)\right).$$

Now for each $n \geq 0$, we put

$$X_n = \bigvee_{i=0}^{n} \mathrm{supp}\left(\mathcal{E}^i(\rho)\right).$$

Then we obtain an increasing sequence

$$X_0 \subseteq X_1 \subseteq \ldots \subseteq X_n \subseteq X_{n+1} \subseteq \ldots$$

of subspaces of $\mathcal{H}$. Let $d_n = \dim X_n$ for every $n \geq 0$. Then

$$d_0 \leq d_1 \leq \cdots \leq d_n \leq d_{n+1} \leq \cdots.$$

Note that $d_n \leq d$ for all n. Thus, there must be some n such that $d_n = d_{n+1}$. Assume that N is the smallest such integer. Then we have

$$0 < \dim \mathrm{supp}(\rho) = d_0 < d_1 < \cdots < d_{N-1} < d_N \leq d$$

and $N \leq d - 1$. On the other hand, both X_N and X_{N+1} are subspaces of $\mathcal{H}$, $X_N \subseteq X_{N+1}$ and $\dim X_N = \dim X_{N+1}$. Thus, $X_N = X_{N+1}$. We can prove that

$$\mathrm{supp}\left(\mathcal{E}^{N+k}(\rho)\right) \subseteq X_N$$

for all $k \geq 1$ by induction on k. So, $\mathcal{R}_C(\rho) = X_N$. $\qquad\square$

5.2.2 Bottom Strongly Connected Components

In classical graph theory, the notion of a bottom strongly connected component (BSCC) plays a key role in the studies of reachability problems. It has also been extensively applied in analysis of Markov chains. In this subsection, we introduce the same notion for the graph defined from a quantum Markov chain. This quantum version of BSCC will be a basis of the reachability analysis algorithms for quantum Markov chains given in the next section.

Strong Connectivity.   The definition of BSCC contains three key words: 'strongly connected', 'component' and 'bottom'. We start from defining 'strongly connected'. Let X be a subspace of $\mathcal{H}$ and $\mathcal{E}$ a quantum operation in $\mathcal{H}$. Then the restriction of $\mathcal{E}$ on X is the quantum operation $\mathcal{E}_X$ in X defined by

$$\mathcal{E}_X(\rho) = P_X \mathcal{E}(\rho) P_X$$

for all $\rho \in \mathcal{D}(X)$, where P_X is the projection onto X. With this notation, we are able to define strong connectivity in a quantum Markov chain.

> **Definition 5.13** Let $\mathcal{C} = \langle \mathcal{H}, \mathcal{E} \rangle$ be a quantum Markov chain. A subspace X of $\mathcal{H}$ is called strongly connected in $\mathcal{C}$ if for any $|\varphi\rangle, |\psi\rangle \in X$, we have
>
> $$|\varphi\rangle \in \mathcal{R}_{\mathcal{C}_X}(\psi) \ and \ |\psi\rangle \in \mathcal{R}_{\mathcal{C}_X}(\varphi), \tag{5.6}$$
>
> where
>
> - $\varphi = |\varphi\rangle\langle\varphi|$ and $\psi = |\psi\rangle\langle\psi|$ are the density operators corresponding to pure states $|\varphi\rangle$ and $|\psi\rangle$, respectively;
> - quantum Markov chain $\mathcal{C}_X = \langle X, \mathcal{E}_X \rangle$ is the restriction of $\mathcal{C}$ on X; and
> - $\mathcal{R}_{\mathcal{C}_X}(\cdot)$ denotes the reachable subspace in $\mathcal{C}_X$.

Intuitively, condition (5.6) means that for any two states $|\varphi\rangle, |\psi\rangle$ in X, $|\varphi\rangle$ is reachable from $|\psi\rangle$ and $|\psi\rangle$ is reachable from $|\varphi\rangle$.

Basic Lattice Theory.   To define the second key word 'component' in BSCC, let us derivate for a while from the main line of exposition and recall several concepts from lattice theory:

- A partial order is a pair $(L, \sqsubseteq)$, where L is a non-empty set, and $\sqsubseteq$ is a binary relation on L such that for any $x, y, z \in L$,

  - Reflexivity: $x \sqsubseteq x$;
  - Transitivity: $x \sqsubseteq y$ and $y \sqsubseteq z$ imply $x \sqsubseteq z$;
  - Anti-symmetry: $x \sqsubseteq y$ and $y \sqsubseteq x$ imply $x = y$.

- Let $(L, \sqsubseteq)$ be a partial order and $K \subseteq L$. An element $x \in L$ is called an upper bound of K if $y \sqsubseteq x$ for every $y \in K$. Furthermore, x is called the least upper bound, written $x = \sqcup K$, when

  - x is an upper bound of K;
  - if y is also an upper bound of K, then $x \sqsubseteq y$.

- An element x of a partial order $(L, \sqsubseteq)$ is called a maximal element of L if for any $y \in L$, $x \sqsubseteq y$ implies $x = y$.
- Let $(L, \sqsubseteq)$ be a partial order. If any two elements $x, y \in L$ are comparable; that is, either $x \sqsubseteq y$ or $y \sqsubseteq x$, then we say that L is linearly ordered by $\sqsubseteq$.
- A partial order $(L, \sqsubseteq)$ is said to be inductive if for any subset K of L that is linearly ordered by $\sqsubseteq$, the least upper bound $\bigsqcup K$ exists in L.

Strongly Connected Components. Now let us return to a quantum Markov chain $\mathcal{C} = \langle \mathcal{H}, \mathcal{E} \rangle$. We write $SC(\mathcal{C})$ for the set of all strongly connected subspaces of $\mathcal{H}$ in $\mathcal{C}$. It is clear that $SC(\mathcal{C})$ with set inclusion $\subseteq$, that is, $(SC(\mathcal{C}), \subseteq)$, is a partial order. Thus, the lattice-theoretic concepts that we just introduced can be applied to it. In particular, we have:

Lemma 5.14 *The partial order $(SC(\mathcal{C}), \subseteq)$ is inductive.*

Exercise 5.7 Prove Lemma 5.14.

Moreover, the Zorn lemma in set theory asserts that every inductive partial order has (at least one) maximal elements. This enables us to introduce the following:

Definition 5.15 A maximal element of $(SC(\mathcal{C}), \subseteq)$ is called a strongly connected component (SCC) of $\mathcal{C}$.

Invariance. Next we define the third key word 'bottom' in BSCC. The notion of invariance defined in Subsection 4.3.3 for quantum automata can be generalised to the case of quantum Markov chains. It will be a key ingredient here for our purpose.

Definition 5.16 We say that a subspace X of $\mathcal{H}$ is invariant under a quantum operation $\mathcal{E}$ if $\mathcal{E}(X) \subseteq X$.

The intuition behind the inclusion $\mathcal{E}(X) \subseteq X$ is that quantum operation $\mathcal{E}$ cannot transfer a state in X into a state outside X.

The two representations of a quantum operation $\mathcal{E}$ given in Theorem 3.40 can be more conveniently used in checking the invariance condition $\mathcal{E}(X) \subseteq X$. Suppose that quantum operation $\mathcal{E}$ has the Kraus representation $\mathcal{E} = \{E_i\}_i$. Then it follows from Proposition 5.4 that X is invariant under $\mathcal{E}$ if and only if it is invariant under the Kraus operators E_i:

$$E_i X \subseteq X$$

for all i.

Exercise 5.8 Find a condition equivalent to $\mathcal{E}(X) \subseteq X$ in terms of the system-environment model (Theorem 3.40 (ii)).

Furthermore, the following theorem presents a useful property of invariant subspaces showing that a quantum operation does not decrease the probability of falling into an invariant subspace.

Theorem 5.17 *Let $C = \langle \mathcal{H}, \mathcal{E} \rangle$ be a quantum Markov chain. If subspace X of $\mathcal{H}$ is invariant under $\mathcal{E}$, then*

$$\mathrm{tr}(P_X \mathcal{E}(\rho)) \geq \mathrm{tr}(P_X \rho)$$

for all $\rho \in \mathcal{D}(\mathcal{H})$.

Proof It suffices to show that

$$\mathrm{tr}(P_X \mathcal{E}(|\psi\rangle\langle\psi|)) \geq \mathrm{tr}(P_X|\psi\rangle\langle\psi|)$$

for each $|\psi\rangle \in \mathcal{H}$. Assume that $\mathcal{E} = \{E_i\}_i$, and $|\psi\rangle = |\psi_1\rangle + |\psi_2\rangle$ where $|\psi_1\rangle \in X$ and $|\psi_2\rangle \in X^\perp$ are unnormalised. Since X is invariant under $\mathcal{E}$, we have $E_i|\psi_1\rangle \in X$ and

$$P_X E_i|\psi_1\rangle = E_i|\psi_1\rangle.$$

Then

$$a := \sum_i \mathrm{tr}\left(P_X E_i|\psi_2\rangle\langle\psi_1|E_i^\dagger\right) = \sum_i \mathrm{tr}\left(E_i|\psi_2\rangle\langle\psi_1|E_i^\dagger P_X\right)$$

$$= \sum_i \mathrm{tr}\left(E_i|\psi_2\rangle\langle\psi_1|E_i^\dagger\right) = \sum_i \langle\psi_1|E_i^\dagger E_i|\psi_2\rangle = \langle\psi_1|\psi_2\rangle = 0.$$

Similarly, it holds that

$$b := \sum_i \mathrm{tr}\left(P_X E_i|\psi_1\rangle\langle\psi_2|E_i^\dagger\right) = 0.$$

Moreover, we have

$$c := \sum_i \mathrm{tr}\left(P_X E_i|\psi_2\rangle\langle\psi_2|E_i^\dagger\right) \geq 0.$$

Therefore,

$$\mathrm{tr}\left(P_X \mathcal{E}(|\psi\rangle\langle\psi|)\right) = \sum_i \mathrm{tr}\left(P_X E_i|\psi_1\rangle\langle\psi_1|E_i^\dagger\right) + a + b + c$$

$$\geq \sum_i \mathrm{tr}\left(P_X E_i|\psi_1\rangle\langle\psi_1|E_i^\dagger\right) = \sum_i \langle\psi_1|E_i^\dagger E_i|\psi_1\rangle$$

$$= \langle\psi_1|\psi_1\rangle = \mathrm{tr}(P_X|\psi\rangle\langle\psi|).$$

$\square$

Bottom Strongly Connected Components. Now we are ready to introduce the key notion of this subsection, namely bottom strongly connected component. It is simply a combination of invariance and strongly connected component defined earlier.

Definition 5.18 Let $C = \langle \mathcal{H}, \mathcal{E} \rangle$ be a quantum Markov chain. Then a subspace X of $\mathcal{H}$ is called a bottom strongly connected component (BSCC) of C if it is an SCC of C and it is invariant under $\mathcal{E}$.

Example 5.19 Consider quantum Markov chain $C = \langle \mathcal{H}, \mathcal{E} \rangle$ with state Hilbert space $\mathcal{H} = \mathrm{span}\{|0\rangle, \ldots, |4\rangle\}$ and quantum operation $\mathcal{E} = \{E_i : i = 1, \ldots, 5\}$ where the Kraus operators are given by

$$E_1 = \frac{1}{\sqrt{2}}(|1\rangle\langle +_{01}| + |3\rangle\langle +_{23}|), \quad E_2 = \frac{1}{\sqrt{2}}(|1\rangle\langle -_{01}| + |3\rangle\langle -_{23}|),$$

$$E_3 = \frac{1}{\sqrt{2}}(|0\rangle\langle +_{01}| + |2\rangle\langle +_{23}|), \quad E_4 = \frac{1}{\sqrt{2}}(|0\rangle\langle -_{01}| + |2\rangle\langle -_{23}|),$$

$$E_5 = \frac{1}{10}(|0\rangle\langle 4| + |1\rangle\langle 4| + |2\rangle\langle 4| + 4|3\rangle\langle 4| + 9|4\rangle\langle 4|),$$

and

$$|\pm_{ij}\rangle = (|i\rangle \pm |j\rangle)/\sqrt{2}. \tag{5.7}$$

It is easy to verify that $B = \mathrm{span}\{|0\rangle, |1\rangle\}$ is a BSCC of C. Indeed, for any $|\psi\rangle = \alpha|0\rangle + \beta|1\rangle \in B$, we have

$$\mathcal{E}(|\psi\rangle\langle\psi|) = (|0\rangle\langle 0| + |1\rangle\langle 1|)/2.$$

Characterisations of BSCCs. The abstract definition of BSCC given in Definition 5.18 is usually not convenient in applications. We have two useful characterisations of BSCCs. The first characterisation is simple and it shows that a BSCC coincides with the reachable space of any pure state in it.

Lemma 5.20 *A subspace X is a BSCC of quantum Markov chain C if and only if*

$$\mathcal{R}_C(|\varphi\rangle\langle\varphi|) = X$$

for any $|\varphi\rangle \in X$.

Proof We only prove the 'only if' part because the "if" part is obvious. Suppose X is a BSCC. By the strong connectivity of X, we have

$$\mathcal{R}_C(|\varphi\rangle\langle\varphi|) \supseteq X$$

for all $|\varphi\rangle \in X$. On the other hand, for any vector $|\varphi\rangle$ in X, using the invariance of X, that is, $\mathcal{E}(X) \subseteq X$, it is easy to show that if $|\psi\rangle$ is reachable from $|\varphi\rangle$ then $|\psi\rangle \in X$. So, it holds that

$$\mathcal{R}_C(|\varphi\rangle\langle\varphi|) \subseteq X. \qquad \square$$

The preceding result can be generalised to the case of multiple BSCCs with the reachable spaces of mixed states.

Lemma 5.21 *Let $X_1, \ldots, X_n$ be a set of pairwise orthogonal BSCCs of quantum Markov chain C, and $\rho \in \mathcal{D}(\mathcal{H})$ such that for each i, $\mathrm{tr}(P_i \rho) > 0$, where P_i is the projector onto X_i. Then we have*

$$\mathcal{R}_C(\rho) = \bigoplus_i X_i.$$

Proof It has been proved in [14, Proposition 14] that for each i,

$$P_i \mathcal{E}(\rho) P_i = P_i \rho P_i,$$

a stronger result than Theorem 5.17. Then by induction, we have

$$P_i \mathcal{E}^n(\rho) P_i = P_i \rho P_i$$

for any n. The result then follows by the fact that

$$\mathcal{R}_C(P_i \rho P_i / \mathrm{tr}(P_i \rho)) = X_i. \qquad \square$$

The second characterisation of BSCCs is based on the notion of fixed point of a quantum operation, defined in the following.

Definition 5.22

(i) A density operator ρ in $\mathcal{H}$ is called a fixed point state of quantum operation $\mathcal{E}$ if $\mathcal{E}(\rho) = \rho$.
(ii) A fixed point state ρ of quantum operation $\mathcal{E}$ is called minimal if for any fixed point state σ of $\mathcal{E}$, it holds that

$$\mathrm{supp}(\sigma) \subseteq \mathrm{supp}(\rho) \text{ implies } \sigma = \rho.$$

The following lemma establishes a close connection between the invariant subspaces under a quantum operation $\mathcal{E}$ and the fixed point states of $\mathcal{E}$.

Lemma 5.23

(i) *If ρ is a fixed point state of $\mathcal{E}$, then $\mathrm{supp}(\rho)$ is invariant under $\mathcal{E}$.*
(ii) *Conversely, if X is invariant under $\mathcal{E}$, then there exists a fixed point state ρ of $\mathcal{E}$ such that $\mathrm{supp}(\rho) \subseteq X$.*

Exercise 5.9 Prove Lemma 5.23.

With the help of Lemma 5.23, we are able to prove that BSCCs coincide with the supports of minimal fixed point states. Indeed, the following theorem is a strengthened version of Lemma 5.23.

Theorem 5.24 *A subspace X is a BSCC of quantum Markov chain $C = \langle \mathcal{H}, \mathcal{E} \rangle$ if and only if there exists a minimal fixed point state ρ of $\mathcal{E}$ such that*

$$\mathrm{supp}(\rho) = X.$$

Proof We first prove the 'if' part. Let ρ be a minimal fixed point state of $\mathcal{E}$ such that $\mathrm{supp}(\rho) = X$. Then by Lemma 5.23, X is invariant under $\mathcal{E}$. To show that X is a BSCC, by Lemma 5.20 it suffices to prove that for any $|\varphi\rangle \in X$,

$$\mathcal{R}_C(|\varphi\rangle\langle\varphi|) = X.$$

Suppose conversely that there exists $|\psi\rangle \in X$ such that $\mathcal{R}_C(|\psi\rangle\langle\psi|) \subsetneq X$. Then by Lemma 5.11 we can show that $\mathcal{R}_C(|\psi\rangle\langle\psi|)$ is invariant under $\mathcal{E}$. By Lemma 5.23, we can find a fixed point state ρ_ψ with

$$\mathrm{supp}(\rho_\psi) \subseteq \mathcal{R}_C(|\psi\rangle\langle\psi|) \subsetneq X.$$

This contradicts the assumption that ρ is minimal.

For the 'only if' part, suppose that X is a BSCC. Then X is invariant under $\mathcal{E}$, and by Lemma 5.23, we can find a minimal fixed point state ρ of $\mathcal{E}$ with $\mathrm{supp}(\rho) \subseteq X$. Take $|\varphi\rangle \in \mathrm{supp}(\rho)$. By Lemma 5.25 we have $\mathcal{R}_C(|\varphi\rangle\langle\varphi|) = X$. But using Lemma 5.23 again we know that $\mathrm{supp}(\rho)$ is invariant under $\mathcal{E}$, so

$$\mathcal{R}_C(|\varphi\rangle\langle\varphi|) \subseteq \mathrm{supp}(\rho).$$

Therefore, $\mathrm{supp}(\rho) = X$.   □

Exercise 5.10 Find BSCCs of Markov chains $\langle \mathcal{H}, \mathcal{E}_{BF} \rangle$, $\langle \mathcal{H}, \mathcal{E}_{PF} \rangle$ and $\langle \mathcal{H}, \mathcal{E}_{BFF} \rangle$ defined in Exercise 5.1.

Relationship Between BSCCs. The structure of a single BSCC is clearly described in Lemma 5.20 and Theorem 5.24. To conclude this section, we further clarify the relationship between two different BSCCs.

Lemma 5.25

   (i) *For any two different BSCCs X and Y of quantum Markov chain C, we have $X \cap Y = \{0\}$ (0-dimensional Hilbert space).*
  (ii) *If X and Y are two BSCCs of C with $\dim X \neq \dim Y$, then they are orthogonal, i.e. $X \perp Y$.*

Proof (i) Suppose conversely that there exists a nonzero vector $|\varphi\rangle \in X \cap Y$. Then by Lemma 5.20, we have

$$X = \mathcal{R}_C(|\varphi\rangle\langle\varphi|) = Y,$$

contradicting the assumption that $X \neq Y$. Therefore $X \cap Y = \{0\}$.

(ii) The proof of this part needs to use Theorem 5.31 and is not involved. For readability, we postpone this part to Appendix 2, Section A2.1. □

5.3 Decomposition of the State Hilbert Space

Many reachability analysis techniques for classical Markov chains are based on the fact that their state spaces can be appropriately decomposed into certain subspaces so that we can deal with these subspaces separately. We will adopt this strategy in reachability analysis of quantum Markov chains. The quantum graph-theoretic results presented in the preceding section provide us with a basis for a series of algorithms for decomposing the state Hilbert spaces of quantum Markov chains. This section is devoted to the development of these algorithms.

5.3.1 Transient Subspaces

Recall that a state in a classical Markov chain is transient if there is a non-zero probability that the process will never return to it, and a state is recurrent if from it the returning probability is 1. It is well known that in a finite-state Markov chain a state is recurrent if and only if it belongs to some BSCC, and thus the state space of the Markov chain can be decomposed into the union of some BSCCs and a transient subset.

One of the major aims of this subsection is to prove a quantum generalisation of the above result. Such a decomposition of the state Hilbert space forms a basis of our algorithms for reachability analysis of quantum Markov chains to be presented in the next section.

In the last section, we already carefully studied a special class of subspaces of the state Hilbert spaces of quantum Markov chains, namely the BSCCs. Now we introduce the notion of transient subspace of a quantum Markov chain. Our definition of quantum transient subspace is motivated by an equivalent characterisation of transient states in a finite-state classical Markov chain: a state is transient if and only if the probability that the system stays at it will eventually become 0. This observation can be directly generalised to the following:

Definition 5.26 A subspace $X \subseteq \mathcal{H}$ is transient in a quantum Markov chain $\mathcal{C} = \langle \mathcal{H}, \mathcal{E} \rangle$ if

$$\lim_{k \to \infty} \mathrm{tr} \left(P_X \mathcal{E}^k(\rho) \right) = 0 \tag{5.8}$$

for any $\rho \in \mathcal{D}(\mathcal{H})$, where P_X is the projection onto X.

Intuitively, $\mathrm{tr} \left(P_X \mathcal{E}^k(\rho) \right)$ is the probability that the system's state falls into the subspace X after executing quantum operation $\mathcal{E}$ for k times. So, Eq. (5.8) means that the probability that the system stays in subspace X is eventually 0.

The Largest Transient Subspace. It is obvious from Definition 5.26 that if subspaces $X \subseteq Y$ and Y is transient then X is transient too. So, it is sufficient to understand the structure of the largest transient subspace. Fortunately, we have an elegant characterisation of the largest transient subspace. To give such a characterisation, we need the following notion.

Definition 5.27 Let $\mathcal{E}$ be a quantum operation in $\mathcal{H}$. Then its asymptotic average is

$$\mathcal{E}_\infty = \lim_{N \to \infty} \frac{1}{N} \sum_{n=1}^{N} \mathcal{E}^n. \tag{5.9}$$

Exercise 5.11 Prove that $\mathcal{E}_\infty$ defined above is a quantum operation.

The following lemma points out a link between fixed point states of a quantum operation and its asymptotic average. This link will be used in the proof of Theorem 5.29.

Lemma 5.28

(i) *For any density operator ρ, $\mathcal{E}_\infty(\rho)$ is a fixed point state of $\mathcal{E}$.*
(ii) *For any fixed point state σ, it holds that* $\mathrm{supp}(\sigma) \subseteq \mathcal{E}_\infty(\mathcal{H})$.

Exercise 5.12 Prove Lemma 5.28.

Now we can give a characterisation of the largest transient subspace in terms of asymptotic average.

Theorem 5.29 *Let $\mathcal{C} = \langle \mathcal{H}, \mathcal{E} \rangle$ be a quantum Markov chain. Then the orthocomplement of the image of $\mathcal{H}$ under the asymptotic average of $\mathcal{E}$:*

$$T_\mathcal{E} = \mathcal{E}_\infty(\mathcal{H})^\perp$$

is the largest transient subspace in $\mathcal{C}$, where $\perp$ stands for orthocomplement (see Definition 3.8(ii)).

Proof Let P be the projection onto the subspace $T_\mathcal{E}$. For any $\rho \in \mathcal{D}(\mathcal{H})$, we put

$$p_k = \mathrm{tr}\left(P \mathcal{E}^k(\rho)\right)$$

for every $k \geq 0$. Since $\mathcal{E}_\infty(\mathcal{H})$ is invariant under $\mathcal{E}$, by Theorem 5.17 we know that the sequence $\{p_k\}$ is non-increasing. Thus, the limit $p_\infty = \lim_{k \to \infty} p_k$ does exist. Furthermore, noting that

$$\mathrm{supp}(\mathcal{E}_\infty(\rho)) \subseteq \mathcal{E}_\infty(\mathcal{H}),$$

we have

$$0 = \mathrm{tr}(P\mathcal{E}_\infty(\rho)) = \mathrm{tr}\left(P \lim_{N \to \infty} \frac{1}{N} \sum_{n=1}^{N} \mathcal{E}^n(\rho)\right)$$

$$= \lim_{N \to \infty} \frac{1}{N} \sum_{n=1}^{N} \mathrm{tr} \left(P \mathcal{E}^n (\rho) \right)$$

$$= \lim_{N \to \infty} \frac{1}{N} \sum_{n=1}^{N} p_n$$

$$\geq \lim_{N \to \infty} \frac{1}{N} \sum_{n=1}^{N} p_\infty = p_\infty.$$

Thus $p_\infty = 0$, and $T_\mathcal{E}$ is transient by the arbitrariness of ρ.

To show that $T_\mathcal{E}$ is the largest transient subspace of C, we first note that

$$\mathrm{supp} \left(\mathcal{E}_\infty (I) \right) = \mathcal{E}_\infty (\mathcal{H}).$$

Let $\sigma = \mathcal{E}_\infty (I/d)$ where $d = \dim \mathcal{H}$. Then by Lemma 5.28, σ is a fixed point state with $\mathrm{supp}(\sigma) = T_\mathcal{E}^\perp$. Suppose Y is a transient subspace. We have

$$\mathrm{tr}(P_Y \sigma) = \lim_{i \to \infty} \mathrm{tr} \left(P_Y \mathcal{E}^i (\sigma) \right) = 0.$$

This implies $Y \perp \mathrm{supp}(\sigma) = T_\mathcal{E}^\perp$. So, we have $Y \subseteq T_\mathcal{E}$. □

5.3.2 BSCC Decomposition

Now we are ready to present the first way of decomposing the state Hilbert space of a quantum Markov chain, namely BSCC decomposition. Let $C = \langle \mathcal{H}, \mathcal{E} \rangle$ be a quantum Markov chain. First, it can be simply divided into two parts,

$$\mathcal{H} = \mathcal{E}_\infty (\mathcal{H}) \oplus T_\mathcal{E},$$

where $\oplus$ stands for (orthogonal) sum (see Definition 3.10). We already know from Theorem 5.29 that $T_\mathcal{E}$ is the largest transient subspace. So, what we need to do next is to examine the structure of $\mathcal{E}_\infty (\mathcal{H})$.

Decomposition of $\mathcal{E}_\infty (\mathcal{H})$. Our procedure for decomposition of $\mathcal{E}_\infty (\mathcal{H})$ is based on the following key lemma that shows how a fixed point state can be subtracted by another.

Lemma 5.30 *Let ρ and σ be two fixed point states of $\mathcal{E}$, and $\mathrm{supp}(\sigma) \subsetneq \mathrm{supp}(\rho)$. Then there exists another fixed point state η such that*

(i) $\mathrm{supp}(\eta) \perp \mathrm{supp}(\sigma)$; *and*
(ii) $\mathrm{supp}(\rho) = \mathrm{supp}(\eta) \oplus \mathrm{supp}(\sigma)$.

Proof See Appendix 2, Section A2.2. □

Intuitively, state η in Lemma 5.30 can be understood as the subtraction of ρ by σ. The proof of this lemma is quite involved; for readability, it is postponed to Section 2.

Now the BSCC decomposition of $\mathcal{E}_\infty(\mathcal{H})$ can be derived simply by repeated applications of Lemma 5.30.

Theorem 5.31 *Let $\mathcal{C} = \langle\mathcal{H},\mathcal{E}\rangle$ be a quantum Markov chain. Then $\mathcal{E}_\infty(\mathcal{H})$ can be decomposed into the direct sum of some orthogonal BSCCs of $\mathcal{C}$.*

Proof We notice that $\mathcal{E}_\infty(I/d)$ is a fixed point state of $\mathcal{E}$ and

$$\mathrm{supp}(\mathcal{E}_\infty(I/d)) = \mathcal{E}_\infty(\mathcal{H})$$

where $d = \dim\mathcal{H}$. Then it suffices to prove the following:

- *Claim*: Let ρ be a fixed point state of $\mathcal{E}$. Then $\mathrm{supp}(\rho)$ can be decomposed into the direct sum of some orthogonal BSCCs.

In fact, if ρ is minimal, then by Theorem 5.24, $\mathrm{supp}(\rho)$ is itself a BSCC and we are done. Otherwise, we apply Lemma 5.30 to obtain two fixed point states of $\mathcal{E}$ with smaller orthogonal supports. Repeating this procedure, we can get a set of minimal fixed point states $\rho_1,\ldots,\rho_k$ with mutually orthogonal supports such that

$$\mathrm{supp}(\rho) = \bigoplus_{i=1}^{k} \mathrm{supp}(\rho_i).$$

Finally, from Lemma 5.23 and Theorem 5.24, we know that each $\mathrm{supp}(\rho_i)$ is a BSCC. $\square$

The BSCC decomposition comes directly from a combination of Theorems 5.29 and 5.31. We see that the state Hilbert space of a quantum Markov chain $\mathcal{C} = \langle\mathcal{H},\mathcal{E}\rangle$ can be decomposed into the direct sum of a transient subspace and a family of BSCCs:

$$\mathcal{H} = B_1 \oplus \cdots \oplus B_u \oplus T_{\mathcal{E}}, \tag{5.10}$$

where B_i's are orthogonal BSCCs of $\mathcal{C}$, and $T_{\mathcal{E}}$ is the largest transient subspace.

Uniqueness of Decomposition. Theorem 5.31 shows the existence of BSCC decomposition for quantum Markov chains. Then a question immediately arises: Is such a decomposition unique? It is well known that the BSCC decomposition of a classical Markov chain is unique. However, it is not the case for quantum Markov chains as shown in the following.

Example 5.32 Let $\mathcal{C} = \langle \mathcal{H}, \mathcal{E} \rangle$ be a quantum Markov chain given as in Example 5.19. Then

$$B_1 = \text{span}\{|0\rangle, |1\rangle\}, \quad B_2 = \text{span}\{|2\rangle, |3\rangle\},$$
$$D_1 = \text{span}\{|+_{02}\rangle, |+_{13}\rangle\}, \quad D_2 = \text{span}\{|-_{02}\rangle, |-_{13}\rangle\}$$

are all BSCCs, where the states $|\pm_{ij}\rangle$ are defined by Eq. (5.7). It is easy to see that $T_{\mathcal{E}} = \text{span}\{|4\rangle\}$ is the largest transient subspace. Furthermore, we have two different BSCC decompositions of $\mathcal{H}$:

$$\mathcal{H} = B_1 \oplus B_2 \oplus T_{\mathcal{E}} = D_1 \oplus D_2 \oplus T_{\mathcal{E}}.$$

Although the BSCC decomposition of a quantum Markov chain is not unique in general, fortunately we have the following weak uniqueness in the sense that any two decompositions have the same number of BSCCs, and the corresponding BSCCs in them must have the same dimension.

Theorem 5.33 *Let $\mathcal{C} = \langle \mathcal{H}, \mathcal{E} \rangle$ be a quantum Markov chain, and let*

$$\mathcal{H} = B_1 \oplus \ldots \oplus B_u \oplus T_{\mathcal{E}} = D_1 \oplus \ldots \oplus D_v \oplus T_{\mathcal{E}}$$

be two BSCC decompositions where B_is and D_is are arranged, respectively, according to the increasing order of the dimensions. Then

(i) *$u = v$; and*
(ii) *$\dim B_i = \dim D_i$ for each $1 \leq i \leq u$.*

Proof For simplicity, we write $b_i = \dim B_i$ and $d_i = \dim D_i$. We prove by induction on i that $b_i = d_i$ for any $1 \leq i \leq \min\{u, v\}$, and thus $u = v$ as well.

First, we claim $b_1 = d_1$. Otherwise let, say, $b_1 < d_1$. Then $b_1 < d_j$ for all j. Thus by Lemma 5.25 (ii), we have

$$B_1 \perp \bigoplus_{j=1}^{v} D_j.$$

This is a contradiction as $B_1 \perp T_{\mathcal{E}}$.

Now suppose we already have $b_i = d_i$ for all $i < n$. We claim $b_n = d_n$. Otherwise let, say, $b_n < d_n$. Then from Lemma 5.25 (ii), we have

$$\bigoplus_{i=1}^{n} B_i \perp \bigoplus_{i=n}^{v} D_i,$$

and consequently,

$$\bigoplus_{i=1}^{n} B_i \subseteq \bigoplus_{i=1}^{n-1} D_i.$$

On the other hand, we have

$$\dim\left(\bigoplus_{i=1}^{n} B_i\right) = \sum_{i=1}^{n} b_i > \sum_{i=1}^{n-1} d_i = \dim\left(\bigoplus_{i=1}^{n-1} D_i\right),$$

a contradiction.   □

It is worth pointing out that in Theorem 5.33, for each $1 \le i \le n$, $\dim B_i = \dim D_i$ actually means that B_i and D_i are the same up to a unitary transformation U_i. However, for $i_1 \ne i_2$, unitary transformations U_{i_1} and U_{i_2} can be different. This is an essential difference between the classical case and the quantum one.

Decomposition Algorithm.   We have proved the existence and weak uniqueness of BSCC decomposition for quantum Markov chains. A basic idea of the BSCC decomposition algorithm is given in the proof of Theorem 5.31. Now we explicitly present it as Algorithm 5, which calls procedure Decompose(X) for a subspace X.

Algorithm 5: Decompose($\mathcal{C}$)

---

input: A quantum Markov chain $\mathcal{C} = \langle \mathcal{H}, \mathcal{E} \rangle$.
output: A set of orthogonal BSCCs $\{B_i\}$ and the largest transient subspace $T_{\mathcal{E}}$
            such that $\mathcal{H} = \left(\bigoplus_i B_i\right) \oplus T_{\mathcal{E}}$.

begin
  $\mathcal{B} \leftarrow$ Decompose($\mathcal{E}_\infty(\mathcal{H})$);
  return $\mathcal{B}$, $\mathcal{E}_\infty(\mathcal{H})^\perp$
end

To settle the complexity of Algorithm 5, we need the following technical lemma.

Lemma 5.34 *Let $\langle \mathcal{H}, \mathcal{E} \rangle$ be a quantum Markov chain with $d = \dim \mathcal{H}$, and $\rho \in \mathcal{D}(\mathcal{H})$. Then*

(i) *The asymptotic average state $\mathcal{E}_\infty(\rho)$ can be computed in time $O(d^6)$.*
(ii) *A density operator basis of the set*

$$\{A \in \mathcal{L}(\mathcal{H}) : \mathcal{E}(A) = A\}$$

of fixed points of $\mathcal{E}$ can be computed in time $O(d^6)$.

Proof For readability, we postpone the lengthy proof of Lemma 5.34 into Appendix 2, Section A2.3.   □

Now the correctness and complexity of Algorithm 5 can be shown in the following.

Procedure Decompose(X)

---

input: A subspace X which is the support of a fixed point state of $\mathcal{E}$.
output: A set of orthogonal BSCCs $\{B_i\}$ such that $X = \bigoplus B_i$.
begin

    $\mathcal{E} \leftarrow P_X \circ \mathcal{E}$;

    $\mathcal{B} \leftarrow$ a density operator basis of the set $\{A \in \mathcal{L}(\mathcal{H}) : \mathcal{E}(A) = A\}$;

    if $|\mathcal{B}| = 1$ **then**

        $\rho \leftarrow$ the unique element of $\mathcal{B}$;

        return $\{\mathrm{supp}(\rho)\}$;

    else

        $\rho_1, \rho_2 \leftarrow$ two arbitrary elements of $\mathcal{B}$;

        $\rho \leftarrow$ positive part of $\rho_1 - \rho_2$;

        $Y \leftarrow \mathrm{supp}(\rho)^{\perp}$;   (* the ortho-complement of $\mathrm{supp}(\rho)$ in X*)

        return Decompose($\mathrm{supp}(\rho)$) $\cup$ Decompose(Y)

    end

end

Theorem 5.35 *Given a quantum Markov chain $\langle \mathcal{H}, \mathcal{E} \rangle$, Algorithm 5 decomposes the Hilbert space $\mathcal{H}$ into the direct sum of a family of orthogonal BSCCs and the largest transient subspace of C in time $O(d^7)$, where $d = \dim \mathcal{H}$.*

Proof   The correctness of Algorithm 5 is easy to prove. Actually, it follows immediately from Theorems 5.29 and 5.31. For the time complexity, we first notice that the non-recursive part of the procedure Decompose(X) runs in time $O(d^6)$. Thus the total complexity of Decompose(X) is $O(d^7)$, as the procedure calls itself at most $O(d)$ times. Algorithm 5 first computes $\mathcal{E}_\infty(\mathcal{H})$, which, as indicated by Lemma 5.34 (i), costs time $O(d^6)$, and then feeds it into the procedure Decompose(X). Thus the total complexity of Algorithm 5 is $O(d^7)$.   □

5.3.3 Periodic Decomposition

We have presented a decomposition of the state space of a quantum Markov chain into the largest transient subspace and some BSCCs. In this section, we further decompose each BSCC subspace according to its periodicity, thus obtaining a refined decomposition of the whole state space. To this end, we need some more notions.

Irreducibility.   We first extend the notion of irreducibility of classical Markov chains to quantum Markov chains. Recall from classical probability theory that an irreducible Markov chain starting from any initial state can reach any other state in a finite number of steps. Straightforwardly, we have

Definition 5.36 A quantum Markov chain $C = \langle \mathcal{H}, \mathcal{E} \rangle$ is called *irreducible* if for any $\rho \in \mathcal{D}(\mathcal{H})$, $\mathcal{R}_C(\rho) = \mathcal{H}$.

To illustrate irreducibility, let us see two simple examples.

Example 5.37 We consider a natural way to encode the classical NOT gate: $0 \rightarrow 1; 1 \rightarrow 0$ into a quantum operation. Let $\mathcal{H} = \mathrm{span}\{|0\rangle, |1\rangle\}$. Then it can be modelled by $\mathcal{E} : \mathcal{D}(\mathcal{H}) \rightarrow \mathcal{D}(\mathcal{H})$ defined as follows:

$$\mathcal{E}(\rho) = |1\rangle\langle 0|\rho|0\rangle\langle 1| + |0\rangle\langle 1|\rho|1\rangle\langle 0|$$

for any $\rho \in \mathcal{D}(\mathcal{H})$. It is easy to check that the quantum Markov chain $\langle \mathcal{H}, \mathcal{E} \rangle$ is irreducible.

Example 5.38 (Amplitude-damping channel) Consider the 2-dimensional amplitude-damping channel modeling the physical processes such as spontaneous emission. Let $\mathcal{H} = \mathrm{span}\{|0\rangle, |1\rangle\}$, and

$$\mathcal{E}(\rho) = E_0 \rho E_0^\dagger + E_1 \rho E_1^\dagger,$$

where

$$E_0 = |0\rangle\langle 0| + \sqrt{1-p}|1\rangle\langle 1|, \qquad E_1 = \sqrt{p}|0\rangle\langle 1|$$

with $p > 0$. Then the quantum Markov chain $C = \langle \mathcal{H}, \mathcal{E} \rangle$ is reducible since, say, $\mathcal{R}_C(|0\rangle\langle 0|) = \mathrm{span}\{|0\rangle\}$.

The following theorem gives a characterisation of irreducibility in terms of BSCCs and fixed points, which indeed provides an effective way to check whether a quantum Markov chain is irreducible.

Theorem 5.39 *Let $C = \langle \mathcal{H}, \mathcal{E} \rangle$ be a quantum Markov chain. The following three statements are equivalent:*

(i) *C is irreducible.*
(ii) *C has $\mathcal{H}$ as a BSCC.*
(iii) *C has a unique fixed point state ρ^* and $\mathrm{supp}(\rho^*) = \mathcal{H}$.*

Exercise 5.13 Prove Theorem 5.39.

With Theorem 5.39, checking whether $\langle \mathcal{H}, \mathcal{E} \rangle$ is reducible can be done by Algorithm 5 given in the previous section. The time complexity is $O(d^7)$, where $\dim(\mathcal{H}) = d$.

As a matter of fact, we note that for any quantum Markov chain C and BSCC B, the restriction of C on B defined in Definition 5.13 is irreducible.

Periodicity. We now further define the notion of periodicity for quantum Markov chains. In a classical Markov chain $\langle S, P \rangle$, the period of a state $s \in S$ is given as

$$\gcd\{m \geq 1 : P^m(s,s) > 0\}.$$

Here, gcd stands for the greatest common divisor. For simplicity, it is assumed that $\gcd(\emptyset) = \infty$. We can directly generalise this notion to quantum Markov chains as follows.

Definition 5.40 Let $C = \langle \mathcal{H}, \mathcal{E} \rangle$ be a quantum Markov chain, and $\rho \in \mathcal{D}(\mathcal{H})$.

(i) The period of ρ, denoted p_ρ, is defined to be

$$\gcd\{m \geq 1 : \operatorname{supp}(\rho) \subseteq \operatorname{supp}(\mathcal{E}^m(\rho))\}.$$

(ii) ρ is said to be aperiodic if its period is 1.
(iii) A subspace X of $\mathcal{H}$ is aperiodic if any state ρ with $\operatorname{supp}(\rho) \subseteq X$ is aperiodic.
(iv) C is said to be *aperiodic* if the whole state space $\mathcal{H}$ is aperiodic.

Any two states in a Markov chain have the same period if they are reachable from each other. The following lemma shows a similar result for quantum Markov chains. Recall from Definition 5.9 that σ is reachable from ρ in C if there is a path from ρ to σ in the quantum graph induced by C.

Proposition 5.41 *Let $C = \langle \mathcal{H}, \mathcal{E} \rangle$ be a quantum Markov chain, and $\rho, \sigma \in \mathcal{D}(\mathcal{H})$. Whenever ρ is reachable from σ and σ is reachable from ρ, we have $p_\rho = p_\sigma$.*

Exercise 5.14 Prove Proposition 5.41.

All the states in a BSCC of a classical Markov chain can reach each other, thus sharing the same period. However, the reachable space of a quantum state is defined to be the subspace *spanned* by the states reachable from it; see Definition 5.10. As a result, quantum states in the reachable space of ρ are not necessarily reachable from ρ in the underlying quantum graph, and thus states in the same BSCC subspace may have different periods. This can be clearly seen from the following example.

Example 5.42 Consider a quantum Markov chain similar to that in Example 5.37, but here we encode the cycle

$$0 \to 1; \ 1 \to 2; \ 2 \to 3; \ 3 \to 0.$$

Let $\mathcal{H} = \operatorname{span}\{|i\rangle : 0 \leq i \leq 3\}$. Then it can be modelled by quantum operation (in Kraus operator-sum form) $\mathcal{E} = \{E_i : i = 0, \ldots, 3\}$ where

$$E_0 = |0\rangle\langle 3|, \quad E_1 = |1\rangle\langle 0|, \quad E_2 = |2\rangle\langle 1|, \quad E_3 = |3\rangle\langle 2|.$$

Again, the quantum Markov chain $\langle \mathcal{H}, \mathcal{E} \rangle$ is irreducible. Moreover, for any $0 \leq i$, $j \leq 3$, let

$$|+_{ij}\rangle = (|i\rangle + |j\rangle)/\sqrt{2}$$

and $\rho = \frac{1}{4}\sum_{i=0}^{3}|i\rangle\langle i|$. It is easy to show that

$$P_{|i\rangle\langle i|} = 4, \quad P_{|+_{02}\rangle\langle+_{02}|} = 2, \quad P_\rho = 1.$$

A Characterisation of Periods. Note that the periods shown in Example 5.42, although different, are all factors of 4, the period of the encoded cycle. Interestingly, we will prove that this observation is indeed true for any BSCC subspace of quantum Markov chains.

First, we show that in the special case of ρ being aperiodic, every quantum state in the reachable space of ρ is indeed reachable from ρ.

Lemma 5.43 *Let $C = \langle \mathcal{H}, \mathcal{E}\rangle$ be a quantum Markov chain and $\rho \in \mathcal{D}(\mathcal{H})$. Then ρ is aperiodic if and only if there exists an integer $M > 0$ such that*

$$\mathrm{supp}(\mathcal{E}^m(\rho)) = \mathcal{R}_C(\rho)$$

for all $m \geq M$.

Proof The sufficiency part is obvious. For the necessity part, let

$$X_i = \mathrm{supp}(\mathcal{E}^i(\rho))$$

for $i \geq 0$. In particular, $X_0 = \mathrm{supp}(\rho)$. Let

$$T_\rho = \{i \geq 1 : X_i \supseteq X_0\}. \tag{5.11}$$

Then from Proposition 5.7, we have that for any $i, j \geq 0$,

$$X_{i+j} = \mathcal{E}^i(X_j), \text{ and} \tag{5.12}$$

$$\text{if } i, j \in T_\rho, \text{ then } i + j \in T_\rho. \tag{5.13}$$

By the assumption that ρ is aperiodic, we have $\gcd(T_\rho) = 1$. From basic number theory, there is a finite subset $\{m_k\}_{k\in K}$ of T_ρ with $\gcd\{m_k\}_{k\in K} = 1$, and an integer $M' > 0$ such that for any $i \geq M'$, there exist positive integers $\{a_k\}_{k\in K}$ with

$$i = \sum_{k\in K} a_k m_k.$$

Thus $i \in T_\rho$ from Eq. (5.13).

Now let $M = M' + d - 1$ where $d = \dim \mathcal{H}$, and take any $m \geq M$. For all $0 \leq i \leq d - 1$, we have shown that $m - i \in T_\rho$; that is, $X_{m-i} \supseteq X_0$. Thus $X_m \supseteq X_i$ from Eq. (5.12), and $X_m \supseteq \mathcal{R}_C(\rho)$ from Theorem 5.12. Therefore, $X_m = \mathcal{R}_C(\rho)$, as the reverse inclusion trivially holds. $\qquad\square$

Based on Lemma 5.43, we can define the *saturation time* of an aperiodic state ρ to be

$$s(\rho) = \min\{n \geq 1 : \operatorname{supp}(\mathcal{E}^m(\rho)) = \mathcal{R}_\mathcal{C}(\rho)\}.$$

The following lemma shows that for any aperiodic BSCC B of a quantum Markov chain, the saturation time for any state in B has a *universal* upper bound, thus strengthening the result shown in Lemma 5.43.

Lemma 5.44 *Let $\mathcal{C} = \langle \mathcal{H}, \mathcal{E} \rangle$ be a quantum Markov chain. A subspace X of $\mathcal{H}$ is an aperiodic BSCC if and only if there exists an integer $M > 0$ such that for all $\rho \in \mathcal{D}(X)$, we have*

$$\operatorname{supp}(\mathcal{E}^m(\rho)) = X$$

for all $m \geq M$.

Proof The sufficiency part is obvious, so we consider the necessity part only. For any $\rho \in \mathcal{D}(X)$, let

$$N(\rho) = \left\{ \sigma \in \mathcal{D}(X) : \|\rho - \sigma\|_1 < \lambda_{min}(\mathcal{E}^{s(\rho)}(\rho)) \right\},$$

where $\|\cdot\|_1$ is the trace norm and $\lambda_{\min}(\tau)$ is the minimum non-zero eigenvalue of τ. Obviously, $N(\rho)$ is an open set. Then $\{N(\rho)\}_{\rho \in \mathcal{D}(X)}$ is an open cover of $\mathcal{D}(X)$. As $\mathcal{D}(X)$ is compact, we can find a finite number of density operators $\{\rho_i\}_{i \in J} \subseteq \mathcal{D}(X)$ such that

$$\mathcal{D}(X) = \bigcup_{i \in J} N(\rho_i).$$

In the following, we show for any $\rho \in \mathcal{D}(X)$ and $\sigma \in N(\rho)$, it holds that

$$\operatorname{supp}(\mathcal{E}^m(\sigma)) = X$$

for all $m \geq s(\rho)$. Then the theorem holds by taking $M = \max_{i \in J} s(\rho_i)$.

Let

$$Y = \operatorname{supp}(\mathcal{E}^{s(\rho)}(\sigma)),$$

and P_Y be the projector onto Y. As X is invariant, $Y \subseteq X$. Let $P_{\bar{Y}} = P_X - P_Y$. Then

$$\begin{aligned}
\operatorname{tr}(P_{\bar{Y}} \mathcal{E}^{s(\rho)}(\rho)) &= \|P_{\bar{Y}} \mathcal{E}^{s(\rho)}(\rho) P_{\bar{Y}}\|_1 \\
&= \|P_{\bar{Y}}(\mathcal{E}^{s(\rho)}(\rho) - \mathcal{E}^{s(\rho)}(\sigma)) P_{\bar{Y}}\|_1 \\
&\leq \|\mathcal{E}^{s(\rho)}(\rho) - \mathcal{E}^{s(\rho)}(\sigma)\|_1 \\
&\leq \|\rho - \sigma\|_1 \\
&< \lambda_{\min}(\mathcal{E}^{s(\rho)}(\rho)).
\end{aligned}$$

By the definition of $\lambda_{\min}$, this is possible only when $Y = X$, since

$$\text{supp}(\mathcal{E}^{s(\rho)}(\rho)) = X.$$

In other words, it holds that

$$\text{supp}(\mathcal{E}^{s(\rho)}(\sigma)) = X.$$

Thus, we obtain

$$\text{supp}(\mathcal{E}^{s(\rho)-1}(\sigma)) \subseteq \text{supp}(\mathcal{E}^{s(\rho)}(\sigma)) \text{ and } \text{supp}(\mathcal{E}^{s(\rho)}(\sigma)) \subseteq \text{supp}(\mathcal{E}^{s(\rho)+1}(\sigma))$$

from Proposition 5.7. So

$$\text{supp}(\mathcal{E}^{s(\rho)+1}(\sigma)) = X.$$

By induction, we can show that $\text{supp}(\mathcal{E}^m(\sigma)) = X$ for all $m \geq s(\rho)$. $\qquad\square$

The next lemma presents a characterisation of the period p_ρ of a quantum state ρ in $\mathcal{C}$ showing that p_ρ is just the minimal number n such that ρ is aperiodic in $\mathcal{C}^n$, the n-repeated application of $\mathcal{C}$.

> **Lemma 5.45** *Let $\mathcal{C} = \langle \mathcal{H}, \mathcal{E} \rangle$ be a quantum Markov chain and $\rho \in \mathcal{D}(\mathcal{H})$ with $p_\rho < \infty$. We set*
>
> $$W_\rho = \{n \geq 1 : \rho \text{ is aperiodic in the quantum Markov chain } \mathcal{C}^n = \langle \mathcal{H}, \mathcal{E}^n \rangle\},$$
>
> *where $\mathcal{E}^n = \mathcal{E} \circ \cdots \circ \mathcal{E}$ stands for repeated application of $\mathcal{E}$ for n times. Then*
>
> $$p_\rho = \min(W_\rho).$$
>
> *Moreover, for any $n \in W_\rho$ and $m \geq 1$, we have $mn \in W_\rho$ as well.*

Proof For simplicity, we denote $p = p_\rho$ and

$$T_k = \{m \geq 1 : \text{supp}(\mathcal{E}^{mk}(\rho)) \supseteq \text{supp}(\rho)\}$$

for any $k \geq 1$. Note that $\gcd(T_1) = p$.

We first prove $p \in W_\rho$. Observe that for any $m \geq 1$, if $m \in T_1$ then $m = m'p$ for some $m' \in T_p$. Thus $\gcd(T_p) \cdot p$ divides $\gcd(T_1)$, and so $\gcd(T_p) = 1$ as desired.

To prove $p = \min(W_\rho)$, let $n \in W_\rho$ be arbitrarily chosen. Then $\gcd(T_n) = 1$. Note that if $m \in T_n$ then $mn \in T_1$. Consequently,

$$n = \gcd(T_n) \cdot n \geq \gcd(T_1) = p.$$

Finally, for any $n \in W_\rho$ and $m \geq 1$, $mn \in W_\rho$ follows directly from Lemma 5.43.

$\qquad\square$

Interestingly, Lemma 5.45 can be generalised from the case of state ρ to a BSCC subspace B. Indeed, such a generalisation provides a way to define the period of a BSCC. Let $C = \langle \mathcal{H}, \mathcal{E} \rangle$ be a quantum Markov chain and B a BSCC of C. We denote by p_B be the number of *peripheral eigenvalues* (eigenvalues with magnitude 1) of $\mathcal{E}$ with the associated eigenvectors supported in B. As B is invariant, these eigenvalues are exactly the peripheral eigenvalues of $\mathcal{E}_B$, the restriction of $\mathcal{E}$ on B.

> **Theorem 5.46** *Let $C = \langle \mathcal{H}, \mathcal{E} \rangle$ be a quantum Markov chain and B a BSCC of C. We set*
>
> $$W_B = \{ n \geq 1 : B \text{ is aperiodic in the quantum Markov chain } C^n = \langle \mathcal{H}, \mathcal{E}^n \rangle \}.$$
>
> *Then*
>
> $$p_B = \min(W_B).$$
>
> *In particular, B is aperiodic if and only if $p_B = 1$.*

Proof Denote $p = p_B$. Note that the quantum Markov chain $C_B = \langle B, \mathcal{E}_B \rangle$ is irreducible. Thus the adjoint map $\mathcal{E}_B^\dagger$ of $\mathcal{E}_B$ is unital, and from [115, Theorem 6.6], the peripheral spectrum of $\mathcal{E}_B^\dagger$ is exactly

$$\{ \exp(2\pi i k / p) : 0 \leq k < p \}.$$

Furthermore, there exist a family of orthogonal projectors $\{ P_0, \ldots, P_{p-1} \}$ such that $\sum_{k=0}^{p-1} P_k = B$, and

$$\mathcal{E}_B^\dagger(P_k) = P_{k \ominus 1}$$

for $k = 0, \ldots, p-1$, where $\ominus$ denotes subtraction modulo p. Note further that the eigenvalues of $\mathcal{E}_B$ are complex conjugate of eigenvalues of $\mathcal{E}_B^\dagger$. We see that $\mathcal{E}_B^p := (\mathcal{E}_B)^p$ has a trivial peripheral spectrum; more precisely, 1 is the only peripheral eigenvalue and its algebraic multiplicity is 1. Furthermore, as C_B is irreducible, by Theorem 5.39 it has a unique fixed point state ρ^* with $\mathrm{supp}(\rho^*) = B$. Note that ρ^* is also a fixed point state of $\mathcal{E}_B^p$, thus the normalised eigenvector associated with eigenvalue 1. Then from [115, Theorems 6.7 and 6.8], there exists $M > 0$ such that

$$\mathrm{supp}(\mathcal{E}^{mp}(\rho)) = \mathrm{supp}(\mathcal{E}_B^{mp}(\rho)) = B$$

for all $m \geq M$ and $\rho \in \mathcal{D}(B)$. It follows from Lemma 5.44 that B is aperiodic in C^p. Thus $p_B \in W_B$.

For any $n \in W_B$, we need to prove $p \leq n$. As B is aperiodic in $C^n = \langle \mathcal{H}, \mathcal{E}^n \rangle$, by Lemma 5.44 there exists an integer $M > 0$ such that

$$\mathrm{supp}(P_k) \subseteq \mathrm{supp}(\mathcal{E}^{mn}(P_k)) = \mathrm{supp}(\mathcal{E}_B^{mn}(P_k))$$

for all $m \geq M$. Thus,

$$0 < \text{tr}(P_k \mathcal{E}_B^{mn}(P_k)) = \text{tr}(\mathcal{E}_B^{\dagger mn}(P_k)P_k) = \text{tr}(P_{k \ominus mn} P_k). \tag{5.14}$$

Therefore, p must be a factor of n, and thus $p \leq n$.   □

In view of Theorem 5.46, we can define p_B as the *period of B* whenever B is a BSCC.

Periodic Decomposition.   Now we are ready to present the main result of this subsection: periodic decomposition for BSCCs, which, combined with Theorem 5.33, provides a refined decomposition for state spaces of quantum Markov chains.

> **Theorem 5.47 (Periodic Decomposition)** *Let $C = \langle \mathcal{H}, \mathcal{E} \rangle$ be a quantum Markov chain. Then every BSCC B of C with period $p = p_B$ can be decomposed uniquely into the direct sum of some mutually orthogonal subspaces*
>
> $$B = B_0 \bigoplus \cdots \bigoplus B_{p-1}$$
>
> *satisfying the following properties:*
>
> (i) *$\mathcal{E}(B_k) = B_{k \oplus 1}$, where $\oplus$ denotes addition modulo p;*
> (ii) *each B_k is an aperiodic BSCC of $C^p = \langle \mathcal{H}, \mathcal{E}^p \rangle$; and*
> (iii) *for any $\rho \in \mathcal{D}(\mathcal{H})$ with $\text{supp}(\rho) \subseteq B$, let*
>
> $$J_\rho = \{k : 0 \leq k < p, \text{tr}(P_{B_k}\rho) > 0\}.$$
>
> *Then p_ρ is the minimal $n \geq 1$ such that $J_\rho = \{i \oplus n : i \in J_\rho\}$. In particular, all states ρ with the support in any single B_i share the same period p.*

Proof   We leave (i) and (ii) as an exercise. For (iii), let

$$J_\rho^n = \{i \oplus n : i \in J_\rho\};$$

in particular, $J_\rho^0 = J_\rho$. Let R_ρ be the set of $n \geq 1$ such that $J_\rho = J_\rho^n$, and $n^* = \min(R_\rho)$. We have to show $n^* = p_\rho$. Note that for any $m, n \in R_\rho$, $m - n \in R_\rho$ whenever $m > n$. Thus,

$$R_\rho = \{mn^* : m \geq 1\}.$$

Moreover, from (i) we have for any $n \geq 0$,

$$\text{supp}(\mathcal{E}^n(\rho)) \subseteq \bigoplus_{k \in J_\rho^n} B_k. \tag{5.15}$$

It then follows that $T_\rho \subseteq R_\rho$ where T_ρ is defined in Eq. (5.11). So n^* is a factor of p_ρ.

We now prove that p_ρ is a factor of n^*. First, from Theorem 5.46, ρ is aperiodic in C^p. Thus by Lemma 5.43,

$$\text{supp}(\mathcal{E}^{mp}(\rho)) = \mathcal{R}_{C^p}(\rho)$$

for a sufficiently large m. On the other hand, from (ii) and Lemma 5.21, we know that

$$\mathcal{R}_{C^p}(\rho) = \bigoplus_{k \in J_\rho} B_k.$$

Then we have from (i) that

$$\text{supp}(\mathcal{E}^{mp + \ell n^*}(\rho)) = \mathcal{R}_{C^p}(\rho)$$

for any $\ell \geq 1$, which implies that p_ρ is a factor of n^*. □

Exercise 5.15 Prove (i) and (ii) of Theorem 5.47.

To conclude this section, let us give a final remark on the periods of quantum states in a BSCC subspace.

Remark 5.48 *Theorem 5.47 confirms the observation we made after Example 5.42. In particular, let $C = \langle \mathcal{H}, \mathcal{E} \rangle$ be a quantum Markov chain and B a BSCC of C. Then*

(i) *There exists an orthonormal basis of B such that every (pure) state in the basis shares the same period which equals period p_B, just like the case in Markov chains.*
(ii) *Superposition of the basis states, a phenomenon which does not exist in Markov chains, is responsible for the fact that other pure states in B might have periods different from p_B; see the state $|+_{02}\rangle$ in Example 5.42. For mixed states, this can be due to probabilistic uncertainty; see the state ρ in Example 5.42. Note that the latter also appears in the classical case.*
(iii) *The period of any quantum state supported in B must be a factor of p_B; conversely, any factor of period p_B can be the period of some quantum state supported in B.*

5.4 Reachability Analysis of Quantum Markov Chains

The graph structures of quantum Markov chains were carefully examined in Section 5.2. Furthermore, the algorithms for BSCC and periodic decomposition of their state Hilbert spaces were presented in Section 5.3. This provides us with necessary mathematical tools for reachability analysis of quantum Markov chains.

In this section, we study several reachability properties of quantum Markov chains and develop algorithms for their analysis based on the results obtained in the preceding two sections.

5.4.1 Reachability Probability

We first consider the simplest reachability property of a quantum Markov chain: a subspace X is reached. The probability of such a reachability is formally defined in the following:

Definition 5.49 Let $\langle \mathcal{H}, \mathcal{E} \rangle$ be a quantum Markov chain, $\rho \in \mathcal{D}(\mathcal{H})$ an initial state and $X \subseteq \mathcal{H}$ a subspace. Then the probability of reaching X, starting from ρ, is

$$\Pr(\rho \vDash \Diamond X) = \lim_{i \to \infty} \mathrm{tr}\left(P_X \widetilde{\mathcal{E}}^i(\rho)\right), \qquad (5.16)$$

where $\widetilde{\mathcal{E}}^i$ is the composition of i copies of $\widetilde{\mathcal{E}}$, and $\widetilde{\mathcal{E}}$ is the quantum operation defined by

$$\widetilde{\mathcal{E}}(\sigma) = P_X \sigma P_X + \mathcal{E}\left(P_{X^\perp} \sigma P_{X^\perp}\right)$$

for all density operator σ.

Obviously, the limit in Definition 5.49 exists, as the probabilities

$$\mathrm{tr}\left(P_X \widetilde{\mathcal{E}}^i(\rho)\right)$$

are non-decreasing in i. Intuitively, $\widetilde{\mathcal{E}}$ can be seen as a procedure that first performs the projective measurement $\{P_X, P_{X^\perp}\}$ and then applies the identity operator $\mathcal{I}$ or $\mathcal{E}$ depending on the measurement outcome.

Computation of Reachability Probability.   Clearly, it is not easy to compute the reachability probability

$$\Pr(\rho \vDash \Diamond X)$$

directly using its defining Eq. (5.16). But it can be computed based on the BSCC decomposition algorithm given in the last section.

We first note that the subspace X in Eq. (5.16) is invariant under $\widetilde{\mathcal{E}}$. Thus $\langle X, \widetilde{\mathcal{E}} \rangle$ is a quantum Markov chain. It is easy to verify that

$$\widetilde{\mathcal{E}}_\infty(X) = X,$$

where $\widetilde{\mathcal{E}}_\infty$ is the asymptotic average of $\widetilde{\mathcal{E}}$ defined according to Eq. (5.9). Then we can decompose X into a set of orthogonal BSCCs according to $\widetilde{\mathcal{E}}$ by Theorem 5.31.

Next, we need to compute the limit probability of hitting a single BSCC. The following lemma shows a connection between it and the probability that the asymptotic average of the initial state lies in the same BSCC.

Lemma 5.50 *Let $\{B_i\}$ be a BSCC decomposition of $\mathcal{E}_\infty(\mathcal{H})$, and P_{B_i} the projection onto B_i. Then for each i, we have*

$$\lim_{k\to\infty} \mathrm{tr}\left(P_{B_i}\mathcal{E}^k(\rho)\right) = \mathrm{tr}\left(P_{B_i}\mathcal{E}_\infty(\rho)\right) \tag{5.17}$$

for all $\rho \in \mathcal{D}(\mathcal{H})$.

Proof We write P for the projection onto $T_\mathcal{E} = \mathcal{E}_\infty(\mathcal{H})^\perp$. Then similar to the proof of Theorem 5.29, we see that the limit

$$q_i := \lim_{k\to\infty} \mathrm{tr}\left(P_{B_i}\mathcal{E}^k(\rho)\right)$$

does exist, and

$$\mathrm{tr}\left(P_{B_i}\mathcal{E}_\infty(\rho)\right) \leq q_i.$$

Moreover, we have

$$1 = \mathrm{tr}\left((I - P)\mathcal{E}_\infty(\rho)\right) = \sum_i \mathrm{tr}\left(P_{B_i}\mathcal{E}_\infty(\rho)\right)$$

$$\leq \sum_i q_i$$

$$= \lim_{k\to\infty} \mathrm{tr}\left((I - P)\mathcal{E}^k(\rho)\right) = 1.$$

This implies $q_i = \mathrm{tr}\left(P_{B_i}\mathcal{E}_\infty(\rho)\right)$ for each i. $\qquad\square$

A combination of Lemma 5.50 and Theorem 5.29 gives us an elegant way to compute the reachability probability of a subspace in a quantum Markov chain.

Theorem 5.51 *Let $\langle\mathcal{H},\mathcal{E}\rangle$ be a quantum Markov chain, $\rho \in \mathcal{D}(\mathcal{H})$, and $X \subseteq \mathcal{H}$ a subspace. Then*

$$\Pr(\rho \models \Diamond X) = \mathrm{tr}\left(P_X\tilde{\mathcal{E}}_\infty(\rho)\right),$$

and this probability can be computed in time $O(d^6)$ where $d = \dim(\mathcal{H})$.

Proof The claim that

$$\Pr(\rho \models \Diamond X) = \mathrm{tr}\left(P_X\tilde{\mathcal{E}}_\infty(\rho)\right)$$

follows directly from Lemma 5.50 and Theorem 5.29. The time complexity of computing reachability probability follows from Lemma 5.34 (i). $\qquad\square$

Exercise 5.16 Elaborate an algorithm for computing reachability probability $\Pr(\rho \models \Diamond X)$ and analyse its complexity.

5.4.2 *Repeated Reachability Probability*

We now consider a kind of more complicated reachability property, namely repeated reachability, of quantum Markov chains. Intuitively, repeated reachability means that a system satisfies a desired condition infinitely often. As we will see in the text that follows, quantum BSCC decomposition can also be used in analysis of repeated reachability of quantum Markov chains.

The notion of repeated reachability for classical Markov chains cannot be straightforwardly generalised to the quantum case. As one can imagine, the major difficulty comes from the way we treat the repeated quantum measurements, which may change the system's state.

A Special Case. To motivate our definition of repeated reachability for quantum Markov chains, let us first consider a special case. If a quantum Markov chain $\langle \mathcal{H}, \mathcal{E} \rangle$ starts from a pure state $|\psi\rangle$, how can we decide whether its evolution sequence

$$|\psi\rangle\langle\psi|, \mathcal{E}(|\psi\rangle\langle\psi|), \mathcal{E}^2(|\psi\rangle\langle\psi|), \ldots$$

reaches a subspace X of $\mathcal{H}$? To do this, certain quantum measurements should be performed on the system. Since a quantum measurement can change the state of the measured system, we have at least two different scenarios.

- *Measure-once:* For each $i \geq 0$, in the i steps of evolution from $|\psi\rangle\langle\psi|$ to $\mathcal{E}^i(|\psi\rangle\langle\psi|)$, the projective measurement $\{P_X, P_{X^\perp}\}$ is performed only at the end.
- *Measure-many:* Measurement $\{P_X, P_{X^\perp}\}$ is performed at each of the i steps of evolution. If the outcome corresponding to P_X is observed, the process terminates immediately; otherwise, it continues with another round of applying $\mathcal{E}$.

The following two lemmas give a simple characterisation of repeated reachability in the above two different scenarios, from which we can see some interesting difference between the two scenarios.

> **Lemma 5.52** *(Measure-once) Let B be a BSCC of quantum Markov chain $\mathcal{C} = \langle \mathcal{H}, \mathcal{E} \rangle$, and X a subspace which is not orthogonal to B. Then for any $|\psi\rangle \in B$, it holds that*
>
> $$\mathrm{tr}\left(P_X \mathcal{E}^i (|\psi\rangle\langle\psi|) \right) > 0$$
>
> *for infinitely many i.*

Proof As X is not orthogonal to B, we can always find a pure state $|\varphi\rangle \in B$ such that $P_X|\varphi\rangle \neq 0$. Now for any $|\psi\rangle \in B$, if there exists N such that

$$\mathrm{tr}\left(P_X \mathcal{E}^k (|\psi\rangle\langle\psi|) \right) = 0$$

for any $k > N$, then

$$|\varphi\rangle \notin \mathcal{R}_{\mathcal{C}}\left(\mathcal{E}^{N+1}(|\psi\rangle\langle\psi|)\right),$$

which means that the reachable space $\mathcal{R}_{\mathcal{C}}\left(\mathcal{E}^{N+1}(|\psi\rangle\langle\psi|)\right)$ is a proper invariant subspace of B. This contradicts the assumption that B is a BSCC. Thus we have

$$\operatorname{tr}\left(P_X \mathcal{E}^i(|\psi\rangle\langle\psi|)\right) > 0$$

for infinitely many i. □

Lemma 5.53 *(Measure-many) Let B be a BSCC of a quantum Markov chain $\mathcal{C} = \langle \mathcal{H}, \mathcal{E} \rangle$, and $X \subseteq B$ a non-trivial subspace of B. Then for any $|\psi\rangle \in B$, we have*

$$\lim_{i\to\infty} \operatorname{tr}\left(\mathcal{G}^i(|\psi\rangle\langle\psi|)\right) = 0,$$

where the quantum operation $\mathcal{G}$ is the restriction of $\mathcal{E}$ in $X^\perp$; that is,

$$\mathcal{G}(\rho) = P_{X^\perp}\mathcal{E}(\rho)P_{X^\perp} \tag{5.18}$$

for all density operators ρ, and $X^\perp$ is the ortho-complement of X in $\mathcal{H}$.

Proof   For any $|\psi\rangle \in B$, we claim that

$$\rho_\psi := \mathcal{G}_\infty(|\psi\rangle\langle\psi|)$$

is a zero operator. Otherwise, it is easy to check that ρ_ψ is a fixed point of $\mathcal{G}$. Furthermore, from the fact that

$$\operatorname{tr}(\mathcal{E}(\rho_\psi)) = \operatorname{tr}(\mathcal{G}(\rho_\psi)) + \operatorname{tr}(P_X\mathcal{E}(\rho_\psi)P_X) = \operatorname{tr}(\rho_\psi) + \operatorname{tr}(P_X\mathcal{E}(\rho_\psi)P_X),$$

we have $\operatorname{tr}(P_X\mathcal{E}(\rho_\psi)) = 0$ as $\mathcal{E}$ is trace-preserving. Thus $P_X\mathcal{E}(\rho_\psi) = 0$, and ρ_ψ is also a fixed point of $\mathcal{E}$. Note that

$$\operatorname{supp}(\rho_\psi) \subseteq X^\perp \cap B.$$

By Theorem 5.24, we see that this contradicts with the assumption that B is a BSCC. Now with the above claim and the fact that $\operatorname{tr}(\mathcal{G}^i(|\psi\rangle\langle\psi|))$ is non-increasing in i, we immediately have

$$\lim_{i\to\infty} \operatorname{tr}\left(\mathcal{G}^i(|\psi\rangle\langle\psi|)\right) = 0.$$ □

Note that quantum operation $\mathcal{G}$ defined in Eq. (5.18) actually models the situation in a single step where $\mathcal{E}$ is applied to the system, then we perform the measurement $\{P_X, P_{X^\perp}\}$, and the outcome corresponds to $X^\perp$. Lemma 5.53 actually shows that if we set X as an absorbing boundary, which is included in BSCC B, then the reachability probability will be absorbed eventually.

Defining Repeated Reachability. Now we turn to consider how to define the notion of repeated reachability in the general case where the initial state is a mixed state expressed as a density operator ρ. First of all, we have the following:

Theorem 5.54 *Let $C = \langle \mathcal{H}, \mathcal{E} \rangle$ be a quantum Markov chain, X a subspace of $\mathcal{H}$, and $\mathcal{G}$ as defined in Eq. (5.18). Then the following two statements are equivalent:*

(i) *The subspace $X^{\perp}$ contains no BSCC.*
(ii) *For any $\rho \in \mathcal{D}(\mathcal{H})$, we have*

$$\lim_{i \to \infty} \mathrm{tr}(\mathcal{G}^i(\rho)) = 0.$$

Proof   Similar to the proof of Lemma 5.53.   □

The foregoing discussions, in particular Lemma 5.53 and Theorem 5.54, provide us with a basis for defining a general form of repeated reachability in a quantum Markov chain.

Let $C = \langle \mathcal{H}, \mathcal{E} \rangle$ be a quantum Markov chain. Note that $\mathcal{E}_{\infty}(\mathcal{H})^{\perp}$ is a transient subspace. So, we can focus our attention on $\mathcal{E}_{\infty}(\mathcal{H})$. The following definition further identifies a subspace only in which repeated reachability of X is actually relevant.

Definition 5.55 Given a subspace X of $\mathcal{E}_{\infty}(\mathcal{H})$, let

$$\mathcal{X}(X) = \left\{ |\psi\rangle \in \mathcal{E}_{\infty}(\mathcal{H}) : \lim_{k \to \infty} \mathrm{tr}\left(\mathcal{G}^k(|\psi\rangle\langle\psi|)\right) = 0 \right\},$$

where $\mathcal{G}$ is defined in Eq. (5.18).

Intuitively, starting from a state $|\psi\rangle$ in $\mathcal{X}(X)$, we repeatedly run quantum operation $\mathcal{E}$, and at the end of each step we perform the measurement $\{P_X, P_{X^{\perp}}\}$. The defining equation of $\mathcal{X}(X)$ means that the probability that the system eventually always falls into $X^{\perp}$ is 0; in other words, the system infinitely often reaches X. It is easy to see that $\mathcal{X}(X)$ is a subspace of $\mathcal{H}$. Therefore, the repeated reachability probability can be properly defined within $\mathcal{X}(X)$.

Definition 5.56 Let $C = \langle \mathcal{H}, \mathcal{E} \rangle$ be a quantum Markov chain, X a subspace of $\mathcal{H}$ and ρ a density operator in $\mathcal{H}$. Then the probability that state ρ satisfies the repeated reachability rep(X) is defined as

$$\Pr(\rho \models \mathrm{rep}(X)) = \lim_{k \to \infty} \mathrm{tr}\left(P_{\mathcal{X}(X)} \mathcal{E}^k(\rho)\right). \tag{5.19}$$

The well-definedness of $\Pr(\rho \vDash \mathrm{rep}(X))$ comes from the fact that $\mathcal{X}(X)$ is invariant under $\mathcal{E}$. By Theorem 5.17 we know that the sequence

$$\left\{ \mathrm{tr}\left(P_{\mathcal{X}(X)}\mathcal{E}^k(\rho)\right)\right\}_{k\geq 0}$$

is non-decreasing, and thus its limit exists. Definition 5.56 is not easy to understand. To give the reader a better understanding of this definition, let us look at the defining equation (5.19) of repeated reachability probability in the following way: First, for any $0 \leq \lambda < 1$, it follows from (5.19) that

$$\Pr(\rho \vDash \mathrm{rep}(X)) \geq \lambda$$

if and only if for any $\epsilon > 0$, there exists N such that for all $k \geq N$, $\mathcal{E}^k(\rho)$ falls into subspace $\mathcal{X}(X)$ with probability $\geq \lambda - \epsilon$. On the other hand, we already noticed above that starting from any state in $\mathcal{X}(X)$, the system can infinitely often reach X. Combining these two observations gives us the intuition that starting from ρ, the system infinitely often reaches X.

> **Exercise 5.17** Compare repeated reachability defined earlier with infinitely often reachability $\mathcal{A} \vDash \mathbf{I}f$ for quantum automaton $\mathcal{A}$ defined in Section 4.4.

The problem of computing repeated reachability probability will be discussed in the next subsection, together with the computation of persistence probability.

5.4.3 Persistence Probability

The aim of this subsection is to study another kind of reachability property of quantum Markov chains, namely persistence. Intuitively, persistence means that a desired condition is always satisfied from a certain point of time.

Defining Persistence. As pointed out in the Subsection 5.4.2, we can focus our attention on $\mathcal{E}_\infty(\mathcal{H})$ because $\mathcal{E}_\infty(\mathcal{H})^\perp$ is a transient subspace. Similar to Definition 5.55, we can identify a subspace where the persistence of X is really relevant.

> **Definition 5.57** Given a subspace X of $\mathcal{E}_\infty(\mathcal{H})$, let
>
> $$\mathcal{Y}(X) = \left\{ |\psi\rangle \in \mathcal{E}_\infty(\mathcal{H}) : (\exists N \geq 0)(\forall k \geq N).\, \mathrm{supp}\left(\mathcal{E}^k(|\psi\rangle\langle\psi|)\right) \subseteq X \right\}.$$

It is clear from its defining equation that $\mathcal{Y}(X)$ consists of the pure states from which the states reachable after some time point N are all in X.

The following lemma gives a characterisation of $\mathcal{X}(X)$ and $\mathcal{Y}(X)$ and also clarifies the relationship between them.

Lemma 5.58 *For any subspace X of $\mathcal{E}_\infty(\mathcal{H})$, both $\mathcal{X}(X)$ and $\mathcal{Y}(X)$ are invariant subspaces of $\mathcal{H}$ under $\mathcal{E}$. Furthermore, we have*

(i) $\mathcal{X}(X) = \mathcal{E}_\infty(X)$;

(ii) $\mathcal{Y}(X) = \bigvee_{B \subseteq X} B = \mathcal{X}(X^\perp)^\perp$, *where B ranges over all BSCCs, and the orthogonal complements are taken in $\mathcal{E}_\infty(\mathcal{H})$.*

Proof   See Appendix 2, Section A2.4.   □

Let us give a simple example to illustrate the subspace $\mathcal{Y}(X)$ defined earlier as well as $\mathcal{X}(X)$ defined in the last subsection. In particular, from the following example the reader can see the difference between them.

Example 5.59   Let us revisit Examples 5.19 and 5.32 where

$$\mathcal{E}_\infty(\mathcal{H}) = \text{span}\{|0\rangle, |1\rangle, |2\rangle, |3\rangle\}.$$

(i) If $X = \text{span}\{|0\rangle, |1\rangle, |2\rangle\}$, then

$$\mathcal{E}_\infty(X^\perp) = \text{supp}(\mathcal{E}_\infty(|3\rangle\langle 3|)) = B_2$$

and $\mathcal{E}_\infty(X) = \mathcal{E}_\infty(\mathcal{H})$. Thus from Lemma 5.58, $\mathcal{Y}(X) = B_1$ and $\mathcal{X}(X) = \mathcal{E}_\infty(\mathcal{H})$.

(ii) If $X = \text{span}\{|3\rangle\}$, then

$$\mathcal{E}_\infty(X^\perp) = B_1 \oplus B_2$$

and $\mathcal{E}_\infty(X) = B_2$. Thus from Lemma 5.58, $\mathcal{Y}(X) = \{0\}$ and $\mathcal{X}(X) = B_2$.

Now we are ready to define persistence probability of a quantum Markov chain.

Definition 5.60   Let $\mathcal{C} = \langle \mathcal{H}, \mathcal{E} \rangle$ be a quantum Markov chain, $X \subseteq \mathcal{H}$ a subspace and ρ a density operator in $\mathcal{H}$. Then the probability that ρ satisfies the persistence property pers(X) is

$$\Pr(\rho \vDash \text{pers}(X)) = \lim_{k \to \infty} \text{tr}\left(P_{\mathcal{Y}(X)} \mathcal{E}^k(\rho) \right).$$

Definition 5.60 deserves a careful explanation. Since $\mathcal{Y}(X)$ is invariant under $\mathcal{E}$, it follows from Theorem 5.17 that the sequence

$$\left\{ \text{tr}\left(P_{\mathcal{Y}(X)} \mathcal{E}^k(\rho) \right) \right\}_{k \geq 0}$$

is non-decreasing, and thus $\Pr(\rho \vDash \text{pers}(X))$ is well defined. The above definition can be understood in a way similar to that given for Definition 5.56. For any $0 \leq \lambda < 1$,

$$\Pr(\rho \vDash \text{pers}(X)) \geq \lambda$$

if and only if for any $\epsilon > 0$, there exists integer N such that for all $k \geq N$, $\mathcal{E}^k(\rho)$ falls into subspace $\mathcal{Y}(X)$ with probability $\geq \lambda - \epsilon$. Furthermore, starting from any state in $\mathcal{Y}(X)$, all the reachable states after some time point must be in X. Therefore, Definition 5.60 coincides with our intuition for persistence that a desired condition always holds after a certain point of time.

Computation of Repeated Reachability and Persistence Probabilities. Now we consider how to compute the repeated reachability and persistence probabilities in a quantum Markov chain. First, combining Theorem 5.51 and Lemma 5.58, we obtain the main result of this subsection.

Theorem 5.61

(i) *The repeated reachability probability is*

$$\Pr(\rho \vDash \text{rep}(X)) = 1 - \text{tr}\left(P_{\mathcal{X}(X)^\perp}\mathcal{E}_\infty(\rho)\right)$$
$$= 1 - \Pr\left(\rho \vDash \text{pers}\left(X^\perp\right)\right).$$

(ii) *The persistence probability is*

$$\Pr(\rho \vDash \text{pers}(X)) = \text{tr}(P_{\mathcal{Y}(X)}\mathcal{E}_\infty(\rho)).$$

We are able to develop an algorithm for computing persistence probability based on Theorem 5.61 (ii). It is presented as Algorithm 6.

Algorithm 6: Persistence(X, ρ)

---

input: A quantum Markov chain $\langle \mathcal{H}, \mathcal{E} \rangle$, a subspace $X \subseteq \mathcal{H}$, and an initial
            state $\rho \in \mathcal{D}(\mathcal{H})$.
output: The probability $\Pr(\rho \vDash \text{pers}(X))$.
begin
$\quad$ $\rho_\infty \leftarrow \mathcal{E}_\infty(\rho)$;
$\quad$ $Y \leftarrow \mathcal{E}_\infty(X^\perp)$;
$\quad$ $P \leftarrow$ the projection onto $Y^\perp$;   (* $Y^\perp$ is the ortho-complement of Y in
$\quad$ $\mathcal{E}_\infty(\mathcal{H})$ *)
$\quad$ **return** $\text{tr}(P\rho_\infty)$;
end

The following theorem shows the correctness and complexity of Algorithm 6.

Theorem 5.62 *Given a quantum Markov chain $\langle \mathcal{H}, \mathcal{E} \rangle$, an initial state $\rho \in \mathcal{D}(\mathcal{H})$, and a subspace $X \subseteq \mathcal{H}$, Algorithm 6 computes persistence probability $\Pr(\rho \vDash \text{pers}(X))$ in time $O(d^8)$, where $d = \dim \mathcal{H}$.*

Proof The correctness of Algorithm 6 follows immediately from Theorem 5.61 (ii). The time complexity is again dominated by the Jordan decomposition used in computing $\mathcal{E}_\infty(\rho)$ and $\mathcal{E}_\infty(X^\perp)$, thus it is $O(d^8)$. $\square$

With Theorem 5.61 (i), Algorithm 6 can also be used to compute repeated reachability probability $\Pr(\rho \vDash \mathrm{rep}(X))$.

5.5 Checking Quantum Markov Decision Processes

We have investigated various properties of quantum Markov chains and developed algorithms for checking them in the previous sections. These results can be naturally generalised to quantum Markov decision processes (qMDPs). This section is devoted to a systematic study of model-checking algorithms for qMDPs. Note that qMDPs can serve as a semantic model of non-deterministic and concurrent quantum programs. The algorithms developed in this section can be applied in termination analysis of these quantum programs.

Recall that a classical Markov decision process (MDP) consists of a set S of states and a set Act of actions. Each action $\alpha \in Act$ corresponds to a probabilistic transition function

$$P_\alpha : S \times S \to [0,1];$$

that is, the pair $\langle S, P_\alpha \rangle$ forms a Markov chain. Thus, the MDP is a triple $\langle S, Act, \{P_\alpha : \alpha \in Act\}\rangle$.

An MDP allows not only probabilistic choice between the system states as a result of performing an action $\alpha \in Act$, but also a non-deterministic choice between actions Act: there might be more than one actions enabled at a single state. Thus, the notion of scheduler is introduced to resolve the non-determinism between enabled actions, depending on previous and current states of the system.

Motivated by the basic ideas of MDPs, we now formally define qMDPs and their schedulers.

Definition 5.63 A qMDP is a 4-tuple:

$$\mathcal{M} = \langle \mathcal{H}, Act, \{\mathcal{E}_\alpha \mid \alpha \in Act\}, \mathbf{M}\rangle,$$

where

- $\mathcal{H}$ is a finite-dimensional Hilbert space, called the state space. The dimension of $\mathcal{H}$ is also called the dimension of $\mathcal{M}$, that is, $\dim \mathcal{M} = \dim \mathcal{H}$.
- Act is a finite set of action names. For each $\alpha \in Act$, there is a corresponding quantum operation $\mathcal{E}_\alpha$ that describes the evolution of the system caused by action α.
- $\mathbf{M}$ is a finite set of quantum measurements. We write Ω for the set of all possible observations from $\mathbf{M}$; that is,

$$\Omega = \{\langle M, m \rangle : M \in \mathbf{M} \text{ and } m \text{ is a possible outcome of } M\}.$$

It is obvious that for each $\alpha \in Act$, the probabilistic transition function P_α in a classical MDP is replaced by a quantum operation $\mathcal{E}_\alpha$ in a qMDP. In addition, a qMDP is equipped with a set $\mathbf{M}$ of quantum measurements. Intuitively, these are the measurements allowed for us to perform on the system in order to acquire classical information about it.

> **Example 5.64** In Example 5.2, the three typical noises on a qubit, bit flip, phase flip and bit-phase flip were treated separately in three different quantum Markov chains $\langle \mathcal{H}, \mathcal{E}_{BF} \rangle, \langle \mathcal{H}, \mathcal{E}_{PF} \rangle$, and $\langle \mathcal{H}, \mathcal{E}_{BPF} \rangle$, respectively. Now we consider the situation where a qubit can be affected by all of these noises, and we are allowed to measure the qubit both in the basis $\{|0\rangle, |1\rangle\}$ and in the basis $\{|+\rangle, |-\rangle\}$. Then the system can be modelled as a qMDP:
>
> $$\mathcal{M} = \langle \mathcal{H}, Act, \{\mathcal{E}_\alpha \mid \alpha \in Act\}, \mathbf{M} \rangle,$$
>
> where $Act = \{BF, PF, BPF\}$, $\mathbf{M} = \{M, M'\}$ and M, M' stand for the measurements in $\{|0\rangle, |1\rangle\}$ and $\{|+\rangle, |-\rangle\}$, respectively.

Moreover, the notion of qMDP can also be regarded as an extension of quantum automaton presented in Definition 4.1 by allowing (1) super-operators instead of only unitary operators in transitions; and (2) measurements at each step to obtain information about the system states.

> **Definition 5.65** A scheduler for a qMDP $\mathcal{M}$ is a function
>
> $$\mathfrak{S} : (Act \cup \Omega)^* \to Act \cup \mathbf{M}.$$

Intuitively, a scheduler selects the next action or measurement based on the past actions and outcomes of measurements.

In particular, when $\mathfrak{S}((Act \cup \Omega)^*) \subseteq Act$, that is, $\mathfrak{S}$ only chooses actions but not measurements, we simply denote $\mathfrak{S} = \alpha_1 \alpha_2 \ldots$ where $\alpha_i = \mathfrak{S}(\alpha_1 \ldots \alpha_{i-1})$ for $i \geq 1$.

We now describe the evolution of a qMDP $\mathcal{M}$ with an initial state $\rho \in \mathcal{D}(\mathcal{H})$ and a scheduler $\mathfrak{S}$. For each word $w \in (Act \cup \Omega)^*$, the state $\rho_w^{\mathfrak{S}}$ of $\mathcal{M}$ and the probability $p_w^{\mathfrak{S}}$ that this state is reached after observing w are defined by induction on the length of w:

- $\rho_\epsilon^{\mathfrak{S}} = \rho$ and $p_\epsilon^{\mathfrak{S}} = 1$, where ϵ is the empty word.
- If $\mathfrak{S}(w) = \alpha \in Act$, then

$$\rho_{w\alpha}^{\mathfrak{S}} = \mathcal{E}_\alpha(\rho_w^{\mathfrak{S}}) \quad \text{and} \quad p_{w\alpha}^{\mathfrak{S}} = p_w^{\mathfrak{S}}.$$

(Note that all the super-operators $\mathcal{E}_\alpha, \alpha \in Act$, are assumed to be trace-preserving.)
- If $\mathfrak{S}(w) = M \in \mathbf{M}$, then for any possible outcome m of M with $\operatorname{tr}(M_m \rho_w^{\mathfrak{S}} M_m^\dagger) > 0$,

$$\rho_{wo}^{\mathfrak{S}} = \frac{M_m \rho_w^{\mathfrak{S}} M_m^\dagger}{\operatorname{tr}(M_m \rho_w^{\mathfrak{S}} M_m^\dagger)} \quad \text{and} \quad p_{wo}^{\mathfrak{S}} = p_w^{\mathfrak{S}} \cdot \operatorname{tr}(M_m \rho_w^{\mathfrak{S}} M_m^\dagger),$$

where $o = \langle M, m \rangle \in \Omega$;
- For the other cases, $p_w^{\mathfrak{S}} = 0$ and $\rho_w^{\mathfrak{S}}$ is not defined.

Furthermore, for each $n \geq 0$, we can define the state of the qMDP $\mathcal{M}$ at step n according to scheduler $\mathfrak{S}$ as the probabilistic combination

$$\rho(n, \mathfrak{S}) = \sum_{w: \, |w|=n \, \wedge \, p_w^{\mathfrak{S}}>0} p_w^{\mathfrak{S}} \rho_w^{\mathfrak{S}}. \tag{5.20}$$

5.5.1 Invariant Subspaces and Reachability Probability

The aim of this section is to study decidability and complexity of reachability analysis for qMDPs. We have seen in the previous sections the key role played by invariant subspaces, in particular BSCCs, in reachability analysis of quantum Markov chains. The counterpart of this notion in qMDPs is the *common* invariant subspace (also called invariant subspace for simplicity). In this subsection, we formally define it and further introduce the notion of reachability with its help.

Invariant Subspaces. Recall that a subspace B is invariant under a super-operator $\mathcal{E}$ if $\mathcal{E}(B) \subseteq B$. Similarly, B is invariant under a measurement $M = \{M_1, \ldots, M_k\}$ if $\mathcal{E}_M(B) \subseteq B$, where $\mathcal{E}_M$ is the super-operator induced by M; that is, for any ρ,

$$\mathcal{E}_M(\rho) = \sum_{i=1}^{k} M_i \rho M_i^\dagger. \tag{5.21}$$

Note that an equivalent condition for B being invariant is

$$\text{supp}(M_i P_B M_i^\dagger) \subseteq B$$

for all $1 \leq i \leq k$, where P_B is the projection onto B. In other words, whenever the state before measurement lies in B, so do all the post-measurement states.

> **Definition 5.66** Let $\mathcal{M} = \langle \mathcal{H}, Act, \{\mathcal{E}_\alpha \mid \alpha \in Act\}, \mathbf{M} \rangle$ be a qMDP and B a subspace of $\mathcal{H}$. Then B is called an invariant subspace of $\mathcal{M}$ if B is invariant under super-operator $\mathcal{E}_\alpha$ for all $\alpha \in Act$, and it is invariant under all measurements $M \in \mathbf{M}$.

Defining Reachability. The reachability problems for MDPs are usually studied in two different scenarios.

- In the finite horizon, we consider whether the system will satisfy a certain property at step n for some n. For instance, suppose a man repeatedly tosses a fair coin. Then at time 10, the probability that he never has a 'head' is 2^{-10}.
- In the infinite horizon, we consider whether the system will eventually satisfy a certain property. For instance, the man who repeatedly tosses a fair coin will eventually get a 'head' with probability 1.

We also consider these two scenarios in qMDPs. The reachability probabilities of qMDPs in the finite horizon and infinite horizon are formally defined in the following.

Definition 5.67 Let $\mathcal{M}$ be a qMDP with state Hilbert space $\mathcal{H}$, ρ an initial state, $\mathfrak{S}$ a scheduler, and B a subspace of $\mathcal{H}$. Then

(i) Finite horizon. The probability that B is reached at step n is

$$\Pr{}^{\mathfrak{S}}(\rho \vDash \Diamond^n B) = \mathrm{tr}(P_B \rho(n, \mathfrak{S})), \tag{5.22}$$

where $\rho(n, \mathfrak{S})$ is given by Eq. (5.20).

(ii) Infinite horizon. If B is invariant, then the probability that B is eventually reached is

$$\Pr{}^{\mathfrak{S}}(\rho \vDash \Diamond B) = \lim_{n \to \infty} \Pr{}^{\mathfrak{S}}(\rho \vDash \Diamond^n B). \tag{5.23}$$

The existence of the limit in Eq. (5.23) is not obvious. It is guaranteed by the following lemma which states that the probability that an invariant subspace is reached is a non-decreasing function of the number of steps.

Lemma 5.68 *Let $\mathcal{M}$ be a qMDP with initial state ρ and B an invariant subspace. Then for any scheduler $\mathfrak{S}$ and $n \geq 0$,*

$$\Pr{}^{\mathfrak{S}}(\rho \vDash \Diamond^{n+1} B) \geq \Pr{}^{\mathfrak{S}}(\rho \vDash \Diamond^n B). \tag{5.24}$$

Exercise 5.18

(i) Prove Lemma 5.68.
(ii) Is inequality (5.24) still true for B that is not invariant? If not, find a counterexample.

Optimal Scheduler.   The optimal scheduler in a classical MDP is defined as the one that can attain the supremum of reachability probability, if there is any. This notion can be easily generalised into the case of qMDPs.

Definition 5.69 Let $\mathcal{M}$ be a qMDP, ρ an initial state, and B an invariant subspace. Then

(i) The supremum reachability probability of B is

$$\Pr{}^{\sup}(\rho \vDash \Diamond B) = \sup_{\mathfrak{S}} \Pr{}^{\mathfrak{S}}(\rho \vDash \Diamond B). \tag{5.25}$$

(ii) If scheduler $\mathfrak{S}_0$ satisfies

$$\Pr{}^{\mathfrak{S}_0}(\rho \vDash \Diamond B) = \Pr{}^{\sup}(\rho \vDash \Diamond B),$$

then $\mathfrak{S}_0$ is called an optimal scheduler for ρ.

5.5.2 Comparison of Classical MDPs, POMDPs and qMDPs

The structures of classical MDPs, partially observable Markov decision processes (POMDPs), and qMDPs are very similar. In this subsection, we employ several simple examples to show some subtle differences between them.

First of all, it is easy to see that MDPs (and also probabilistic automata) and POMDPs can both be encoded as qMDPs. For example, the MDP $\langle S, Act, \{P_\alpha : \alpha \in Act\}\rangle$ can be simulated by a qMDP $\langle \mathcal{H}, Act, \{\mathcal{E}_\alpha \mid \alpha \in Act\}, \mathbf{M}\rangle$, where

- $\mathcal{H} = \text{span}\{|s\rangle : s \in S\}$.
- For any $\alpha \in Act$, whenever $P_\alpha = [p_{st}]_{s,t \in S}$, we have

$$\mathcal{E}_\alpha = \left\{\sqrt{p_{st}}|t\rangle\langle s| : s, t \in S\right\}.$$

  Note that here $\mathcal{E}_\alpha$ is given in terms of its Kraus operators.
- $\mathbf{M} = \{M\}$, where $M = \{|s\rangle\langle s| : s \in S\}$ is the measurement according to the orthonormal basis $\{|s\rangle : s \in S\}$.

Existence of Optimal Schedulers.   It is well known that for any given MDP and any set of target states, there exists a memoryless scheduler that is optimal for all initial states. In the quantum case, however, optimal schedulers may not exist at all.

Example 5.70 Consider a qMDP $\mathcal{M} = \langle \mathcal{H}, Act, \{\mathcal{E}_\alpha \mid \alpha \in Act\}, \mathbf{M}\rangle$, where $\mathcal{H} = \text{span}\{|0\rangle, |1\rangle, |2\rangle, |3\rangle\}$, $\mathbf{M} = \emptyset$, $Act = \{\alpha, \beta\}$ and

$$\mathcal{E}_\alpha = \left\{\frac{1}{\sqrt{2}}|0\rangle\langle 0|, \frac{1}{\sqrt{2}}|1\rangle\langle 0|, |1\rangle\langle 1|, |2\rangle\langle 2|, |3\rangle\langle 3|\right\},$$

$$\mathcal{E}_\beta = \{|3\rangle\langle 0|, |2\rangle\langle 1|, |2\rangle\langle 2|, |3\rangle\langle 3|\}.$$

Let $\rho_0 = |0\rangle\langle 0|$ and $B = \text{span}\{|2\rangle\}$. Then

$$\Pr^{\mathfrak{S}}(\rho_0 \models \Diamond B) < \Pr^{\sup}(\rho_0 \models \Diamond B) = 1$$

for all schedulers $\mathfrak{S}$. Indeed, if $\mathfrak{S} = \alpha^\omega$, then

$$\Pr^{\mathfrak{S}}(\rho_0 \models \Diamond B) = 0.$$

Otherwise, let $\mathfrak{S} = \gamma_1\gamma_2 \ldots$ and k be the first index such that $\gamma_k = \beta$. Then

$$\Pr^{\mathfrak{S}}(\rho_0 \models \Diamond B) = 1 - 0.5^{k-1} < 1.$$

Obviously, the non-existence of optimal schedulers in Example 5.70 is due to the lack of precise information about the current quantum state. If we could determine whether it is $|0\rangle$ or $|1\rangle$, then appropriate actions would be taken accordingly: α for $|0\rangle$ and β for $|1\rangle$. Note that this probabilistic uncertainty about system states also prohibits POMDPs to always have optimal schedulers.

However, as the following example shows, superposition presented in the system states can also contribute to the non-existence of optimal scheduler for qMDPs.

Example 5.71 Let $\mathcal{M}$, ρ_0, B be defined as in Example 5.70 except that $\mathcal{E}_\alpha = \{U, |2\rangle\langle 2|, |3\rangle\langle 3|\}$, where

$$U = \cos\theta(|0\rangle\langle 0| + |1\rangle\langle 1|) + \sin\theta(|0\rangle\langle 1| - |1\rangle\langle 0|)$$

and $\theta = 0.6$. Note that the set $\{U^n|0\rangle : n \in \mathbb{N}\}$ is dense on the unit circle

$$\{a|0\rangle + b|1\rangle : a, b \subset \mathbb{R}, a^2 + b^2 = 1\}.$$

For any $\epsilon > 0$, there exists n, such that

$$\mathcal{E}_\alpha^n(|1\rangle\langle 1|) = |\psi_n\rangle\langle\psi_n|$$

with $|\langle 1|\psi_n\rangle| > \sqrt{1-\epsilon}$. Thus, we have

$$\mathrm{Pr}^{\mathfrak{S}}(\rho_0 \vDash \Diamond B) > 1 - \epsilon$$

for $\mathfrak{S} = \alpha^n\beta^\omega$, which implies

$$\mathrm{Pr}^{\sup}(\rho_0 \vDash \Diamond B) = 1.$$

However, since $U^m|0\rangle \neq |1\rangle$ for any m, there is no optimal scheduler.

It should be noted that in Example 5.71, there is no probabilistic uncertainty in any transition of the system. However, no scheduler can bring the initial state $|0\rangle$ to $|1\rangle$ exactly.

Robustness of Qualitative Analysis.   Recall that for MDPs and POMDPs, when considering the qualitative reachability problem, we are only concerned with if a certain entry of the probability matrix is positive, but not its exact value. However, as the following example shows, a small perturbation of the non-zero entries of a super-operator can make things very different.

Example 5.72 Let $\mathcal{M}$, ρ_0, B be defined as in Example 5.71 except that $\theta = \pi/4$. Since $U^2|1\rangle = -|2\rangle$, we have

$$\mathrm{Pr}_{\mathcal{M}}^{\mathfrak{S}_0}(\rho_0 \vDash \Diamond B) = 1$$

for $\mathfrak{S}_0 = \alpha^2\beta^\omega$. However, for any rational number $\epsilon > 0$, $\cos(\pi/4 + \epsilon) \neq 0$. Thus for any integers k and j, we have $k\theta' \neq (j + 0.5)\pi$ where $\theta' = \pi/4 + \epsilon$. Let $\mathcal{M}'$ be a qMDP obtained from $\mathcal{M}$ by changing θ to θ'. Then for any scheduler $\mathfrak{S}$ of $\mathcal{M}'$, we have

$$\mathrm{Pr}_{\mathcal{M}'}^{\mathfrak{S}}(\rho_0 \vDash \Diamond B) < 1.$$

5.5.3 Reachability in the Finite Horizon

Now we start to carefully study decidability of reachability analysis for qMDPs. For the cases where it is decidable, we will present an algorithm for solving the problem. This subsection deals with qMDPs in the finite horizon.

Quantitative Analysis.   Let us first consider the quantitative analysis problem for reachability of qMDPs.

> **Theorem 5.73** *The following problem is undecidable:*

- *Given a qMDP $\mathcal{M}$, an initial state ρ, a subspace B of $\mathcal{H}$, and $p \in [0, 1]$, determine if there are a scheduler $\mathfrak{S}$ and a non-negative integer n such that*

$$\Pr^{\mathfrak{S}}(\rho \vDash \Diamond^n B) \sim p,$$

where $\sim \in \{>, \geq, <, \leq\}$.

Proof Note that any probabilistic finite automaton can be encoded as a qMDP. The theorem then follows immediately from the undecidability of the corresponding emptiness problem for probabilistic finite automata [97]. □

Qualitative Analysis.   For qualitative analysis, we have two variants.

> **Problem 5.1** *Given a qMDP $\mathcal{M}$ and a subspace B,*
>
> (i) *Are there a scheduler $\mathfrak{S}$ and an integer n such that $\Pr^{\mathfrak{S}}(\rho \vDash \Diamond^n B) = 1$ for all initial states ρ?*
> (ii) *Are there a scheduler $\mathfrak{S}$ and an integer n such that $\Pr^{\mathfrak{S}}(\rho \vDash \Diamond^n B) = 1$ for a given initial state ρ?*

Before we show the results about this problem for qMDPs, let us recall the ones about MDPs. The counterpart of Problem 5.1(ii) for classical MDPs can be stated as follows:

- Given an MDP $\mathcal{M}$ with a finite set S of states, an initial state s_0 and $B \subseteq S$, decide whether there exist a scheduler $\mathfrak{S}$ and an integer n such that for any possible sequence of states $s_0 s_1 s_2 \ldots$ under $\mathfrak{S}$, there exists $j < n$ such that $s_j \in B$.

The polynomial-time decidability of this problem immediately follows from the fact that an optimal scheduler for maximum reachability problem of an MDP can be found in polynomial time [7]. The only thing we need to do is to check whether there exists a cycle in all states reachable from s_0 in $S \backslash B$. The same result is true for the counterpart of Problem 5.1(i) for MDPs.

Let us now come back to qMDPs. The following theorem indicates that the classical and quantum situations are very different.

Theorem 5.74 *Both Problems 5.1(i) and 5.1(ii) with $|Act| \geq 2$ and B invariant are undecidable.*

Proof Our proof technique is a reduction from the matrix mortality problem which can be simply stated as follows:

- Given a finite set of matrices $G = \{M_i \in \mathbb{Z}^{n \times n} : 1 \leq i \leq k\}$, is there any sequence $j_1, \ldots, j_m$ such that $M_{j_m} M_{j_{m-1}} \ldots M_{j_1} = 0$?

It is known [63] that this problem is undecidable for $k \geq 2$. Now, for a set G of matrices as earlier, we construct a qMDP $\mathcal{M}$ as follows.

- Let $\mathcal{H} = \text{span}\{|1\rangle, \ldots, |2n\rangle\}$.
- Let $Act = \{1, 2, \ldots, k\}$. For each $i \in Act$, let $\mathcal{E}_i = \{A_i, B_i, C_i\}$ where

$$A_i = \frac{1}{\sqrt{r_i}} \begin{pmatrix} M_i & 0 \\ 0 & 0 \end{pmatrix}, \quad B_i = \begin{pmatrix} 0 & 0 \\ 0 & I_{n \times n} \end{pmatrix}, \quad C_i = \begin{pmatrix} 0 & 0 \\ \sqrt{I - M_i^\dagger M_i / r_i} & 0 \end{pmatrix},$$

and r_i is a positive integer such that $I - M_i^\dagger M_i / r_i$ is positive semi-definite.
- $\mathbf{M} = \emptyset$.

Let $\mathfrak{S} = j_1 j_2 \ldots \in Act^\omega$. It is easy to show that for any initial state

$$\rho = \begin{pmatrix} \rho_a & * \\ * & \rho_b \end{pmatrix},$$

it holds that

$$\rho(m, \mathfrak{S}) = \begin{pmatrix} A \rho_a A^\dagger & 0 \\ 0 & * \end{pmatrix},$$

where

$$A = M_{j_m} \ldots M_{j_1} / \sqrt{r_{j_m} \ldots r_{j_1}}.$$

Now let $B = \text{span}\{|n+1\rangle, \ldots, |2n\rangle\}$. Then there exists a scheduler $\mathfrak{S}$ such that

$$\text{Pr}^\mathfrak{S}(\rho \models \Diamond^m B) = 1$$

for all initial states ρ if and only if there exists $j_1, \ldots, j_m \in Act$ such that $M_{j_m} \ldots M_{j_1} = 0$. Since the matrix mortality problem is undecidable for $k \geq 2$, Problem 5.1(i) is undecidable with $|Act| \geq 2$ and B invariant.

The reduction still works if we take the initial state to be $I/2n$. Therefore, Problem 5.1(ii) is undecidable too. $\qquad\square$

5.5.4 Reachability in the Infinite Horizon

Now we turn to consider the case of infinite horizon. First, note that both the limit problem and the quantitative value problem of probabilistic automata are undecidable [30]. We have the following corresponding results for supremum reachability probability of qMDPs.

Theorem 5.75 *The following two problems are undecidable: Given a qMDP* $\mathcal{M}$, *an initial state* ρ, *and an invariant subspace* B,

(i) *(Qualitative reachability) decide whether* $\text{Pr}^{\text{sup}}(\rho \vDash \Diamond B) = 1$.
(ii) *(Quantitative reachability) decide whether* $\text{Pr}^{\text{sup}}(\rho \vDash \Diamond B) > p$ *for a given* $p \in$ $(0, 1)$.

Exercise 5.19 Prove Theorem 5.75.

Furthermore, from the fact that quantitative existence problem in probabilistic automata is undecidable [30], we deduce that the corresponding problem in qMDPs is undecidable as well. However, as the following theorem shows, the qualitative existence problem in qMDPs is also undecidable. This is in sharp contrast with the results for the classical cases, because it is known that this problem is in P for MDPs, and is EXPTIME-Complete for POMDPs.

Theorem 5.76 *The following two problems are undecidable: Given a qMDP* $\mathcal{M}$, *an initial state* ρ, *and an invariant subspace* B,

(i) *(Qualitative existence) decide whether* $\text{Pr}^{\mathfrak{S}}(\rho \vDash \Diamond B) = 1$ *for some scheduler* $\mathfrak{S}$.
(ii) *(Quantitative existence) decide whether* $\text{Pr}^{\mathfrak{S}}(\rho \vDash \Diamond B) > p$ *for some scheduler* $\mathfrak{S}$, *for a given* $p \in (0, 1)$.

Proof The undecidability of quantitative existence problem is from the corresponding result for probabilistic automata. For qualitative existence analysis, we reduce from the finite horizon reachability problem of qMDPs. Let $\mathcal{M} = \langle \mathcal{H}, Act, \{\mathcal{E}_\alpha \mid \alpha \in Act\}, \mathbf{M} \rangle$ be a qMDP with $\mathbf{M} = \emptyset$, and B an invariant subspace. We construct a new qMDP $\mathcal{M}' = \langle \mathcal{H}', Act', \{\mathcal{E}'_\alpha : \alpha \in Act'\}, \emptyset \rangle$ as follows:

- $\mathcal{H}' = \mathcal{H} \oplus \text{span}\{|f\rangle, |s\rangle\}$.
- $Act' = Act \cup \{\kappa\}$ for a fresh action κ.
- For any $\alpha \in Act'$ and $\sigma \in \mathcal{D}(\mathcal{H}')$,

$$
\mathcal{E}'_\alpha(\sigma) = \begin{cases} \mathcal{E}_\alpha(P_\mathcal{H} \sigma P_\mathcal{H}) + \sum_{x \in \{f,s\}} |x\rangle\langle x|\sigma|x\rangle\langle x|, & \text{if } \alpha \in Act; \\ \text{tr}(\sigma P_{B^s})|s\rangle\langle s| + [1 - \text{tr}(\sigma P_{B^s})]|f\rangle\langle f|, & \text{if } \alpha = \kappa, \end{cases}
$$

where $P_{B^s} = P_B + |s\rangle\langle s|$.

It is easy to see that $\text{span}\{|f\rangle\}$ and $\text{span}\{|s\rangle\}$ are both invariant subspaces of $\mathcal{M}'$, and the only way to go into these two subspaces is to perform $\mathcal{E}'_\kappa$. Moreover, once $\mathcal{E}'_\kappa$ is applied, the system state will completely lie in these two subspaces for ever. Therefore, for any initial state $\rho \in \mathcal{D}(\mathcal{H})$, the following two statements are equivalent:

(i) There exist a scheduler $\mathfrak{S}$ for $\mathcal{M}$ and an integer n such that $\Pr^{\mathfrak{S}}(\rho \vDash \Diamond^n B) = 1$.
(ii) There exists a scheduler $\mathfrak{S}'$ for $\mathcal{M}'$ such that $\Pr^{\mathfrak{S}'}(\rho \vDash \Diamond B') = 1$, where $B' = \mathrm{span}\{|s\rangle\}$.

Since the first problem is proved to be undecidable (Theorem 5.74), so is the second one. □

Note that initial state ρ is given in the problems considered in Theorem 5.76. We now propose a variant of qualitative existence problem where the initial state can be taken arbitrarily.

Problem 5.2 *Given a qMDP $\mathcal{M}$ and an invariant subspace B, is there a scheduler $\mathfrak{S}$ such that $\Pr^{\mathfrak{S}}(\rho \vDash \Diamond B) = 1$ for all initial states ρ?*

Before studying this problem, let us first point out that the classical counterparts of these two versions of qualitative existence problems – the one in Theorem 5.76 with a given initial state ρ and the one in Problem 5.2 with all initial states – have the same hardness, because MDPs are assumed to have only a finite number of states, which can be checked one by one. However, the quantum versions are very different due to the fact that the state Hilbert space of a qMDP is a continuum.

Solving Problem 5.2 requires certain technical preparations. We state them as the following two lemmas.

Lemma 5.77 *Let $\langle \mathcal{H}, \mathcal{E} \rangle$ be a quantum Markov chain, and X a subspace of $\mathcal{H}$. Then for any subspace Y of $\mathcal{H}$,*

$$Y \subseteq \mathcal{E}^\dagger(X)^\perp \quad iff \quad \mathcal{E}(Y) \subseteq X^\perp, \tag{5.26}$$

where $\mathcal{E}^\dagger$ stands for the dual of super-operator $\mathcal{E}$. In particular, we have

- $\mathcal{E}(\mathcal{E}^\dagger(X)^\perp) \subseteq X^\perp$.
- *If X is invariant, then*

$$X \subseteq \mathcal{E}^\dagger(X^\perp)^\perp \cap \mathcal{E}^\dagger(X).$$

Proof For any subspace Y,

$$Y \subseteq \mathcal{E}^\dagger(X)^\perp$$
$$\text{iff} \quad \mathrm{tr}(P_Y \mathcal{E}^\dagger(P_X)) = 0$$
$$\text{iff} \quad \mathrm{tr}(\mathcal{E}(P_Y) P_X) = 0$$
$$\text{iff} \quad \mathcal{E}(Y) \subseteq X^\perp.$$

Then $\mathcal{E}(\mathcal{E}^\dagger(X)^\perp) \subseteq X^\perp$ follows easily.

If X is invariant, then $\mathcal{E}(X) \subseteq X$, and $X \subseteq \mathcal{E}^\dagger(X^\perp)^\perp$ follows from Eq. (5.26). Furthermore, for any $|\psi\rangle \in \mathcal{E}^\dagger(X)^\perp$, it holds that

$$\mathrm{tr}(P_X \mathcal{E}(|\psi\rangle\langle\psi|)) = 0.$$

Thus, $\mathrm{tr}(P_X |\psi\rangle\langle\psi|) = 0$ from Theorem 5.17, and then $|\psi\rangle \in X^\perp$. So, $X \subseteq \mathcal{E}^\dagger(X)$ follows. □

For a finite sequence $s = s_1 s_2 \dots s_k \in Act^*$, we denote $\mathcal{E}_s = \mathcal{E}_{s_k} \circ \cdots \circ \mathcal{E}_{s_2} \circ \mathcal{E}_{s_1}$, the composition of these quantum operations.

Lemma 5.78 *Let $\mathcal{M} = \langle \mathcal{H}, Act, \{\mathcal{E}_\alpha \mid \alpha \in Act\}, \mathbf{M} \rangle$ be a qMDP with $|\mathbf{M}| = \emptyset$, B an invariant subspace, and $\mathfrak{S} = s^\omega$ for some $s \in Act^*$. If $\mathcal{E}_s^\dagger(B) = \mathcal{H}$, then for any ρ, it holds that*

$$\mathrm{Pr}^{\mathfrak{S}}(\rho \vDash \Diamond B) = 1.$$

Proof Note that $\mathcal{C} = \langle \mathcal{H}, \mathcal{E}_s \rangle$ is a quantum Markov chain with B being an invariant subspace of it. We claim that there does not exist a BSCC included in $B^\perp$. Otherwise, suppose that $B' \subseteq B^\perp$ is such a BSCC. Then $\mathcal{E}_s(B') \subseteq B^\perp$, and from Lemma 5.77, $B' \subseteq \mathcal{E}_s^\dagger(B)^\perp$, contradicting that $\mathcal{E}_s^\dagger(B) = \mathcal{H}$. The lemma then follows from Theorem 5.54. □

Now we are ready to present our results about Problem 5.2.

Theorem 5.79 *Given a qMDP $\mathcal{M} = \langle \mathcal{H}, Act, \{\mathcal{E}_\alpha \mid \alpha \in Act\}, \mathbf{M} \rangle$ and an invariant subspace B of $\mathcal{M}$, the following two statements are equivalent:*

(i) *There is a scheduler $\mathfrak{S}$ such that $\mathrm{Pr}^{\mathfrak{S}}(\rho \vDash \Diamond B) = 1$ for all initial states ρ.*
(ii) *There is no invariant subspace of $\mathcal{M}$ included in $B^\perp$.*

Furthermore, if (ii) holds, then there exists an optimal finite-memory scheduler $\mathfrak{S} = s^\omega$ for some $s \in Act^*$.

Proof The proof of (i) $\Rightarrow$ (ii) is easy. We now show (ii) $\Rightarrow$ (i) for the special case of $\mathbf{M} = \emptyset$. Assume that there is no invariant subspace of $\mathcal{M}$ included in $B^\perp$. To simplify notation, we denote $X_s = \mathcal{E}_s^\dagger(B)$ for $s \in Act^*$. Let

$$D = \{\dim X_s : s \in Act^*\}$$

and $s \in \arg\max D$. We claim that $X_s = \mathcal{H}$, and then (i) follows by Lemma 5.78. Otherwise, let $Y = \mathcal{E}_s(X_s^\perp)$. For any $u \in Act^*$, we know

$$X_{su} = \mathcal{E}_s^\dagger(\mathcal{E}_u^\dagger(B)) \supseteq \mathcal{E}_s^\dagger(B) = X_s$$

from the fact that $\mathcal{E}_u^\dagger(B) \supseteq B$. Thus, $X_s = X_{su}$ from the maximum dimension of X_s, and so it holds that

$$X_s^\perp = X_{su}^\perp = \mathcal{E}_s^\dagger(X_u)^\perp.$$

Then from Lemma 5.77, we have $Y \subseteq X_u^\perp$ and $\mathcal{E}_u(Y) \subseteq \mathcal{E}_u(X_u^\perp) \subseteq B^\perp$.

Let

$$\mathcal{F} = \frac{1}{|Act|} \sum_{\alpha \in Act} \mathcal{E}_\alpha,$$

and $C_\mathcal{F} = \langle \mathcal{H}, \mathcal{F} \rangle$ be a quantum Markov chain. We have proved $\mathcal{E}_u(Y) \subseteq B^\perp$ for any $u \in Act^*$. Thus $\mathcal{R}_{C_\mathcal{F}}(Y)$ is an invariant subspace of $\mathcal{M}$ included in $B^\perp$, contradicting the assumption (ii).

For the general case where $\mathbf{M} \neq \emptyset$, we construct a new qMDP $\mathcal{M}'$ on $\mathcal{H}$ with $Act' = Act \cup \mathbf{M}$ and $\mathbf{M}' = \emptyset$, where for each $M \in \mathbf{M}$ the super-operator $\mathcal{E}_M$ is defined in Eq. (5.21). The theorem then follows from a similar argument as presented earlier. $\qquad\square$

By Theorem 5.79, Problem 5.2 is reduced to the existence of certain invariant subspace of qMDPs. Based on it, we can develop an algorithm for checking existence of the optimal scheduler. It is presented as Algorithm 7.

Algorithm 7: Find a universally optimal scheduler

input: A qMDP $\mathcal{M} = \langle \mathcal{H}, Act, \{\mathcal{E}_\alpha \mid \alpha \in Act\}, \mathbf{M}\rangle$ and an invariant subspace $B \subsetneq \mathcal{H}$.

output: A string $s \in (Act \cup \mathbf{M})^*$ which witness if there is a universally optimal scheduler.

begin

$\quad d \leftarrow \dim \mathcal{H}; \quad s \leftarrow \epsilon;$

$\quad S \leftarrow \bigcup_{i=1}^d (Act \cup \mathbf{M})^i;$

$\quad$**repeat**

$\quad\quad$ Let $u^* \in \arg\max\{\dim X_{su} : u \in S\};$

$\quad\quad s' \leftarrow s; \quad s \leftarrow su^*;$

$\quad$**until** $\dim X_s = \dim X_{s'};$

$\quad$**if** $\dim X_s < d$ **then**

$\quad\quad$| **return** ϵ

$\quad$**else**

$\quad\quad$| **return** s

$\quad$**end**

end

The correctness and complexity of Algorithm 7 is shown in the following:

Theorem 5.80 *Given a qMDP* $\mathcal{M} = \langle \mathcal{H}, Act, \{\mathcal{E}_\alpha \mid \alpha \in Act\}, \mathbf{M} \rangle$ *and an invariant subspace* B *of* $\mathcal{M}$,

(i) *Algorithm 7 returns* ϵ *if there does not exist a scheduler* $\mathfrak{S}$ *such that* $\mathrm{Pr}^{\mathfrak{S}}(\rho \models \Diamond B) = 1$ *for all initial states* ρ. *Otherwise it returns* $s \neq \epsilon$ *such that* $\mathfrak{S}^* = s^\omega$ *is such a universally optimal scheduler.*

(ii) *The time complexity of Algorithm 7 is* $O(d^7 N^d)$, *where* $N = |Act| + |\mathbf{M}|$.

Proof The correctness of the algorithm follows directly from the proof of Theorem 5.79. The loop repeats at most d times as the dimension of X_s increases at least 1 before termination. For each iteration, the complexity of computing X_{su} for each u is $O(d^6)$, since there are at most d^2 matrix × vector multiplications and each costs $O(d^4)$. Thus the complexity of the whole algorithm is $O(d \cdot N^d \cdot d^6) = O(d^7 N^d)$. $\qquad\qquad\qquad\qquad\qquad\qquad\qquad\qquad\qquad\qquad\qquad\qquad\quad\Box$

5.6 Final Remarks

To conclude this chapter, we would like to point out the limitation of the current research discussed here and some problems for future research.

(i) Although temporal logical notations are used in Definitions 5.49 and 5.67, we have not formally defined a temporal logic for specifying dynamic properties of quantum Markov chains and decision processes. Indeed, an appropriate temporal logic for this purpose is still missing in the literature. The reader can see a more detailed discussion about this issue in the final remarks of the last chapter.

(ii) All algorithms for reachability analysis of quantum automata and quantum Markov chains and decision processes presented in Chapter 4 and this chapter are classical; that is, they are developed to be executed on classical computers. It is a very interesting research topic to develop quantum algorithms for the same purpose that can improve the complexities of the corresponding algorithms given in Chapter 4 and this chapter.

5.7 Bibliographic Remarks

The earliest motivation of research on reachability of quantum Markov chains came from quantum program analysis. Termination of quantum **while**-loops with unitary transformations as their loop bodies was first studied in [118]. The main results of [118] were generalised to the case of general quantum loops with super-operators as their loop bodies in [123], where quantum Markov chains were adopted as their semantic model. Naturally, termination analysis of these quantum programs leads to reachability problem of quantum Markov chains. Furthermore, an analysis for termination of nondeterministic quantum programs was carried out by Li et al. [81], generalising several results by Hart, Sharir and Pnueli [67] for probabilistic programs. Termination of concurrent quantum programs with fairness conditions was studied by Yu et al. [123].

However, the materials in this chapter are exposed from the viewpoint of model checking rather than program analysis. Theorem 5.12 was first proved in [123]. The other results in Sections 5.2 through 5.4 except Subsection 5.3.3 are taken from Ying et al. [120]. Subsection 5.3.3 is based on Guan et al. [61]. The results presented in Section 5.5 are from [121].

It should be pointed out that some of the main results in [61, 120, 121, 123] were obtained independently by other authors in different contexts. There are quite extensive literature on quantum Markov chains and decision processes, and here is a (far from complete) list of recent references: [3, 10, 14, 26–28, 47, 107].

6

Model Checking Super-Operator-Valued Markov Chains

In the previous two chapters, we studied the techniques for checking (reachability of) quantum automata and quantum Markov chains and decision processes. The system's dynamics there had been gradually generalised from unitary transformations to a single super-operator and then to a family of super-operators that are executed in an interleaving manner.

This chapter is devoted to studying a class of more complex quantum systems modelled as so-called super-operator-valued Markov chains (SVMCs). The dynamics of these systems is described also by a family of super-operators as in a quantum Markov decision process, but their executions are arranged according to a directed graph rather than being simply interleaving.

SVMCs can also be viewed in a different way as a generalisation of classical Markov chains. Roughly speaking, a Markov chain can be seen as a directed graph where a real number in the unit interval is associated with each edge, which can be thought of as the probability that the action represented by the edge occurs. In an SVMC, such a real number is replaced by a (unnecessarily trace-preserving) super-operator. As will be shown by examples, this new Markov chain model turns out to be useful in modelling the high-level structure of quantum programs and quantum communication protocols.

Since the directed graph underlying an SVMC is a classical structure, a temporal logic for specifying its dynamic properties can be naturally defined according to the graph: the time points in the execution of actions are represented by the nodes of the graph, and the effect of executing an action is modelled by the super-operator associated with the corresponding edge. Just like the temporal logics used for specifying properties of probabilistic systems, such a logic is quantitative rather than qualitative (Boolean-valued).

In this chapter, we will introduce the mathematical tools needed in analysis of quantum systems modelled as SVMCs and develop a series of algorithms for checking temporal logic properties of them.

6.1 Super-Operator-Valued Markov Chains

We first define the model of SVMCs. In such a model, we have to distinguish two levels of states. At the higher level, by a state we mean a node of the directed graph underlying an SVMC. So, the state space of this level is classical. However, the transitions between these classical states are labelled by super-operators that are understood as quantum operations performed on a (fixed) quantum system. Then at the lower level, we have a Hilbert space $\mathcal{H}$ as the state space of this quantum system. Throughout this chapter, we assume that $\mathcal{H}$ is finite dimensional.

Algebra of Super-Operators. As a preparation, let us examine the algebraic structure of super-operators on $\mathcal{H}$. Let $SO(\mathcal{H})$ be the set of (trace-nonincreasing) super-operators on $\mathcal{H}$, ranged over by $\mathcal{E}, \mathcal{F}, \ldots$. Obviously, both $(SO(\mathcal{H}), 0, +)$ and $(SO(\mathcal{H}), \mathrm{Id}, \circ)$ are monoids, where Id and 0 are the identity and null super-operators on $\mathcal{H}$, respectively, and $\circ$ is the composition of super-operators defined by

$$(\mathcal{E} \circ \mathcal{F})(\rho) = \mathcal{E}(\mathcal{F}(\rho))$$

for any $\rho \in \mathcal{D}(\mathcal{H})$, where $\mathcal{D}(\mathcal{H})$ is the set of density operators on $\mathcal{H}$. We always omit the symbol $\circ$ and write $\mathcal{E}\mathcal{F}$ directly for $\mathcal{E} \circ \mathcal{F}$. The operation $\circ$ is (both left and right) distributive with respect to $+$:

$$\mathcal{E}(\mathcal{F}_1 + \mathcal{F}_2) = \mathcal{E}\mathcal{F}_1 + \mathcal{E}\mathcal{F}_2, \quad (\mathcal{F}_1 + \mathcal{F}_2)\mathcal{E} = \mathcal{F}_1\mathcal{E} + \mathcal{F}_2\mathcal{E}.$$

Thus $(SO(\mathcal{H}), +, \circ)$ forms a semiring.

Furthermore, we define the 'trace order' $\precsim$ on $SO(\mathcal{H})$ by letting $\mathcal{E} \precsim \mathcal{F}$ if for any $\rho \in \mathcal{D}(\mathcal{H})$,

$$\mathrm{tr}(\mathcal{E}(\rho)) \leq \mathrm{tr}(\mathcal{F}(\rho)).$$

Intuitively, $\mathcal{E} \precsim \mathcal{F}$ if and only if the success probability of performing $\mathcal{E}$ is always not greater than that of performing $\mathcal{F}$, whatever the initial state is. Let $\approx$ be $\precsim \cap \succsim$; that is,

$$\mathcal{E} \approx \mathcal{F} \text{ iff } \mathcal{E} \precsim \mathcal{F} \text{ and } \mathcal{E} \succsim \mathcal{F}.$$

It is obvious that $\approx$ is an equivalence relation.

Lemma 6.1 shows that the order $\precsim$ is preserved by the right application of composition.

Lemma 6.1 *Let* $\mathcal{E}, \mathcal{F}, \mathcal{G} \in SO(\mathcal{H})$. *If* $\mathcal{E} \precsim \mathcal{F}$, *then* $\mathcal{E}\mathcal{G} \precsim \mathcal{F}\mathcal{G}$.

Exercise 6.1

(i) Prove Lemma 6.1.
(ii) Is the order $\precsim$ preserved by the left application of composition? If so, prove it; if not, find a counter-example.

Definition and Examples of Super-Operator-Valued Markov Chains. With the notions introduced in the preceding text, we are ready to define the key model of this section. We assume a finite set AP of atomic propositions. It is worth noting that atomic propositions considered in this chapter are about classical states, instead of quantum states in Chapter 4.

> **Definition 6.2 (Super-Operator-Valued Markov Chain)** A labelled super-operator-valued Markov chain (SVMC for short) $\mathcal{M}$ is a tuple $(S, \mathbf{Q}, L)$, in which
>
> - S is a finite set of (classical) states.
> - $\mathcal{H}$ is a finite dimensional Hilbert space.
> - $\mathbf{Q} : S \times S \to \mathcal{SO}(\mathcal{H})$ is a transition super-operator matrix where for each $s \in S$,
>
> $$\sum_{t \in S} \mathbf{Q}[s, t] \approx \mathcal{I}.$$
>
> - $L : S \to 2^{AP}$ is a labelling function.

The transition super-operator matrix $\mathbf{Q}$ in an SVMC is functionally analogous to the transition probability matrix in a classical Markov chain (MC). Actually, it is more expressible than MC, since an SVMC would be an MC when $\mathcal{H}$ is 1-dimensional.

To further show the expressiveness of SVMCs, we present some examples, which cover quantum programs with simple loops, recursive quantum programs, and quantum communication protocols.

> **Example 6.3** (Quantum Loop Programs) A simple quantum loop program reads as follows:
>
> $$l_0 : q := \mathcal{F}(q);$$
> $$l_1 : \textbf{while } M[q] \textbf{ do}$$
> $$l_2 : \qquad q := \mathcal{E}(q);$$
> $$l_3 : \textbf{end}$$
>
> where $M = 0 \cdot |0\rangle\langle 0| + 1 \cdot |1\rangle\langle 1|$. The intuitive meaning of this program is as follows. We first initialise at line l_0 the state of the quantum system q by a trace-preserving super-operator $\mathcal{F}$. At line l_1, the two-outcome projective measurement M is applied to q. If outcome 0 is observed, then the program terminates at line l_3; otherwise it proceeds to l_2 where a trace-preserving super-operator $\mathcal{E}$ is performed on q, and then the program returns to line l_1 and another iteration continues.
>
> We now construct an SVMC to describe the program. Let $\mathcal{H} = \text{span}\{|0\rangle, |1\rangle\}$, $S = \{l_i : 0 \leq i \leq 3\}$, and $\mathbf{Q}$ be defined as
>
> $$\mathbf{Q}(l_0, l_1) = \mathcal{F}, \quad \mathbf{Q}(l_1, l_3) = \mathcal{E}^0 = \{|0\rangle\langle 0|\}, \quad \mathbf{Q}(l_1, l_2) = \mathcal{E}^1 = \{|1\rangle\langle 1|\},$$
>
> $$\mathbf{Q}(l_2, l_1) = \mathcal{E}, \quad \mathbf{Q}(l_3, l_3) = \text{Id}.$$

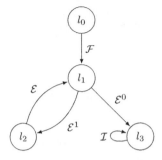

Figure 6.1 The SVMC for a quantum loop program.

Furthermore, let $AP = S$ and for each $s \in S$, $L(s) = \{s\}$. The SVMC is depicted in Figure 6.1.

Example 6.4 (Recursive Quantum Programs) Suppose Alice and Bob want to randomly choose a leader between them, by taking a qubit system q as the coin. The protocol of Alice goes as follows. She first measures the system q according to the observable

$$M_A = 0 \cdot |\psi\rangle\langle\psi| + 1 \cdot |\psi^{\perp}\rangle\langle\psi^{\perp}|,$$

where $\{|\psi\rangle, |\psi^{\perp}\rangle\}$ is an orthonormal basis of $\mathcal{H}_q$. If the outcome 0 is observed, then she is the winner. Otherwise, she gives the qubit q to Bob and lets him decide. Bob's protocol goes similarly, except that his measurement is

$$M_B = 0 \cdot |\varphi\rangle\langle\varphi| + 1 \cdot |\varphi^{\perp}\rangle\langle\varphi^{\perp}|$$

for another orthonormal basis $\{|\varphi\rangle, |\varphi^{\perp}\rangle\}$ of $\mathcal{H}_q$ so that $|\langle\psi|\varphi\rangle| \notin \{0, 1\}$.

We can describe such a protocol as the following quantum program with procedure calls.

Global variables *winner* : string, q : **qubit**	
Program Alice	**Program** Bob
switch $M_A[q]$ **do**	**switch** $M_B[q]$ **do**
case 0 :	**case** 0 :
winner := 'A';	*winner* := 'B';
case 1 :	**case** 1 :
Call Bob;	Call Alice;
end	**end**

The semantics of this program can be described by an SVMC depicted in Figure 6.2, where the transition super-operator matrix $\mathbf{Q}$ is given by

$$\mathbf{Q}[s_a, t_a] = \{|\psi\rangle\langle\psi|\}, \quad \mathbf{Q}[s_a, s_b] = \{|\psi^{\perp}\rangle\langle\psi^{\perp}|\},$$
$$\mathbf{Q}[s_b, t_b] = \{|\varphi\rangle\langle\varphi|\}, \quad \mathbf{Q}[s_b, s_a] = \{|\varphi^{\perp}\rangle\langle\varphi^{\perp}|\}.$$

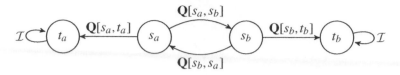

Figure 6.2 The SVMC for a leader election protocol.

Intuitively, the state s_a (resp. s_b) corresponds to the position in the program where Alice (reps. Bob) is about to perform the measurement M_A (resp. M_B), while the state t_a (resp. t_b) corresponds to Alice (resp. Bob) being selected as the winner.

It is easy to validate

$$\mathbf{Q}[s_a,t_a] + \mathbf{Q}[s_a,s_b] \approx \mathcal{I} \quad \text{and} \quad \mathbf{Q}[s_b,s_a] + \mathbf{Q}[s_b,t_b] \approx \mathcal{I},$$

which ensure the normalisation condition of $\mathbf{Q}$.

Example 6.5 (Quantum Key-Distribution Protocol) BB84, the first quantum key distribution protocol developed by Bennett and Brassard in 1984 [15], provides a provably secure way to create a private key between two parties, say, Alice and Bob. The basic BB84 protocol goes as follows:

(i) Alice randomly creates two strings of bits $\tilde{B}_a$ and $\tilde{K}_a$, each with size n.
(ii) Alice prepares a string of qubits $\tilde{q}$, with size n, such that the ith qubit of $\tilde{q}$ is $|x_y\rangle$ where x and y are the ith bits of $\tilde{B}_a$ and $\tilde{K}_a$, respectively, and $|0_0\rangle = |0\rangle$, $|0_1\rangle = |1\rangle$, $|1_0\rangle = |+\rangle = (|0\rangle + |1\rangle)/\sqrt{2}$, and $|1_1\rangle = |-\rangle = (|0\rangle - |1\rangle)/\sqrt{2}$.
(iii) Alice sends the qubit string $\tilde{q}$ to Bob.
(iv) Bob randomly generates a string of bits $\tilde{B}_b$ with size n.
(v) Bob measures each qubit received from Alice according to the basis determined by the bits he generated: if the ith bit of $\tilde{B}_b$ is k then he measures the ith qubit of $\tilde{q}$ with $\{|k_0\rangle, |k_1\rangle\}$, $k = 0, 1$. Let the measurement results be $\tilde{K}_b$, which is also a string of bits with size n.
(vi) Bob sends his choice of measurement bases $\tilde{B}_b$ back to Alice, and upon receiving the information, Alice sends her bases $\tilde{B}_a$ to Bob.
(vii) Alice and Bob determine at which positions the bit strings $\tilde{B}_a$ and $\tilde{B}_b$ are equal. They discard the bits in $\tilde{K}_a$ and $\tilde{K}_b$ where the corresponding bits of $\tilde{B}_a$ and $\tilde{B}_b$ do not match.

After the execution of the basic BB84 protocol, the remaining bits of $\tilde{K}_a$ and $\tilde{K}_b$ should be the same, provided that the communication channels used are perfect, and no eavesdropper exists.

The SVMC for the basic BB84 protocol in the simplest case of $n = 1$ is depicted in Figure 6.3, where $Set^{|\psi\rangle}$ is the 1-qubit super-operator which sets the target qubit to $|\psi\rangle$, $\mathcal{X} = \{X\}$ and $\mathcal{Z} = \{Z\}$ are respectively the Pauli-X and Pauli-Z super-operators, and $\mathcal{E}^i = \{|i\rangle\langle i|\}$, $i = 0, 1, +, -$. We use the subscripts for the s-states to denote the choices of the basis B_a of Alice, the key K_a generated by Alice, and the basis

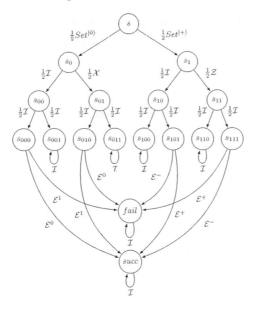

Figure 6.3 The SVMC for the basic BB84 protocol when $n = 1$.

B_b guessed by Bob. For example, in s_0, $B_a = 0$; in s_{01}, $B_a = 0$ and $K_a = 1$; and in s_{101}, $B_a = B_b = 1$ and $K_a = 0$. Let $AP = S \cup \{abort\}$ and $L(s) = \{abort\}$ if $s \in \{s_{001}, s_{011}, s_{100}, s_{110}\}$, meaning that at these states Alice and Bob's bases differ, so the protocol will be aborted without generating any key. For other states s, we let $L(s) = \{s\}$ naturally.

We use the states *succ* and *fail* to denote the successful and unsuccessful termination of BB84 protocol, respectively. We take the state s_{101} as an example to illustrate the basic idea. As the bases of Alice and Bob are both $\{|+\rangle, |-\rangle\}$ at s_{101}, they will regard the key bit as the final key generated by the protocol. Thus if the outcome of Bob's measurement is 0, which corresponds to the super-operator $\mathcal{E}^+$, then the protocol succeeds since Alice and Bob indeed share the same key bit 0; otherwise the protocol fails as they end up with different bits: Alice with 0 while Bob with 1. That explains why we have $\mathbf{Q}[s_{101}, succ] = \mathcal{E}^+$ while $\mathbf{Q}[s_{101}, fail] = \mathcal{E}^-$.

6.2 Positive Operator–Valued Measures on SVMCs

A prerequisite for defining probabilistic temporal logics for a classical MC is a suitable probability measure on the set of infinite paths. Such a measure was introduced by Vardi [109] by first defining the probabilities corresponding to cylinder sets of finite paths. The probability measure is then extended to the σ-algebra generated by these cylinder sets, by using the Carathéodory–Hahn extension theorem.

The aim of this section is to define a proper positive operator–valued measure for SVMCs, constructed similarly to Vardi's probability measure. For a better understanding, we suggest the reader to review Subsection 2.4.2 before reading this section.

Definition of Positive Operator–Valued Measures.   Let

$$\mathcal{P}(\mathcal{H}) = \{M \in \mathcal{L}(\mathcal{H}) : 0 \sqsubseteq M \sqsubseteq I\},$$

where I and 0 are the identity and zero operators on $\mathcal{H}$, respectively, be the quantum analogy of the unit interval $[0,1]$ in probability measures. Here the Löwner partial order between linear operators is defined by letting $M \sqsubseteq N$ if and only if $N - M$ is positive. Let $\mathcal{P}(\mathcal{H})^n$ be the set of n-size row vectors over $\mathcal{P}(\mathcal{H})$, and extend the Löwner order $\sqsubseteq$ componentwise to it. Then we have

> **Lemma 6.6** *The set* $(\mathcal{P}(\mathcal{H})^n, \sqsubseteq)$ *is a complete partial order set with the least element* $(0, \dots, 0)$.

> **Exercise 6.2** Prove Lemma 6.6.

The notion of positive operator–valued measure is a straightforward generalisation of probability measure where a real number value of probability is replaced by a positive operator representing a quantum effect.

> **Definition 6.7 (Positive Operator–Valued Measure)** Let (Ω, Σ) be a measurable space; that is, Ω is a nonempty set and Σ a σ-algebra over Ω. A function $\Delta : \Sigma \to \mathcal{P}(\mathcal{H})$ is said to be a positive operator–valued measure (POVM) if Δ satisfies the following properties:
>
> (i) $\Delta(\Omega) = I$, and
> (ii) $\Delta\left(\biguplus_i A_i\right) = \sum_i \Delta(A_i)$ for any pairwise disjoint and countable sequence A_1, $A_2, \dots$ in Σ.
>
> We call the triple (Ω, Σ, Δ) a (positive operator–valued) measure space.

In physics literatures, POVMs are widely used to provide a mathematical description for quantum measurements, and in most cases, the sample space Ω (the set of measurement outcomes) is assumed to be discrete, or even finite. POVMs enjoy some similar properties satisfied by probabilistic measures, which are collected in Lemma 6.8.

> **Lemma 6.8** *Let* (Ω, Σ, Δ) *be a measure space. Then*
>
> (i) $\Delta(\emptyset) = 0$.
> (ii) $\Delta(A^c) + \Delta(A) = I$ *where* A^c *is the complement set of* A *in* Ω.

(iii) *(Monotonicity) for any $A, A' \in \Sigma$, if $A \subseteq A'$ then $\Delta(A) \sqsubseteq \Delta(A')$.*
(iv) *(Continuity) for any sequence $A_1, A_2, \ldots$ in Σ,*

- If $A_1 \subseteq A_2 \subseteq \ldots$, then $\Delta(A_1) \sqsubseteq \Delta(A_2) \sqsubseteq \ldots$, and

$$\Delta \left(\bigcup_{i \geq 1} A_i \right) = \lim_{i \to \infty} \Delta(A_i);$$

- If $A_1 \supseteq A_2 \supseteq \ldots$, then $\Delta(A_1) \sqsupseteq \Delta(A_2) \sqsupseteq \ldots$, and

$$\Delta \left(\bigcap_{i \geq 1} A_i \right) = \lim_{i \to \infty} \Delta(A_i).$$

Proof We only prove the first item of (iv), and other conclusions are left to the reader as an exercise. Suppose $A_1 \subseteq A_2 \subseteq \ldots$. Let

$$B_n = A_n \setminus \bigcup_{i < n} A_i$$

for $n = 1, 2, \ldots$. Then each pair B_i and B_j are disjoint provided that $i \neq j$, and for each n, $A_n = \biguplus_{i \leq n} B_i$. Thus,

$$\Delta(A_n) = \sum_{i \leq n} \Delta(B_i)$$

by the additivity of Δ. Finally,

$$\Delta \left(\bigcup_{i \geq 1} A_i \right) = \Delta \left(\biguplus_{i \geq 1} B_i \right) = \sum_{i \geq 1} \Delta(B_i) = \lim_{n \to \infty} \Delta(A_n).$$

Here the existence of the limit is guaranteed by Lemma 6.6. □

Positive Operator–Valued Measures Determined by SVMCs. We now consider how to construct a POVM from an SVMC that is appropriate for quantitatively reasoning about its behaviour. Let $\mathcal{M} = (S, \mathbf{Q}, L)$ be an SVMC. Similar to the cases of transition systems (see Section 2.1) and classical Markov chains (see Subsection 2.4.2), we can define

- A path $\pi = s_0 s_1 \ldots$ of $\mathcal{M}$ is an infinite sequence of states in S.
- A finite path $\widehat{\pi}$ is a finite-length prefix of a path; and its length, denoted $|\widehat{\pi}|$, is defined to be the number of states in it.

- We denote by $\pi(i)$ the ith state of a path π, and $\widehat{\pi}(i)$ the ith state of a finite path $\widehat{\pi}$ if $i < |\widehat{\pi}|$.

Note that we index the states in a path or finite path from 0. The sets of all infinite and finite paths of $\mathcal{M}$ starting in state s are denoted $\text{Path}^{\mathcal{M}}(s)$ and $\text{Path}^{\mathcal{M}}_{fin}(s)$, respectively.

For each $s \in S$ we construct a POVM $\Delta_s^{\mathcal{M}}$ as follows. As the first step, for any finite path $\widehat{\pi} = s_0 \ldots s_n \in \text{Path}^{\mathcal{M}}_{fin}(s)$, we define

$$m_s(\widehat{\pi}) = \begin{cases} I, & \text{if } n = 0; \\ \mathbf{Q}[s_0, s_1]^\dagger \circ \cdots \circ \mathbf{Q}[s_{n-1}, s_n]^\dagger(I), & \text{otherwise,} \end{cases}$$

where $\mathbf{Q}[s, t]^\dagger$ denotes the adjoint of $\mathbf{Q}[s, t]$. Next, for each $\widehat{\pi} \in \text{Path}^{\mathcal{M}}_{fin}(s)$ we define the cylinder set $Cyl(\widehat{\pi}) \subseteq \text{Path}^{\mathcal{M}}(s)$ as

$$Cyl(\widehat{\pi}) = \{\pi \in \text{Path}^{\mathcal{M}}(s) : \widehat{\pi} \text{ is a prefix of } \pi\};$$

that is, the set of all infinite paths from s with $\widehat{\pi}$ as a prefix. Let

$$\mathfrak{S}^{\mathcal{M}}(s) = \{Cyl(\widehat{\pi}) : \widehat{\pi} \in \text{Path}^{\mathcal{M}}_{fin}(s)\} \cup \{\emptyset\}$$

and $\Delta_s^{\mathcal{M}}$ be a mapping from $\mathfrak{S}^{\mathcal{M}}(s)$ to $\mathcal{P}(\mathcal{H})$ defined by letting $\Delta_s^{\mathcal{M}}(\emptyset) = 0$ and

$$\Delta_s^{\mathcal{M}}(Cyl(\widehat{\pi})) = m_s(\widehat{\pi}). \tag{6.1}$$

The reader should have noticed that the preceding construction is very similar to that given in Subsection 2.4.2. The only difference is that real numbers used there are replaced by positive operators here.

Example 6.9 Let us revisit the SVMC presented in Example 6.4. For the finite paths $s_a t_a$ and $s_a s_b s_a t_a$, their corresponding operators under $\Delta_{s_a}^{\mathcal{M}}$ are

$$\Delta_{s_a}^{\mathcal{M}}(Cyl(s_a t_a)) = \mathbf{Q}[s_a, t_a]^\dagger(I) = |\psi\rangle\langle\psi|$$
$$\Delta_{s_a}^{\mathcal{M}}(Cyl(s_a s_b s_a t_a)) = \mathbf{Q}[s_a, s_b]^\dagger \circ \mathbf{Q}[s_b, s_a]^\dagger \circ \mathbf{Q}[s_a, t_a]^\dagger(I)$$
$$= \mathbf{Q}[s_a, s_b]^\dagger \circ \mathbf{Q}[s_b, s_a]^\dagger(|\psi\rangle\langle\psi|)$$
$$= |\langle\psi|\varphi^\perp\rangle|^2 \cdot \mathbf{Q}[s_a, s_b]^\dagger(|\varphi^\perp\rangle\langle\varphi^\perp|)$$
$$= |\langle\psi|\varphi^\perp\rangle|^2 \cdot |\langle\psi^\perp|\varphi^\perp\rangle|^2 \cdot |\psi^\perp\rangle\langle\psi^\perp|.$$

Our second step is to extend the mapping $\Delta_s^{\mathcal{M}}$ defined earlier to a POVM on the σ-algebra of infinite paths generated by cylinder extensions of finite paths. This can be done by a procedure similar to Vardi's work for classical MCs [109] (see also Subsection 2.4.2). More precisely, we have:

Theorem 6.10 *(Extension Theorem) The mapping* $\Delta_s^{\mathcal{M}}$ *defined in Eq. (6.1) can be uniquely extended to a POVM, denoted also by* $\Delta_s^{\mathcal{M}}$, *on the σ-algebra generated by* $\mathfrak{S}^{\mathcal{M}}(s)$.

Proof of Extension Theorem. The remaining part of this section is devoted to a proof of Theorem 6.10. This proof is quite involved; for the first reading, the reader can skip it and directly move to the next section.

To prove Theorem 6.10, we need some definitions and results from vector measures [40]. Let Ω be a non-empty set. A semi-algebra $\mathfrak{S}$ on Ω is a subset of the power set 2^{Ω} with the following properties:

(i) $\emptyset \in \mathfrak{S}$;
(ii) $A, B \in \mathfrak{S}$ implies $A \cap B \in \mathfrak{S}$;
(iii) $A, B \in \mathfrak{S}$ implies that $A \backslash B = \biguplus_{i=1}^{n} A_i$ for some disjoint $A_1, \dots, A_n \in \mathfrak{S}$.

An algebra is a semi-algebra which is further closed under union and subtraction; a σ-algebra is an algebra which is also closed under complement and countable union. Given a semi-algebra $\mathfrak{S}$, we denote by $\mathcal{R}(\mathfrak{S})$ (resp. $\sigma(\mathfrak{S})$) the algebra (resp. σ-algebra) generated by $\mathfrak{S}$; that is, the intersection of all algebras (resp. σ-algebras) which contain $\mathfrak{S}$ as a subset. Obviously, $\sigma(\mathfrak{S}) = \sigma(\mathcal{R}(\mathfrak{S}))$.

Recall also that a Banach space is a complete normed vector space.

Definition 6.11 Let $T \subseteq 2^{\Omega}$, and δ a function from T to a Banach space $\mathcal{B}$. We call δ a countably additive vector measure, or vector measure for simplicity, if for any sequence $(A_i)_{i \geq 1}$ of pairwise disjoint members of T such that $\biguplus_{i \geq 1} A_i \in T$, it holds that

$$\delta \left(\biguplus_{i \geq 1} A_i \right) = \sum_{i \geq 1} \delta(A_i).$$

Definition 6.12 Let $\mathcal{R}$ be an algebra on Ω and $\delta : \mathcal{R} \to \mathcal{B}$ a vector measure. Let μ be a finite non-negative real-valued measure on $\mathcal{R}$. Then δ is said to be μ-continuous if for any sequence $(A_i)_{i \geq 1}$ in $\mathcal{R}$,

$$\lim_i \mu(A_i) = 0 \text{ implies } \lim_i \delta(A_i) = 0.$$

The main tool used for proving a similar extension theorem in the case of classical MCs is the Carathéodory–Hahn extension theorem. But here we need its generalisation proved by Kluvanek in vector measure theory.

Theorem 6.13 (Carathéodory–Hahn–Kluvanek Extension Theorem) *Let $\mathcal{R}$ be an algebra on Ω and $\delta : \mathcal{R} \to \mathcal{B}$ a bounded vector measure. If there exists a finite and non-negative real-valued measure μ on $\mathcal{R}$ such that δ is μ-continuous, then*

δ can be uniquely extended to a vector measure $\delta' : \sigma(\mathcal{R}) \to \mathcal{B}$ on the σ-algebra generated by $\mathcal{R}$ such that

$$\delta'(A) = \delta(A) \text{ for all } A \in \mathcal{R}.$$

We are now ready to prove Theorem 6.10. To do this, we first note that the set $\text{Herm}(\mathcal{H})$ of Hermitian operators on $\mathcal{H}$ is a Banach space, and $\mathfrak{S}^{\mathcal{M}}(s)$ is a semi-algebra on $\text{Path}^{\mathcal{M}}(s)$. Then we have the following lemma.

Lemma 6.14 *The mapping* $\Delta_s^{\mathcal{M}}$ *defined in Eq. (6.1), regarded as a mapping from* $\mathfrak{S}^{\mathcal{M}}(s)$ *to* $\text{Herm}(\mathcal{H})$, *is a bounded vector measure.*

Proof We only need to check that $\Delta_s^{\mathcal{M}}$ is countably additive. Let $\emptyset \neq A = \biguplus_{i \geq 1} A_i$ for a disjoint sequence $(A_i)_{i \geq 1}$ in $\mathfrak{S}^{\mathcal{M}}(s)$ and $A \in \mathfrak{S}^{\mathcal{M}}(s)$. We need to show

$$\Delta_s^{\mathcal{M}}(A) = \sum_{i \geq 1} \Delta_s^{\mathcal{M}}(A_i). \tag{6.2}$$

We claim that there are only finitely many nonempty sets in the sequence $(A_i)_{i \geq 1}$. We prove this claim by contradiction. Suppose $A = Cyl(\widehat{\pi}_0)$, and for each $i \geq 1$, $A_i = Cyl(\widehat{\pi}_i)$ whenever $A_i \neq \emptyset$ where $\widehat{\pi}_i \in \text{Path}_{fin}^{\mathcal{M}}(s)$, and $\widehat{\pi}_0$ is a prefix of each $\widehat{\pi}_i$ for $i \geq 1$. By the fact that A_is are disjoint, $\widehat{\pi}_i$ cannot be a prefix of $\widehat{\pi}_j$ for distinct $i, j \geq 1$. Let $\Pi = \{\widehat{\pi}_i : i \geq 1, A_i \neq \emptyset\}$. For any $\widehat{\pi} \in \text{Path}_{fin}^{\mathcal{M}}(s)$, let

$$Ind_{\widehat{\pi}} = \{i \geq 1 : A_i \neq \emptyset, Cyl(\widehat{\pi}) \supseteq A_i\}, \text{ and}$$

$$K = \{\widehat{\pi} \in \text{Path}_{fin}^{\mathcal{M}}(s) : Ind_{\widehat{\pi}} \text{ is infinite}\}.$$

Obviously, $K \cap \Pi = \emptyset$. Note that $\widehat{\pi}_0 \in K$, and for any $\widehat{\pi} \in K$, since

$$Ind_{\widehat{\pi}} = \biguplus_{t \in S} Ind_{\widehat{\pi}t},$$

there exists $t_{\widehat{\pi}} \in S$ such that $\widehat{\pi} t_{\widehat{\pi}} \in K$. Thus we can extend $\widehat{\pi}_0$ to an infinite path $\pi \in \text{Path}^{\mathcal{M}}(s)$ such that any finite-length prefix $\widehat{\pi}$ of π with $|\widehat{\pi}| \geq |\widehat{\pi}_0|$ is not included in Π. Then for any i, $\pi \notin A_i$, contradicting the fact that $\pi \in A$.

With the claim, we can assume without loss of generality that $A_i \neq \emptyset$ if and only if $i \leq n$ for some n. Let $N = \max\{|\widehat{\pi}_i| : 1 \leq i \leq n\}$ and $\Pi_N = \{\widehat{\pi} \in \Pi : |\widehat{\pi}| = N\}$. Obviously, we can partition Π_N into several disjoint subsets such that each one contains exactly $|S|$ elements with the same $N - 1$-length prefix; that is, there exists a set $\{\widehat{\pi}_1', \dots, \widehat{\pi}_{I_N}'\}$ such that for each $1 \leq i \leq I_N$, $|\widehat{\pi}_i'| = N - 1$, and

$$\Pi_N = \biguplus_{i=1}^{I_N} \Pi_N^i, \text{ where } \Pi_N^i = \{\widehat{\pi}_i' t : t \in S\}.$$

We delete Π_N from Π and add $\widehat{\pi}'_i$, $1 \leq i \leq I_N$, into it. Denote by $\Pi_{\leq N-1}$ the resultant set. Then each element in $\Pi_{\leq N-1}$ has length less than N, and it is easy to check that

$$\sum_{\widehat{\pi} \in \Pi_N} m_s(\widehat{\pi}) = \sum_{i=1}^{I_N} m_s(\widehat{\pi}'_i), \text{ thus } \sum_{\widehat{\pi} \in \Pi} m_s(\widehat{\pi}) = \sum_{\widehat{\pi} \in \Pi_{\leq N-1}} m_s(\widehat{\pi}).$$

Proceeding in this way, we can construct a sequence of sets $\Pi_{\leq i}, |\widehat{\pi}_0| < i \leq N$, such that for any i,

$$\sum_{\widehat{\pi} \in \Pi_{\leq i}} m_s(\widehat{\pi}) = \sum_{\widehat{\pi} \in \Pi_{\leq i-1}} m_s(\widehat{\pi}),$$

where $\Pi_{\leq N} = \Pi$. Note that $\Pi_{\leq |\widehat{\pi}_0|} = \{\widehat{\pi}_0\}$. We finally have

$$\sum_{i \geq 1} \Delta_s^{\mathcal{M}}(A_i) = \sum_{\widehat{\pi} \in \Pi} m_s(\widehat{\pi}) = m_s(\widehat{\pi}_0) = \Delta_s^{\mathcal{M}}(A).$$

That completes the proof of the lemma. $\qquad\qquad\square$

Proof of Theorem 6.10 Let $\mathcal{R} = \mathcal{R}(\mathfrak{S}^{\mathcal{M}}(s))$ be the algebra generated by $\mathfrak{S}^{\mathcal{M}}(s)$. Obviously, we have

$$\mathcal{R} = \left\{ A : A = \biguplus_{i=1}^{n} A_i \text{ for some } n \geq 0, A_i \in \mathfrak{S}^{\mathcal{M}}(s) \right\}.$$

We extend the mapping $\Delta_s^{\mathcal{M}}$ to $\mathcal{R}$ by defining

$$\Delta_s^{\mathcal{M}} \left(\biguplus_{i=1}^{n} A_i \right) = \sum_{i=1}^{n} \Delta_s^{\mathcal{M}}(A_i),$$

which turns out to be a bounded vector measure from $\mathcal{R}$ to $\mathrm{Herm}(\mathcal{H})$. Let μ_s be a mapping defined as follows:

- $\mu_s(\emptyset) = 0$, and for any $A = Cyl(\widehat{\pi}) \in \mathfrak{S}^{\mathcal{M}}(s)$,

$$\mu_s(A) = \mathrm{tr}(m_s(\widehat{\pi}) \cdot \rho),$$

  where $\rho = I/(\dim \mathcal{H})$ is the maximally mixed state in $\mathcal{D}(\mathcal{H})$;
- For any disjoint sets $A_1, \ldots, A_n$ in $\mathfrak{S}^{\mathcal{M}}(s)$,

$$\mu_s \left(\biguplus_{i=1}^{n} A_i \right) = \sum_{i=1}^{n} \mu_s(A_i).$$

Then μ_s is indeed a finite and non-negative real-valued measure on $\mathcal{R}$, since

$$\mu_s(\text{Path}^{\mathcal{M}}(s)) = \mu_s(Cyl(s)) = \text{tr}(I \cdot \rho) = 1.$$

Note that if $\lim_{i \to \infty} \text{tr}(M_i \cdot \rho) = 0$, where $(M_i)_{i \geq 1}$ is a sequence of positive operators, then $\lim_{i \to \infty} M_i = 0$, which means that $\Delta_s^{\mathcal{M}}$ is μ_s-continuous.

Now using Theorem 6.13, we can extend $\Delta_s^{\mathcal{M}}$ uniquely to a vector measure $\Delta_s^{\mathcal{M}} : \sigma(\mathfrak{S}^{\mathcal{M}}(s)) \to \text{Herm}(\mathcal{H})$. In the following, we show that the extended measure actually has values in $\mathcal{P}(\mathcal{H})$. By the additivity of $\Delta_s^{\mathcal{M}}$, it suffices to show $0 \sqsubseteq \Delta_s^{\mathcal{M}}(A)$ for all $A \in \sigma(\mathfrak{S}^{\mathcal{M}}(s))$; that is, for any $\rho \in \mathcal{D}(\mathcal{H})$, $\text{tr}(\Delta_s^{\mathcal{M}}(A) \cdot \rho) \geq 0$. Let $\mu_\rho : \sigma(\mathfrak{S}^{\mathcal{M}}(s)) \to \mathbb{R}$ be defined as

$$\forall A \in \sigma(\mathfrak{S}^{\mathcal{M}}(s)) : \mu_\rho(A) = \text{tr}(\Delta_s^{\mathcal{M}}(A) \cdot \rho).$$

Then obviously, μ_ρ is a real-valued measure over $\sigma(\mathfrak{S}^{\mathcal{M}}(s))$ and its restriction on $\mathfrak{S}^{\mathcal{M}}(s)$, denoted $\mu_\rho|_{\mathfrak{S}^{\mathcal{M}}(s)}$, is a probabilistic measure. Now from Carathéodory Theorem for probabilistic measures, $\mu_\rho|_{\mathfrak{S}^{\mathcal{M}}(s)}$ can be uniquely extended to a probabilistic measure μ_ρ' over $\sigma(\mathfrak{S}^{\mathcal{M}}(s))$. Then we have

$$\text{tr}(\Delta_s^{\mathcal{M}}(A) \cdot \rho) = \mu_\rho(A) = \mu_\rho'(A) \geq 0$$

by the uniqueness of such extension.   □

Relationship Between POVM and Vardi's Probability Measure. As we saw in Section 2.4, probabilistic model checking computes the *probability* of a given property; it requires a concrete initial distribution attached to the model. In contrast, in this chapter we compute a *positive operator* (POVM value) corresponding to the property that is independent of initial quantum states. A natural question then arises: What is the relationship between these two approaches?

In this section, we answer this question by showing that the POVM defined in the previous section for a given SVMC $\mathcal{M}$, when applied on an initial quantum state ρ, gives exactly Vardi's probability measure defined for a corresponding classical MC obtained by equipping $\mathcal{M}$ with ρ in a natural way.

Given an SVMC $\mathcal{M} = (S, \mathbf{Q}, L)$, a classical state $s \in S$, and a quantum state $\rho \in \mathcal{D}(\mathcal{H})$, we can construct a (countably infinite state) Markov chain $\mathcal{M}_{s,\rho} = (\overline{S}, P)$ where $\overline{S} \subseteq S \times (\mathcal{D}(\mathcal{H}) \cup \{0\})$ and $P : \overline{S} \times \overline{S} \to [0, 1]$ are defined as follows:

(i) $\langle s, \rho \rangle \in \overline{S}$.
(ii) If $\langle r, \sigma \rangle \in \overline{S}$ then $\langle t, \tau \rangle \in \overline{S}$ for all $t \in S$, where

$$\tau = \frac{\mathbf{Q}[r, t](\sigma)}{\text{tr}(\mathbf{Q}[r, t](\sigma))}$$

and

$$P(\langle r, \sigma \rangle, \langle t, \tau \rangle) = \mathrm{tr}(\mathbf{Q}[r, t](\sigma)).$$

In this chapter, with a slight abuse of notation, we let $\frac{\tau}{\mathrm{tr}(\tau)} = 0$ whenever $\mathrm{tr}(\tau) = 0$.

(iii) $\overline{S}$ is the smallest set satisfying (i) and (ii), and for all $\langle r, 0 \rangle \in \overline{S}$, $P(\langle r, 0 \rangle, \langle r, 0 \rangle) = 1$.

Now for any $\pi = s_0 s_1 \ldots \subset S^\omega$ with $s_0 = s$, it is easy to see that the path $\pi_\rho = \langle s_0, \rho_0 \rangle \langle s_1, \rho_1 \rangle \cdots \in \overline{S}^\omega$ where $\rho_0 = \rho$, and for all $i \geq 1$,

$$\rho_i = \frac{\mathbf{Q}[s_{i-1}, s_i](\rho_{i-1})}{\mathrm{tr}(\mathbf{Q}[s_{i-1}, s_i](\rho_{i-1}))}.$$

Conversely, any π_ρ in $\overline{S}^\omega$ determines a unique path π in S^ω by omitting the quantum state part. For any $A \subseteq S^\omega$, let

$$A_\rho = \{\pi_\rho \in \overline{S}^\omega : \pi \in A\}.$$

Then $A \in \sigma(\mathfrak{S}^\mathcal{M}(s))$ if and only if $A_\rho \in \sigma(\mathfrak{S}^{\mathcal{M}_{s,\rho}}(\langle s, \rho \rangle))$.

Theorem 6.15 *For any SVMC $\mathcal{M} = (S, \mathbf{Q}, L)$, $s \in S$, and $\rho \in \mathcal{D}(\mathcal{H})$, $\mathcal{M}_{s,\rho}$ defined above is indeed a Markov chain. Furthermore, for any measurable set $A \in \sigma(\mathfrak{S}^\mathcal{M}(s))$,*

$$\mathrm{tr}(\Delta_s^\mathcal{M}(A) \cdot \rho) = \mathbf{P}^{\mathcal{M}_{s,\rho}}(A_\rho), \tag{6.3}$$

where $\mathbf{P}^{\mathcal{M}_{s,\rho}}$ is Vardi's probability measure defined on $\mathcal{M}_{s,\rho}$.

Proof For any $\langle r, \sigma \rangle \in \overline{S}$ with $\sigma \neq 0$, we calculate

$$\sum_{\langle t, \tau \rangle \in \overline{S}} P(\langle r, \sigma \rangle, \langle t, \tau \rangle) = \sum_{t \in S} \mathrm{tr}(\mathbf{Q}[r, t](\sigma))$$

$$= \mathrm{tr}\left(\left[\sum_{t \in S} \mathbf{Q}[r, t]\right](\sigma)\right)$$

$$= \mathrm{tr}(\sigma) = 1,$$

which guarantees that $\mathcal{M}_{s,\rho}$ is an MC.

To prove Eq. (6.3), it suffices to show it for cylinder sets in $\mathfrak{S}^\mathcal{M}(s)$. For any finite path $\widehat{\pi} = s_0 \ldots s_n \in \mathrm{Path}_{fin}^\mathcal{M}(s)$, let $\widehat{\pi}_\rho = \langle s_0, \rho_0 \rangle \cdots \langle s_n, \rho_n \rangle$ be defined similarly to π_ρ above. It is easy to show by mutual induction on $i \leq n$ that

$$\rho_i = \frac{(\mathbf{Q}[s_{i-1}, s_i] \circ \cdots \circ \mathbf{Q}[s_0, s_1](\rho)}{\mathrm{tr}((\mathbf{Q}[s_{i-1}, s_i] \circ \cdots \circ \mathbf{Q}[s_0, s_1](\rho))}. \tag{6.4}$$

and

$$\mathbf{P}^{\mathcal{M}_{s,\rho}}(Cyl(\widehat{\pi}_\rho^i)) = \mathrm{tr}\,(\mathbf{Q}[s_{i-1}, s_i] \circ \cdots \circ \mathbf{Q}[s_0, s_1](\rho)) \tag{6.5}$$

where $\widehat{\pi}_\rho^i = \langle s_0, \rho_0 \rangle \cdots \langle s_i, \rho_i \rangle$ is the $i + 1$th prefix of $\widehat{\pi}_\rho$. Then

$$\begin{aligned}
\mathrm{tr}(\Delta_s^{\mathcal{M}}(Cyl(\widehat{\pi})) \cdot \rho) &= \mathrm{tr}\,\left(\mathbf{Q}[s_0, s_1]^\dagger \circ \cdots \circ \mathbf{Q}[s_{n-1}, s_n]^\dagger(I) \cdot \rho\right) \\
&= \mathrm{tr}\,(\mathbf{Q}[s_{n-1}, s_n] \circ \cdots \circ \mathbf{Q}[s_0, s_1](\rho)) \\
&= \mathbf{P}^{\mathcal{M}_{s,\rho}}(Cyl(\widehat{\pi}_\rho)).
\end{aligned}$$

That completes the proof of the theorem. $\qquad\qquad\qquad\qquad\qquad\qquad\square$

6.3 Positive Operator–Valued Temporal Logic

In this section, we define the quantum extensions of probabilistic temporal logics for description of the dynamic properties of quantum systems modelled as SVMCs. In particular, we are interested in two popular logics, namely computation tree logic (CTL) and linear temporal logic (LTL), which are respectively the topics of the following two subsections.

The reader should briefly review Section 2.2 and Subsection 2.4.2 in order to better understand this section.

6.3.1 *Quantum Computation Tree Logic*

We first introduce a quantum extension of the probabilistic computation tree logic (PCTL) [65], which in turn is an extension of the classical computation tree logic CTL [43].

> **Definition 6.16** The syntax of quantum computation tree logic (QCTL) is as follows:
>
> $$\Phi ::= a \mid \neg\Phi \mid \Phi \wedge \Phi \mid \mathbb{Q}_{\sim M}[\phi]$$
> $$\phi ::= \mathbf{X}\Phi \mid \Phi\mathbf{U}\Phi,$$
>
> where $a \in AP$ is an atomic proposition, $\sim \in \{\sqsubseteq, \sqsupseteq, =\}$, and $M \in \mathcal{P}(\mathcal{H})$. We call Φ a *state formula* and ϕ a *path formula*.

As can be seen from the definition, our logic is very similar to PCTL; the only difference is that the formula $\mathbb{P}_{\sim p}[\phi]$ in PCTL, which asserts that the probability of paths from a certain state satisfying the path formula ϕ is constrained by $\sim p$ where $0 \le p \le 1$, is replaced in QCTL by $\mathbb{Q}_{\sim M}[\phi]$, which asserts that the POVM value corresponding to paths from a certain state satisfying the formula ϕ is constrained by $\sim M$ where $0 \sqsubseteq M \sqsubseteq I$. Note that $\mathbb{P}_{\sim p}[\phi]$ is a special case of $\mathbb{Q}_{\sim M}[\phi]$ by taking M as $p \cdot I$.

Definition 6.17 Let $\mathcal{M} = (S, \mathbf{Q}, L)$ be an SVMC. For any state $s \in S$, the satisfaction relation $\models$ is defined inductively by

$$
\begin{aligned}
s &\models a & \text{iff} && a &\in L(s); \\
s &\models \neg\Phi & \text{iff} && s &\not\models \Phi; \\
s &\models \Phi \wedge \Psi & \text{iff} && s &\models \Phi \text{ and } s \models \Psi; \\
s &\models \mathbb{Q}_{\sim M}[\phi] & \text{iff} && Q^{\mathcal{M}}(s, \phi) &\sim M,
\end{aligned}
$$

where

$$
Q^{\mathcal{M}}(s, \phi) = \Delta_s^{\mathcal{M}}(\{\pi \in \text{Path}^{\mathcal{M}}(s) \mid \pi \models \phi\}),
$$

and for any path $\pi \in \text{Path}^{\mathcal{M}}(s)$,

$$
\begin{aligned}
\pi &\models \mathbf{X}\Phi & \text{iff} && \pi(1) &\models \Phi \\
\pi &\models \Phi\mathbf{U}\Psi & \text{iff} && \exists i &\in \mathbb{N}.(\pi(i) \models \Psi \wedge \forall j < i.(\pi(j) \models \Phi)).
\end{aligned}
$$

Similar to PCTL, we can check that for each path formula ϕ and each state s in an SVMC $\mathcal{M}$, the set

$$
\{\pi \in \text{Path}^{\mathcal{M}}(s) \mid \pi \models \phi\}
$$

is in the σ-algebra generated by $\mathfrak{S}^{\mathcal{M}}(s)$. As usual, we introduce some syntactic sugars to simplify notations:

- the falsity $\texttt{ff} := a \wedge \neg a$, the tautology $\texttt{tt} := \neg\texttt{ff}$;
- the disjunction $\Psi_1 \vee \Psi_2 := \neg(\neg\Psi_1 \wedge \neg\Psi_2)$; and
- the *eventually* operator $\Diamond\Psi := \texttt{tt}\mathbf{U}\Psi$, and the *always* operator $\Box\Psi := \neg\Diamond\neg\Psi$.

Example 6.18 We revisit the examples in the previous section, to show the expressive power of QCTL.

(i) Example 6.3. The QCTL formula $\mathbb{Q}_{\supseteq M}[\Diamond l_3]$ asserts that the POVM value corresponding to the event that the loop program in Example 6.3 terminates is lower bounded by M. That is, for each i,

$$
l_i \models \mathbb{Q}_{\supseteq M}[\Diamond l_3]
$$

means that starting with any initial quantum state ρ and program line l_i, the termination probability is not less than $\text{tr}(M\rho)$. In particular, the property that it terminates everywhere can be described as $\mathbb{Q}_{=I}[\Diamond l_3]$.

(ii) Example 6.4. The QCTL formula $\mathbb{Q}_{\supseteq M}[\Diamond t_a]$ (resp. $\mathbb{Q}_{\supseteq M}[\Diamond t_b]$) asserts that the POVM value corresponding to that the leader election protocol terminates with Alice (resp. Bob) being the winner is lower bounded by M.

(iii) Example 6.5. The correctness of the basic BB84 protocol can be stated as

$$
s \models \mathbb{Q}_{=0}[\Diamond fail] \wedge \mathbb{Q}_{=\frac{1}{2}I}[\Diamond succ],
$$

meaning that the protocol never (with probability 0) fails, and with probability a half, it will successfully terminate at a shared key.

6.3.2 Linear Temporal Logic

We now turn to consider another kind of temporal logic; namely linear temporal logic (LTL). Its syntax has already been given in Chapter 2. We restate it here for easy reference:

$$\psi ::= a \mid \neg\psi \mid \psi_1 \wedge \psi_2 \mid \mathbf{X}\psi \mid \psi_1\mathbf{U}\psi_2,$$

where $a \in AP$.

Definition 6.19 For any infinite sequence $\pi \in (2^{AP})^\omega$, the satisfaction relation $\models$ is defined inductively by

$$\pi \models a \quad \text{iff} \quad a \in L(\pi(0));$$
$$\pi \models \neg\psi \quad \text{iff} \quad \pi \not\models \psi;$$
$$\pi \models \psi_1 \wedge \psi_2 \quad \text{iff} \quad \pi \models \psi_1 \text{ and } \pi \models \psi_2;$$
$$\pi \models \mathbf{X}\psi \quad \text{iff} \quad \pi|_1 \models \psi;$$
$$\pi \models \psi_1\mathbf{U}\psi_2 \quad \text{iff} \quad \exists i \in \mathbb{N}.(\pi|_i \models \psi_2 \wedge \forall j < i.(\pi|_j \models \psi_1)),$$

where $\pi|_i$ is the $i+1$th postfix of π; that is, $\pi|_i = A_i A_{i+1}\ldots$ whenever $\pi = A_0 A_1\ldots$.

Syntactic sugars such as ff, tt, disjunction, and the eventually and always operators are also defined for LTL formulas.

Example 6.20 The properties stated in Example 6.18 can also be expressed using LTL formulas. For example, in the leader election protocol, $\Diamond t_a$ represents the event that Alice is eventually elected as the winner.

6.4 Algorithms for Checking Super-Operator-Valued Markov Chains

This section is devoted to developing algorithms for model checking properties described by QCTL or LTL formulas against SVMCs.

6.4.1 Model Checking QCTL Formulas

Let us start from QCTL model checking. It would be helpful for the reader to review Section 2.3 and Subsection 2.4.3 because the algorithms presented in this and the next subsections are essentially generalisations of the algorithms presented there.

QCTL Model-Checking Problem. As in the classical case, given a state s in an SVMC $\mathcal{M} = (S, \mathbf{Q}, L)$ and a state formula Φ expressed in QCTL, model checking if s satisfies Φ is essentially determining whether s belongs to the satisfaction set $Sat(\Phi)$ which is defined inductively as follows:

$$Sat(a) = \{s \in S : a \in L(s)\},$$
$$Sat(\neg\Psi) = S\backslash Sat(\Psi),$$
$$Sat(\Psi \wedge \Phi) = Sat(\Psi) \cap Sat(\Phi),$$
$$Sat(\mathbb{Q}_{\sim A}[\phi]) = \{s \in S : \mathcal{Q}^{\mathcal{M}}(s,\phi) \sim A\}.$$

QCTL Model-Checking Algorithm.   The algorithm for checking most of the QCTL formulae are the same as in probabilistic model checking. The only difference is the case of $\mathbb{Q}_{\sim A}[\phi]$. In the following, we will elaborate how to employ the results presented in previous sections to calculate the satisfaction sets for such kind of formulae. To this end, we need to compute $\mathcal{Q}^{\mathcal{M}}(s,\phi)$ for the following two cases.

Case 1: $\phi = \mathbf{X}\Phi$. By Definition 6.17,

$$\{\pi \in \text{Path}^{\mathcal{M}}(s) : \pi \models \mathbf{X}\Phi\} = \biguplus_{t\in Sat(\Phi)} Cyl(st).$$

Thus

$$\mathcal{Q}^{\mathcal{M}}(s,\mathbf{X}\Phi) = \Delta_s^{\mathcal{M}}\left(\biguplus_{t\in Sat(\Phi)} Cyl(st)\right) = \sum_{t\in Sat(\Phi)} \Delta_s^{\mathcal{M}}(Cyl(st))$$
$$= \sum_{t\in Sat(\Phi)} \mathbf{Q}[s,t]^\dagger(I).$$

This can be calculated easily, since by the recursive nature of the definition, we can assume that $Sat(\Phi)$ is already known.

Case 2: $\phi = \Phi\mathbf{U}\Psi$. In this case, we define for any $s \in S$ and $k \geq 0$,

$$\Pi_s = \{\pi \in \text{Path}^{\mathcal{M}}(s) : \pi \models \Phi\mathbf{U}\Psi\},$$

$$\Pi_s^k = \{\pi \in \text{Path}^{\mathcal{M}}(s) : \exists i \leq k.(\pi(i) \models \Psi \wedge \forall j < i.(\pi(j) \models \Phi))\}.$$

Obviously, the sequence $(\Pi_s^k)_{k\geq 0}$ is non-decreasing with respect to $\subseteq$, and $\bigcup_{k\geq 0} \Pi_s^k = \Pi_s$. Thus from Lemma 6.8 (iv),

$$\Delta_s^{\mathcal{M}}(\Pi_s) = \lim_{k\to\infty} \Delta_s^{\mathcal{M}}(\Pi_s^k). \tag{6.6}$$

By induction on k, we can show that for each k and s, $\Pi_s^k = \emptyset$ or it is the disjoint union of some cylinder sets; specifically, we have

$$\Pi_s^k = \biguplus_{\widehat{\pi}\in A_s^k} Cyl(\widehat{\pi}),$$

where

$$
A_s^k = \begin{cases}
\{s\}, & \text{if } s \in Sat(\Psi); \\
\emptyset, & \text{if } (s \notin Sat(\Phi) \cup Sat(\Psi)) \vee (k = 0 \wedge s \notin Sat(\Psi)); \\
\biguplus_{t \in S} s A_t^{k-1}, & \text{if } (s \in Sat(\Phi) \backslash Sat(\Psi)) \wedge k \geq 1,
\end{cases}
$$

where $s A_t^{k-1}$ denotes the set of strings obtained by prepending s to strings in A_t^{k-1}. So in the first two cases, $\Delta_s^{\mathcal{M}}(\Pi_s^k) = I$ and 0 respectively, and if $s \in Sat(\Phi) \backslash Sat(\Psi)$ and $k \geq 1$, we have

$$
\Delta_s^{\mathcal{M}}(\Pi_s^k) = \sum_{\widehat{\pi} \in A_s^k} \Delta_s^{\mathcal{M}}(Cyl(\widehat{\pi}))
$$

$$
= \sum_{t \in S} \sum_{\widehat{\pi}' \in A_t^{k-1}} m_s(s\widehat{\pi}') = \sum_{t \in S} \sum_{\widehat{\pi}' \in A_t^{k-1}} \mathbf{Q}[s,t]^\dagger(m_t(\widehat{\pi}'))
$$

$$
= \sum_{t \in S} \sum_{\widehat{\pi}' \in A_t^{k-1}} \mathbf{Q}[s,t]^\dagger(\Delta_t^{\mathcal{M}}(Cyl(\widehat{\pi}'))) = \sum_{t \in S} \mathbf{Q}[s,t]^\dagger(\Delta_t^{\mathcal{M}}(\Pi_t^{k-1})).
$$

$$
(6.7)
$$

Let $S^? = Sat(\Phi) \backslash Sat(\Psi)$. We have the following theorem that describes a way of computing the satisfaction set as the fixed point of a family of super-operators.

Theorem 6.21 *Let $f : \mathcal{L}(\mathcal{H})^{S^?} \to \mathcal{L}(\mathcal{H})^{S^?}$ be a mapping such that for any $X \in \mathcal{L}(\mathcal{H})^{S^?}$ and $s \in S^?$,*

$$
f(X)_s = \sum_{t \in S^?} \mathbf{Q}[s,t]^\dagger(X_t) + \sum_{t \in Sat(\Psi)} \mathbf{Q}[s,t]^\dagger(I).
$$

Then

(i) *$f(X)$ has a unique least fixed point, denoted by μf, in $\mathcal{P}(\mathcal{H})^{S^?}$ with respect to the order $\sqsubseteq$;*

(ii) *For all $s \in S^?$, $(\mu f)_s = \mathcal{Q}^{\mathcal{M}}(s, \Phi U \Psi)$;*

(iii) *Given any $M \in \mathcal{P}(\mathcal{H})$ and $s \in S^?$, whether*

$$
M \sim (\mu f)_s \quad \text{for } \sim \in \{\sqsubseteq, \sqsupseteq, =\}
$$

can be decided in time $O(|S|^4 d^8)$ where $d = \dim \mathcal{H}$ is the dimension of $\mathcal{H}$.

Proof For (i), we check that $f(X)$ indeed maps $\mathcal{P}(\mathcal{H})^{S^?}$ into $\mathcal{P}(\mathcal{H})^{S^?}$. Let $X \in \mathcal{P}(\mathcal{H})^{S^?}$. Then for any $s \in S^?$,

$$
f(X)_s \sqsubseteq \sum_{t \in S^?} \mathbf{Q}[s,t]^\dagger(I) + \sum_{t \in Sat(\Psi)} \mathbf{Q}[s,t]^\dagger(I) \sqsubseteq \sum_{t \in S} \mathbf{Q}[s,t]^\dagger(I) = I,
$$

where the first inequality is from the fact that $X_t \sqsubseteq I$, and the last equality is from the normalisation condition

$$\sum_{t \in S} \mathbf{Q}[s,t] \approx \mathcal{I}.$$

Note further that the function f is Scott continuous with respect to the partial order $\sqsubseteq$. Then by Lemma 6.6 and Kleene fixed point theorem, $f(X)$ has a (unique) least fixed point which can be written as

$$\mu f = \lim_{k \to \infty} f^k(\vec{0}),$$

where $\vec{0} \in \mathcal{P}(\mathcal{H})^{S^?}$ is given by $\vec{0}_s = 0$ for all $s \in S^?$.
 For (ii), note that

$$Q^{\mathcal{M}}(s, \Phi U \Psi) = \Delta_s^{\mathcal{M}}(\Pi_s).$$

Then from Eq. (6.6), it suffices to show by induction that for any $k \geq 0$ and $s \in S^?$,

$$\Delta_s^{\mathcal{M}}(\Pi_s^k) = f^k(\vec{0})_s. \qquad (6.8)$$

Fix arbitrarily $s \in S^?$. When $k = 0$, we have

$$f^0(\vec{0})_s = 0 = \Delta_s^{\mathcal{M}}(\Pi_s^0)$$

as $s \notin Sat(\Psi)$. Now suppose Eq. (6.8) holds for k. Then

$$\Delta_s^{\mathcal{M}}(\Pi_s^{k+1}) = \sum_{t \in S} \mathbf{Q}[s,t]^\dagger (\Delta_t^{\mathcal{M}}(\Pi_t^k))$$

$$= \sum_{t \in S^?} \mathbf{Q}[s,t]^\dagger (\Delta_t^{\mathcal{M}}(\Pi_t^k)) + \sum_{t \in Sat(\Psi)} \mathbf{Q}[s,t]^\dagger (I)$$

$$= \sum_{t \in S^?} \mathbf{Q}[s,t]^\dagger (f^k(\vec{0})_t) + \sum_{t \in Sat(\Psi)} \mathbf{Q}[s,t]^\dagger (I)$$

$$= f(f^k(\vec{0}))_s = f^{k+1}(\vec{0})_s,$$

where the first equation is from Eq. (6.7), and the third one from the induction hypothesis.
 The proof of (iii) is too involved and we postpone it to Appendix 3, Section A3.1.   □

Complexity of QCTL Model Checking. Recall from Subsection 2.4.3 that the overall time complexity for model checking a PCTL formula Φ against a classical Markov chain with n states is linear in $|\Phi|$ and polynomial in n, where the size $|\Phi|$

is defined to be the number of logical connectives and temporal operators in Φ plus the sum of the sizes of the temporal operators [76].

We now consider the complexity of the QCTL model-checking algorithm. Let $d = \dim \mathcal{H}$. The greatest extra cost of our algorithm is the until operator but from Theorem 6.21 it is of the order $n^4 d^8$. Thus the complexity for model checking a QCTL formula Φ against an SVMC is again linear in $|\Phi|$ and polynomial in n and d. Thus we have

> **Theorem 6.22** *Given an SVMC $\mathcal{M} = (S, \mathbf{Q}, L)$, $s \in S$, and a QCTL formula Φ, the model-checking problem $s \models \Phi$ can be solved in time $O(poly(n) \cdot poly(d) \cdot |\Phi|)$ where $n = |S|$ and $d = \dim \mathcal{H}$.*

> **Remark 6.23** *Note that in the classical case, we can compute the set*
>
> $$Sat(\mathbb{P}_{=0}[\Phi U \Psi])$$
>
> *from the underlying graph of the MC. Consequently, the derived equation system has a unique solution. However, as shown in Exercise 6.3, such a method does not work in the quantum case.*
>
> *Nevertheless, we can still simplify the calculation by identifying some S^0 and S^1 such that*
>
> $$S \backslash (Sat(\Psi) \cup Sat(\Phi)) \subseteq S^0 \subseteq Sat(\mathbb{Q}_{=0}[\Phi U \Psi])$$
>
> *and*
>
> $$Sat(\Psi) \subseteq S^1 \subseteq Sat(\mathbb{Q}_{=1}[\Phi U \Psi]),$$
>
> *which are calculated by Algorithms 8 and 9, respectively. Then we can set $S^? = S \backslash (S^0 \cup S^1)$ in Theorem 6.21.*

Algorithm 8: An algorithm to calculate S^0.

---

    input: $Sat(\Phi)$ and $Sat(\Psi)$.
    output: A subset S^0 of S such that
               $S \backslash Sat(\Psi) \backslash Sat(\Phi) \subseteq S^0 \subseteq Sat(\mathbb{Q}_{=0}[\Phi U \Psi])$.
    begin
        $R \leftarrow \{s : \text{no direct path from } s \text{ to states in } Sat(\Psi)\}$;
        $R \leftarrow R \cup (S \backslash Sat(\Phi) \backslash Sat(\Psi))$;
        $done \leftarrow$ **false**;
        while $done = $ **false do**
            $R' \leftarrow R \cup \{s \in S \backslash R : \sum_{t \in R} \mathbf{Q}[s, t] + \mathbf{Q}[s, s] \approx \mathrm{Id}\}$;
            if $(R' = R)$ **then** $done \leftarrow$ **true**;
            $R \leftarrow R'$;
        end
        return R;
    end

Algorithm 9: An algorithm to calculate S^I.

---

input: $Sat(\Phi)$ and $Sat(\Psi)$.

output: A subset S^I of S such that $Sat(\Psi) \subseteq S^I \subseteq Sat(\mathbb{Q}_{=I}[\Phi\mathbf{U}\Psi])$.

begin

$\quad \mid$ $R \leftarrow Sat(\Psi)$;

$\quad \mid$ $done \leftarrow$ **false**;

$\quad \mid$ **while** $done =$ **false do**

$\quad \mid \quad \mid$ $R' \leftarrow R \cup \{s \in Sat(\Phi) \backslash R : \sum_{t \in R} \mathbf{Q}[s,t] + \mathbf{Q}[s,s] \approx \mathrm{Id}\}$;

$\quad \mid \quad \mid$ **if** $(R' = R)$ **then** $done \leftarrow$ **true**;

$\quad \mid \quad \mid$ $R \leftarrow R'$;

$\quad \mid$ **end**

$\quad \mid$ **return** R;

end

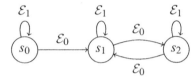

Figure 6.4 An SVMC showing non-uniqueness of solutions to the equation system in Theorem 6.21.

Exercise 6.3 Let an SVMC as defined in Figure 6.4, where $\mathcal{E}_i = \{|i\rangle\langle i|\}$ for $i = 0, 1$. Let $Sat(\Phi) = \{s_1\}$ and $Sat(\Psi) = \{s_2\}$. Then

$$Sat(\mathbb{Q}_{=0}[\Phi\mathbf{U}\Psi]) = \{s_0\}, \quad Sat(\mathbb{Q}_{=I}[\Phi\mathbf{U}\Psi]) = \{s_2\}.$$

Prove that the equation $X_{s_1} = \mathcal{E}_1^\dagger(X_{s_1}) + \mathcal{E}_0^\dagger(I)$ has more than one solutions.

Example 6.24 This example is devoted to model checking the properties listed in Example 6.18 against the SVMCs of Examples 6.3, 6.4, and 6.5.

(i) Quantum loop program. We only check the property $\mathbb{Q}_{\sqsupseteq M}[\lozenge l_3]$. Let $\mathcal{F} = \{|+\rangle\langle i| : i = 0, 1\}$ be the super-operator which sets the target qubit to $|+\rangle = (|0\rangle + |1\rangle)/\sqrt{2}$, $\mathcal{E}^i = \{|i\rangle\langle i|\}$, $i = 0, 1$, and $\mathcal{E} = \mathcal{X}$ the Pauli-X super-operator. We first calculate that $Sat(l_3) = \{l_3\}$ and $Sat(\mathtt{tt}) = \{l_0, l_1, l_2, l_3\}$. So $S^? = \{l_0, l_1, l_2\}$. We proceed as follows:

$$X_{l_0} = \sum_{i=0}^{1} |i\rangle\langle+|X_{l_1}|+\rangle\langle i| = \langle+|X_{l_1}|+\rangle \cdot I, \tag{6.9}$$

$$X_{l_1} = \mathcal{E}^1(X_{l_2}) + \mathcal{E}^0(I) = \langle 1|X_{l_2}|1\rangle \cdot |1\rangle\langle 1| + |0\rangle\langle 0|, \tag{6.10}$$

$$X_{l_2} = \mathcal{E}^\dagger(X_{l_1}) = \sigma_x \cdot X_{l_1} \cdot \sigma_x. \tag{6.11}$$

Inserting Eq. (6.11) into Eq. (6.10), we have

$$X_{l_1} = \langle 0 | X_{l_1} | 0 \rangle \cdot | 1 \rangle \langle 1 | + | 0 \rangle \langle 0 |,$$

which implies $X_{l_1} = I$. Then $X_{l_0} = X_{l_2} = I$ as well, and so

$$l_i \models \mathbb{Q}_{\sqsupseteq M}[\Diamond\, l_3]$$

for all $0 \le i \le 3$ and $M \sqsubseteq I$.

(ii) Recursive quantum program. Consider the path formula $\Diamond l_a$. Let $|\psi\rangle = |0\rangle$, $|\psi^\perp\rangle = |1\rangle$, $|\varphi\rangle = |+\rangle$, and $|\varphi^\perp\rangle = |-\rangle$. Then the equation system goes as follows:

$$X_{s_a} = |0\rangle\langle 0| + |1\rangle\langle 1| X_{s_b} |1\rangle\langle 1|,$$
$$X_{s_b} = |-\rangle\langle -| X_{s_a} |-\rangle\langle -|.$$

Thus $X_{s_a} = |0\rangle\langle 0| + \frac{1}{3}|1\rangle\langle 1|$, and $X_{s_b} = \frac{2}{3}|-\rangle\langle -|$, which implies

$$s_a \models \mathbb{Q}_{= |0\rangle\langle 0| + \frac{1}{3}|1\rangle\langle 1|}[\Diamond t_a] \quad \text{and} \quad s_b \models \mathbb{Q}_{= \frac{2}{3}|-\rangle\langle -|}[\Diamond t_a].$$

(iii) BB84 protocol. We will compute $Q^{\mathcal{M}}(s, \Diamond succ)$ and $Q^{\mathcal{M}}(s, \Diamond fail)$ separately. For $Q^{\mathcal{M}}(s, \Diamond succ)$, we first obtain from Algorithms 8 and 9 that $S^0 = \{s_{001}, s_{011}, s_{100}, s_{110}, fail\}$, and $S^I = \{succ\}$. Then Table 6.1 calculates $\Delta_t^{\mathcal{M}}(\Pi_t^k)$ in Eq. (6.6) for each $t \in S^? = S \backslash S^0 \backslash S^I$ and $0 \le k \le 4$. For example, the item $\Delta_s^{\mathcal{M}}(\Pi_s^4)$ is calculated as follows:

$$\Delta_s^{\mathcal{M}}(\Pi_s^4) = \mathbf{Q}[s, s_0]^\dagger (\Delta_{s_0}^{\mathcal{M}}(\Pi_{s_0}^3) + \mathbf{Q}[s, s_1]^\dagger (\Delta_{s_1}^{\mathcal{M}}(\Pi_{s_1}^3)$$
$$= \frac{1}{4}[(Set^{|0\rangle})^\dagger (|0\rangle\langle 0|) + (Set^{|+\rangle})^\dagger (|+\rangle\langle +|)]$$
$$= \frac{1}{4}(I + I) = \frac{1}{2}I.$$

Note further that $\Delta_t(\Pi_t^k) = \Delta_t(\Pi_t^4)$ for any $t \in S^?$ and $k > 4$. Thus we have

$$Q^{\mathcal{M}}(s, \Diamond succ) = \frac{1}{2}I.$$

Table 6.1 *Values for $\Delta_t(\Pi_t^k)$, $t \in S^?$, and $0 \le k \le 4$ in the basic BB84 protocol.*

k \ t	s_0	s_1	s_{00}	s_{01}	s_{10}	s_{11}	s_{000}	s_{010}	s_{101}	s_{111}
0	0	0	0	0	0	0	0	0	0	0
1	0	0	0	0	0	0	0	$|0\rangle\langle 0|$	$|1\rangle\langle 1|$	$|+\rangle\langle +|$	$|-\rangle\langle -|$
2	0	0	0	$\frac{1}{2}|0\rangle\langle 0|$	$\frac{1}{2}|1\rangle\langle 1|$	$\frac{1}{2}|+\rangle\langle +|$	$\frac{1}{2}|-\rangle\langle -|$	$|0\rangle\langle 0|$	$|1\rangle\langle 1|$	$|+\rangle\langle +|$	$|-\rangle\langle -|$
3	0	$\frac{1}{2}|0\rangle\langle 0|$	$\frac{1}{2}|+\rangle\langle +|$	$\frac{1}{2}|0\rangle\langle 0|$	$\frac{1}{2}|1\rangle\langle 1|$	$\frac{1}{2}|+\rangle\langle +|$	$\frac{1}{2}|-\rangle\langle -|$	$|0\rangle\langle 0|$	$|1\rangle\langle 1|$	$|+\rangle\langle +|$	$|-\rangle\langle -|$
4	$\frac{1}{2}I$	$\frac{1}{2}|0\rangle\langle 0|$	$\frac{1}{2}|+\rangle\langle +|$	$\frac{1}{2}|0\rangle\langle 0|$	$\frac{1}{2}|1\rangle\langle 1|$	$\frac{1}{2}|+\rangle\langle +|$	$\frac{1}{2}|-\rangle\langle -|$	$|0\rangle\langle 0|$	$|1\rangle\langle 1|$	$|+\rangle\langle +|$	$|-\rangle\langle -|$

Similarly, we can compute that $Q^{\mathcal{M}}(s, \Diamond fail) = 0$, thus

$$s \models Q_{=0}[\Diamond fail] \wedge Q_{=\frac{1}{2}I}[\Diamond succ],$$

as expected.

6.4.2 Model Checking LTL Properties

It has been shown in the previous section how QCTL properties can be verified. In this section, we describe the model-checking techniques of LTL formulas, which allow to express and analyse a wide range of relevant properties, such as repeated reachability, reachability in a restricted order, nested Until properties, or conjunctions of such properties.

LTL Model-Checking Problem for SVMCs. The LTL model-checking problem can be stated as follows. Given an SVMC $\mathcal{M} = (S, Q, L)$, $s \in S$, and an LTL formula ψ, compute

$$\mathrm{Qr}_s^{\mathcal{M}}(\psi) := \Delta_s^{\mathcal{M}}(\{\pi \in \mathrm{Path}^{\mathcal{M}}(s) \mid L(\pi) \models \psi\}).$$

Again, we can check that for any ψ and each state s in an SVMC $\mathcal{M}$, the set

$$\{\pi \in \mathrm{Path}^{\mathcal{M}}(s) \mid L(\pi) \models \psi\}$$

is in the σ-algebra generated by $\mathbb{G}^{\mathcal{M}}(s)$.

Parity SVMCs. We have seen in Chapter 2 that an LTL formula can be transformed into a (non-deterministic) Buchi automaton. For our purpose of model checking on SVMCs, however, we use parity automaton, which is a deterministic one, to represent LTL formulas. Note that other deterministic ω-automata will also do the same task.

Definition 6.25 (Parity Automaton) A *(deterministic) parity automaton* (PA) is a tuple $\mathcal{A} = (A, \bar{a}, t, \mathrm{pri})$, where

  (i) A is a finite set of automaton states, and $\bar{a} \in A$ is the *initial state*.
 (ii) $t \colon A \times 2^{AP} \to A$ is a *transition function*.
(iii) $\mathrm{pri} \colon A \to \mathbb{N}$ is a *priority function*. Here $\mathbb{N}$ denotes the set of natural numbers.

A *path* of $\mathcal{A}$ is an infinite sequence $\sigma = a_0 L_0 a_1 L_1 \ldots \in (A \times 2^{AP})^{\omega}$ such that $a_0 = \bar{a}$ and for all $i \geq 0$, $t(a_i, L_i) = a_{i+1}$. We extend the priority function to paths by setting

$$\mathrm{pri}(\sigma) := \liminf_{i \to \infty} \mathrm{pri}(a_i).$$

We use Path$^{\mathcal{A}}$ to denote the set of all paths of $\mathcal{A}$. The *language* accepted by $\mathcal{A}$ is defined as

$$\mathcal{L}(\mathcal{A}) := \{ L_0 L_1 \ldots \in (2^{AP})^{\omega} \mid \exists \sigma = a_0 L_0 a_1 L_1 \ldots \in \text{Path}^{\mathcal{A}}. \, \text{pri}(\sigma) \text{ is even} \}.$$

For an LTL formula ψ, we denote by $\mathcal{A}_\psi$ the PA that accepts the words satisfying ψ; that is,

$$\mathcal{L}(\mathcal{A}_\psi) = \{ \eta \in (2^{AP})^{\omega} \mid \eta \models \psi \}.$$

Effective means to transform LTL formulas to parity automata exists in, say, [98, 102, 104].

We also need to consider SVMCs with parity conditions.

Definition 6.26 (Parity SVMC) An SVMC $\mathcal{M} = (S, \mathbf{Q}, L)$ is called a parity SVMC (PSVMC) if it is equipped with a priority function pri: $S \to \mathbb{N}$. We define the *value* of $\mathcal{M}$ in $s \in S$ as

$$\text{Val}^{\mathcal{M}}(s) = \Delta_s^{\mathcal{M}}(\{ \pi \in \text{Path}^{\mathcal{M}} \mid \text{pri}(\pi) \text{ is even} \}).$$

Here again, we set

$$\text{pri}(\pi) := \liminf_{i \to \infty} \text{pri}(s_i)$$

provided that $\pi = s_0 s_1 s_2 \ldots$. When the labelling function L is irrelevant, we also denote such an SVMC by $(S, \mathbf{Q}, \text{pri})$.

In the following, we describe how to combine an SVMC under consideration with a PA representing the property we are concerned with.

Definition 6.27 (SVMC-PA Product) The *product* of an SVMC $\mathcal{M} = (S, \mathbf{Q}, L)$ and a PA $\mathcal{A} = (A, \bar{a}, t, \text{pri})$ with the same set AP of atomic propositions is a PSVMC $\mathcal{M} \otimes \mathcal{A} := (S', \mathbf{Q}', \text{pri}')$ where

    (i) $S' = S \times A$.
    (ii) $\mathbf{Q}'[(s, a), (s', a')] = \mathbf{Q}[s, s']$ if $t(a, L(s)) = a'$, and 0 otherwise.
    (iii) $\text{pri}'((s, a)) = \text{pri}(a)$.

By the assumption that $\mathcal{A}$ is deterministic, it is easy to check that for any $(s, a) \in S'$,

$$\sum_{(s', a') \in S'} \mathbf{Q}'[(s, a), (s', a')] = \sum_{s' \in S} \mathbf{Q}[s, s'] \approx \text{Id}.$$

Thus the product $\mathcal{M} \otimes \mathcal{A}$ defined above is indeed a PSVMC. The following lemma shows that the value of this product is exactly the POVM value corresponding to the property under consideration in the original model.

Lemma 6.28 *Given an SVMC $\mathcal{M} = (S, \mathbf{Q}, L)$ and an LTL formula ψ, we have for any $s \in S$,*

$$\mathrm{Qr}_s^{\mathcal{M}}(\psi) = \mathrm{Val}^{\mathcal{M}'}((s, \bar{a})),$$

where $\mathcal{M}' := \mathcal{M} \otimes \mathcal{A}_\psi$ and $\bar{a}$ is the initial state of $\mathcal{A}_\psi$.

Proof Let $\mathcal{A}_\psi = (A, \bar{a}, t, \mathrm{pri})$ and $\mathcal{M}' = (S', \mathbf{Q}', \mathrm{pri}')$. We first show that for any $s \in S$ there is a bijection between the following two sets:

$$R_s := \{\, \pi \in \mathrm{Path}^{\mathcal{M}}(s) \mid L(\pi) \in \mathcal{L}(\mathcal{A}_\psi) \,\},$$

$$R'_s := \{\, \pi' \in \mathrm{Path}^{\mathcal{M}'}((s, \bar{a})) \mid \mathrm{pri}'(\pi') \text{ is even} \,\}.$$

Let $\pi = s_0 s_1 \ldots \in R_s$. According to Definition 6.25, there is a unique sequence $a_0 a_1 \ldots$ with $a_0 = \bar{a}$ such that $a_0 L(s_0) a_1 L(s_1) \ldots$ is a path of $\mathcal{A}_\psi$ with the priority being even. Let π' be defined such that for all $i \geq 0$, $\pi'(i) = (s_i, a_i)$. Then by definition, $\mathrm{pri}'(\pi')$ is even, so $\pi' \in R'_s$.

Let $\pi' \in R'_s$. Then there are $\pi := s_0 s_1 \ldots \in \mathrm{Path}^{\mathcal{M}}$ and $a_0 a_1 \ldots \in A^\omega$ with $s_0 = s$ and $a_0 = \bar{a}$ such that for each $i \geq 0$, $\pi'(i) = (s_i, a_i)$. By Definition 6.27, $t(a_i, L(s_i)) = a_{i+1}$. Thus $\sigma := a_0 L(s_0) a_1 L(s_1) \ldots \in \mathrm{Path}^{\mathcal{A}_\psi}$. Furthermore, note that $\mathrm{pri}(\sigma) = \mathrm{pri}'(\pi')$ is even. Thus $\pi \in R_s$.

Finally, it is easy to observe that the bijection between R_s and R'_s preserves the super-operators of finite path prefixes. That is, for each $\pi \in R_s$ and its corresponding path $\pi' \in R'_s$, and for each $i \geq 0$,

$$\mathbf{Q}[\pi(i), \pi(i+1)] = \mathbf{Q}'[\pi'(i), \pi'(i+1)].$$

Thus we have

$$\Delta_s^{\mathcal{M}}(R_s) = \Delta_{(s, \bar{a})}^{\mathcal{M}'}(R'_s),$$

which implies

$$\mathrm{Qr}_s^{\mathcal{M}}(\psi) = \mathrm{Val}^{\mathcal{M}'}((s, \bar{a}))$$

by noting that $L(\pi) \in \mathcal{L}(\mathcal{A}_\psi)$ if and only if $L(\pi) \models \psi$. □

Basic Idea of LTL Model-Checking Algorithm for SVMCs. By Lemma 6.28, the LTL model-checking problem for SVMCs boils down to computing values of PSVMCs. Thus in the following, we only focus on the latter problem.

Up to now, the model checking method works as for classical Markov chains. What would fail is the subsequent part which consists of the evaluation of the PSVMC. The idea for model checking in terms of classical parity Markov chains (PMC) is quite simple: a path of a PMC is accepted if the lowest priority occurring infinitely often is even. Starting from s, the probability that s' is visited infinitely often is 1 if s and s' are in the same BSCC. The probability that a state which is not contained in any BSCC (a transient state) will be visited infinitely often is 0. Thus, model checking for PMCs can be performed as follows.

(i) Identify the set of BSCCs using a graph-based algorithm, and let $ACC = \emptyset$.
(ii) For each BSCC B, check whether the lowest priority occurring on a state of B is even. If yes, add B to ACC, $ACC \leftarrow ACC \cup B$.
(iii) For any state s, if $s \in ACC$, then $\mathrm{Val}^{\mathcal{M}}(s) = 1$. Otherwise, $\mathrm{Val}^{\mathcal{M}}(s)$ is the probability that s reaches any state in ACC. That is, if s is a state of a BSCC $B \not\subseteq ACC$, then $\mathrm{Val}^{\mathcal{M}}(s) = 0$; and values of transient states can be computed by solving a linear equation system.

Note that a PSVMC also has a set of classical states, and the transition super-operators also induce an underlying graph over these states. Thus a natural question is: Can we define the notion of BSCC in terms of the underlying graph structure for a PSVMC, just as in the classical case, and employ the above technique to calculate its values? Unfortunately, this idea does not work, as the following example shows.

Example 6.29 Consider the two parity Markov chains in Figure 6.5. On the left is a classical one with $0 < p < 1$, while the right is a quantum one with $\mathcal{E}_0 := \{|0\rangle\langle 0|\}$ and $\mathcal{E}_1 := \{|1\rangle\langle 1|\}$. Obviously, both models have the same classical state space, and have exactly the same underlying graph. Thus they have the same set of BSCCs, if we would define BSCCs for PSVMCs according to the underlying graphs. However, we will see that this BSCC technique does not help in the evaluation of PSVMCs.

In the classical model, s_0 is a transient state which will eventually reach the only BSCC $\{s_1, s_2\}$. Thus, the priority with which s_0 is labelled is irrelevant. From any state of the BSCC, the probability that both states are visited infinitely often is 1. Thus, the probability that from either state the lowest priority 0 is reached infinitely often is 1, and thus the value of the parity Markov chain is also 1.

In contrast, in the quantum model, note that for $i \in \{0, 1\}$ it holds $\mathcal{E}_i \mathcal{E}_i = \mathcal{E}_i$ and $\mathcal{E}_i \mathcal{E}_{1-i} = 0$. It is easy to check that if we start from s_0, the infinite path $(s_0)^\omega$, with the corresponding *non-zero* POVM value

$$\lim_{n \to \infty} \mathcal{E}_1^n(I) = |1\rangle\langle 1|,$$

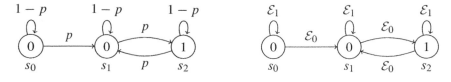

Figure 6.5 Example showing that BSCC decomposition for the underlying graph does not work for model checking PSVMCs. The number inside a state denotes its priority.

never leaves to the set $\{s_1, s_2\}$. Thus s_0 should not be considered as a transient state at all. Furthermore, as the priority of $(s_0)^\omega$ is 0, this path also contributes to the value of the PSVMC. On the other hand, if we start from s_1, there are two infinite paths with non-zero measure, namely $(s_1)^\omega$ with the corresponding POVM value $|1\rangle\langle 1|$ and priority 0, and $(s_1 s_2)^\omega$ with the corresponding POVM value $|0\rangle\langle 0|$ and priority 0. Thus, the value of the PSVMC in state s_1 is $|0\rangle\langle 0| + |1\rangle\langle 1| = I$. However, if we start from s_2 we have $(s_2)^\omega$ with the corresponding POVM value $|1\rangle\langle 1|$ and priority 1, and $(s_2 s_1)^\omega$ with the corresponding POVM value $|0\rangle\langle 0|$ and priority 0. Thus, the value in s_2 is $|0\rangle\langle 0|$, different from the one in s_1.

Thus, algorithms based on BSCC decomposition of the underlying graph do not work for PSVMCs: neither are BSCCs reached with certainty, nor do all states of a BSCC have the same value. In addition, the value of a BSCC state might be neither 0 nor I. Rather surprisingly, by encoding the behavior of $\mathcal{M}$ into a quantum Markov chain acting on the *extended Hilbert space* which is the tensor product of the classical state space and the quantum one, the notion of BSCC *subspaces* defined in Chapter 5 can be used to compute PSVMC values.

Let $\mathcal{M} = (S, \mathbf{Q}, \mathrm{pri})$ be a PSVMC on $\mathcal{H}$ with

$$\mathbf{Q}[s, t] = \{ E_i^{s,t} \mid i \in I^{s,t} \}.$$

We define a super-operator

$$\mathcal{E}_{\mathcal{M}} = \{ |t\rangle\langle s| \otimes E_i^{s,t} \mid s, t \in S, i \in I^{s,t} \} \tag{6.12}$$

acting on $\mathcal{H}_c \otimes \mathcal{H}$, where $\mathcal{H}_c$ is a $|S|$-dimensional Hilbert space with an orthonormal basis $\{ |s\rangle \mid s \in S \}$. It is easy to check that $\mathcal{E}_{\mathcal{M}}$ is trace-preserving, so $(\mathcal{E}_{\mathcal{M}}, \mathcal{H}_c \otimes \mathcal{H})$ is indeed a quantum Markov chain. Let

$$\mathcal{E}_{\mathcal{M}}^\infty = \lim_{N \to \infty} \frac{1}{N} \sum_{n=1}^{N} \mathcal{E}_{\mathcal{M}}^n.$$

As $\mathcal{E}_{\mathcal{M}}$ is trace-preserving, $\mathcal{E}_{\mathcal{M}}^\infty$ is well defined.

The following lemma shows that for quantum Markov chains derived from PSVMCs, the classical and quantum systems will remain separable (disentangled) during the evolution, provided that the initial state is in a product form.

Lemma 6.30 *Let* $\mathcal{M} = (S, \mathbf{Q}, \mathrm{pri})$ *be a PSVMC on* $\mathcal{H}$, $s \in S$, *and* $\rho \in \mathcal{D}(\mathcal{H})$. *Then for any* $n \geq 0$, $\mathcal{E}_{\mathcal{M}}^n(|s\rangle\langle s| \otimes \rho)$ *is block diagonal according to the classical states. Specifically,*

$$\mathcal{E}_{\mathcal{M}}^n(|s\rangle\langle s| \otimes \rho) = \sum_{t \in S} |t\rangle\langle t| \otimes \mathbf{Q}^n[s, t](\rho).$$

Exercise 6.4 Prove Lemma 6.30.

Bottom Strongly Connected Components (BSCCs).　From the form of $\mathcal{E}_M$ presented in Eq. (6.12), it is easy to show that for any fixed point state σ of $\mathcal{E}_M$, that is, $\mathcal{E}_M(\sigma) = \sigma$, it also has the form

$$\sigma = \sum_{s \in S} |s\rangle\langle s| \otimes \sigma_s.$$

Therefore, any BSCC B of $\mathcal{E}_M$ can be spanned by some pure states of the form $|s\rangle|\psi\rangle$ where $s \in S$ and $|\psi\rangle \in \mathcal{H}$. Let

$$C(B) = \{ s \in S \mid |s\rangle|\psi\rangle \in B \text{ for some } |\psi\rangle \in \mathcal{H} \}$$

be the set of classical states supported in B.

Exploiting the *classical-quantum separation* (Lemma 6.30) of super-operators derived from PSVMCs, we are going to show some nice properties of their BSCC decomposition, which are key to our later discussion. First, we see that two BSCCs X and Y are orthogonal, denoted $X \perp Y$, unless they have the same set of support classical states.

Lemma 6.31　*For any two BSCCs X and Y of $\mathcal{E}_M$, if $C(X) \neq C(Y)$ then $X \perp Y$.*

Proof　See Appendix 3, Section A3.2.　　　　　　　　　　　　　　　　$\square$

Given $k \in \mathbb{N}$, let $\mathcal{BSCC}_k$ be the span of all BSCCs of $\mathcal{E}_M$ with the minimal priority being k; that is,

$$\mathcal{BSCC}_k = \bigvee \{ B \text{ is a BSCC of } \mathcal{E}_M : \min\{ \mathsf{pri}(s) \mid s \in C(B) \} = k \}.$$

Similarly, let $\mathcal{BSCC}_{k-}$ and $\mathcal{BSCC}_{k+}$ be the spans of all BSCCs with the minimal priority being less than and larger than k, respectively. Then by Lemma 6.31, $\mathcal{BSCC}_k$, $\mathcal{BSCC}_{k-}$ and $\mathcal{BSCC}_{k+}$ are pairwise orthogonal. Thus the state space $\mathcal{H}_c \otimes \mathcal{H}$ can be decomposed *uniquely* into

$$\mathcal{H} = T \oplus \mathcal{BSCC}_k \oplus \mathcal{BSCC}_{k-} \oplus \mathcal{BSCC}_{k+},$$

where T is the maximum transient subspace of $\mathcal{E}_M$. In the following, we denote by P_T, P_k, P_{k-} and P_{k+} the projections onto T, $\mathcal{BSCC}_k$, $\mathcal{BSCC}_{k-}$ and $\mathcal{BSCC}_{k+}$, respectively. Then:

$$P_T + P_k + P_{k-} + P_{k+} = I_{\mathcal{H}_c \otimes \mathcal{H}},$$

the identity operator on $\mathcal{H}_c \otimes \mathcal{H}$.

We now present some key lemmas which are essential for our discussion. For readability, the proofs of these technical lemmas are postponed to Appendix 3, Section A3.3–A3.6. Let

$$S_k := \{ s \in S \mid \mathsf{pri}(s) = k \}, \qquad S_{k+} := \{ s \in S \mid \mathsf{pri}(s) > k \},$$

and similarly for S_{k^-}. We also denote by $\Diamond$ and $\Box$ the well-known 'Eventually' and 'Always' modal operators respectively applied on set of states. That is, say,

$$\Diamond S_k := \{ \pi \in S^\omega \mid \exists i \geq 0, \pi(i) \in S_k \}.$$

Furthermore, we let

$$\Delta^\mathcal{M}(E) := \sum_{s \in S} |s\rangle\langle s| \otimes \Delta_s^\mathcal{M}(E)$$

whenever E is a measurable subset of S^ω.

Lemma 6.32 *Let* $\mathcal{M} = (S, \mathbf{Q}, \mathrm{pri})$ *be a* PSVMC *on* $\mathcal{H}$.

(i) *For any* $\widehat{\pi} = s_0 s_1 \ldots s_n$ *and a measurable subset E of S^ω, let*

$$\widehat{\pi}^\frown E := \{ s_0 \ldots s_{n-1} \pi \mid \pi \in E \wedge \pi(0) = s_n \}$$

be the set of words formed by concatenation of the n-length prefix of $\widehat{\pi}$ with those words in E starting with the last state of $\widehat{\pi}$. Then

$$\Delta^\mathcal{M}(\widehat{\pi}^\frown E) = \mathcal{P}_{s_0}\mathcal{E}_\mathcal{M}^\dagger \cdots \mathcal{P}_{s_{n-1}}\mathcal{E}_\mathcal{M}^\dagger(|s_n\rangle\langle s_n| \otimes \Delta_{s_n}^\mathcal{M}(E)),$$

where $\mathcal{P}_s$ is the projection super-operator $\mathcal{P}_s := \{P_s\}$ and $P_s := |s\rangle\langle s| \otimes I$. In particular,

$$\Delta^\mathcal{M}(Cyl(\widehat{\pi})) = \mathcal{P}_{s_0}\mathcal{E}_\mathcal{M}^\dagger \cdots \mathcal{P}_{s_{n-1}}\mathcal{E}_\mathcal{M}^\dagger(P_{s_n}).$$

(ii) *For any $k \in \mathbb{N}$ and $s \in S$, let*

$$R_{k,s} = \Delta_s^\mathcal{M}(\{ \pi \in \mathrm{Path}^\mathcal{M} \mid \mathrm{pri}(\pi) = k \}), \tag{6.13}$$

and $R_k = \sum_{s \in S} |s\rangle\langle s| \otimes R_{k,s}$. Then for any $n \geq 0$, $R_k = \mathcal{E}_\mathcal{M}^{n\dagger}(R_k)$. In particular, R_k is a fixed point of $\mathcal{E}_\mathcal{M}^{\infty\dagger}$:

$$R_k = \mathcal{E}_\mathcal{M}^{\infty\dagger}(R_k).$$

Proof See Appendix 3, Section A3.3. $\qquad\qquad\qquad\qquad\qquad\qquad\qquad$ □

Lemma 6.33 *For any $k \in \mathbb{N}$,*

(i) $P_x \cdot \Delta^\mathcal{M}(\Diamond S_x) \cdot P_x = P_x$ *for $x \in \{k, k^-, k^+\}$.*
(ii) $P_x \cdot \Delta^\mathcal{M}(\Diamond S_y) \cdot P_x = 0$ *for $x, y \in \{k, k^-, k^+\}$ with $y < x$, where we let $k^- < k < k^+$.*

Proof See Appendix 3, Section A3.4. $\qquad\qquad\qquad\qquad\qquad\qquad\qquad$ □

Lemma 6.34 *For any $x \in \{k, k^-, k^+\}$, $P_x \cdot \Delta^\mathcal{M}(\Box\Diamond S_x) \cdot P_x = P_x$.*

Proof See Appendix 3, Section A3.5. $\qquad\qquad\qquad\qquad\qquad\qquad\qquad$ □

The following lemma is crucial for our purpose. Note that for any $\rho \in \mathcal{D}(\mathcal{H})$, $\text{tr}(R_{k,t} \cdot \rho)$ denotes the probability that k is the lowest priority infinitely often reachable from the initial state $|t\rangle\langle t| \otimes \rho$, where $R_{k,t}$ is defined in Eq. (6.13). This lemma essentially says that such a probability will be 1 if starting from $\mathcal{BSCC}_k$ (provided that $\text{tr}(\rho) = 1$; otherwise, the probability is $\text{tr}(\rho)$), and it will be 0 if starting from either $\mathcal{BSCC}_{k^-}$ or $\mathcal{BSCC}_{k^+}$. Thus $\mathcal{BSCC}_k$ for each k acts like the standard BSCCs in classical Markov chains.

Lemma 6.35 *For any $x \in \{k, k^-, k^+\}$,*

$$P_x R_k P_x = \delta_{x,k} P_x,$$

where $\delta_{x,k} = 1$ if $x = k$ and 0 otherwise.

Proof See Appendix 3, Section A3.6.   □

With Lemmas 6.30 to 6.35, we are now ready to prove the main theorem of this section.

Theorem 6.36 *Let $\mathcal{M} = (S, \mathbf{Q}, \text{pri})$ be a PSVMC. Then for any $s \in S$,*

$$\text{Val}^{\mathcal{M}}(s) = \mathcal{E}_s^{\dagger} \circ \mathcal{E}_{\mathcal{M}}^{\infty \dagger}(P_{\text{even}}),$$

where

$$P_{\text{even}} := \sum_{\{k \in \text{pri}(S) | k \text{ is even}\}} P_k,$$

and $\mathcal{E}_s := \{|s\rangle \otimes I\}$.

Proof For any even k and $\rho \in \mathcal{D}(\mathcal{H})$, let

$$\rho_s^{\infty} = \mathcal{E}_{\mathcal{M}}^{\infty}(\mathcal{E}_s(\rho))$$

which is a fixed point state of $\mathcal{E}_{\mathcal{M}}$. Then by Lemma 6.31 and Theorem 5.29, $P_T \rho_s^{\infty} P_T = 0$, and ρ_s^{∞} is block diagonal with respect to $\mathcal{BSCC}_k$, $\mathcal{BSCC}_{k^-}$ and $\mathcal{BSCC}_{k^+}$; that is,

$$\rho_s^{\infty} = P_k \rho_s^{\infty} P_k + P_{k^-} \rho_s^{\infty} P_{k^-} + P_{k^+} \rho_s^{\infty} P_{k^+}.$$

Thus from Lemma 6.35,

$$\begin{aligned} \text{tr}(R_{k,s} \cdot \rho) &= \text{tr}(R_k \cdot P_k \rho_s^{\infty} P_k) + \text{tr}(R_k \cdot P_{k^-} \rho_s^{\infty} P_{k^-}) + \text{tr}(R_k \cdot P_{k^+} \rho_s^{\infty} P_{k^+}) \\ &= \text{tr}(P_k \cdot \rho_s^{\infty}). \end{aligned}$$

Then $R_{k,s} = \mathcal{E}_s^{\dagger} \circ \mathcal{E}_{\mathcal{M}}^{\infty \dagger}(P_k)$, and so $\text{Val}^{\mathcal{M}}(s) = \mathcal{E}_s^{\dagger} \circ \mathcal{E}_{\mathcal{M}}^{\infty \dagger}(P_{\text{even}})$, as expected.   □

Example 6.37 (Example 6.29 revisited) Let $\mathcal{M}$ be the PSVMC depicted on the right of Figure 6.5 where $\mathcal{E}_0 = \{|0\rangle\langle0|\}$ and $\mathcal{E}_1 = \{|1\rangle\langle1|\}$. Then the super-operator encoding $\mathcal{M}$ is

$$
\begin{aligned}
\mathcal{E}_{\mathcal{M}} = \quad & \{|s_1\rangle\langle s_0|\} \otimes \mathcal{E}_0 + \{|s_0\rangle\langle s_0|\} \otimes \mathcal{E}_1 \\
+ \, & \{|s_1\rangle\langle s_1|\} \otimes \mathcal{E}_1 + \{|s_2\rangle\langle s_1|\} \otimes \mathcal{E}_0 \\
+ \, & \{|s_1\rangle\langle s_2|\} \otimes \mathcal{E}_0 + \{|s_2\rangle\langle s_2|\} \otimes \mathcal{E}_1,
\end{aligned}
$$

the maximal transient space of $\mathcal{E}_{\mathcal{M}}$ is $T = \mathrm{span}\{|s_0\rangle|0\rangle\}$, and the BSCCs are

$$
\begin{aligned}
B_1 &= \mathrm{span}\{|s_0\rangle|1\rangle\}, & B_2 &= \mathrm{span}\{|s_1\rangle|1\rangle\}, \\
B_3 &= \mathrm{span}\{|s_1\rangle|0\rangle, |s_2\rangle|0\rangle\}, & B_4 &= \mathrm{span}\{|s_2\rangle|1\rangle\}.
\end{aligned}
$$

Thus $\mathcal{BSCC}_0 = \bigvee\{B_1, B_2, B_3\}$, and

$$
P_0 = |s_0\rangle\langle s_0| \otimes |1\rangle\langle1| + |s_1\rangle\langle s_1| \otimes I + |s_2\rangle\langle s_2| \otimes |0\rangle\langle0|.
$$

Furthermore, we calculate that for any $n \geq 1$,

$$
\mathcal{E}_{\mathcal{M}}^{2n-1} = \mathcal{F}_0 \otimes \mathcal{E}_0 + \mathcal{F} \otimes \mathcal{E}_1, \qquad \mathcal{E}_{\mathcal{M}}^{2n} = \mathcal{F}_1 \otimes \mathcal{E}_0 + \mathcal{F} \otimes \mathcal{E}_1,
$$

where $\mathcal{F}_0 = \{|s_1\rangle\langle s_0|, |s_2\rangle\langle s_1|, |s_1\rangle\langle s_2|\}$, $\mathcal{F}_1 = \{|s_2\rangle\langle s_0|, |s_1\rangle\langle s_1|, |s_2\rangle\langle s_2|\}$, and $\mathcal{F} = \{|s_0\rangle\langle s_0|, |s_1\rangle\langle s_1|, |s_2\rangle\langle s_2|\}$. Thus

$$
\mathcal{E}_{\mathcal{M}}^{\infty} = \frac{\mathcal{F}_0 + \mathcal{F}_1}{2} \otimes \mathcal{E}_0 + \mathcal{F} \otimes \mathcal{E}_1,
$$

$$
\mathcal{E}_{\mathcal{M}}^{\infty\,\dagger}(P_0) = I \otimes |0\rangle\langle0| + (|s_0\rangle\langle s_0| + |s_1\rangle\langle s_1|) \otimes |1\rangle\langle1|.
$$

Note that $\mathcal{E}_s = \{|s\rangle \otimes I\}$. It follows that

$$
\mathrm{Val}^{\mathcal{M}}(s) = \mathcal{E}_s^{\dagger} \circ \mathcal{E}_{\mathcal{M}}^{\infty\,\dagger}(P_0) = \begin{cases} I & \text{if } s = s_0 \vee s = s_1 \\ |0\rangle\langle0| & \text{if } s = s_2, \end{cases}
$$

coinciding with the informal discussion given in Example 6.29.

Algorithm for Computing PSVMCs. Now we are ready to propose an algorithm to compute the values of a PSVMC.

First, we recall that the matrix representation of a super-operator $\mathcal{E} = \{E_i \mid i \in I\}$ is denoted

$$
M_{\mathcal{E}} = \sum_{i \in I} E_i \otimes E_i^*.
$$

Let $M_{\mathcal{E}} = KJK^{-1}$ be the Jordan decomposition of $M_{\mathcal{E}}$ where $J = \bigoplus_k J_{\lambda_k}$ and J_{λ_k} is a Jordan block corresponding to the eigenvalue λ_k. Define

$$
J^{\infty} = \bigoplus_{\{k \mid \lambda_k = 1\}} J_{\lambda_k}. \tag{6.14}
$$

Algorithm 10: Compute the values of a PSVMC

---

input: A PSVMC $\mathcal{M} = (S, \mathbf{Q}, \mathrm{pri})$ on $\mathcal{H}$ and a classical state $s \in S$.
output: $\mathrm{Val}^{\mathcal{M}}(s)$.
begin
    (* Compute $\mathcal{E}_{\mathcal{M}}$ and $\mathcal{E}_{\mathcal{M}}^{\infty}$ *)
    $\mathcal{E}_{\mathcal{M}} \leftarrow 0$;
    for $t, t' \in S$ **do**
        $\mathcal{E}_{\mathcal{M}} \leftarrow \mathcal{E}_{\mathcal{M}} + \{|t'\rangle\langle t|\} \otimes \mathbf{Q}[t, t']$;
    end
    $\mathcal{E}_{\mathcal{M}}^{\infty} \leftarrow$
        the super-operator determined by its matrix representation in Eq. (6.14);

    (* Compute P_{even} *)
    $P_{\mathrm{even}} \leftarrow 0$;
    $I_c \leftarrow \sum_{t \in S} |t\rangle\langle t|$;
    $\mathcal{B} \leftarrow \mathrm{GetBSCCs}(\mathcal{E}_{\mathcal{M}}, I_c \otimes I_{\mathcal{H}})$;
    for $B \in \mathcal{B}$ **do**
        if $\min\{\mathrm{pri}(t) \mid t \in C(B)\}$ *is* even **then**
            $P_{\mathrm{even}} \leftarrow P_{\mathrm{even}} + P_B$ where P_B is the projector onto B;
        end
    end

    $M \leftarrow \mathcal{E}_{\mathcal{M}}^{\infty\,\dagger}(P_{\mathrm{even}})$;
    return $\langle s| \otimes I \cdot M \cdot |s\rangle \otimes I$
end

Then $K J^{\infty} K^{-1}$ is the matrix representation of

$$\mathcal{E}^{\infty} = \lim_{N \to \infty} \frac{1}{N} \sum_{n=1}^{N} \mathcal{E}^n.$$

Theorem 6.38 *Given a PSVMC $\mathcal{M} = (S, \mathbf{Q}, \mathrm{pri})$ on $\mathcal{H}$ and a classical state $s \in S$, Algorithm 10 computes $\mathrm{Val}^{\mathcal{M}}(s)$ in time $O(n^8 d^8)$, where $n = |S|$ and $d = \dim \mathcal{H}$.*

Proof   The correctness of Algorithm 10 directly follows from Theorem 6.36. The procedure GetBSCCs which, given a super-operator $\mathcal{E}$ and an invariant subspace of $\mathcal{E}$, outputs a complete set of orthogonal BSCCs in that subspace is a revised version of the procedure Decompose from Section 5.3.

    The most expensive part in Algorithm 10 is computing $\mathcal{E}_{\mathcal{M}}^{\infty}$, the super-operator corresponding to the matrix representation given in Eq. (6.14). We do it by the following steps:

Procedure GetBSCCs($\mathcal{E}, P$)

---

input: A super-operator $\mathcal{E}$ acting on $\hat{\mathcal{H}}$, and a projector P to some invariant subspace $\mathcal{H}_P \subseteq \hat{\mathcal{H}}$ of $\mathcal{E}$.

output: A complete set of orthogonal BSCCs of $\mathcal{E}$ in $\mathcal{H}_P$.

begin

$\quad$ $\mathcal{X} \leftarrow$ a basis of $\{ X \in \mathcal{L}(\mathcal{H}_P) \mid \mathcal{E}(X) = X \}$;

$\quad$ $F \leftarrow \varnothing$;

$\quad$ **for** $X \in \mathcal{X}$ **do**

$\quad\quad$ $X_R \leftarrow (X + X^\dagger)/2$; $X_I \leftarrow (X - X^\dagger)/2i$;

$\quad\quad$ $P_R^+ \leftarrow$ the projector onto eigenspace of X_R with positive eigenvalues;

$\quad\quad$ $P_I^+ \leftarrow$ the projector onto eigenspace of X_I with positive eigenvalues;

$\quad\quad$ $X_R^+ \leftarrow P_R^+ X_R P_R^+$; $X_R^- \leftarrow X_R^+ - X_R$;

$\quad\quad$ $X_I^+ \leftarrow P_I^+ X_I P_I^+$; $X_I^- \leftarrow X_I^+ - X_I$;

$\quad\quad\quad\quad\quad\quad\quad\quad$ (* All of them are positive semidefinite, and

$\quad\quad$ $X = X_R^+ - X_R^- + i(X_I^+ - X_I^-)$ *)

$\quad\quad$ **for** $Y \in \{X_R^+, X_R^-, X_I^+, X_I^-\} \wedge Y \neq 0$ **do**

$\quad\quad\quad$ $F \leftarrow F \cup \{Y/\mathrm{tr}(Y)\}$;$\quad\quad\quad$ (* Fixed point states of $\mathcal{E}$ *)

$\quad\quad$ **end**

$\quad$ **end**

$\quad$ **if** $|F| = 1$ **then**

$\quad\quad$ **return** $\{\mathrm{supp}(Y)\}$;$\quad\quad\quad\quad\quad\quad$ (* Y is the only element of F *)

$\quad$ **else**

$\quad\quad$ $Y_1, Y_2 \leftarrow$ two arbitrary different elements of F;

$\quad\quad$ $P^+ \leftarrow$ the projector onto eigenspace of $Y_1 - Y_2$ with positive eigenvalues;

$\quad\quad$ $P^- \leftarrow P - P^+$;

$\quad\quad$ $\mathcal{E}^+ \leftarrow \mathcal{P}^+ \circ \mathcal{E}$;$\quad\quad\quad\quad\quad$ (* $\mathcal{P}^+$ is the super-operator $\{P^+\}$ *)

$\quad\quad$ $\mathcal{E}^- \leftarrow \mathcal{P}^- \circ \mathcal{E}$;$\quad\quad\quad\quad\quad$ (* $\mathcal{P}^-$ is the super-operator $\{P^-\}$ *)

$\quad\quad$ **return** GetBSCCs($\mathcal{E}^+, P^+$) $\cup$ GetBSCCs($\mathcal{E}^-, P^-$);

$\quad$ **end**

end

(i) Compute the matrix representation M of $\mathcal{E}_M$. The time complexity is

$$\sum_{s,t \in S} m_{s,t} d^4 = O(n^2 d^6),$$

where $m_{s,t} := |I^{s,t}| \leq d^2$ is the number of Kraus operators in $\mathbf{Q}[s,t]$.

(ii) Compute the matrix representation of $\mathcal{E}_{\mathcal{M}}^{\infty}$ using Eq. (6.14). Note that the time complexity of Jordan decomposition is $O(m^4)$ for an $m \times m$ matrix, and the matrix M has size $n^2 d^2 \times n^2 d^2$. This step takes time $O(n^8 d^8)$.

(iii) Convert the matrix representation to $\mathcal{E}_{\mathcal{M}}^{\infty}$, which takes time $O(n^4 d^4)$.

Finally, for the procedure GetBSCCs($\mathcal{E}_{\mathcal{M}}, I_{\hat{\mathcal{H}}}$) where $I_{\hat{\mathcal{H}}} = \mathcal{H}_c \otimes \mathcal{H}$, the most time-consuming step is to compute the null space of the matrix $I_{\hat{\mathcal{H}}} \otimes I_{\hat{\mathcal{H}}} - M$. This can be done by Gaussian elimination with complexity being $O((n^2 d^2)^3) = O(n^6 d^6)$. Note that each recursive call of the procedure decreases the dimension of the subspace by at least one. The complexity of computing GetBSCCs($\mathcal{E}_{\mathcal{M}}, I_{\hat{\mathcal{H}}}$) is $O(n^7 d^7)$. □

At the first glance, the time complexity $O(n^8 d^8)$ of Algorithm 10 looks very high. However, note that a typical super-operator on a d-dimensional Hilbert space has up to d^2 Kraus operators each of them being a $d \times d$ complex matrix. Thus the input size K of a PSVMC $\mathcal{M} = (S, \mathbf{Q}, \text{pri})$ is actually $O(n^2 d^4)$. Thus the time complexity of Algorithm 10 is indeed $O(K^4)$.

Note that the decomposition of M (the matrix representation of $\mathcal{E}_{\mathcal{M}}$) into Jordan blocks, for the purpose of computing $\mathcal{E}_{\mathcal{M}}^{\infty}$, is quite expensive. Therefore, for a practical implementation, an approximate approach might be preferable. Specifically, from

$$\mathcal{E}_{\mathcal{M}}^{\infty} = \lim_{N \to \infty} \frac{1}{N} \sum_{n=1}^{N} \mathcal{E}_{\mathcal{M}}^n$$

we can derive its matrix representation $M^{\infty} = \lim_{N \to \infty} M_N$ where

$$M_N := \frac{1}{N} \sum_{n=1}^{N} M^n.$$

We then compute $M_0, M_1, M_2, \ldots$ until we have reached an N for which

$$\|M_N - M_{N-1}\|_{\max} < \varepsilon$$

for a predefined precision ε, so as to obtain an approximation of M^{∞}. Note that M_N can be computed using a dynamic programming approach by means of the equality

$$M_N = \begin{cases} M & \text{if } N = 1, \\ \frac{1}{N}((N-1)M_{N-1} + M^N) & \text{if } N > 1. \end{cases}$$

In stochastic model checking, such value iteration based approaches are commonly used.

Figure 6.6 The SVMC $\mathcal{M}$ and parity automaton $\mathcal{A}$ for Example 6.39.

Example 6.39 As a complete example, let an SVMC $\mathcal{M}$ be depicted in Figure 6.6 (left) where $AP = \{s_0, s_1\}$ and for each s, $L(s) = \{s\}$. Let

$$\psi = \Box(s_0 \wedge \neg s_1),$$

with the corresponding parity automaton $\mathcal{A}$ shown on the right side of Figure 6.6 where for simplicity, we use a logic formula to represent a set of transitions. For example, $a_1 \xrightarrow{\text{true}} a_1$ means that for any $L \subseteq AP$, $a_1 \xrightarrow{L} a_1$. Then the product $\mathcal{M} \otimes \mathcal{A}$ of $\mathcal{M}$ and $\mathcal{A}$ can be depicted as in Figure 6.7. It is easy to calculate that the maximal transient space of $\mathcal{E}_{\mathcal{M} \otimes \mathcal{A}}$ is

$$T = \text{span}\{|s_0, a_0, 1\rangle, |s_1, a_0, +\rangle, |s_1, a_0, -\rangle, |s_0, a_1, 1\rangle, |s_1, a_1, -\rangle\},$$

and the BSCCs are $B_1 = \text{span}\{|s_0, a_0, 0\rangle\}$, $B_2 = \text{span}\{|s_0, a_1, 0\rangle\}$, and $B_3 = \text{span}\{|s_1, a_1, +\rangle\}$. Note that $\text{pri}(a_0) = 0$ and $\text{pri}(a_1) = 1$. Thus $BSCC_0 = B_1$, and $P_{\text{even}} = |s_0, a_0, 0\rangle\langle s_0, a_0, 0|$. Furthermore, we calculate that

$$\mathcal{E}^{\dagger}_{\mathcal{M} \otimes \mathcal{A}}(P_{\text{even}}) = P_{\text{even}},$$

and so

$$\mathcal{E}^{\infty\dagger}_{\mathcal{M} \otimes \mathcal{A}}(P_{\text{even}}) = P_{\text{even}}$$

as well. Let $\mathcal{E}_{(s, a_0)} = \{|s, a_0\rangle \otimes I\}$. Then

$$\text{Qr}^{\mathcal{M}}_s(\psi) = \text{Val}^{\mathcal{M} \otimes \mathcal{A}}((s, a_0)) = \mathcal{E}^{\dagger}_{(s, a_0)}(P_{\text{even}}) = \begin{cases} |0\rangle\langle 0| & \text{if } s = s_0, \\ 0 & \text{if } s = s_1. \end{cases}$$

6.5 Bibliographic Remarks

The materials presented in this chapter are mainly drawn from [48] and [51]. However, we restate all the results using positive-operator valued measure (POVM). Compared with the super-operator valued measure proposed in [48] and [51], POVM is conceptually more succinct and easy to manipulate. Furthermore, these two measures have the same power in describing the probability of satisfying any given temporal logic formula, when the SVMC is fed with an initial quantum state.

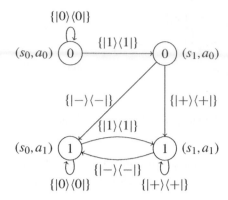

Figure 6.7　The product SVMC of $\mathcal{M}$ and $\mathcal{A}$ shown in Figure 6.6.

It should be pointed out that the model of SVMCs was also proposed by Gudder [62] in a slightly different way, but the problem of model checking SVMCs was not considered there.

Analysis of recursive quantum programs (see [117], section 3.4) was considered only as an example in this chapter. This problem was much more carefully studied in [52] by introducing a quantum generalisation of Etessami and Yannakakis's recursive Markov chains [46], namely recursive super-operator-valued Markov chains (RSVMCs for short); in particular, some techniques for reachability analysis of RSVMCs were developed there.

7

Conclusions and Prospects

This book systematically exposes the existing results of model checking quantum systems. However, the subject is still at an early stage of its development and far from maturity. As we already pointed out on several occasions, some crucial parts of it are missing and to be developed in future research. In particular, in Chapters 4 and 5, we only studied algorithms for checking several classes of reachability properties of quantum automata and quantum Markov chains and decision processes. Their more sophisticated dynamic properties were untouched in this book, because an appropriate temporal logic suitable for specifying these properties does not exist in the literature. Moreover, even for the results presented in the book, there seems still very large room for improvement.

In this concluding chapter, we briefly discuss several possible directions for the further development of the subject.

7.1 State Space Explosion

As is well known, the major practical hurdle in model checking classical systems is the so-called *state space explosion problem* – the combinatorial explosion of states [7, 34, 35]. Certainly, this problem cannot be avoided and it is even more serious in model checking quantum systems. Roughly speaking, we have the following correspondence:

$$
\begin{array}{ccc}
\begin{array}{c} \text{the states of} \\ \text{a classical system} \end{array} & \Leftrightarrow & \begin{array}{c} \text{(a family of) basis states} \\ \text{of a quantum system} \end{array} \\[2ex]
\begin{array}{c} \text{the size of the state space} \\ \text{of a classical system} \end{array} & \Leftrightarrow & \begin{array}{c} \text{the dimension of the state} \\ \text{Hilbert space of a quantum system} \end{array}
\end{array}
$$

But there is one more freedom in a quantum system: the choice of basis states in the aforementioned correspondence is not unique. Indeed, there are infinitely many different possible choices of basis states. Such a freedom comes from the superposition principle in quantum mechanics: the linear combination of a family of states is a state of the same system. The linearity defined by the superposition principle is a double-edged sword in model checking quantum systems: on one hand, it implies that the state space of a quantum system must be a continuum and thus uncountably infinite. Moreover, as pointed out in Section 1.3, linearity of quantum systems brings us with essential difficulties in designing model-checking algorithms for them: linearity should be carefully preserved by the algorithms. On the other hand, as we saw in Chapters 4 and 5, linearity often provides us with a possibility of reducing the problem of model checking a quantum system to only checking its basis states. This enables us to keep the complexity of model-checking algorithms for quantum systems at a similar level of those for classical and/or probabilistic systems.

   Many approaches have been proposed to mitigate the state space explosion problem in model checking classical systems, including symbolic model checking [25], bounded model checking [20], abstraction and reduction (see e.g., chapters 7 and 8 of [7]). It is obviously an interesting topic for future research to see how they can be extended to quantum systems.

7.2 Applications

Classical model checking has been successfully and widely used in verification and testing of hardware and software in computing and communication industry. However, model checking for quantum systems is currently only an area of theoretical research. Nevertheless, in this section, we discuss some of its potential applications.

7.2.1 Verification and Testing of Quantum Circuits

As the recent rapid progress in quantum hardware made by industries like Google and IBM, hardware verification is emerging as an important issue in quantum computing. Indeed, a series of testing and verification techniques have already been developed for quantum circuits in the past 15 years. Equivalence checking is arguably the most important formal verification technique being employed in the design flows of classical computing hardware. The problem of equivalence checking of quantum circuits has already been studied by several authors; for example, an algorithm for checking equivalence of (combinational) quantum circuits was developed in [111] based on a quantum variant of BDDs, called QuIDD, and the notion of miter circuit was generalised in [116] to reversible miter so that various simplification techniques of quantum circuits can be used in equivalence checking.

It is well known that classical model-checking techniques have been very successfully applied in hardware verification (see [42, 74] for a survey). As a simple example, equivalence checking of sequential circuits can be reduced to a reachability problem for a product automaton (see e.g., [91], chapter 9). Recently, the notion of sequential quantum circuit was defined in [114]. But it is still unclear how the reachability analysis techniques developed in Chapter 4 for quantum automata can be used in equivalence checking of sequential quantum circuits. Furthermore, is it possible to apply the reachability analysis techniques for quantum Markov chains and decision processes presented in Chapter 5 for (approximate) equivalence checking of quantum circuits with noisy gates?

7.2.2 Verification and Analysis of Quantum Cryptographic Protocols

Classical model checking has been particularly successfully applied in verification and analysis of security protocols, because they are usually small but subtle and difficult to analyse in the presence of adversaries [13]. Indeed, the earliest researches on model checking quantum systems targeted verification of the correctness and security of quantum cryptographic protocols. This line of research was already briefly discussed in Section 1.4, and the reader who is interested in it can consult a good survey [55] for more details. Here, we would like to point out that both the ways of modelling quantum communicating systems and specifying properties of these systems in these early studies are quite different from those developed in this book. It is certainly worthy to explore the possibility of applying the results presented in this book to quantum cryptography.

There exist two other formal methods applied in verification and analysis of quantum cryptographic protocols in the literature:

- Several process algebras have been employed to model quantum cryptographic protocols, and correctness and security of the protocols are then defined and verified based on the bisimulation semantics of the process algebras [1, 6, 37, 50, 73].
- Relational Hoare logic [11, 16] has been extended to the quantum setting [12, 81, 108] for reasoning about security of quantum cryptographic protocols.

It is interesting to understand the advantages and disadvantages of model checking, program logics and process algebras and how to effectively combine them in reasoning about quantum systems, in particular, quantum cryptographic protocols. The first attempt in this direction is [39], where model-checking techniques developed in [57] is used to verify quantum communicating processes modelled in a process algebra [56].

7.2.3 Verification and Analysis of Quantum Programs

Different from the earliest research on model checking quantum systems targeting verification of quantum cryptographic protocols (see Section 1.4), the techniques presented in Chapters 4 and 5 of this book were first motivated by termination analysis of quantum programs.

Termination analysis of quantum **while**-loops with unitary transformations as the loop bodies was initially studied in [118]. In [123], several major results in [118] were generalised into the case in which the loop bodies can be general quantum operations (i.e. super-operators); in particular, quantum Markov chains are identified as the semantic model of this kind of quantum loops, and termination analysis of quantum loops is reduced to a certain reachability problem of quantum Markov chains. Furthermore, termination analysis of non-deterministic and concurrent quantum programs was studied by Li et al. [83] and Yu et al. [123], respectively, as a reachability problem of quantum Markov decision processes; for example, repeated reachability defined in Section 5.4.2 for quantum Markov chains and its extension for quantum Markov decision processes are particularly useful in specifying a fairness condition for a (concurrent) quantum program consisting of a group of processes, which requires that each process participates in the computation infinitely often provided it is enabled. Indeed, the main results of [83, 123] are quantum generalisations of some results of Hart, Sharir and Pnueli [67, 105] for (nondeterministic and concurrent) probabilistic programs.

Super-operator-valued Markov chains (SVMCs) studied in Chapter 6 were designed to model the higher-level structure of quantum programs (and quantum communication protocols). Furthermore, a quantum generalisation of Etessami and Yannakakis's recursive Markov chains [46], namely recursive super-operator-valued Markov chains, was defined and some techniques for their reachability analysis were developed in [52]. These techniques can be used for termination analysis of recursive quantum programs (see [117], section 3.4 and chapter 7). Another class of analysis techniques for classical recursive programs are based on pushdown automata; see, for example, [45]. A notion of pushdown quantum automata was introduced in [58], but it is still not clear how this kind of pushdown quantum automata can be used in the analysis of recursive quantum programs.

Up to now, applications of model checking in verification and analysis of quantum programs still have not gone beyond termination analysis. On the other hand, testing and debugging techniques for quantum programs are emerging recently [69, 78, 84, 90]. We can expect that as in classical computing, debugging, testing, logical proof and model checking will be combined to guarantee correctness of quantum programs.

7.3 Tools: Model Checkers for Quantum Systems

All of the potential applications discussed in Section 7.2 will heavily depend on the implementation of automatic tools: model checkers for quantum systems. Although this area is not totally empty, it is at the very beginning.

The first model checker for quantum systems was presented in [57], where only those systems that can be modelled as quantum circuits expressible in the stabiliser formalism [59] are dealt with, and the checked properties are specified using a subset of the quantum computation tree logic QCTL defined in [8, 9]. Both the system's model and checked properties there are fundamentally different from those considered in this book.

A model checker QPMC for super-operator-valued Markov chains (SVMCs) studied in Chapter 6 was described in [49]. The reader can find a command-line version of QPMC at http://iscasmc.ios.ac.cn/tool/. Presently, it can only check CTL (computational tree logic) properties of SVMCs, but an extension that can also check LTL (linear temporal logic) properties of SVMCs will be launched soon. A model checker implementing the algorithms for reachability analysis of quantum automata and quantum Markov chains and decision processes presented in Chapters 4 and 5 is under development by a team at the Institute of Software, Chinese Academy of Sciences, and a preliminary version will be announced soon at http://qsoft.ios.ac.cn/tools/.

There are numerous problems to be solved in implementing efficient model checkers for quantum systems. Besides the state space explosion problem discussed in Section 7.1, another key factor that has a significant influence on the efficiency of model checkers for quantum systems is the involved heavy computation of high-dimensional matrices. To mitigate this issue, perhaps we can borrow some of the many ideas proposed by researchers in the area of (classical) simulation of many-body quantum physics. In particular, tensor networks (see [94] for an introduction) have been widely employed in simulations of large quantum circuits on (classical) supercomputers. We can anticipate that tensor networks will play a role in model checking quantum systems similar to that played by data structure BDDs (binary decision diagrams) in classical model checking.

7.4 From Model Checking Quantum Systems to Quantum Model Checking

The reader should have noticed that all of the principles and algorithms developed in this book are directed towards classical computers to check the properties of quantum systems. It is natural to ask: can quantum computers do better in model checking quantum systems (or even classical systems)? This is a wide open problem, but the success of quantum simulation suggests that it might be a direction worth pursuing in future research. At this time, we do not have a clear idea about it, but would like to raise the following two slightly more specific questions:

- Quantum simulation (or more precisely, simulation of quantum systems using quantum computers) has been identified as one of the most important applications of quantum computing from the very beginning (see e.g. [53, 85]; also see [93] for an introduction), and afterwards several new quantum simulation algorithms have been proposed (see e.g. [17, 31]). How can the design ideas of these algorithms be incorporated into model checking quantum systems?
- We have observed in Chapters 4, 5 and 6 that linear algebraic computations (e.g. computing the inner product of two large vectors) are indispensable components of our algorithms for model checking quantum systems. So, can the idea of the HHL (Harrow–Hassidim–Lloyd) algorithm for systems of linear equations [66] (or even HHL itself used as a subroutine) provide us with a quantum speedup for model checking quantum systems?

Appendix 1

Proofs of Technical Lemmas in Chapter 4

In this appendix, for the convenience of the reader, we review some mathematical tools needed in Chapter 4 and provide the proofs omitted there.

A1.1 Proof of Lemma 4.36

Given a unitary operator U, let $\{e^{2\pi i \phi_j}\}_{j \in J}$ be the set of its eigenvalues and P_j the projection on the eigenspace of U associated with $e^{2\pi i \phi_j}$. Let

$$R = \{(j,k) \in J \times J : \phi_j - \phi_k \text{ is rational}\}.$$

For any $(j,k) \in R$ with $\phi_j \neq \phi_k$, there exist coprime integers $m_{j,k}$ and $n_{j,k}$ such that

$$\phi_j - \phi_k = m_{j,k}/n_{j,k}.$$

Let $p = lcm\{n_{j,k} : (j,k) \in R\}$, where $n_{j,k} = 1$ when $\phi_j = \phi_k$.

We now prove that for any subspace K, $U^p K = K$ whenever $U^n K = K$ for some $n \geq 1$. Suppose $U^n K = K$. This implies that the restriction of U^n to subspace K is also a unitary operator that is diagonalisable. Then there exists an orthonormal basis of K with each state being an eigenstate of U^n. Let $|\psi\rangle$ be an arbitrary state in this basis such that $U^n |\psi\rangle = \lambda |\psi\rangle$ for some $\lambda \neq 0$. Let

$$J_\psi = \{j \in J : P_j |\psi\rangle \neq 0\}.$$

Then $|\psi\rangle = \sum_{j \in J_\psi} P_j |\psi\rangle$, and from $U^n |\psi\rangle = \lambda |\psi\rangle$ we have

$$\sum_{j \in J_\psi} e^{2\pi i n \phi_j} P_j |\psi\rangle = \lambda \sum_{j \in J_\psi} P_j |\psi\rangle.$$

Thus for any $j, k \in J_\psi$,

$$e^{2\pi i n \phi_j} = e^{2\pi i n \phi_k},$$

and so $(j,k) \in R$. Now by the definition of p, we know

$$e^{2\pi i p \phi_j} = e^{2\pi i p \phi_k}$$

as well. Thus $|\psi\rangle$ is an eigenvalue of U^p from the arbitrariness of j and k. It then follows that $U^p K = K$.

Note that we have actually proved $p \geq p_U$. We now show $p \leq p_U$. For any $(j,k) \in R$, let $|\psi\rangle \in \mathcal{H}$ such that $J_\psi = \{j,k\}$ and $K = \text{span}\{|\psi\rangle\}$. From

$$e^{2\pi i p \phi_j} = e^{2\pi i p \phi_k},$$

it is easy to check that $U^p K = K$, and so $U^{p_U} K = K$ from the definition of p_U. Thus

$$e^{2\pi i p_U \phi_j} = e^{2\pi i p_U \phi_k}$$

as well. This means that p_U is a common multiplier of $n_{j,k}$ for all $(j,k) \in R$, so $p \leq p_U$.

Finally, note that the computation of $p_U = p$ boils down to computing the eigenvalues of U, which can be done in time $O(d^3)$.

A1.2 Proof of Lemma 4.39

We prove Lemma 4.39 in two different cases.

- **Case 1**: Condition (i) in Theorem 4.38 is not satisfied by $\mathbb{X}$. Let

$$\mathbb{Y} = \{Y_i \in \mathbb{X} : \exists \alpha \in Act.U_\alpha Y_i \notin \mathbb{X}\}, \tag{A1.1}$$

Y_{i_0} be a subspace in $\mathbb{Y}$ with the largest dimension, and $U_{\alpha_0} Y_{i_0} \notin \mathbb{X}$. We claim that $U_{\alpha_0} Y_{i_0} \not\subseteq Y_j$ for any $Y_j \in \mathbb{X}$. Otherwise, let $U_{\alpha_0} Y_{i_0} \subseteq Y_{j_0}$. Obviously, $U_{\alpha_0} Y_{i_0} \neq Y_{j_0}$, thus $\dim Y_{j_0} > \dim Y_{i_0}$ and so $Y_{j_0} \notin \mathbb{Y}$. It is easy to prove by induction on n that all the subspaces $U_{\alpha_0}^n Y_{j_0}, n = 0, 1, \ldots$, are in $\mathbb{X}$. So, there exist n_1 and n_2 such that $n_2 > n_1$ and

$$U_{\alpha_0}^{n_1} Y_{j_0} = U_{\alpha_0}^{n_2} Y_{j_0}.$$

Consequently, Y_{i_0} is a proper subset of

$$U_{\alpha_0}^{-1} Y_{j_0} = U_{\alpha_0}^{n_2 - n_1 - 1} Y_{j_0},$$

which is in $\mathbb{X}$. This contradicts the assumption that $Y_i \not\subseteq Y_j$ for all $i \neq j$.

Now for Y_{i_0}, we set

$$W_j = Y_{i_0} \cap U_{\alpha_0}^{-1} Y_j,$$

where $j = 1, 2, \ldots q$. Then each W_j is a proper subspace of Y_{i_0}. On the other hand, from the definition of $Sat(\mathbf{I}f)$, one can easily verify that $U_\alpha |\psi\rangle \in Sat(\mathbf{I}f)$ for all $|\psi\rangle \in Sat(\mathbf{I}f)$ and $\alpha \in Act$. Thus, for any state $|\psi\rangle \in Sat(\mathbf{I}f) \cap Y_{i_0}$, we know that $U_{\alpha_0}|\psi\rangle \in Sat(\mathbf{I}f) \subseteq \bigcup \mathbb{X}$. So $|\psi\rangle$ is in some $U_{\alpha_0}^{-1} Y_j$. Moreover, we have

$$|\psi\rangle \in Y_{i_0} \cap U_{\alpha_0}^{-1} Y_j = W_j,$$

and thus Eq. (4.17) holds for $i = i_0$.

- **Case 2**: Condition (i) in Theorem 4.38 is satisfied by $\mathbb{X}$ but condition (ii) is not. Then we can find a simple loop

$$Y_{r_0} \overset{U_{\alpha_1}}{\to} Y_{r_1} \overset{U_{\alpha_2}}{\to} \cdots \overset{U_{\alpha_{k-1}}}{\to} Y_{r_{k-1}} \overset{U_{\alpha_k}}{\to} Y_{r_0}, \tag{A1.2}$$

such that $Y_{r_i} \not\subseteq V_t$ for all $i \in \{0, 1, \ldots, k-1\}$ and $t \in \{1, 2, \ldots, m\}$. For each i, we write

$$T_i = U_{\alpha_i} \ldots U_{\alpha_1} U_{\alpha_k} \ldots U_{\alpha_{i+1}},$$

where the addition is taken modulo k. Then it holds that

$$T_i^n Y_{r_i} = Y_{r_i} \not\subseteq V_t,$$

and $Y_{r_i} \not\subseteq T_i^n K(T_i, V_t)$ for all $n \geq 0$, where $K(T_i, V_t)$ is defined as in Theorem 4.37.(i). Let $p_i = p_{T_i}$ be the period of T_i. For any $i \in \{0, 1, \ldots, k-1\}$, $n \in \{0, 1, \ldots, p_i - 1\}$, and $t \in \{1, 2, \ldots, m\}$, put

$$R_{i,t,n} = U_{\alpha_1}^{-1} U_{\alpha_2}^{-1} \ldots U_{\alpha_i}^{-1} T_i^n K(T_i, V_t).$$

Then $Y_{r_0} \not\subseteq R_{i,t,n}$ and $R'_{i,t,n} := Y_{r_0} \cap R_{i,t,n}$ is a proper subspace of Y_{r_0}.

Now we have to show that the set of subspaces $R'_{i,t,n}$ satisfies Eq. (4.17). For any state $|\psi_0\rangle \in Sat(\mathbf{I}f) \cap Y_{r_0}$, let $\pi = |\psi_0\rangle|\psi_1\rangle \cdots$ be the path of $\mathcal{A}$ by repeatedly and consecutively performing $U_{\alpha_1}, U_{\alpha_2}, \ldots, U_{\alpha_k}$ starting from $|\psi\rangle$. Since $\pi \models \mathbf{I}f$, we have $|\psi_n\rangle \in [\![f]\!]$ for infinitely many n. This implies that there exist $i \in \{0, 1, \ldots, k-1\}$ and $t \in \{1, 2, \ldots, m\}$ such that $|\psi_{kn+i}\rangle \in V_t$ for infinitely many n. Thus the set $\{n : T_i^n|\psi_i\rangle \in V_t\}$ is infinite. According to the result of the subsection 4.6.1, we have $|\psi_i\rangle \in T^n K(T_i, V_t)$ for some $n \in \{0, 1, \ldots, p_i - 1\}$. That is, $|\psi_0\rangle \in R_{i,t,n}$.

A1.3 Skolem's Problem for Linear Recurrence Sequences

Skolem's problem was used in Section 4.7 for proving undecidability of certain reachability in quantum automata. In this section and the next one, for convenience of the reader, we recall several results about Skolem's problem needed there. A linear recurrence sequence is a sequence $\{a_n\}_{n=0}^{\infty}$ satisfying a linear recurrence relation given as follows:

$$a_{n+d} = c_{d-1}a_{n+d-1} + c_{d-2}a_{n+d-2} + \cdots + c_0 a_n, \tag{A1.3}$$

for all $n \geq 0$, where $d, c_0, c_1, \ldots, c_{d-1}$ are all fixed constants with $c_0 \neq 0$. Here, d is called the order of this relation.

For a linear recurrence sequence $\{a_n\}_{n=0}^{\infty}$. Let

$$Z = \{n \in \mathbb{N} \mid a_n = 0\} \tag{A1.4}$$

be the set of indices of its null elements. The problem of characterising Z is usually called *Skolem's Problem*. It was first studied by Skolem [106] in 1934. His result was generalised by Mahler [86] and Lech [77].

Theorem A1.1 (Skolem–Mahler–Lech) *In a field of characteristic 0, for any linear recurrence sequence $\{a_n\}_{n=0}^{\infty}$, the set Z of indices of its null elements is semilinear; that is, it is the union of a finite set and finitely many arithmetic progressions.*

Skolem's problem was further considered in terms of decidability. The problem of deciding whether or not Z is infinite was solved by Berstel and Mignotte [18] who found an algorithm for generating all arithmetic progressions used in Theorem A1.1. The problem of deciding the finiteness of the complement of Z was studied by Salomaa and Soittola [103]. Their results are summarised as the following:

Theorem A1.2 (Berstel–Mignotte-Salomaa–Soittola) *For linear recurrence sequences $\{a_n\}_{n=0}^{\infty}$, it is decidable whether or not*

(i) *Z is infinite;*
(ii) *$Z = \mathbb{N}$;*
(iii) *Z contains all except finitely many natural numbers.*

The following emptiness problem dual to item (ii) in Theorem A1.2 was also considered in the literature, but it is still open; for details, we refer to [64, 95].

Problem A1.1 *Given a linear recurrence sequence $\{a_n\}_{n=0}^{\infty}$, decide whether or not Z is empty.*

A1.4 Skolem's Problem in Matrix Form

In this section, we continue our discussion about Skolem's problem, and in particular, show a useful connection between the quantum reachability problem and Skolem's problem. The linear recurrence relation equation (A1.3) can be written in a matrix form:

$$a_n = u^T M^n v, \tag{A1.5}$$

where M is the $d \times d$ matrix

$$
\begin{bmatrix}
c_{d-1} & c_{d-2} & \cdots & c_1 & c_0 \\
1 & 0 & \cdots & 0 & 0 \\
0 & 1 & \cdots & 0 & 0 \\
\vdots & \vdots & \vdots & \ddots & \vdots \\
0 & 0 & \cdots & 1 & 0
\end{bmatrix},
$$

and

$$u = [1,0,\ldots,0]^T, \qquad v = [a_{d-1}, a_{d-2}, \ldots, a_0]^T$$

are d-dimensional column vectors. Here, T stands for transpose.

On the other hand, if $\{a_n\}_{n=0}^{\infty}$ is given in the form of Eq. (A1.5) for general u,v and M of dimension d, then the minimal polynomial $g(x)$ of M is of order at most d, and $g(M) = 0$. Thus, a linear recurrence relation of order no greater than d is satisfied by $\{a_n\}_{n=0}^{\infty}$. Therefore, Skolem's problem can be equivalently considered in terms of the matrix form equation (A1.5).

Now let us return to the Problem of Checking Reachability in Section 4.6. We only consider a very special case: (1) $|Act| = 1$, that is, there is only one unitary operator U_α of $\mathcal{A}$, (2) $f = V$ is a subspace of $\mathcal{H}$, and (3) $\dim \mathcal{H}_{ini} = \dim V^{\perp} = 1$. Let $|\psi_0\rangle \in \mathcal{H}_{ini}$ and $|\varphi\rangle \in V^{\perp}$. Then we have

$$\mathcal{L}(\mathcal{A}, f) = \{n \in \mathbb{N} \mid \langle \varphi | U_\alpha^n | \psi_0 \rangle = 0\}.$$

It is actually the set Z in Eq. (A1.4) if we think of U_α, $|\varphi\rangle$ and $|\psi_0\rangle$ as M, u, and v in Eq. (A1.5), respectively. From Lemma 4.32, the emptiness of Z (Problem A1.1), and the properties (i), (ii) and (iii) of Z in Theorem A1.2 are equivalent to the following satisfaction relations:

$$\mathcal{A} \models \mathbf{F}V, \qquad \mathcal{A} \models \mathbf{I}V, \qquad \mathcal{A} \models \mathbf{G}V, \qquad \mathcal{A} \models \mathbf{U}V,$$

respectively. From this point of view, our decidability for a general f (Theorem 4.35) is somewhat a generalization of the decidable results (Theorem A1.2) of Skolem's problem where f is taken to be a subspace.

We further consider an undecidable result relevant to Skolem's problem. Instead of $\{M^n \mid n \in \mathbb{N}\}$ in Eq. (A1.5), there is a semi-group generated by a finite number of matrices $M_1, M_2, \ldots, M_k$, written as $\langle M_1, M_2, \ldots, M_k \rangle$. Then the emptiness problem can be generalised as follows:

Problem A1.2 *Provided $d \times d$ matrices $M_1, M_2, \ldots, M_k$ and d-dimensional vectors u and v, decide whether or not $\exists M \in \langle M_1, M_2, \ldots, M_k \rangle$ s.t. $u^T M v = 0$.*

The above problem was proved to be undecidable in [29] and [97], through a reduction from the Post's Correspondence Problem (PCP) [99]. Similar to the discussion in the preceding section, we can choose M_i as unitary operators and u, v as quantum states, and then the emptiness of $\mathcal{L}(\mathcal{A}, f)$ for $f = V$ and $\dim \mathcal{H}_{ini} = \dim V^\perp = 1$ but with $|Act| > 1$ being allowed can be regarded as a special case of Problem A1.2. In fact, this problem was also proved to be undecidable by Blondel et al. [21].

Theorem A1.3 (Blondel–Jeandel–Koiran–Portier) *It is undecidable whether or not $\mathcal{L}(\mathcal{A}, V)$ is empty, given a quantum automaton $\mathcal{A}$ and a subspace V with $\dim \mathcal{H}_{ini} = \dim V^\perp = 1$.*

A1.5 Constructing Quantum Automata from Minsky Machines

In this section, we complete the proof of Theorem 4.42 by providing a detailed construction of quantum automaton $\mathcal{A}$ briefly described in Subsection 4.7.2 as well as atomic propositions V and W in Eq. (4.21).

A1.5.1 Encoding Classical States into Quantum States

This subsection is the first step of constructing quantum automaton $\mathcal{A}$. We show how to encode the states of $\mathcal{M}$ into quantum states in a finite dimensional Hilbert space.

First, we use qubit states in the 2-dimensional Hilbert space $\mathcal{H}_2 = \text{span}\{|0\rangle, |1\rangle\}$ to encode natural numbers. Consider the following unitary operator acting on $\mathcal{H}_2$:

$$G = |+\rangle\langle+| + e^{i\theta}|-\rangle\langle-|,$$

where

$$|\pm\rangle = (|0\rangle \pm |1\rangle)/\sqrt{2} \quad \text{and} \quad e^{i\theta} = (3 + 4i)/5.$$

It is easy to see that for any integer n,

$$G^n|0\rangle = |0\rangle \Leftrightarrow n = 0.$$

So for each integer n, we can use $G^n|0\rangle$ to encode n. Moreover, operator G can be thought of as the successor function $g(n) = n + 1$.

Now, let $\mathcal{H}_a = \mathcal{H}_b = \mathcal{H}_2$ and we use states in $\mathcal{H}_a$ and $\mathcal{H}_b$ to encode the counters a and b, respectively. Specifically, for each value n of $c \in \{a, b\}$, the corresponding state is $|\phi_n\rangle = G_c^n|0\rangle \in \mathcal{H}_c$.

We simply encode the instruction labels l as orthonormal quantum states $|l\rangle$ and construct the Hilbert space $\mathcal{H}_L = \text{span}\{|l\rangle | l \in L\}$. Then a state (a, b, x) of $\mathcal{M}$ can be encoded as the quantum state

$$|\phi_a\rangle|\phi_b\rangle|x\rangle \in \mathcal{H}_a \otimes \mathcal{H}_b \otimes \mathcal{H}_L.$$

Moreover, the computation $\sigma_\mathcal{M}$ of $\mathcal{M}$ is encoded as the sequence σ_0 of quantum states. We note that $\mathcal{M}$ terminates if and only if $x_i = l_m$ for some state (a_i, b_i, x_i) in $\sigma_\mathcal{M}$. This condition is equivalent to $|\psi_i\rangle \in V_0$, where

$$V_0 = \mathcal{H}_a \otimes \mathcal{H}_b \otimes \text{span}\{|l_m\rangle\}. \tag{A1.6}$$

So the termination of $\mathcal{M}$ is reduced to reachability of σ_0 as follows:

Lemma A1.4 *$\mathcal{M}$ terminates if and only if $\sigma_0 \models FV_0$.*

Exercise A1.1 Prove Lemma A1.4.

A1.5.2 Simulating Classical Transitions by Unitary Operators

In this subsection, we construct unitary operators of quantum automaton $\mathcal{A}$ to encode the state transitions of $\mathcal{M}$. For any state (a, b, x) of $\mathcal{M}$, we consider the transition from this state to its successor. We need to consider the following two cases, separately:

(i) $x \in L_{1a} \cup L_{1b} \cup L'_{2a} \cup L'_{2b} \cup L''_{2a} \cup L''_{2b} \cup \{l_m\}$. Then from the definition of L, x is of form

$$x : \quad c \leftarrow c + e; \text{ goto } y,$$

where $c \in \{a, b\}$, $y \in L$ and $e = 1, 0, -1$ for $l \in L_{1c}$, $L'_{2c} \cup \{l_n\}$, L''_{2c}, respectively. So the successor of (a, b, x) is as $(\tilde{a}, \tilde{b}, y)$, where $\tilde{a} = a + e$, $\tilde{b} = b$ for $c = a$ and $\tilde{a} = a$, $\tilde{b} = b + e$ for $c = b$. We construct a unitary operator corresponding to x:

$$U_x = O_c^e \otimes O_{xy},$$

where $O_a = G_a \otimes I_b$ and $O_b = I_a \otimes G_b$ are unitary operators on $\mathcal{H}_a \otimes \mathcal{H}_b$, and O_{xy} is a unitary operator on $\mathcal{H}_L$ satisfying $O_{xy}|x\rangle = |y\rangle$. Obviously, we have

$$|\phi_{\tilde{a}}\rangle|\phi_{\tilde{b}}\rangle|y\rangle = U_x|\phi_a\rangle|\phi_b\rangle|x\rangle$$

for any a, b. So U_x is what we want.

(ii) $x \in L_{2a} \cup L_{2b}$. Then x is of the form

$$x : \quad \text{if } c = 0 \text{ then goto } y; \text{ else goto } z;$$

where $c \in \{a, b\}$, $y \in L'_{2c}$ and $z \in L''_{2c}$. The successor of (a, b, x) is (a, b, y) for $c = 0$, and is (a, b, z) for $c \neq 0$. We construct two unitary operators corresponding to x:

$$U_{x0} = I_a \otimes I_b \otimes O_{xy} \text{ and } U_{x1} = I_a \otimes I_b \otimes O_{xz},$$

where $O_{xy}|x\rangle - |y\rangle$ and $O_{xz}|x\rangle = |z\rangle$. Thus, U_{x0} is used when $c = 0$, and U_{x1} is used when $c \neq 0$.

Now, we only need to specifically construct the unitary operator O_{xy} for given $x, y \in L$. To this end, we construct for each $l \in L$ a new quantum state $|\hat{l}\rangle$ to be the result of $O_{xy}|l\rangle$ (for $x \neq l$). Formally, we construct a new state space $\hat{\mathcal{H}}_L = \text{span}\{|\hat{l}\rangle : x \in L\}$ and extend $\mathcal{H}_L$ to

$$\mathcal{H}_{2L} = \mathcal{H}_L \oplus \hat{\mathcal{H}}_L = \text{span}\{|l\rangle, |\hat{l}\rangle | l \in L\}.$$

Then O_{xy} is defined in $\mathcal{H}_{2L}$ as

$$O_{xy}|x\rangle = |y\rangle, \ O_{xy}|l\rangle = |\hat{l}\rangle \ (\forall l \in L, l \neq x),$$
$$O_{xy}|\hat{y}\rangle = |\hat{x}\rangle, \ O_{xy}|\hat{l}\rangle = |l\rangle \ (\forall l \in L, l \neq y). \tag{A1.7}$$

Notably, O_{xy} satisfies the following property:

$$O_{xy}|z\rangle \in \hat{\mathcal{H}}_L, \forall z \in L \text{ and } z \neq x. \tag{A1.8}$$

Now we can put the ingredients prepared in the last section and this one together to define quantum automaton $\mathcal{A}$ as follows:

- The state space is $\mathcal{H} = \mathcal{H}_a \otimes \mathcal{H}_b \otimes \mathcal{H}_{2L}$.
- The unitary operators are $\{U_\alpha | \alpha \in Act\}$, where

$$Act = \{x0, x1 | x \in L_{2a} \cup L_{2b}\} \cup L \setminus (L_{2a} \cup L_{2b}).$$

- The initial state is $|\psi_0\rangle = |0\rangle |0\rangle |l_0\rangle$.

From the construction of the unitary operators, we see that the sequence σ_0 of quantum states defined by Eq. (4.23) is achievable in $\mathcal{A}$.

A1.5.3 Construction of V and W

This subsection is the last step to achieve Eq. (4.21); that is, we define the two atomic propositions V and W (subspaces of the state Hilbert space of quantum automaton $\mathcal{A}$).

First, we find a way to distinguish σ_0 from other paths of $\mathcal{A}$. Specifically, we consider a state $|\psi_n\rangle = |\phi_{a_n}\rangle |\phi_{b_n}\rangle |x_n\rangle$ in σ_0 to be transformed by a 'mismatched' unitary operator in $\{U_\alpha | \alpha \in Act\}$; namely, this unitary operator transforms $|\psi_n\rangle$ into a state $|\psi'\rangle$ other than $|\psi_{n+1}\rangle$. Each unitary operator in $\mathcal{A}$ is of the form U_y, U_{y0}, or U_{y1}, where y is the corresponding instruction. If $y \neq x_n$, then it is definitely mismatched. It follows from Eq. (A1.8) that $|\psi'\rangle \in \hat{V}$, where $\hat{V} = \mathcal{H}_a \otimes \mathcal{H}_b \otimes \hat{\mathcal{H}}_L$.

Now we only need to consider the case of $y = x_n$. We have $x_n \in L_{2a} \cup L_{2b}$, because there are two unitary operators corresponding to x_n: the one mismatched and the one not. For $x_n \in L_{2a}$, there are two cases:

(i) $a_n = 0$ and the mismatched unitary operator is $U_{x_n 1}$. From the definition of $U_{x_n 1}$, we have

$$|\psi'\rangle = U_{x_n 1}|0\rangle |\phi_{b_n}\rangle |x_n\rangle = |0\rangle |\phi_{b_n}\rangle |z\rangle,$$

where $z \in L''_{2a}$. We write

$$V_{2a} = \text{span}\{|0\rangle\} \otimes \mathcal{H}_b \otimes \text{span}\{|l\rangle : l \in L''_{2a}\}.$$

Then $|\psi'\rangle \in V_{2a}$.

(ii) $a_n > 0$ and the mismatched one is $U_{x_n 0}$. From the definition of $U_{x_n 0}$, we have

$$|\psi'\rangle = U_{x_n 0}|\phi_{a_n}\rangle |\phi_{b_n}\rangle |x_n\rangle = |\phi_{a_n}\rangle |\phi_{b_n}\rangle |y\rangle,$$

where $y \in L'_{2a}$. We write

$$V_{1a} = \mathcal{H}_a \otimes \mathcal{H}_b \otimes \text{span}\{|l\rangle : l \in L'_{2a}\},$$
$$W_a = \text{span}\{|0\rangle\} \otimes \mathcal{H}_b \otimes \text{span}\{|l\rangle : l \in L'_{2a}\}.$$

Then $|\psi'\rangle \in V_{1a}\backslash W_a$.

Similarly, for $x_n \in L_{2b}$ we can prove that $|\psi'\rangle \in V_{2b}$ for $b_n = 0$ and $|\psi'\rangle \in V_{1b}\backslash W_b$ for $b_n > 0$, where

$$V_{1b} = \mathcal{H}_a \otimes \mathcal{H}_b \otimes \text{span}\{|l\rangle : l \in L'_{2b}\},$$
$$V_{2b} = \mathcal{H}_a \otimes \text{span}\{|0\rangle\} \otimes \text{span}\{|l\rangle : l \in L''_{2b}\},$$
$$W_b = \mathcal{H}_a \otimes \text{span}\{|0\rangle\} \otimes \text{span}\{|l\rangle : l \in L'_{2b}\}.$$

We have actually proved that a state

$$|\psi'\rangle \in \hat{V} \cup (V_{1a}\backslash W_a) \cup (V_{1b}\backslash W_b) \cup V_{2a} \cup V_{2b} \qquad (A1.9)$$

is always reachable in computation paths of $\mathcal{A}$ other than σ_0. On the other hand, it is also easy to verify that such a state cannot be in σ_0. So σ_0 can be distinguished by this reachability property.

Now we put

$$V = V_0 + \hat{V} + V_{1a} + V_{1b} + V_{2a} + V_{2b},$$
$$W = W_a + W_b,$$

where V_0 is defined by Eq. (A1.6). Then we have

Lemma A1.5 *For all paths p in $\mathcal{A}$ with state sequences $\sigma(p) \neq \sigma_0$, we have $\sigma(p) \models F(V \wedge \neg W)$.*

Proof We only need to note that the union of the five sets in Eq. (A1.9) is included in $\{0\} \cup (V\backslash W)$, and then this result is straightforward from our preceding discussion. □

Moreover, we have the following:

Lemma A1.6 $\sigma_0 \models F(V \wedge \neg W)$ *iff* $\sigma_0 \models FV_0$.

Proof It suffices to prove that for any state $|\psi_n\rangle$ in σ_0,

$$|\psi_n\rangle \in V\backslash W \text{ iff } |\psi_n\rangle \in V_0.$$

The 'if' part is obvious since $V_0 \subseteq V$ and $V_0 \cap W = \{0\}$. We now prove the 'only if' part. As $|\psi_n\rangle = |\phi_{a_n}\rangle |\phi_{b_n}\rangle |x_n\rangle$ is a state in σ_0, (a_n, b_n, x_n) is a state in $\sigma_\mathcal{M}$ and thus $x_n \in L$. From the definition of L and Eq. (4.20), $|\psi_n\rangle$ is checked in the following cases of x_n:

$$x_n \in L_{1a} \cup L_{1b} \cup L_{2a} \cup L_{2b}, \text{ thus } |\psi_n\rangle \notin V;$$
$$x_n \in L'_{1a} \Rightarrow a_n = 0, \text{ thus } |\psi_n\rangle \in W_a;$$

$$x_n \in L'_{1b} \Rightarrow b_n = 0, \text{ thus } |\psi_n\rangle \in W_b;$$
$$x_n \in L''_{2a} \Rightarrow a_n \neq 0, \text{ thus } |\psi_n\rangle \notin V;$$
$$x_n \in L''_{2b} \Rightarrow b_n \neq 0, \text{ thus } |\psi_n\rangle \notin V.$$

None of them satisfies $|\psi_n\rangle \in V \setminus W$. So the only possibility is $x_n = l_m$, and then $|\psi_n\rangle \in V_0$.

$\square$

Finally, we obtain Eq. (4.21) by simply combining Lemmas A1.4, A1.5 and A1.6. Undecidability of $\mathcal{A} \models \mathbf{F}f$ is so proved, even for the simple form of $f = V \wedge \neg W$.

Appendix 2

Proofs of Technical Lemmas in Chapter 5

In this appendix, we provide the proofs of several technical lemmas omitted in Chapter 5.

A2.1 Proof of Lemma 5.25 (ii)

We are going to show that any two BSCCs X, Y of a quantum Markov chain are orthogonal provided dim $X \neq$ dim Y. This proof requires some technical preparations. The next lemma shows that every complex matrix can be represented by four positive matrices.

> **Lemma A2.1** *For any matrix A, there are positive matrices B_1, B_2, B_3, B_4 such that*
>
> (i) $A = (B_1 - B_2) + i(B_3 - B_4)$; *and*
> (ii) $tr B_i^2 \leq tr(A^\dagger A)$ $(i = 1, 2, 3, 4)$.

Proof We can take Hermitian operators

$$(A + A^\dagger)/2 = B_1 - B_2, \quad -i(A - A^\dagger)/2 = B_3 - B_4,$$

where B_1, B_2 are positive operators with orthogonal supports, and B_3, B_4 are also positive operators with orthogonal supports. Then it holds that

$$
\begin{aligned}
\sqrt{tr B_1{}^2} &= \sqrt{tr(B_1{}^\dagger B_1)} \\
&\leq \sqrt{tr(B_1{}^\dagger B_1 + B_2{}^\dagger B_2)} \\
&= \|((A + A^\dagger)/2 \otimes I)|\Phi\rangle\| \\
&\leq (\|(A \otimes I)|\Phi\rangle\| + \|(A^\dagger \otimes I)|\Phi\rangle\|)/2 \\
&= \sqrt{tr(A^\dagger A)}.
\end{aligned}
$$

It is similar to prove that $tr B_i{}^2 \leq tr(A^\dagger A)$ for $i = 2, 3, 4$. □

An operator A (not necessarily a partial density operator as in Definition 5.22 (i)) in $\mathcal{H}$ is called a fixed point of quantum operation $\mathcal{E}$ if $\mathcal{E}(A) = A$. The following lemma shows that fixed points can be preserved by the positive matrix decomposition given in Lemma A2.1.

Lemma A2.2 *Let $\mathcal{E}$ be a quantum operation in $\mathcal{H}$ and A a fixed point of $\mathcal{E}$. If we have*

(i) $A = (X_+ - X_-) + i(Y_+ - Y_-)$;
(ii) X_+, X_-, Y_+, Y_- *are all positive matrices; and*
(iii) $\mathrm{supp}(X_+) \perp \mathrm{supp}(X_-)$ *and* $\mathrm{supp}(Y_+) \perp \mathrm{supp}(Y_-)$,

then X_+, X_-, Y_+, Y_- are all fixed points of $\mathcal{E}$.

Exercise A2.1 Prove Lemma A2.2.

Now we are ready to prove Lemma 5.25 (ii). Suppose without any loss of generality that $\dim X < \dim Y$. By Theorem 5.24, we know that there are two minimal fixed point states ρ and σ with $\mathrm{supp}(\rho) = X$ and $\mathrm{supp}(\sigma) = Y$. Note that for any $\lambda > 0$, $\rho - \lambda\sigma$ is also a fixed point of $\mathcal{E}$. We can take λ sufficiently large such that

$$\rho - \lambda\sigma = \Delta_+ - \Delta_-,$$

with $\Delta_\pm$ being positive, $\mathrm{supp}(\Delta_-) = \mathrm{supp}(\sigma)$, and $\mathrm{supp}(\Delta_+) \perp \mathrm{supp}(\Delta_-)$. Let P be the projection onto Y. It follows from Lemma A2.2 that both Δ_+ and Δ_- are fixed points of $\mathcal{E}$. Then

$$P\rho P = \lambda P\sigma P + P\Delta_+ P - P\Delta_- P = \lambda\sigma - \Delta_-$$

is a fixed point state of $\mathcal{E}$ too. Note that $\mathrm{supp}(P\rho P) \subseteq Y$, σ is the minimal fixed point state and $\mathrm{supp}(\sigma) = Y$. Therefore, we have $P\rho P = p\sigma$ for some $p \geq 0$. Now if $p > 0$, then by Proposition 5.4 (iii) we obtain:

$$Y = \mathrm{supp}(\sigma) = \mathrm{supp}(P\rho P) = span\{P|\psi\rangle : |\psi\rangle \in X\}.$$

This implies $\dim Y \leq \dim X$, contradicting our assumption. Thus we have $P\rho P = 0$, which implies $X \perp Y$.

A2.2 Proof of Lemma 5.30

Roughly speaking, this lemma asserts that a fixed point state of $\mathcal{E}$ can be decomposed into two orthogonal fixed point states. The proof technique for Lemma 5.25 (ii) showing that two BSCCs are orthogonal can be used in the proof of this lemma. First, we note that for any $\lambda > 0$, $\rho - \lambda\sigma$ is also a fixed point of $\mathcal{E}$, and thus we can take λ sufficiently large such that

$$\rho - \lambda\sigma = \Delta_+ - \Delta_-,$$

with $\Delta_\pm$ being positive, $\mathrm{supp}(\Delta_-) = \mathrm{supp}(\sigma)$, and $\mathrm{supp}(\Delta_+)$ is the orthogonal complement of $\mathrm{supp}(\Delta_-)$ in $\mathrm{supp}(\rho)$. By Lemma A2.2, both Δ_+ and Δ_- are fixed points of $\mathcal{E}$. Let $\eta = \Delta_+$. We have

$$\mathrm{supp}(\rho) = \mathrm{supp}(\rho - \lambda\sigma) = \mathrm{supp}(\Delta_+) \oplus \mathrm{supp}(\Delta_-) = \mathrm{supp}(\eta) \oplus \mathrm{supp}(\sigma).$$

A2.3 Proof of Lemma 5.34

For part (i), we are required to figure out the complexity for computing the asymptotic average $\mathcal{E}_\infty(\rho)$ of a density operator ρ. To this end, we first present a lemma about the matrix representation of the asymptotic average of a quantum operation.

Lemma A2.3 *Let $M = SJS^{-1}$ be the Jordan decomposition of M where*

$$J = \bigoplus_{k=1}^{K} J_k(\lambda_k) = diag\,(J_1(\lambda_1), \ldots, J_K(\lambda_K)),$$

and $J_k(\lambda_k)$ is the Jordan block corresponding to the eigenvalue λ_k. Define

$$J_\infty = \bigoplus_{k \text{ s.t. } \lambda_k = 1} J_k(\lambda_k)$$

and $M_\infty = SJ_\infty S^{-1}$. Then M_∞ is the matrix representation of $\mathcal{E}_\infty$.

Exercise A2.2 Prove Lemma A2.3.

Now we can prove part (i) of Lemma 5.34. We know from [36] that the time complexity of Jordan decomposition for a $d \times d$ matrix is $O(d^4)$. So, we can compute the matrix representation M_∞ of $\mathcal{E}_\infty$ in time $O(d^8)$. Furthermore, $\mathcal{E}_\infty(\rho)$ can be computed using the correspondence:

$$(\mathcal{E}_\infty(\rho) \otimes I_{\mathcal{H}})\,|\Psi\rangle = M_\infty(\rho \otimes I_{\mathcal{H}})|\Psi\rangle,$$

where $|\Psi\rangle = \sum_{i=1}^{d} |i\rangle|i\rangle$ is the (unnormalised) maximally entangled state in $\mathcal{H} \otimes \mathcal{H}$.

For part (ii), we need to settle the complexity for finding the density operator basis of the set of fixed points of $\mathcal{E}$; that is, {matrices $A : \mathcal{E}(A) = A$}. We first notice that this density operator basis can be computed in the following three steps:

(a) Compute the matrix representation M of $\mathcal{E}$. The time complexity is $O(md^4)$, where $m \le d^2$ is the number of operators E_i in the Kraus representaion $\mathcal{E} = \sum_i E_i \circ E_i^\dagger$.
(b) Find a basis $\mathcal{B}$ for the null space of the matrix $M - I_{\mathcal{H} \otimes \mathcal{H}}$, and transform them into matrix forms. This can be done by Guassian elimination with complexity being $O((d^2)^3) = O(d^6)$.
(c) For each basis matrix A in $\mathcal{B}$, compute positive matrices X_+, X_-, Y_+, Y_- such that $\text{supp}(X_+) \perp \text{supp}(X_-)$, $\text{supp}(Y_+) \perp \text{supp}(Y_-)$, and

$$A = X_+ - X_- + i(Y_+ - Y_-).$$

Let Q be the set of non-zero elements in $\{X_+, X_-, Y_+, Y_-\}$. Then by Lemma A2.2, every element of Q is a fixed point state of $\mathcal{E}$. Replace A by elements of Q after normalisation. Then the resultant $\mathcal{B}$ is the required density operator basis. At last, we make the elements in $\mathcal{B}$ linearly independent. This can be done by removing the redundant elements in $\mathcal{B}$ using Guassian elimination. The computational complexity of this step is $O(d^6)$.

So, we see that the total complexity for computing the density operator basis of {matrices $A : \mathcal{E}(A) = A$} is $O(d^6)$.

A2.4 Proof of Lemma 5.58

We first prove the following technical lemma.

Lemma A2.4 *Let S be an invariant subspace of $\mathcal{E}_\infty(\mathcal{H})$ under $\mathcal{E}$. Then for any density operator ρ with $\text{supp}(\rho) \subseteq \mathcal{E}_\infty(\mathcal{H})$ and any integer k, we have*

$$\text{tr}(P_S \mathcal{E}^k(\rho)) - \text{tr}(P_S \rho),$$

where P_S is the projection onto S.

Proof By Lemma 5.30, there exists an invariant subspace T such that $\mathcal{E}_\infty(\mathcal{H}) = S \oplus T$, where S and T are orthogonal. Then by Theorem 5.17, we have

$$\text{tr}(P_S \mathcal{E}^k(\rho)) \geq \text{tr}(P_S \rho) \text{ and } \text{tr}(P_T \mathcal{E}^k(\rho)) \geq \text{tr}(P_T \rho).$$

Furthermore, it follows that

$$1 \geq \text{tr}(P_S \mathcal{E}^k(\rho)) + \text{tr}(P_T \mathcal{E}^k(\rho))$$
$$\geq \text{tr}(P_S \rho) + \text{tr}(P_T \rho) = \text{tr}(\rho) = 1.$$

Thus we have

$$\text{tr}(P_S \mathcal{E}^k(\rho)) = \text{tr}(P_S \rho). \qquad \square$$

Now we can prove Lemma 5.58. For any pure state $|\varphi\rangle$, we write the corresponding density operator $\varphi = |\varphi\rangle\langle\varphi|$. First of all, we show that $\mathcal{Y}(X)$ is a subspace. Let $|\psi_i\rangle \in \mathcal{Y}(X)$ and α_i be complex numbers, $i = 1,2$. Then by the definition of $\mathcal{Y}(X)$ there exists N_i such that for any $j \geq N_i$, supp $(\mathcal{E}^j(\psi_i)) \subseteq X$. Let

$$|\psi\rangle = \alpha_1|\psi_1\rangle + \alpha_2|\psi_2\rangle \text{ and } \rho = |\psi_1\rangle\langle\psi_1| + |\psi_2\rangle\langle\psi_2|.$$

Then $|\psi\rangle \in \text{supp}(\rho)$, and from Propositions 5.4 (i), (ii) and (iv) we have

$$\text{supp}\left(\mathcal{E}^j(\psi)\right) \subseteq \text{supp}\left(\mathcal{E}^j(\rho)\right) = \text{supp}\left(\mathcal{E}^j(\psi_1)\right) \vee \text{supp}\left(\mathcal{E}^j(\psi_2)\right)$$

for any $j \geq 0$. So, we have supp $(\mathcal{E}^j(\psi)) \subseteq X$ for all $j \geq N \stackrel{\triangle}{=} \max\{N_1, N_2\}$, and thus $|\psi\rangle \in \mathcal{Y}(X)$.

We divide the rest of proof into the following six claims:

- Claim 1: $\mathcal{Y}(X) \supseteq \bigvee\{B \subseteq X : B \text{ is a BSCC}\}$.

  For any BSCC $B \subseteq X$, from Lemmas 5.28 (ii) and 5.23 we have $B \subseteq \mathcal{E}_\infty(\mathcal{H})$. Furthermore, as B is a BSCC, it holds that

$$\text{supp}\left(\mathcal{E}^i(\psi)\right) \subseteq B \subseteq X$$

for any $|\psi\rangle \in B$ and any i. Thus $B \subseteq \mathcal{Y}(X)$, and the claim follows from the fact that $\mathcal{Y}(X)$ is a subspace.

- Claim 2: $\mathcal{Y}(X) \subseteq \bigvee\{B \subseteq X : B \text{ is a BSCC}\}$.

  For any $|\psi\rangle \in \mathcal{Y}(X)$, note that $\rho_\psi \stackrel{\triangle}{=} \mathcal{E}_\infty(\psi)$ is a fixed point state. Let $Z = \text{supp}(\rho_\psi)$. We claim that $|\psi\rangle \in Z$. This is obvious if $Z = \mathcal{E}_\infty(\mathcal{H})$. Otherwise, as $\mathcal{E}_\infty\left(\frac{I_\mathcal{H}}{d}\right)$ is a fixed point state and

$$\mathcal{E}_\infty(\mathcal{H}) = \text{supp}\left(\mathcal{E}_\infty\left(\frac{I_\mathcal{H}}{d}\right)\right),$$

by Lemma 5.30 we have $\mathcal{E}_\infty(\mathcal{H}) = Z \oplus Z^\perp$, where $Z^\perp$, the ortho-complement of Z in $\mathcal{E}_\infty(\mathcal{H})$, is also invariant. As Z is again a direct sum of some orthogonal BSCCs, by Lemma 5.50 we have

$$\lim_{i \to \infty} \mathrm{tr}\left(P_Z \mathcal{E}^i(\psi)\right) = \mathrm{tr}(P_Z \mathcal{E}_\infty(\psi)) = 1;$$

that is,

$$\lim_{i \to \infty} \mathrm{tr}\left(P_{Z^\perp} \mathcal{E}^i(\psi)\right) = 0.$$

Together with Theorem 5.17, this implies $\mathrm{tr}(P_{Z^\perp}\psi) = 0$, and so $|\psi\rangle \in Z$.

By the definition of $\mathcal{Y}(X)$, there exists $M \geq 0$, such that $\mathrm{supp}\left(\mathcal{E}^i(\psi)\right) \subseteq X$ for all $i \geq M$. Thus

$$Z = \mathrm{supp}\left(\lim_{N \to \infty} \frac{1}{N} \sum_{i=1}^{N} \mathcal{E}^i(\psi)\right)$$

$$= \mathrm{supp}\left(\lim_{N \to \infty} \frac{1}{N} \sum_{i=M}^{N} \mathcal{E}^i(\psi)\right) \subseteq X.$$

Furthermore, since Z can be decomposed into the direct sum of some BSCCs, we have

$$|\psi\rangle \in Z \subseteq \bigvee \{B \subseteq X : B \text{ is a BSCC}\}.$$

Thus, Claim 2 is proved.

- Claim 3: $\mathcal{Y}(X^\perp)^\perp \subseteq \mathcal{X}(X)$.

First, from Claims 1 and 2 above we have $\mathcal{Y}(X^\perp) \subseteq X^\perp$, and

$$X' \stackrel{\triangle}{=} \mathcal{Y}(X^\perp)^\perp$$

is invariant. Thus $X \subseteq \mathcal{Y}(X^\perp)^\perp$, and $\mathcal{E}$ is also a quantum operation in the subspace X'. We now consider quantum Markov chain $\langle X', \mathcal{E} \rangle$. Claim 1 implies that any BSCC in $X^\perp$ is also contained in $\mathcal{Y}(X^\perp)$. Therefore, there is no BSCC in $X' \cap X^\perp$. By Theorem 5.54, for any $|\psi\rangle \in X'$, we obtain

$$\lim_{i \to \infty} \mathrm{tr}\left[(P_{X^\perp} \circ \mathcal{E})^i(\psi)\right] = 0.$$

Thus $|\psi\rangle \in \mathcal{X}(X)$ by definition, and the claim is proved.

- Claim 4: $\mathcal{X}(X) \subseteq \mathcal{Y}(X^\perp)^\perp$.

Similar to Claim 3, we have $\mathcal{Y}(X^\perp) \subseteq X^\perp$ and $\mathcal{Y}(X^\perp)$ is invariant. Let P be the projection onto $\mathcal{Y}(X^\perp)$. Then $P_{X^\perp} P P_{X^\perp} = P$. For any $|\psi\rangle \in \mathcal{X}(X)$, we have

$$\mathrm{tr}\left(P\left(P_{X^\perp} \circ \mathcal{E}\right)(\psi)\right) = \mathrm{tr}\left(P_{X^\perp} P P_{X^\perp} \mathcal{E}(\psi)\right)$$
$$= \mathrm{tr}(P\mathcal{E}(\psi)) \geq \mathrm{tr}(P\psi),$$

where the last inequality is derived by Theorem 5.17. Therefore

$$0 = \lim_{i \to \infty} \mathrm{tr}\left((P_{X^\perp} \circ \mathcal{E})^i(\psi)\right)$$
$$\geq \lim_{i \to \infty} \mathrm{tr}\left(P\left(P_{X^\perp} \circ \mathcal{E}\right)^i(\psi)\right) \geq \mathrm{tr}(P\psi),$$

and so $|\psi\rangle \in \mathcal{Y}(X^\perp)^\perp$.

- Claim 5: $\bigvee \{B \subseteq X : B \text{ is a BSCC}\} \subseteq \mathcal{E}_\infty(X^\perp)^\perp$.

  Suppose that $B \subseteq X$ is a BSCC. Then we have $\text{tr}(P_B I_{X^\perp}) = 0$. It follows from Lemma A2.4 that

$$\text{tr}\left(P_B \mathcal{E}^i(I_{X^\perp})\right) = 0$$

for any $i \geq 0$. Thus

$$\text{tr}(P_B \mathcal{E}_\infty(I_{X^\perp})) = 0.$$

This implies $B \perp \mathcal{E}_\infty(X^\perp)$. Therefore, $B \subseteq \mathcal{E}_\infty(X^\perp)^\perp$. Then the claim follows from the fact that $\mathcal{E}_\infty(X^\perp)^\perp$ is a subspace.

- Claim 6: $\mathcal{E}_\infty(X^\perp)^\perp \subseteq \bigvee \{B \subseteq X : B \text{ is a BSCC}\}$.

  We first note that $\mathcal{E}_\infty(X^\perp)^\perp$ can be decomposed into direct sum of BSCCs B_i. For any B_i, we have

$$\text{tr}(P_{B_i} \mathcal{E}_\infty(I_{X^\perp})) = 0.$$

Thus, $\text{tr}(P_{B_i} I_{X^\perp}) = 0$ and $B_i \perp X^\perp$. Therefore, $B_i \subseteq X$, and the claim is proved.

Finally, we observe that the invariance of $\mathcal{X}(X)$ and $\mathcal{Y}(X)$ is already included in Claims 1 and 2. This completes the proof.

Appendix 3

Proofs of Technical Lemmas in Chapter 6

In this appendix, we provide the proofs omitted in Chapter 6.

A3.1 Proof of Theorem 6.21 (iii)

We first recall some basic results from linear algebra. Let M be a squared matrix and $M = SJS^{-1}$ its Jordan decomposition, where S is a non-singular matrix,

$$J = diag(J_{n_1}(\lambda_1), J_{n_2}(\lambda_2), \ldots, J_{n_k}(\lambda_k)),$$

and each $J_{n_i}(\lambda_i)$ is an $n_i \times n_i$-Jordan block with eigenvalue λ_i. Let

$$\tilde{M} = S\tilde{J}S^{-1},$$

where $\tilde{J}$ is obtained from J by replacing each Jordan block whose associated eigenvalue has absolute value greater than or equal to 1 with the zero block of the same size; that is $\tilde{J} = diag(\tilde{J}_1, \tilde{J}_2, \ldots, \tilde{J}_k)$ where

$$\tilde{J}_i = \begin{cases} 0_{n_i \times n_i}, & \text{if } |\lambda_i| \geq 1; \\ J_{n_i}(\lambda_i), & \text{otherwise.} \end{cases}$$

Lemma A3.1 *Let $J = J_n(\lambda)$ be an $n \times n$-Jordan block with eigenvalue λ and $|\lambda| \geq 1$, and y an n-dimensional (column) vector. If $\sum_{m=0}^{\infty} J^m y = 0$, then $y = 0$.*

Proof Note that for any $m \geq 0$,

$$J^m = \begin{pmatrix} \lambda^m & \binom{m}{1}\lambda^{m-1} & \cdots & \binom{m}{n-1}\lambda^{m-n+1} \\ 0 & \lambda^m & \cdots & \binom{m}{n-2}\lambda^{m-n+2} \\ \vdots & \ddots & \vdots & \vdots \\ 0 & \cdots & 0 & \lambda^m \end{pmatrix}.$$

The result follows easily by inspection. $\qquad\qquad\square$

Lemma A3.2 *Let M be a $d \times d$ complex matrix and x a d-dimensional vector. If $\sum_{m=0}^{\infty} M^m x$ exists, then for each $m \geq 0$, $M^m x = \tilde{M}^m x$.*

Proof Suppose $\sum_{m=0}^{\infty} M^m x$ exists. Then $\lim_{m \to \infty} M^m x = 0$. Since $M^m = S J^m S^{-1}$, we have

$$\lim_{m \to \infty} S J^m x = 0.$$

Decompose Sx according to the blocks of J as $Sx = (y_1, \dots, y_k)^T$, where y_i has dimension n_i. Then

$$S J^m x = \left(J_{n_1}^m(\lambda_1) \cdot y_1, \dots, J_{n_k}^m(\lambda_k) \cdot y_k \right),$$

and for each i,

$$\lim_{m \to \infty} J_{n_i}^m(\lambda_i) \cdot y_i = 0.$$

From Lemma A3.1 we deduce that $y_i = 0$ for each i whenever $|\lambda_i| \geq 1$. Thus $S J^m x = S \tilde{J}^m x$, and $M^m x = \tilde{M}^m x$. □

Corollary A3.3 *For any x and M,*

$$\sum_{m=0}^{\infty} M^m x = (I - \tilde{M})^{-1} x,$$

provided that the limit exists.

Proof Observe that the spectral radius of $\tilde{M}$ is strictly less than 1. The result then follows from Lemma A3.2. □

Recall that Eq. (3.13) gives the matrix representation of a single super-operator. We further extend this definition to a matrix of super-operators. Let $\mathbf{Q} = (\mathcal{E}_{i,j})$ be an $m \times n$-matrix of super-operators. Then the matrix representation of $\mathbf{Q}$, denoted $M_{\mathbf{Q}}$, is defined as the block matrix

$$M_{\mathbf{Q}} = \begin{pmatrix} M_{\mathcal{E}_{1,1}} & \cdots & M_{\mathcal{E}_{1,n}} \\ \vdots & \ddots & \vdots \\ M_{\mathcal{E}_{m,1}} & \cdots & M_{\mathcal{E}_{m,n}} \end{pmatrix},$$

where for each i and j, $M_{\mathcal{E}_{i,j}}$ is the matrix representation of $\mathcal{E}_{i,j}$. Furthermore, let $|\Psi\rangle = \sum_{k \in K} |kk\rangle$ be a (un-normalised) maximally entangled state in $\mathcal{H} \otimes \mathcal{H}$. Then the vector representation of a linear operator $A \in L(\mathcal{H})$ is defined as

$$vec(A) = (A \otimes I_{\mathcal{H}}) |\Psi\rangle.$$

It is easy to check that

$$A = \sum_{k \in K} (I \otimes \langle k|) \cdot vec(A) \cdot \langle k|. \tag{A3.1}$$

This notion is then extended to vector of linear operators in a similar way.

Lemma A3.4 *Let $M_{\mathcal{E}}$ be the matrix representation of $\mathcal{E} \in SO(\mathcal{H})$. Then for any $A \in L(\mathcal{H})$, we have*

$$vec(\mathcal{E}(A)) = M_{\mathcal{E}} \cdot vec(A).$$

Exercise A3.1 Prove Lemma A3.4.

We are now ready to prove Theorem 6.21 (iii). Let $\mathbf{A} \in \mathcal{L}(\mathcal{H})^{S^?}$ such that $\mathbf{A}_s = \sum_{t \in Sat(\Psi)} \mathbf{Q}[s,t]^\dagger(I)$. Let $\mathbf{T}$ be a matrix of super-operators such that $\mathbf{T}[s,t] = \mathbf{Q}[s,t]^\dagger$ for all $s,t \in S^?$. With Lemma A3.4, it is easy to prove by induction that for any $k \geq 1$,

$$vec(f^k(\vec{0})) = \sum_{m=0}^{k-1} M_{\mathbf{T}}^m \cdot vec(\mathbf{A}),$$

and thus

$$vec(\mu f) = \sum_{m=0}^{\infty} M_{\mathbf{T}}^m \cdot vec(\mathbf{A}) = (I - \tilde{M}_{\mathbf{T}})^{-1} \cdot vec(\mathbf{A}). \tag{A3.2}$$

from Corollary A3.3.

With the vector representation of μf, we can recover $(\mu f)_s$ by Eq. (A3.1), and then decide whether $M \sim (\mu f)_s$ easily. Note that the time complexity for Jordan decomposition of an $n \times n$ matrix is n^4. The foregoing decision procedure takes time $O(|S|^4 d^8)$, where $d = \dim(\mathcal{H})$ is the dimension of $\mathcal{H}$.

A3.2 Proof of Lemma 6.31

Suppose $C(X) \neq C(Y)$, and, without loss of generality, let $s \in C(Y) \backslash C(X)$. Let ρ_X and ρ_Y be the fixed point states corresponding to X and Y, respectively. Since

$$\mathcal{E}_\mathcal{M}(\rho_X + \rho_Y) = \rho_X + \rho_Y,$$

we know that $(\rho_X + \rho_Y)/2$ is a fixed point state corresponding to $Z := X \vee Y$. Thus Z can be decomposed into the direct sum of some orthogonal BSCCs:

$$Z = X \oplus Z_1 \oplus \cdots \oplus Z_n.$$

We claim that $n = 1$. Otherwise, for any i, $\dim Z_i < \dim Y$ because

$$\sum_i \dim Z_i + \dim X = \dim Z \leq \dim X + \dim Y,$$

and thus $Y \perp Z_i$ by Lemma 5.25. This means $Y = X$, a contradiction. Now let $|s\rangle|\psi\rangle \in Y$. Since $s \notin C(X)$, we have $|s\rangle|\psi\rangle \perp X$, and thus $|s\rangle|\psi\rangle \in Z_1$. On the other hand, since both Y and Z_1 are BSCCs,

$$Y = Z_1 = \mathcal{R}(|s\rangle\langle s| \otimes |\psi\rangle\langle\psi|).$$

Here $\mathcal{R}(\cdot)$ denotes the reachability space; see Definition 5.10. Thus $X \perp Y$.

A3.3 Proof of Lemma 6.32

The first clause is easy to prove by induction. For (ii), note that $\mathrm{pri}(\pi) = \mathrm{pri}(\pi')$ for any suffix π' of π. Let

$$E_k = \{ \pi \in \mathrm{Path}^\mathcal{M} \mid \mathrm{pri}(\pi) = k \}.$$

Then for any $n \geq 0$,

$$E_k = \biguplus_{\widehat{\pi} \in S^n} \widehat{\pi}^\frown E_k.$$

Now from (i),

$$R_k = \sum_{s_0, \ldots, s_n \in S} \mathcal{P}_{s_0} \mathcal{E}_{\mathcal{M}}^\dagger \cdots \mathcal{P}_{s_{n-1}} \mathcal{E}_{\mathcal{M}}^\dagger (|s_n\rangle\langle s_n| \otimes \Delta_{s_n}^{\mathcal{M}}(E_k))$$

$$= (\mathcal{E}_{\mathcal{M}}^\dagger)^n \left(\sum_{s_n \in S} |s_n\rangle\langle s_n| \otimes \Delta_{s_n}^{\mathcal{M}}(E_k) \right) = \mathcal{E}_{\mathcal{M}}^{n\dagger}(R_k).$$

A3.4 Proof of Lemma 6.33

For clause (i), note that

$$\Box \neg S_x = \bigcap_{n \geq 0} \biguplus_{\widehat{\pi} \in (S \backslash S_x)^{n+1}} Cyl(\widehat{\pi}).$$

Thus from Lemma 6.32, for any $n \geq 0$,

$$\Delta^{\mathcal{M}}(\Box \neg S_x) \sqsubseteq \sum_{s_0, \ldots, s_n \notin S_x} \mathcal{P}_{s_0} \mathcal{E}_{\mathcal{M}}^\dagger \cdots \mathcal{P}_{s_{n-1}} \mathcal{E}_{\mathcal{M}}^\dagger (\mathcal{P}_{s_n})$$

$$= (\mathcal{P}_{S_x^c} \mathcal{E}_{\mathcal{M}}^\dagger)^n (\mathcal{P}_{S_x^c}),$$

where $\mathcal{P}_{S_x^c} = \sum_{s \notin S_x} \mathcal{P}_s$ and $\mathcal{P}_{S_x^c} = \{\mathcal{P}_{S_x^c}\}$. Note that for each BSCC $B \subseteq BSCC_x$, there exists a state $|s\rangle|\psi\rangle \in B$ with $s \in S_x$ such that

$$\text{supp}(\mathcal{E}_{\mathcal{M}}^\infty(|s\rangle\langle s| \otimes |\psi\rangle\langle\psi|)) = \mathcal{R}(|s\rangle\langle s| \otimes |\psi\rangle\langle\psi|) = B.$$

Thus, $\mathcal{E}_{\mathcal{M}}^\infty(G) \supseteq BSCC_x$, where $G := \mathcal{H}_{S_x} \otimes \mathcal{H} \cap BSCC_x$ and $\mathcal{H}_{S_x} = \text{span}\{|s\rangle \mid s \in S_x\}$. From Theorem 5.29, we know that for any $\rho \in \mathcal{D}(\mathcal{H}_c \otimes \mathcal{H})$ with $\text{supp}(\rho) \subseteq BSCC_x$,

$$\lim_{n \to \infty} \text{tr}((\mathcal{P}_{G^\perp} \mathcal{E}_{\mathcal{M}})^n(\rho)) = 0.$$

Note that $G^\perp \subseteq \mathcal{H}_{S_x}^\perp \otimes \mathcal{H}$. Thus we have

$$\lim_{n \to \infty} P_x (\mathcal{P}_{S_x^c} \mathcal{E}_{\mathcal{M}}^\dagger)^n (\mathcal{P}_{S_x^c}) P_x = 0,$$

and so

$$P_x \cdot \Delta^{\mathcal{M}}(\Diamond S_x) \cdot P_x = P_x - P_x \cdot \Delta^{\mathcal{M}}(\Box \neg S_x) \cdot P_x = P_x,$$

as desired.

For clause (ii), note that

$$\Diamond S_y = \bigcup_{n \geq 0} \bigcup \{Cyl(\widehat{\pi}) \mid |\widehat{\pi}| = n + 1 \wedge \widehat{\pi}(n) \in S_y\}.$$

Thus by Lemma 6.32,

$$\Delta^{\mathcal{M}}(\Diamond S_y) \sqsubseteq \sum_{n \geq 0} \sum_{s_0,\dots,s_{n-1} \in S} \sum_{s_n \in S_y} P_{s_0} \mathcal{E}_{\mathcal{M}}^{\dagger} \cdots P_{s_{n-1}} \mathcal{E}_{\mathcal{M}}^{\dagger}(P_{s_n})$$

$$= \sum_{n \geq 0} \mathcal{E}_{\mathcal{M}}^{\dagger n}(P_{S_y}),$$

where $P_{S_y} = \sum_{s \in S_y} P_s$. Since $\mathcal{BSCC}_x$ is an invariant space of $\mathcal{E}_{\mathcal{M}}$, we have for any $n \geq 0$,

$$\mathcal{E}_{\mathcal{M}}^{n}(\mathcal{BSCC}_x) \subseteq \mathcal{BSCC}_x,$$

which is orthogonal to P_{S_y} whenever $y < x$. Thus $P_x \cdot \Delta^{\mathcal{M}}(\Diamond S_y) \cdot P_x = 0$.

A3.5 Proof of Lemma 6.34

Note that

$$\Diamond\Box\neg S_x = \bigcup_{n \geq 0} \biguplus_{\widehat{\pi} \in S^{n+1}} \widehat{\pi}^{\frown}\Box\neg S_x.$$

Thus from Lemma 6.32,

$$\Delta^{\mathcal{M}}(\Diamond\Box\neg S_x) \sqsubseteq \sum_{n \geq 0} \sum_{t' \in S} \mathcal{E}_{\mathcal{M}}^{\dagger n}(|t'\rangle\langle t'| \otimes \Delta_{t'}^{\mathcal{M}}(\Box\neg S_x)). \qquad (A3.3)$$

Since $\mathcal{BSCC}_x$ is an invariant space of $\mathcal{E}_{\mathcal{M}}$, we have for any $n \geq 0$,

$$\mathcal{E}_{\mathcal{M}}^{n}(\mathcal{BSCC}_x) \subseteq \mathcal{BSCC}_x.$$

Furthermore, from Lemma 6.33,

$$P_x \cdot \Delta^{\mathcal{M}}(\Box\neg S_x) \cdot P_x = 0.$$

Thus

$$P_x \cdot \Delta^{\mathcal{M}}(\Diamond\Box\neg S_x) \cdot P_x = 0,$$

and that completes the proof of the lemma.

A3.6 Proof of Lemma 6.35

When $x = k$, we note that for any path π, $\mathrm{pri}(\pi) < k$ implies $\pi \models \Diamond S_{k-}$, and $\mathrm{pri}(\pi) > k$ implies $\pi \models \neg\Box\Diamond S_k$. Thus

$$R_k = \Delta^{\mathcal{M}}(\{\pi \in \mathrm{Path}^{\mathcal{M}}(t) \mid \mathrm{pri}(\pi) = k\})$$

$$\sqsupseteq I - \Delta^{\mathcal{M}}(\Diamond S_{k-}) - \Delta^{\mathcal{M}}(\neg\Box\Diamond S_k),$$

and $P_k R_k P_k = P_k$ from Lemmas 6.33 and 6.34. For $x \neq k$, note that $\mathrm{pri}(\pi) = k$ implies $\pi \models \Diamond S_k$ and $\pi \models \neg\Box\Diamond S_{k-}$. Then we have

$$R_k \sqsubseteq I - \Delta^{\mathcal{M}}(\Box\Diamond S_{k-}),$$

and so $P_{k-} R_k P_{k-} = 0$ from Lemma 6.34. Similarly, from $R_k \sqsubseteq \Delta^{\mathcal{M}}(\Diamond S_k)$ and Lemma 6.33, we derive $P_{k+} R_k P_{k+} = 0$.

References

[1] P. Adao and P. Mateus. A process algebra for reasoning about quantum security. *Electronic Notes in Theoretical Computer Science*, 170:3–21, 2007.

[2] A. V. Aho and J. E. Hopcroft. *The Design and Analysis of Computer Algorithms*, 1st ed. Addison-Wesley Longman, 1974.

[3] V. V. Albert. Asymptotics of quantum channels: Conserved quantities, an adiabatic limit, and matrix product states. *Quantum*, 3:151, 2019.

[4] A. Ambainis and A. Yakaryılmaz. Automata and quantum computing. arXiv:1507.01988, 2015.

[5] E. Ardeshir-Larijani, S. J. Gay and R. Nagarajan. Equivalence checking of quantum protocols. In *International Conference on Tools and Algorithms for the Construction and Analysis of Systems*, pp. 478–92. Springer, 2013.

[6] E. Ardeshir-Larijani, S. J. Gay and R. Nagarajan. Verification of concurrent quantum protocols by equivalence checking. In *International Conference on Tools and Algorithms for the Construction and Analysis of Systems*, pp. 500–14. Springer, 2014.

[7] C. Baier and J.-P. Katoen. *Principles of Model Checking*. MIT Press, 2008.

[8] P. Baltazar, R. Chadha and P. Mateus. Quantum computation tree logic: Model checking and complete calculus. *International Journal of Quantum Information*, 6(02):219–36, 2008.

[9] P. Baltazar, R. Chadha, P. Mateus and A. Sernadas. Towards model-checking quantum security protocols. In *2007 First International Conference on Quantum, Nano, and Micro Technologies (ICQNM'07)*, p. 14. IEEE, 2007.

[10] J. Barry, D. T. Barry and S. Aaronson. Quantum partially observable Markov decision processes. *Physical Review A*, 90(3):032311, 2014.

[11] G. Barthe, B. Grégoire and S. Zanella Béguelin. Formal certification of code-based cryptographic proofs. In *Proceedings of POPL*, vol. 44, pp. 90–101. ACM, 2009.

[12] G. Barthe, J. Hsu, M. Ying, N. Yu and L. Zhou. Relational reasoning for quantum programs. In *Proceedings of POPL*. ACM, 2020.

[13] D. Basin, C. Cremers and C. Meadows. Model checking security protocols. In E. M. Clarke, T. A. Henzinger, H. Veith, and B. Bloem, eds., *Handbook of Model Checking*, pp. 727–62. Springer, 2011.

[14] B. Baumgartner and H. Narnhofer. The structures of state space concerning quantum dynamical semigroups. *Reviews in Mathematical Physics*, 24(2):1250001, 2012.

[15] C. H. Bennett and G. Brassard. Quantum cryptography: Public key distribution and coin tossing. In *Proceedings of IEEE International Conference on Computers, Systems, and Signal Processing*, pp. 175–79, 1984.

[16] N. Benton. Simple relational correctness proofs for static analyses and program transformations. In *Proceedings of POPL*, vol. 39, pp. 14–25. ACM, 2004.

[17] D. W. Berry, G. Ahokas, R. Cleve and B. C. Sanders. Efficient quantum algorithms for simulating sparse hamiltonians. *Communications in Mathematical Physics*, 270(2):359–71, 2007.

[18] J. Berstel and M. Mignotte. Deux propriétés décidables des suites récurrentes linéaires. *Bulletin de la Société Mathématique de France*, 104:175–84, 1976.

[19] A. Biere, A. Cimatti, E. M. Clarke, O. Strichman, Y. Zhu, et al. Bounded model checking. *Advances in Computers*, 58(11):117–48, 2003.

[20] G. Birkhoff and J. Von Neumann. The logic of quantum mechanics. *Annals of Mathematics*, pp. 823–43, 1936.

[21] V. D. Blondel, E. Jeandel, P. Koiran and N. Portier. Decidable and undecidable problems about quantum automata. *SIAM Journal on Computing*, 34(6):1464–73, 2005.

[22] H.-P. Breuer and F. Petruccione. *The Theory of Open Quantum Systems*. Oxford University Press on Demand, 2002.

[23] T. A. Brun. A simple model of quantum trajectories. *American Journal of Physics*, 70(7):719–37, 2002.

[24] G. Bruns and J. Harding. Algebraic aspects of orthomodular lattices. In B. Coecke, D. Moore, and A. Wilce, eds., *Current Research in Operational Quantum Logic*, pp. 37–65. Springer, 2000.

[25] J. R. Burch, E. M. Clarke, K. L. McMillan, D. L. Dill and L.-J. Hwang. Symbolic model checking: 1020 states and beyond. *Information and Computation*, 98(2):142–70, 1992.

[26] D. Burgarth, G. Chiribella, V. Giovannetti, P. Perinotti and K. Yuasa. Ergodic and mixing quantum channels in finite dimensions. *New Journal of Physics*, 15(7):073045, 2013.

[27] R. Carbone and Y. Pautrat. Irreducible decompositions and stationary states of quantum channels. *Reports on Mathematical Physics*, 77(3):293–313, 2016.

[28] R. Carbone and Y. Pautrat. Open quantum random walks: reducibility, period, ergodic properties. In *Annales Henri Poincaré*, vol. 17, pp. 99–135. Springer, 2016.

[29] J. Cassaigne and J. Karhumäki. Examples of undecidable problems for 2-generator matrix semigroups. *Theoretical Computer Science*, 204(1-2):29–34, 1998.

[30] K. Chatterjee and T. Henzinger. Probabilistic automata on infinite words: Decidability and undecidability results. In A. Bouajjani and W.-N. Chin, eds., *Automated Technology for Verification and Analysis*, vol. 6252 of *Lecture Notes in Computer Science*, pp. 1–16. Springer, 2010.

[31] A. M. Childs. On the relationship between continuous-and discrete-time quantum walk. *Communications in Mathematical Physics*, 294(2):581–603, 2010.

[32] J. I. Cirac and P. Zoller. Goals and opportunities in quantum simulation. *Nature Physics*, 8(4):264, 2012.

[33] E. M. Clarke and E. A. Emerson. Design and synthesis of synchronization skeletons using branching time temporal logic. In *Workshop on Logic of Programs*, pp. 52–71. Springer, 1981.

[34] E. M. Clarke, T. A. Henzinger, H. Veith and R. Bloem. *Handbook of Model Checking*, vol. 10. Springer, 2018.

[35] E. M. Clarke Jr, O. Grumberg, D. Kroening, D. Peled and H. Veith. *Model Checking*. MIT Press, 2018.

[36] T. H. Cormen, C. E. Leiserson, R. L. Rivest and C. Stein. *Introduction to Algorithms*. MIT Press, 2009.

[37] T. Davidson, S. Gay, R. Nagarajan and I. Puthoor. Analysis of a quantum error correcting code using quantum process calculus. *Electronic Proceedings in Theoretical Computer Science*, 95:67–80, 2012.

[38] T. A. Davidson. *Formal Verification Techniques Using Quantum Process Calculus*. PhD thesis, University of Warwick, 2012.

[39] T. A. Davidson, S. J. Gay, H. Mlnarik, R. Nagarajan and N. Papanikolaou. Model checking for communicating quantum processes. *IJUC*, 8(1):73–98, 2012.

[40] J. Diestel and J. Uhl. *Vector Measures*. American Mathematical Society, 1977.

[41] J. P. Dowling and G. J. Milburn. Quantum technology: The second quantum revolution. *Philosophical Transactions of the Royal Society of London. Series A: Mathematical, Physical and Engineering Sciences*, 361(1809):1655–74, 2003.

[42] C. Eisner and D. Fisman. Functional specification of hardware via temporal logic. In *Handbook of Model Checking*, pp. 795–829. Springer, 2018.

[43] E. A. Emerson. Temporal and modal logic. In *Formal Models and Semantics*, pp. 995–1072. Elsevier, 1990.

[44] K. Engesser, D. M. Gabbay and D. Lehmann. *Handbook of Quantum Logic and Quantum Structures: Quantum Structures*. Elsevier, 2007.

[45] J. Esparza and S. Schwoon. A bdd-based model checker for recursive programs. In *International Conference on Computer Aided Verification*, pp. 324–36. Springer, 2001.

[46] K. Etessami and M. Yannakakis. Recursive Markov chains, stochastic grammars, and monotone systems of nonlinear equations. *Journal of the ACM (JACM)*, 56(1):1, 2009.

[47] F. Fagnola and R. Rebolledo. On the existence of stationary states for quantum dynamical semigroups. *Journal of Mathematical Physics*, 42(3):1296–1308, 2001.

[48] Y. Feng, E. M. Hahn, A. Turrini, and S. Ying. Model checking omega-regular properties for quantum markov chains. In *28th International Conference on Concurrency Theory (CONCUR 2017)*, pp. 35:1–35:16. Schloss Dagstuhl-Leibniz-Zentrum fuer Informatik, 2017.

[49] Y. Feng, E. M. Hahn, A. Turrini and L. Zhang. Qpmc: A model checker for quantum programs and protocols. In *International Symposium on Formal Methods*, pp. 265–72. Springer, 2015.

[50] Y. Feng and M. Ying. Toward automatic verification of quantum cryptographic protocols. In *26th International Conference on Concurrency Theory (CONCUR 2015)*, pp. 441–55, 2015.

[51] Y. Feng, N. Yu and M. Ying. Model checking quantum markov chains. *Journal of Computer and System Sciences*, 79(7):1181–98, 2013.

[52] Y. Feng, N. Yu and M. Ying. Reachability analysis of recursive quantum Markov chains. In *International Symposium on Mathematical Foundations of Computer Science*, pp. 385–96. Springer, 2013.

[53] R. P. Feynman. Simulating physics with computers. *International Journal of Theoretical Physics*, 21(6):467–88, 1982.

[54] S. Gay, R. Nagarajan and N. Papanikolaou. Probabilistic model–checking of quantum protocols. arXiv preprint quant-ph/0504007, 2005.

[55] S. Gay, R. Nagarajan and N. Papanikolaou. Specification and verification of quantum protocols. In I. Mackie and S. Gay, eds., *Semantic Techniques in Quantum Computation*, pp. 414–72. Cambridge University Press, 2010.

[56] S. J. Gay and R. Nagarajan. Communicating quantum processes. In *Proceedings of the 32Nd ACM SIGPLAN-SIGACT Symposium on Principles of Programming Languages*, POPL'05, pp. 145–57. ACM, 2005.

[57] S. J. Gay, R. Nagarajan and N. Papanikolaou. Qmc: A model checker for quantum systems. In *International Conference on Computer Aided Verification*, pp. 543–47. Springer, 2008.

[58] M. Golovkins. Quantum pushdown automata. In *International Conference on Current Trends in Theory and Practice of Computer Science*, pp. 336–46. Springer, 2000.

[59] D. E. Gottesman. *Stabilizer Codes and Quantum Error Correction*. PhD thesis, California Institute of Technology, 1997.

[60] R. B. Griffiths. Consistent histories and quantum reasoning. *Physical Review A*, 54(4):2759, 1996.

[61] J. Guan, Y. Feng and M. Ying. Decomposition of quantum Markov chains and its applications. *Journal of Computer and System Sciences*, 95:55–68, 2018.

[62] S. Gudder. Quantum Markov chains. *Journal of Mathematical Physics*, 49(7):072105, 2008.

[63] V. Halava. Decidable and undecidable problems in matrix theory. Technical Report, Turku Centre for Computer Science, 1997.

[64] V. Halava, T. Harju, M. Hirvensalo and J. Karhumäki. Skolem's problem: On the border between decidability and undecidability. Technical Report 683, Turku Centre for Computer Science, 2005.

[65] H. Hansson and B. Jonsson. A logic for reasoning about time and reliability. *Formal Aspects of Computing*, 6(5):512–35, 1994.

[66] A. W. Harrow, A. Hassidim and S. Lloyd. Quantum algorithm for linear systems of equations. *Physical Review Letters*, 103(15):150502, 2009.

[67] S. Hart, M. Sharir and A. Pnueli. Termination of probabilistic concurrent programs. In *Proceedings of the 9th ACM SIGPLAN-SIGACT Symposium on Principles of programming languages*, pp. 1–6. ACM, 1982.

[68] J. Heath, M. Kwiatkowska, G. Norman, D. Parker and O. Tymchyshyn. Probabilistic model checking of complex biological pathways. In *International Conference on Computational Methods in Systems Biology*, pp. 32–47. Springer, 2006.

[69] Y. Huang and M. Martonosi. Statistical assertions for validating patterns and finding bugs in quantum programs. In *Proceedings of the 46th International Symposium on Computer Architecture*, pp. 541–53. ACM, 2019.

[70] C. J. Isham and N. Linden. Quantum temporal logic and decoherence functionals in the histories approach to generalized quantum theory. *Journal of Mathematical Physics*, 35(10):5452–476, 1994.

[71] G. Kalmbach. *Orthomodular Lattices*. Academic Press, 1983.

[72] A. Kondacs and J. Watrous. On the power of quantum finite state automata. In *Proceedings 38th Annual Symposium on Foundations of Computer Science*, pp. 66–75. IEEE, 1997.

[73] T. Kubota, Y. Kakutani, G. Kato, Y. Kawano and H. Sakurada. Semi-automated verification of security proofs of quantum cryptographic protocols. *Journal of Symbolic Computation*, 73:192–220, 2016.

[74] R. P. Kurshan. Transfer of model checking to industrial practice. In *Handbook of Model Checking*, pp. 763–93. Springer, 2018.

[75] M. Kwiatkowska, G. Norman and D. Parker. Probabilistic symbolic model checking with PRISM: A hybrid approach. *International Journal on Software Tools for Technology Transfer*, 6(2):128–42, 2004.

[76] M. Kwiatkowska, G. Norman and D. Parker. Stochastic model checking. In *International School on Formal Methods for the Design of Computer, Communication and Software Systems*, pp. 220–70. Springer, 2007.

[77] C. Lech. A note on recurring series. *Arkiv för Matematik*, 2(5):417–21, 1953.

[78] G. Li, L. Zhou, N. Yu, Y. Ding, M. Ying and Y. Xie. Poq: Projection-based runtime assertions for debugging on a quantum computer. arXiv preprint arXiv:1911.12855, 2019.

[79] L. Li and D. Qiu. Determination of equivalence between quantum sequential machines. *Theoretical Computer Science*, 358(1):65–74, 2006.

[80] L. Li and D. Qiu. Determining the equivalence for one-way quantum finite automata. *Theoretical Computer Science*, 403(1):42–51, 2008.

[81] Y. Li and D. Unruh. Quantum relational hoare logic with expectations. arXiv:1903.08357, 2019.

[82] Y. Li and M. Ying. (Un)decidable problems about reachability of quantum systems. In *International Conference on Concurrency Theory*, pp. 482–96. Springer, 2014.

[83] Y. Li, N. Yu and M. Ying. Termination of nondeterministic quantum programs. *Acta informatica*, 51(1):1–24, 2014.

[84] J. Liu, G. Byrd and H. Zhou. Quantum circuits for dynamic runtime assertions in quantum computation. In *25th International Conference on Architectural Support for Programming Languages and Operating Systems (ASPLOS 2020)*. ACM, 2020.

[85] S. Lloyd. Universal quantum simulators. *Science*, 273(5278):1073–78, 1996.

[86] K. Mahler. *Eine arithmetische Eigenschaft der Taylor-koeffizienten rationaler Funktionen*. Noord-Hollandsche Uitgevers Mij, 1935.

[87] P. Mateus, J. Ramos, A. Sernadas and C. Sernadas. Temporal logics for reasoning about quantum systems. In I. Mackie and S. Gay, eds., *Semantic Techniques in quantum computation*, pp. 389–413. Cambridge University Press, 2010.

[88] P. Mateus and A. Sernadas. Weakly complete axiomatization of exogenous quantum propositional logic. *Information and Computation*, 204(5):771–94, 2006.

[89] M. L. Minsky. *Computation: Finite and Infinite Machines*. Prentice-Hall, 1967.

[90] A. Miranskyy and L. Zhang. On testing quantum programs. In *2019 IEEE/ACM 41st International Conference on Software Engineering: New Ideas and Emerging Results (ICSE-NIER)*, pp. 57–60. IEEE, 2019.

[91] P. Molitor and J. Mohnke. *Equivalence Checking of Digital Circuits: Fundamentals, Principles, Methods*. Springer Science+Business Media, 2007.

[92] C. Moore and J. P. Crutchfield. Quantum automata and quantum grammars. *Theoretical Computer Science*, 237(1-2):275–306, 2000.

[93] M. A. Nielsen and I. Chuang. *Quantum Computation and Quantum Information*. Cambridge University Press, 2000.

[94] R. Orús. A practical introduction to tensor networks: Matrix product states and projected entangled pair states. *Annals of Physics*, 349:117–58, 2014.

[95] J. Ouaknine and J. Worrell. Decision problems for linear recurrence sequences. In *International Workshop on Reachability Problems*, pp. 21–8. Springer, 2012.

[96] N. K. Papanikolaou. *Model Checking Quantum Protocols*. PhD thesis, University of Warwick, 2009.

[97] A. Paz. *Introduction to Probabilistic Automata*. Academic Press, 2014.

[98] N. Piterman. From nondeterministic Büchi and Streett automata to deterministic parity automata. In *21st Annual IEEE Symposium on Logic in Computer Science (LICS'06)*, pp. 255–64. IEEE, 2006.

[99] E. L. Post. A variant of a recursively unsolvable problem. *Journal of Symbolic Logic*, 12(2):55–6, 1947.

[100] D. Qiu, L. Li, X. Zou, P. Mateus and J. Gruska. Multi-letter quantum finite automata: Decidability of the equivalence and minimization of states. *Acta Informatica*, 48(5-6):271, 2011.

[101] J.-P. Queille and J. Sifakis. Specification and verification of concurrent systems in cesar. In *International Symposium on programming*, pp. 337–51. Springer, 1982.

[102] S. Safra. On the complexity of omega-automata. In *29th Annual Symposium on Foundations of Computer Science*, pp. 319–27. IEEE, 1988.

[103] A. Salomaa and M. Soittola. Automata-theoretic aspects of formal power series. *Bulletin of the American Mathematical Society*, 1:675–78, 1979.

[104] S. Schewe. Tighter bounds for the determinisation of Büchi automata. In *International Conference on Foundations of Software Science and Computational Structures*, pp. 167–81. Springer, 2009.

[105] M. Sharir, A. Pnueli and S. Hart. Verification of probabilistic programs. *SIAM Journal on Computing*, 13(2):292–314, 1984.

[106] T. Skolem. Ein Verfahren zur Behandlung gewisser exponentialer Gleichungen und diophantischer Gleichungen. In *Proceedings of the 8th Congress of Scandinavian Mathematicians*, pp. 163–88. Stockholm, 1934.

[107] V. Umanità. Classification and decomposition of quantum Markov semigroups. *Probability Theory and Related Fields*, 134(4):603–23, 2006.

[108] D. Unruh. Quantum relational hoare logic. In *Proceedings of POPL*, vol. 33, pp. 1–31. ACM, 2019.

[109] M. Y. Vardi. Automatic verification of probabilistic concurrent finite state programs. In *26th Annual Symposium on Foundations of Computer Science*, pp. 327–38. IEEE, 1985.

[110] M. Y. Vardi and P. Wolper. An automata-theoretic approach to automatic program verification. In *Proceedings of the First Symposium on Logic in Computer Science*, pp. 322–31. IEEE Computer Society, 1986.

[111] G. F. Viamontes, I. L. Markov and J. P. Hayes. Checking equivalence of quantum circuits and states. In *2007 IEEE/ACM International Conference on Computer-Aided Design*, pp. 69–74. IEEE, 2007.

[112] L. Vigano, M. Volpe and M. Zorzi. A branching distributed temporal logic for reasoning about entanglement-free quantum state transformations. *Information and Computation*, 255:311–33, 2017.

[113] Q. Wang, J. Liu and M. Ying. Equivalence checking of quantum finite-state machines. arXiv preprint arXiv:1901.02173, 2019.

[114] Q. Wang and M. Ying. Equivalence checking of sequential quantum circuits. arXiv preprint arXiv:1811.07722, 2018.

[115] M. M. Wolf. Quantum channels & operations: Guided tour. Lecture notes available at www-m5.ma.tum.de/foswiki/pub/M5/Allgemeines/MichaelWolf/QChannelLecture.pdf, 5, 2012.

[116] S. Yamashita and I. L. Markov. Fast equivalence-checking for quantum circuits. In *Proceedings of the 2010 IEEE/ACM International Symposium on Nanoscale Architectures*, pp. 23–8. IEEE Press, 2010.

[117] M. Ying. *Foundations of Quantum Programming*. Morgan Kaufmann, 2016.

[118] M. Ying and Y. Feng. Quantum loop programs. *Acta Informatica*, 47(4):221–50, 2010.

[119] M. Ying, Y. Li, N. Yu and Y. Feng. Model-checking linear-time properties of quantum systems. *ACM Transactions on Computational Logic (TOCL)*, 15(3):22, 2014.

[120] S. Ying, Y. Feng, N. Yu and M. Ying. Reachability probabilities of quantum markov chains. In *International Conference on Concurrency Theory*, pp. 334–48. Springer, 2013.

[121] S. Ying and M. Ying. Reachability analysis of quantum Markov decision processes. *Information and Computation*, 263:31–51, 2018.

[122] N. Yu. Quantum temporal logic. arXiv preprint arXiv:1908.00158, 2019.

[123] N. Yu and M. Ying. Reachability and termination analysis of concurrent quantum programs. In M. Koutny and I. Ulidowski, eds., *CONCUR 2012: Concurrency Theory*, vol. 7454 of *Lecture Notes in Computer Science*, pp. 69–83. Springer, 2012.

Index